Covert Operations

THE MIDDLE AGES SERIES

Ruth Mazo Karras, General Editor
Edward Peters, Founding Editor

A complete list of books in the series
is available from the publisher.

Covert Operations

The Medieval Uses of Secrecy

Karma Lochrie

PENN

University of Pennsylvania Press

Philadelphia

10   9   8   7   6   5   4   3   2   1

Published by
University of Pennsylvania Press
Philadelphia, Pennsylvania 19104-4011

Library of Congress Cataloging-in-Publication Data
Lochrie, Karma.
      Covert operations : the medieval uses of secrecy / Karma Lochrie.
         p.   cm. — (The Middle Ages series)
      Includes bibliographical references (p.   ) and index.
      ISBN 0-8122-3473-1 (acid-free paper)
         1. English literature — Middle English, ca. 1100–1500 — History and criticism.
      2. Women and literature — England — History — To 1500.   3. Women — England —
      History — Middle Ages, 500–1500.   4. Marriage customs and rites, Medieval.
      5. England — Social conditions — 1066–1485.   6. Science, Medieval, in literature.
      7. Law, Medieval, in literature.   8. Marriage in literature.   9. Secrecy in literature.
      10. Gossip in literature.   11. Sodomy in literature.   I. Title.   II. Series.
      PR275.W6L63   1999
      820.9'001 — dc21   98-11694
                                                                                                CIP

Contents

Introduction, or Dark Matter

I have grown to love secrecy. It seems to be the one thing that can make modern life mysterious or marvellous to us. The commonest thing is delightful if one only hides it.
— Oscar Wilde, *The Picture of Dorian Gray*[1]

My decision to study secrets and practices of concealment in the Middle Ages did not evolve out of the desire to make modern life mysterious and marvelous, as Basil Hallward would have it. Nor did the subject of my project elicit the delight and enthusiasm that Oscar Wilde attributes to the secret. When I was asked what I was writing at a reception toward the end of my work on the project and I explained that it was about medieval secrets, my interrogator responded, "Oh, is that anything like dark matter?" I did not know at the time what dark matter in physics was, but I knew somehow that the metaphor was appropriate. Secrets and secrecy in any culture, medieval or modern, inhabit the realm between what is said or seen and what is not, just as dark matter in physics designates that realm of matter that seems most un-matter-like, that occupies the invisible realm of physical properties, like the spaces between stars. To try to talk about secrets is something like trying to describe the spaces between stars, at least for the physics-challenged person such as myself.

Michel Foucault, D. A. Miller, Sissela Bok, Evelyn Fox Keller, and Eve Kosofsky Sedgwick are among the contemporary theoreticians of secrecy, and they, too, refer to the paradoxical property of secrecy, that it implies its own revelation, that it limns the explicit statement and the body of knowledge, that it structures identity and subjectivity. Foucault traces the history of sexuality to practices of secrecy in medieval confession, which he describes as a silence that "functions alongside the things said. There is no binary division to be made between what one says and what one does not say."[2] Like dark matter, secrecy functions within discourses, such as the most verbose of them all in Foucault's judgment, confession. But secrecy and the secrets it keeps also mark boundaries of knowledge, such as the secrets of nature, life, and death that used to constitute, according to Sissela Bok, "what human beings care most to protect and to probe: the exalted, the dangerous, the shameful; the sources of power and creation; the fragile and the intimate."[3] When divine, natural, and epistemological secrets no longer structure what human beings care to protect and to probe, Wilde might have argued, we must create secrets and secretive technologies to make modern life mysterious and marvelous.

Yet this same technology of secrecy in its medieval and modern incarnations also structures power relations, including those produced by religious institutions, cultural practices, social idioms, and individual behavior. D. A. Miller and Eve Sedgwick are interested in this kind of secrecy as the sort of "dark matter" of particular historical periods and cultures, in both its sense of that which functions within and alongside cultural discourses and of that which operates negatively and often invisibly to exclude, oppress, and control some knowledges, some peoples, and some discourses over others. Both theorists call for cultural and historical studies of secrecy, including its social functions, its subtle workings, and its powerfully debilitating effects for the modern subject. Miller speculates that a study of the kinds of knowledge that secrecy covers would "tell us much about a given culture or historical period." Miller is careful to redirect attention away from the secrets that usually engage our attention to the practices of concealment that cultures exert upon different subjects and in different ways:

Instead of the question "What does secrecy cover?" we had better ask "What covers secrecy?" What, that is, takes secrecy for its field of operations? In a world where the explicit exposure of the subject would manifest how thoroughly he has been inscribed within a socially given totality, secrecy would be the spiritual exercise by which the subject is allowed to conceive of himself as resistance: a friction in the smooth functioning of the social order, a margin to which its far-reaching discourse does not reach.[4]

In a culture such as ours, however, where secrecy structures the subject according to oppositions between private and public, inside and outside, subject and object, the secretive subject is less a resistant one than an "open secret" caught in the very network that has excluded her in the first place. This is one of the dilemmas of the modern gay subject, as Eve Sedgwick so exhaustively theorizes it — one that proves Wilde's formula for modernity has its costs as well as its marvels.

In the course of her analysis of the closet as a trope of gay identity, Sedgwick proposes that this "defining structure for gay oppression in this century" is actually implicated in a larger historical and cultural practice of secrecy, allying the closet with other secrecy technologies:

I want to argue that a lot of the energy of attention and demarcation that has swirled around issues of homosexuality since the end of the nineteenth century, in Europe and the United States, has been impelled by the distinctively indicative relation of homosexuality to wider mappings of secrecy and disclosure, and of the private and the public, that were and are critically problematical for the gender, sexual, and economic structures of the heterosexist culture at large, mappings whose enabling but dangerous incoherence has become oppressively, durably condensed in certain figures of homosexuality. "The closet" and "coming out," now verging on all-purpose phrases for the potent crossing and recrossing of almost any politically charged lines of representation, have been the gravest and most magnetic of those figures.[5]

Sedgwick would have us understand the closet in terms of its historical relationships and affiliations with that wider mapping of secrecy and other dangerous incoherences that are always the legacies of secret technologies. Even if the modern structures of identity such as the closet are not to be found in pre-modern worlds where sexual identities had not yet been invented, there are genealogies to be traced in the historical trajectories of secrecy and its capacity for reinventing the marvelous and mysterious, along with the dangerous and exclusionary, for different cultures.

The dark matter of medieval practices of secrecy has little explicitly to do with the gay closets of the twentieth century or Basil Hallward's key to making modern life mysterious and marvelous. Nevertheless, my own interest in secrecy begins with modern structures of secrecy, whether it is the durably oppressive epistemological structure of the closet for gay identity or the personal strategy of resistance to which Wilde and Miller refer in decidedly different registers. Inevitably, all scholarly books emerge from the writer's own dark matter, including those aspects she can identify and those she still cannot. The choice of secrecy as the focus of a book about the Middle Ages never struck me as strange, even though it seems to strike others so. My interest in medieval mysticism, with its esoteric languages of otherworldly experience and its covert forms of cultural transgression, after all, first led me to medieval secrets generally. What is most marvelous and mysterious about the Middle Ages is, like Wilde's self-fashioned modern life or Miller's questionings, what it kept secret, where it kept secrets, and how its secrecy worked.

I have never assumed, however, that the secrets and secrecy I am studying in medieval culture are solely medieval creations or habitudes; they are as much about me as they are about the Middle Ages. Secrecy is never a solitary activity. "Secrets are always located in particular social contexts," including the context of medievalist and the Middle Ages, though it may not always seem particularly social.[6] As I shall discuss later in this book, Michel de Certeau describes secrecy as a "play between actors," and I am aware that in this particular play I am as much a seeker after medieval secrets as a concealer.[7] The incumbent pressure on a book about secrecy to make grand revelations as well as *not* to be secretive is daunting, and it constitutes part of the social relations and play among myself, my book, and the Middle Ages that I am endeavoring to engage as well as to create.

The title of my book is, perhaps, guilty itself of secrecy, since the term "covert operations" nearly always alludes somewhat mysteriously to intentionally concealed activities. I use the well-known phrase to emphasize the operations rather than the objects of secrecy. I am more interested in how, where, and why the Middle Ages kept secrets than I am in what secrets it kept. For one of the tricks of secrecy is to call our attention to the supposed secrets as the locus of truth, rather than to the operations that make them appear to be truths and the social relationships that are negotiated through them. The secrets always distract us, too, from the power relations that surround and give meaning to them. The covert operations are much more diverse and ideological than the secrets themselves would suggest. As Sedgwick argues, they are implicated in gender, culture, and class ideologies in different historical periods. Finally, as I have already indicated, it is not through the secrets themselves but through the operations of concealment that we can begin to understand contemporary strategies of concealment and the social networks they organize. From the secrets and coversions of the Middle Ages, the present is challenged to address and possibly even to reframe its own understanding of its mysteries and its marvels, its power technologies and its oppressions.[8]

The chapters of this book represent particular historical sites of covert operations in medieval culture, including confession, gossip, books of secrets, medieval law, and sodomitic discourse. In each chapter I examine first the cultural activity and discourse of a particular type or logics of secrecy and then investigate how this covert logic becomes textualized in a particular literary work. Except in Chapter 3, where I am looking at the textual formulations of secrecy in medieval books of secrets, each chapter is divided into two parts. In the first part I draw upon a variety of theoretical and historical sources to construct a framework for understanding the operations of secrecy and the ideologies they enable and support. In the second part I select one Middle English text as a sort of case study of that particular covert operation, not so much as a way of illustrating it but as a way of trying it out and complicating it. The cultural sites and the literary texts I have chosen are selective; they are not the whole story. With the breadth of my focus and method, I cannot pretend to cover all the kinds and permutations of medieval secrets and secrecy, nor all the literary texts in which we can see them played out. Rather, I hope to have selected crucially important sites of investigation that become complicated in interesting ways by the literary texts I bring to bear on them. Likewise, I expect the bringing of particular medieval literary texts to the hermeneutic of covert operations to open those texts up in significant ways. If this part of my book is successful, not only will these texts become new, de-familiarized, and complicated, but other medieval texts I have not discussed will suddenly become configured in the reader's mind in relation to secrecy.

Another strategy I have adopted throughout the book is the juxtaposition of contemporary and medieval cultural operations and media. The first chapter, for example, positions Foucault's remarks about contemporary man as a "confessing animal" with an article from the *New York Times* on the modern, trouble-free confessional box. My discussion of secret knowledges in Chapter 3 also begins with a remark from an exhibit of African art in which a Ghanaian elder performs the very covert operation that I describe in medieval books of secrets. And in Chapter 5 I use Susan Streitfeld's film, *Female Perversions*, as a way of thinking about sodomitic discourse in the Middle Ages. My purpose throughout the book is not to imply some trans-historical truth about the secrecy I am investigating but to use the medieval cultural formations of secrecy to resist the present, forcing it into unfamiliar but not necessarily unrelated territories. In one sense, I would like to think that I am tapping the creative potential of the Middle Ages to help us re-think our present, rather than insisting upon the difference that modernity makes, idealizing the medieval past, or sponsoring a universalist historical truth.[9] My book is not the first to attempt to position such a rearticulation of the Middle Ages and the present, but I think it is the first to undertake this by clustering so many diverse cultural practices together. Secrecy as a cultural operation is not limited to sexual constructions, acts, or identities but travels freely among medieval and postmodern discourses alike. It is positively verbose, and this verbosity can tell us much about ourselves, our histories, our social world—including "its alliances and divisions, social spaces that are shared and those that are partitioned off from others"—and perhaps most importantly, the workings of power and individual resistance.[10] The indelibility of the trajectories of cultural secrets and the violence of their plots become more visible, and it is hoped, less powerful in the process.

While secrecy and secrets may be elusive stuff, like dark matter, they are easily defined for this project. If we take secrecy to mean intentional concealment that structures social and power relationships, it is apparent enough how insignificant actual secrets are by comparison. Nevertheless, as the five chapters here illustrate, there are many types of secrecy, many social configurations it endorses, and as many discursive formulations it structures. In spite of these differences, however, secrecy always serves the dual purpose of constituting one set of knowledges, discourses, or social agents and also disempowering others.[11] While contemporary American society constitutes its notions of autonomy and privacy in terms of secrecy, the Middle Ages was just beginning to fashion subjectivity and institutional power through secrecy.

In spite of the pervasiveness of secrecy in modern culture, though, very little has been written to theorize secrecy either for cultures or for literatures. As a result, I have been compelled to theorize it myself using a range of contemporary theories. Such selective and sometimes eclectic use of contemporary theories might strike the reader as haphazard or, worse, desperate, but because secrecy covers everything from confession to women's gossip to sodomitic discourse, I insist that such eclecticism is necessary. It is true that some of the theorists, such as Catharine MacKinnon, are incompatible with some of the other theorists I use in the rest of the book, but there is no direct conflict among them in the way that I am using them. That is to say, MacKinnon's theory of privacy does not conflict with Sedgwick's ideas about secrecy or Foucault's theory of confession or Michel de Certeau's analysis of the problematics of secrecy in sixteenth- and seventeenth-century mysticism. There may even be a queer complementarity among these otherwise conflicting theoretical standpoints because the authors are describing quite different operations of secrecy. While the ideological agendas and directions of their work might differ radically, their insights about secrecy do not necessarily invoke those implications and agendas. I do not wish, for example, for my use of MacKinnon's statement to endorse somehow all of her political views, and I do not see why it should. In any case, I am aware of the trickiness of negotiating such disparate theorists and of placing them in relationships to each other that they would find uncomfortable. If I have done this fairly and responsibly, however, my book should reflect the richness of their interactions and their sometimes strange conjunctions.

The trajectory of medieval secrets to modernity's marvel and mystery begins in confession. Chapter 1 takes up Foucault's remarks about confessional secrecy and the creation of Christian subjectivity in the first volume of *The History of Sexuality*. Although Foucault's remarks have become foundational to contemporary histories of sexuality and queer theory, little attention has actually been paid to his remarks about confession as they relate to his genealogy of sexuality. This chapter begins with a critique of Foucault's Middle Ages and, in particular, his analysis of confession as a historical practice. Although I am indebted to his discussion of the role of secrecy in confession, I find his understanding of the Middle Ages and confession to be problematic at best and riddled with contradictions. In the second part of this chapter, I examine the operations of secrecy as they are elaborated and codified in confessional manuals, summa, and sermons. It is here that Foucault's analysis of the power relations between the one who listens and the one who tells, between concealing and revealing, and between self-publication and renunciation becomes extremely cogent. Finally, in the third part of the chapter, I take the dynamics of secrecy that I have sketched out in the second section into a consideration of *Sir Gawain and the Green Knight*, where confession is not what it seems to be. Foucault alluded to a "metamorphosis in literature" that accompanied the new technology of confession in Western culture, and Lee Patterson calls confession "one of the central modes of self-representation available in late-medieval England."[12] Yet there has been little attempt by medieval scholars to assess and explore this mode, except in isolated texts. My examination of *Sir Gawain and the Green Knight* endeavors to trace the poem's own subversion of confession even as it employs confessional secrecies. It suggests that confession was not only a literary mode but a contested and vexed cultural discourse, one that the *Gawain* poet cannot help using even as he dismantles it. The operations of secrecy are paramount in this poem, not only in the proliferation of confession in it but in the representation of courtly love. Ultimately, secrecy haunts the poem's narrative structure, its plot, and its meaning.

The second chapter takes up the devolution of confession into gossip that occurs at the end of *Sir Gawain and the Green Knight* and explores the medieval representation of gossip. Gender ideology is not necessarily constitutive of confession, but it is conducive to the operations of secrecy, as my analysis of *Sir Gawain* demonstrates. In Chapter 2 I suggest that gossip is confession's stigmatized parody, its debased "other" that marks the feminine, especially women's bodies and their speech. Drawing upon Patricia Spacks's important study of *Gossip*, I also bring some language theory and remarks of Martin Heidegger and Roland Barthes to bear on a theory of medieval gossip as the secret language of a marginal group. The mimicry of confession that gossip performs consists of its strategic use of secrecy to authorize itself, to fashion a discourse of truth, to negotiate power relations in medieval culture. As the abjected discourse of medieval culture, however, gossip serves as a resistant discourse that mocks and mimics patriarchal discourse, as, for example, in the Wife of Bath's Prologue. At the same time, gossip uses secrecy — and the endlessness and excesses of discourses that depend on it — in order to threaten masculine poetics. I examine two examples of this insurrectionary potential of gossip in a late medieval poem called "The Gossips" in which a male narrator voyeuristically attempts to expose the secret tavern activities and discourse of the town gossips. My main literary case study of gossip is Chaucer's *House of Fame*, a text that most readers might not associate with the thematics or operations of gossip, but which I argue is crucially about the relationship between women's secrets, their gossip, and masculine poetics.

Chapter 3 shifts the book's focus to the fields of medieval science and medicine with their books of secrets. Secrecy is the subject of these treatises, obviously, but it is also a rhetorical device and primary discursive mode by which culturally transmitted knowledge is authorized and configured. First the Pseudo-Aristotelian *Secret of Secrets* texts are examined for their strategies of coversion framed in an epistolary dialogue between Alexander and Aristotle. These texts, which collect advice to kings, regimens for health, and natural philosophy, were immensely popular in the Middle Ages, and they came to model the scientific method, at least according to Roger Bacon. I am interested in how Aristotle hyperbolically invokes secrecy for the purpose of transmitting to Alexander, the recent conqueror of the Persians, the secrets of the Persians' culture, and of the secrets of statecraft so that he may maintain his control over them. I am not only interested in Aristotle's use of secrecy to create a masculine, colonialist rhetoric that Bacon rationalizes for all scientific discourse, but also in the illustrative parables he includes in an otherwise mundane collection of information. In these stories I show how the secrets of the treatise encode a masculine fear of the feminine and the East that secrecy neutralizes and transforms for masculine use.

This kind of ideological use of secrecy is even more apparent in Pseudo-Albert the Great's *The Secrets of Women*. Here what gets designated as the secret is women's bodies, their sexualities, and their devious natures, which it is the task of religious men (the narrator and reader) to expose and defuse. Within this covert rhetoric, Pseudo-Albert engages in a coy master-disciple game that depends upon the exchange of women's secrets. The dangers of women's secrets are implicit throughout the treatise, though women themselves are said to be ignorant of the very powerful secrets that they *are*. A distinction between *being* and *having* the secret underlies both treatises, forming the peculiar power relations that govern both. This genre of the medieval book of secrets, like the Pseudo-Aristotelian one, is important not only for its significant popularity but for its composition of a kind of knowledge transmission that defines women — or Persians — as secrets so that they can be exchanged among masculine masters and disciples in an erotic homosocial network.

Chapter 4 turns from the discursive realms of the previous two chapters to the legal and social configurations of married women as secrets in the Middle Ages. Beginning with French legal terminology for wife, *covert de baron* (woman who is "covered" by a baron), I flesh out the semantic range and implications of the wife's status in medieval society. Playing on the term, I suggest that the medieval wife was more the husband's secret than his protected possession by drawing upon the laws governing wives' ownership of property, contractual capacities, and their work. The legal coversion of women in medieval culture, I argue, can be understood in terms of Catharine MacKinnon's feminist critique of privacy, in which she claims that our modern American valorization of privacy depends upon the equation of women and privacy and, at the same time, a fundamental denial of privacy to women. In other words, women can *be* it, but not *have* it. I substitute secrecy for her privacy to frame my discussion of women and their work in medieval society. Chaucer's Miller's Tale is the intriguing focus for my study of the translation of "covert women" in medieval culture in masculine texts. Here, too, as we saw in Chapter 3, men engage in the coversion of women, including their speech and bodies, in order to authorize and constitute a masculine poetics and to contain homosexual tendencies in that poetics, as well as in courtly love and fabliaux.

The power of secrets not only to render mysteries and cultural marvels but to abject is most evident in medieval discourse of sodomy. Chapter 5 addresses the recently recuperated discourse that was often singled out for the necessity of maintaining it under the strictest secrecy. Confessional manuals, penitential treatises, and medieval theology all create a secret of sodomy in order to contain and control its threats. My analysis of this secretive discourse, however, critiques the current practice of ignoring gender in the medieval construction of sodomy. Using Susan Streitfeld's 1997 film, *Female Perversions*, I argue that "perversions are never what they seem to be," in either postmodernity or the Middle Ages. Beginning with the Parson's definition of sodomy in the last tale of the *Canterbury Tales*, I demonstrate how utterly confused the category actually was, as well as how gendered it was. I maintain that it was viewed not primarily as a disorder of sexual acts but as a "female perversion," or rather, a gender perversion that mimics femininity. Far from designating a single type of sexual activity between men, the term included women as well as men, though medieval scholarship generally disregards this fact. In addition to being a gendered perversion that was seen to derive from female perversity, sodomy as an unnatural vice was more affiliated with heterosexual sex acts than it was opposed to them. Three arguments emerge from this analysis: that sodomy was primarily a gendered category, that women were included in it even if most contemporary studies render them invisible, and that heteronormativity could not have existed for the Middle Ages, given the medieval conception of the corruption and perversion of all desire. John Gower's *Confessio Amantis* provides a fascinating demonstration of both the impossibility of naturalized, normative heterosexuality and the complicity of unnatural and natural sex acts. While most scholars attempt to moralize Gower's critique of courtly love in the poem, I argue for the poem's subversion of its own penitential structure and exposure of the incoherence of normative hetero-love or -sex in the fractured medieval world of his time. From Gower to Streitfeld the secrets change, but their harmful effects and residues are everywhere visible.

If D. A. Miller is right — that we can learn a great deal about any cultural or historical period by the things it keeps secret, by what takes secrecy as its field of operations — what does the Middle Ages have to tell us through its covert operations and its secrets? I have focused throughout this book on the particular ways in which secrecy structured gender ideology in the representation of women's gossip, women's bodies and sexuality, legal terminology governing wives, and sodomy. I have also argued throughout that secrecy supports masculine regimes of knowledge, discourse, and power, even though it also abjects men as well as women. The practice of concealment found in confession is not explicitly a gendered one, although I have shown how it can be deployed as such in my analysis of *Sir Gawain and the Green Knight*. Gender is, clearly, one of secrecy's more successful covert operations in the Middle Ages. Yet I am aware that this conclusion is also partly a result of the cultural sites I have chosen for this book, and besides, it is not the conclusion that interests me. It is too simplistic, and it does not account for the multiform ways in which secrecy works, the complicated system of alliances and divisions it creates, the power relations it frames, or the individual invisibilities it fosters.

As I have already said, I think that the study of secrecy helps us to understand our own personal and public constraints and the ways in which society benefits and encourages them. To see contemporary closetedness, for example, in terms of medieval laws governing wives can be useful for enlarging our vision of oppression and developing strategies of resistance to it. The medieval closet — what it kept secret and structured its regimes of knowledge and ignorance around — has much in common with contemporary secrecies, and while the recognition of this resemblance might not ultimately render life more mysterious or marvelous, it at least offers an awareness that prevents us from seeing our present in too narrow or insufficiently compassionate a light.

Tongues Untied

Confession and Its Secrets

. . . the confession became one of the West's most highly valued techniques for producing truth. We have since become a singularly confessing society. The confession has spread its effects far and wide. It plays a part in justice, medicine, education, family relationships, and love relations, in the most ordinary affairs of everyday life, and in the most solemn rites; one confesses one's crimes, one's sins, one's thoughts and desires, one's illnesses and troubles; one goes about telling, with the greatest precision, whatever is most difficult to tell.

> — Michel Foucault, *History of Sexuality*, Vol. 1 [1]

With their lead-lined walls, double doors, heating, cooling and ventilation systems and a special screen to block spit and bad breath, Genuflex confessionals have little in common with the creaky, musty, old-fashioned boxes where churchgoers knelt in darkness to whisper their sins into the ear of the parish priest. . . . A deluxe model, which sells for almost $8,000, offers lighting, a place for the parishioner to sit as well as kneel, and an opening in the wall for those who don't care for the secrecy of the traditional screen. The entire structure is soundproofed, even the keyhole. "We have taken the antique confessionals, which were oppressive, places of sins, spoken and unspoken, where there was no dialogue, and we have transformed them into places where you can talk," Mr. Lion [owner of Genuflex] said. [2]

From Michel Foucault to Genuflex, the Middle Ages-inspired habit of confessing goes New Age. The truth technology of confession — its requirement of secrecy, interrogation, and concealment — has been complemented by the improved technology of the confessional box. Now secrecy is no longer dependent on fallible human discretion alone; instead, our confessions are physically secured from exposure to the world outside. At the same time, ironically, the new confessional, courtesy of Genuflex, dispenses with the outdated secrecy of the screen separating priest from penitent, with its one-way whisperings, in favor of dialogue. Only the screen to protect both subjects from the spit and bad breath of the other serves as a reminder of the "oppressive places of sins." Confession has found a new home, one that accommodates the one who confesses with ventilation, appropriate temperature control, and comfort as a way of encouraging talk. The results are no secret: "Priests tell me that they have had an increase in people coming to confess with these new confessionals," says the owner of Genuflex, Mr. Lion. His trade secret in marketing confessionals is simple: "My secret is that I go out there and sell."[3]

Foucault would not have been surprised at this development in the technology of the confessional box to service the truth technology designed by the medieval church. For the concept of self and the discourse of confession that produces it remain intact — not only intact but positively flourishing. Before the talk-show explosion of the 1980s and 1990s and the advent of the memoir, as well as the increasing accessibility of psychotherapy, Foucault argued that confession already was not so much a Catholic obligation as it was a modern discourse embracing medicine, psychology, education — everything from " the most ordinary affairs of everyday life" to "the most solemn rites." In contrast to the image of confession fostered by Genuflex as oppressive, degrading, and frightening, contemporary confession, even without Genuflex comfort, is characterized by "immense verbosity" that funds our pleasure, our liberation, and our systems of power and knowledge. In short, confession has become the modern discourse of self and society: "Western man has become a confessing animal."[4]

Foucault traces this discursive enthusiasm produced by confession in its medieval and modern forms to the Christian sacrament instituted by the Fourth Lateran Council of 1215 and to medieval theology, which "tended to make flesh into the root of all evil, shifting the most important moment of transgression from the act itself to the stirrings — so difficult to perceive and formulate — of desire."[5] This locating of sin in the flesh, along with the categorizing and codifying of all desires and effects associated with it, established sex and sexuality at the center of the regime of discourses produced by confession, according to Foucault. Confession promised to "lay bare the unbroken nervure of the flesh"; at the same time "sex was taken charge of, tracked down as it were, by a discourse that aimed to allow it no obscurity, no respite."[6]

Sex becomes "something akin to a secret whose discovery is imperative," and confession provides the means of discovery, as well as the presumption of concealment. Hence the paradox that sex is both the thing that is hidden and the thing that must be expressed, at first, for the absolution it earns, later, for the mental therapy it provides, and always, for the pleasure it brings. As Foucault argues repeatedly in his first volume of the *History of Sexuality*, confession created an elaborate discourse of secrecy that extended beyond the confidentiality of the confessional to construct our very understanding of the human subject and subjectivity.

This is where my interest in secrecy begins, with Foucault's theory of confession in the Middle Ages as a discourse of secrecy that proliferated and extended beyond the sacramental act itself. As I have reread Foucault, I have also become aware of how much theory of the history of sexuality is crucially bound up in this theory of confession. Sex "as we know it" is essentially the creation of medieval confessional discourse — not the liberation from Victorian repression, as psychoanalysis would have us think — but the secret that simply *must* speak its name, that will not shut up. Foucault revolutionized thinking about sexuality by calling attention to its construction through a host of discourses — medical, scientific, psychoanalytic — and by tracking its changing affiliations with acts and identities. It is no exaggeration to credit Foucault with the recent developments in queer theory and politics and to identify a certain devotion among current sexual historians and queer theorists. Perhaps the most outright of these is David Halperin who confesses, "As far as I'm concerned, the guy was a fucking saint."[7]

Without wishing to deny scholars their hagiographies or queer theory its founding father, I find much that is troubling in Foucault's theory of confession and sexuality and in his vision of the Middle Ages in general. As a medievalist and feminist scholar with queer interests, I cannot ignore three disturbing aspects of Foucault's *History of Sexuality*: his nostalgic representation of the Middle Ages as the modern's "other," his own complex and paradoxical relationship to confession, and finally, his reduction of confessional discourse to the subject of sex. After presenting Foucault's theory of confession and sexuality along with my critique in this first segment of the chapter, I will pursue his idea of the institutionalization of secrecy in medieval confession and its effects, particularly the way the Middle Ages transformed confession into literature, creating its own pleasures, truths, and technologies of the self. It should be understood that my critique of Foucault that follows does not ignore or discount my own indebtedness to his work, nor is it meant to unsettle Foucault's deserved place in contemporary queer theory and politics. My purpose is to problematize Foucault and, in the process, to challenge queer theory and medieval histories of sexuality, without denying ourselves pleasure, at least as Foucault defines it to mean that experience that fragments and dissociates the subject from itself.[8] In this case, our collective pleasure will be constituted by fracturing our identifications as scholars with a certain prevailing idea of Foucault's work.

Confessions of the Flesh I:
Foucault and *The History of Sexuality*, Vol. 4

Foucault's history of sexuality is inseparable from his version of the Middle Ages and his analysis of its chief contribution to the creation of modern subjectivity: confession. His work on the history of sexuality in the first three volumes, but especially volume 1, is responsible for de-naturalizing sexuality and revealing its construction, reconstituting sexuality from a site of liberation to one of contestation, and developing a strategy of resistance for scholarly and political intervention.[9] Equally important is his description of the workings of power, a theme that embraces his work on sexuality, madness, and prison systems. A critique of psychoanalysis, including its methods and its "repressive hypothesis" about sexuality, is also a legacy of Foucault's work, although contemporary queer theory often brings the two into a conjunction that is itself queer. Ultimately, Foucault's name and his work are associated with the historical and constructionist studies of sexuality, particularly as they map its discursive terrains and the power relations it entails. Foucault's account of modernity as a confessing society dedicated to "speaking of it [sex] *ad infinitum*, while exploiting it as *the* secret," has interestingly provoked more such talk about sexuality in scholarship than it has studies of why we are so obsessed and confessed on the subject.[10]

In an interview conducted while he was at Berkeley in April 1983, Foucault discussed his work in progress, including his fourth volume of the *History of Sexuality*, which was to focus on the Middle Ages. The interviewer began by alluding to his first volume and asking the philosopher, "Do you still think that understanding sexuality is central for understanding who we are?" As the founder of modern queer studies whose name is associated with sex and sexuality, Foucault's response is puzzling: "I must confess that I am much more interested in problems about techniques of the self and things like that rather than sex . . . sex is boring."[11] While this statement may not seem consistent with Foucault's three-volume work on the subject, it is consistent with his later work, particularly during the time that he was writing his fourth volume on the Middle Ages, and with his interest in confession. Yet this declaration is not an isolated one, for Foucault admits in other interviews that he was so bored with his plan for the six-volume series on the history of sexuality that he was forced to reconceptualize the project.[12]

At the same time, Foucault's remarks about sex and sexuality in the Middle Ages are peculiar, if not un-Foucaultian. The first appears in his discussion of confession as the medieval discourse about sex: "The Middle Ages had organized around the theme of the flesh and the practice of penance a discourse that was markedly unitary."[13] What marks the difference between the medieval and the modern is the epistemic break that occurs in the centuries following the Middle Ages when "this relative uniformity was broken apart, scattered, and multiplied in an explosion of distinct discursivities which took form in demography, biology, medicine, psychiatry, psychology, ethics, pedagogy, and political criticism." Such a characterization of medieval confession is suspicious given Foucault's own efforts to resist and interrogate such monolithic narratives of any historical period. More seriously, his view of the unitary discourse of sex provides the medieval "other" to his conception of modernity and its myriad and proliferated sexual discourses all structured by confession. At the same time, Foucault establishes a link between modernity and its radically different medieval past through the practice of confession. If Foucault is wrong about the Middle Ages, his modernity and his historical narrative of sexuality need to be questioned.

Before looking at confessional discourse in order to test Foucault's theory, I want to pose another remark of his that is more baffling in light of his argument about the discursivity of sexuality, his resistance to the "naturalness" of sexuality as a category, and his critique of the confessional discourse that made a secret of sexuality in the first place: "Never did sexuality enjoy a more immediately natural understanding and never did it know a greater 'felicity of expression' than in the Christian world of fallen bodies and of sin." The proof, Foucault maintains, can be found in the mystical tradition that "was incapable of dividing the continuous forms of desire, of rapture, of penetration, of ecstasy, of that outpouring which leaves us spent."[14] Suddenly in Foucault's work, the Middle Ages becomes that prediscursive — and hence, by definition, pre-modern — origin of sexuality, when it enjoyed its most "natural" understanding and expression. Mystical transport is idealized and de-ideologized in this remark, rendering it the sole place and moment when sexuality was not yet codified or regulated, when it was somehow even exempt from the homogenizing effects of confession. The nostalgia of these two comments is not only surprising and disturbing, but it renders Foucault's work on the Middle Ages — and by necessity, modernity — suspect. As the natural, felicitous, unitary "other" to modern proliferated discourses about sex, the Middle Ages has nothing to gain from Foucault's nostalgia. Modernity, on the other hand, both does and doesn't:

What characterizes modern sexuality from Sade to Freud is not its having found the language of its logic or of its natural process, but rather, through the violence done by such languages, its having been "denatured" — cast into an empty zone where it achieves whatever meager form is bestowed upon it by the establishment of its limits. Sexuality points to nothing beyond itself, no prolongation, except in a frenzy which disrupts it. We have not in the least liberated sexuality, though we have, to be exact, carried it to its limits.[15]

The difference that modernity makes is that it has "denatured" the natural felicitous expression of medieval mystical sex and cast it adrift from meaning, pointing to nothing beyond sex itself. We still have confession, but this too, apparently, has proliferated into that empty zone that points to nothing beyond itself — beyond the mere compulsion to confess. The difference is that the denaturing of sexuality provides modernity with a language that is coextensive with the death of God and with the interior limit that compensates for the loss of the divine.[16] Sexuality provides the modern experience of transgression — of surpassing the world of limits exposed by the death of God.

The othering of the Middle Ages that permits Foucault's narrative of modern sexuality is, as I have suggested, problematic. What is missing from his own nostalgic vision of the Middle Ages and from contemporary theory that relies on Foucault is an understanding of how confession as a discourse constructs our notion of sexuality. Foucault's first volume plainly locates our modern habits of thinking and talking about sexuality in the medieval habits of confession, but scholars continue to ignore this crucial part of his theory. The liberatory effects of Foucault's analysis of sexuality continue to be argued in spite of the fact that he views modern sexuality as a "regime of discourses" created by medieval confession.[17] If Foucault taught us that we cannot have the sex without the discourse, it is time to inquire into the discourse responsible for modern sexuality as we know it: confession.

Unfortunately, Foucault's fourth volume of his *History of Sexuality* on the Middle Ages has never been published, although he had completed the writing of it when he died in 1984. In his first volume and in interviews and essays published late in his life, Foucault provides an outline of his ideas about confession and its relationship to sexuality, even if he was not always consistent on these topics, as I have already suggested. The projected title for volume 4 on the Middle Ages was to be *Les Aveux de la chair*, or "Confessions of the Flesh," uniting his twin themes of the flesh and confession in volume 1 on medieval sexuality. His choice of words for confession, *les aveux* rather than *les confessions*, is instructive, for, as he explains in his *History of Sexuality*, Vol. 1, the concept of "avowal" is key to the new technology of the self, the body and its pleasures, and truth-telling constituted by the medieval confessional regime. In place of the earlier meaning of *avowal* as "a guarantee of the status, identity, and value granted to one person by another" whereby people vouched for each other, the term came to mean "someone's acknowledgment of his own actions and thoughts" in the context of medieval confession.[18] This changing significance is reflected in literature, too, according to Foucault: "We have passed from a pleasure to be recounted and heard, centering on the heroic or marvelous narration of 'trials' of bravery or sainthood, to a literature ordered according to the infinite task of extracting from the depths of oneself, in between the words, a truth which the very form of confession holds out like a shimmering mirage."[19]

Codified in the Fourth Lateran Council of 1215 and in the vast literature of penitential and instructional manuals for parish priests and for lay people, the system of Christian confession, or avowal, constituted a unique truth obligation for the individual and a collection of power mechanisms for religious and civic institutions. Foucault argues that not only was the individual responsible for moral and religious truths, but now one was also obligated to "seek [out] and state the truth about oneself." This process of self-doubt and self-analysis is ultimately endless, "in the sense that one must be forever extending as far as possible the range of one's thoughts, however insignificant and innocent they may appear to be," writes Foucault.[20]

The "avowals of the flesh" alluded to in Foucault's projected title for his fourth volume in the *History of Sexuality* thus constitute what he calls "Christian technologies of the self."[21] The implicit truth of this technology that it is designed to uncover is sexuality, according to Foucault. From his first volume to his unpublished fourth, Foucault's interest in self technologies gradually supersedes that of his interest in sexuality itself — to the point, as he jokingly asserts in the interview quoted, that "sex is boring." This new focus in Foucault's later work is not so much a moderation in his philosophical interests as it might first appear to be, for the three published volumes of the *History of Sexuality* pursue a larger subject than the title designates. Avowal as confession and the struggles of the flesh are, in fact, the focal points of Foucault's first volume, as well as of his late work and projected fourth volume on medieval sexuality.[22] Sexuality itself becomes less and less the subject of Foucault's history, as Foucault himself recognized more than once in his late interviews and essays.[23]

The first volume in conjunction with Foucault's later work, including his lectures, essays, and interviews, provides a patchwork narrative of how medieval confession eventually produced not only the Christian subject, but the discourse of contemporary society that constructs sexuality and just about everything else. Foucault saw in the medieval institution of the church, the practice of penance, and confessional technologies "the idea of a self which one had to renounce."[24] The Christian subject is the result of two complementary processes of institutional interrogation and control and of individual renunciation and avowal:

> This form of power [i.e., that of the Church] cannot be exercised without knowing the inside of people's minds, without exploring their souls, without making them reveal their innermost secrets. It implies a knowledge of the conscience and an ability to direct it.[25]

The paradigm of Christian subjectivization tailored to this institutional regime is of a self that must be "renounced and deciphered" because of the ineluctable concupiscence lodged in the flesh.[26]

> This subjectivization is linked with a process of self-knowledge which makes the obligation to seek and state the truth about oneself an indispensable and perma- nent condition of this [Cassian's] asceticism; and if there is subjectivization, it also involves an indeterminate objectivization of the self by the self-indeterminate in the sense that one must be forever extending as far as possible the range of one's thoughts, however insignificant and innocent they may appear to be.[27]

Foucault describes a dual movement — or splitting — of the self in its strug- gle with the flesh and the obligation to avow those struggles: subjectiviza- tion, a process of self-knowledge and self-disclosure, and objectivization, a suspiciousness about one's every thought and vigilant interrogation of one's secrets. Accounting for one's range of thought signifies an extension of scope of self from soul, body, and will to the meandering, deceptive, and potentially destructive movements of thought.

Such a complicity of knowledge, power, and subjectivization is not without its pleasures, either.[28] For the obligation to reveal is lined with the duty to conceal, and in the interaction of the two, a dynamic pleasure is enacted: "pleasure in the truth of pleasure, the pleasure of knowing that truth, of discovering and exposing it, the fascination of seeing it and telling it, of captivating and capturing others by it, of confiding it in secret, of luring it out in the open — the specific pleasure of the true discourse on pleasure."[29] If we have become "a singularly confessing society" as Foucault maintains, it is not exclusively because of the efforts of the medieval church to institutionalize its own power over the individual soul. Instead, it is the cluster of pleasures that confession produces — in the "truth of pleasure," hiding and discovering our secrets, captivating others with our disclosures, luring the truth out into the open, seeing it, and, most importantly, telling it endlessly and with the greatest relish. Nevertheless, this pleasure is merely the effect of the discourse and technology of the self fashioned by the medieval church.

The quasi-juridical regime of confession licensed two crucial developments in Western culture: a new Christian technology of the self and a discourse tailored to the requirements of the medieval church's power. The Christian technology of the self is based on the notion of *gouvernement*, extracting from the individual a particularly sinister regimen of "unconditional obedience, uninterrupted self-examination, and exhaustive confession," in Foucault's judgment.[30] The subject is rendered an obscure text to be deciphered by "sophisticated practices of attentiveness, concern, decipherment and verbalization." The truth of the self, therefore, always demands self-rupture in the form of an avowal that "I am not who I am."[31]

The agent of negation here — that which brings the "not myself" into play — is sexuality for Foucault. In an essay on "Sexuality and Solitude," Foucault cites a comment by Peter Brown that we must come to understand why sexuality became the "seismograph of our subjectivity" in Christianity.[32] Foucault theorizes that sexuality is the measure of Christian identity as the result of the inextricable linking of "sexuality, subjectivity, and truth" in the medieval regulation and practice of confession.[33] In his introduction to the *History of Sexuality*, he charts the course from the medieval pastoral injunction to confess to the modern incitement to sexual discourse:

A twofold evolution tended to make the flesh into the root of all evil, shifting the most important moment of transgression from the act itself to the stirrings — so difficult to perceive and formulate — of desire. For this was an evil that afflicted the whole man, and in the most secret of forms: "Examine diligently, therefore, all the faculties of your soul: memory, understanding, and will. Examine with precision all your senses as well. . . . Examine, moreover, all your thoughts, every word you speak, and all your actions. Examine even unto your dreams, to know if, once awakened, you did not give them your consent. And finally, do not think that in so sensitive and perilous a matter as this, there is anything trivial or insignificant."[34]

Confession, therefore, is intimately linked to the theory of the flesh, with its illicit desires, thoughts, dreams, sensual stirrings, and its access to the soul. As a discourse, confession mirrored that "most secret of forms" of evil, the flesh. In order to capture the secret truth of the human soul, confession itself must take place in secret and in strictest confidence.

From this medieval injunction to examine diligently everything down to the most trivial, it is a short distance to what Foucault calls the "most highly valued technique for producing truth" in the quotation at the beginning of this chapter. Not only does confession now structure knowledge systems, human relationships, and everything else from the solemn to the ordinary, but it sets up a ritualized power relationship conducted through secrecy between the one who confesses and the one who keeps the secrets. In the Middle Ages this was the priest and the penitent. Secrecy thus becomes a function of the power relationship, the pleasures of confession, and the makings of the Christian subject, rather than a function of the secrets supposedly confided. Confessional secrecy is guaranteed and validated not through its authority or its tradition, "but by the bond, the basic intimacy in discourse, between the one who speaks and what he is speaking about." This intimacy, in turn, is key to the production of truth, knowledge, power, and the self at once:

The confession is a ritual discourse in which the speaking subject is also the subject of the statement; it is also a ritual that unfolds within a power relationship, for one does not confess without the presence (or virtual presence) of a partner who is not simply the interlocutor but the authority who requires the confession, prescribes and appreciates it, and intervenes in order to judge, punish, forgive, console, and reconcile; a ritual in which the truth is corroborated by the obstacles and resistances it has had to surmount in order to be formulated; and finally a ritual in which the expression alone, independently of its external consequences, produces intrinsic modifications in the person who articulates it: it exonerates, redeems, and purifies him; it unburdens him of his wrongs, liberates him, and promises him salvation.[35]

The power relationship that exonerates, redeems, and purifies depends upon that paradox that "the agency of domination does not reside in the one who speaks (for it is he who is constrained), but in the one who listens and says nothing; not in the one who knows and answers, but in the one who questions and is not supposed to know."[36] Psychotherapy, medicine, education — all are systems based on this power relationship formed during the Middle Ages by the laws and practice of confession. Man has become a confessing animal only because secrecy has become a primary discourse of knowledge systems extending back to medieval confession.

Foucault's account of confession as it was linked to the theology of the flesh is a powerful one for its ability to describe the way in which secrecy generated an "unrelenting system" of talk; the Church extended its power; Christian subjectivity was conceived; and modern technologies of the self were discursively produced. A prevailing assumption underlying Foucault's analysis is problematic, however, namely his equation of the flesh with sex. This narrow reading of confessional manuals, penitentials, and theology leads Foucault to the alarming statement quoted at the outset of this chapter that medieval discourse about sex was "markedly unitary" in its confessional form. Not only does he make the mistake of reducing the multiple and complex designations of the medieval term "the flesh" to a single referent, "sex," but he disastrously homogenizes the discourse of confession and penance to a single, unitary meaning.[37] Finally, this account of confession permits Foucault his two other unFoucaultian moves of rendering modernity in binary opposition to the Middle Ages, as a multiplicity of sexual discourses replacing the single, unitary medieval one, and of taking nostalgic refuge in an imaginary, pre-discursive, natural medieval experience of sexuality. The continuous forms of desire and rapture that Foucault finds in the mystical tradition represent a greater "felicity of expression" and natural understanding than the post-confessional discursive age of sexuality. Finally, sexuality itself becomes discreet from other avowals of the flesh in a Foucaultian history of sexuality, subsuming all other categories of sin to itself.

In addition to these problems with Foucault's theory of confession and the construction of sexuality, there is the further problem of his own attitude towards his subjects. His nostalgia for that "other" Middle Ages that marks the difference modernity will make exists in unsettling conjunction with Foucault's own critique of this same period, when sexuality became the measure of the self's renunciation and of its integrity. A similar incongruity exists in Foucault's approach to confession. For in addition to that "singular imperialism" to tell the truth about oneself, submit to pastoral authority, obey completely the confessor's direction, and renounce the self entirely, Foucault found something appealing in confession and its principle of self-renunciation. At the end of his Howison lectures at the University of California at Berkeley in 1980, Foucault attributed a "great richness" to the Christian technology of the self, that is, self-sacrifice, concluding that "no truth about the self [is] without the sacrifice of the self."[38] Yet neither self-sacrifice nor the kind of mystical experience of sexuality was possible without confessional discourse, as he himself had already shown.

Foucault further associated this same self-renunciation with the act of writing, including his own. In his 1969 essay, "Qu'est-ce qu'un auteur?" and his 1980 "Talk with philosophers," Foucault asserts that writing in the modern period, like early Christian asceticism, is a practice of self-negation: "The negation of the self is the nucleus of the literary experience of the modern world."[39] His own writing, he observes elsewhere, participates in this same ascetic activity, as he describes it in the introduction to *The Archaeology of Knowledge*: "I am no doubt not the only one who writes in order to have no face."[40] Foucault does not abjure confession here, nor its effects, self-renunciation; in fact, he actively seeks the latter in his writing. In the Howison lectures, Foucault questions whether this technology of the self inherited from medieval Christianity is necessary or desirable. He further speculates that "maybe the problem is to change those technologies or maybe to get rid of those technologies, and then, to get rid of the sacrifice which is linked to those technologies."[41]

Foucault's work on confession and medieval sexuality, for all its suggestiveness, is plagued with inconsistencies, contradictions, and even nostalgia. At the same time, his construction of modernity so crucial to contemporary histories of sexuality and queer theory is based on an "othering" of the Middle Ages, that time when sex enjoyed its most natural, felicitous expression, before confessional discourse had its way with sex. Even then, confession somehow managed to produce across very different cultures and traditions a "markedly unitary" discourse that would fragment and proliferate, becoming modern sexuality "as we know it" and the primary technology for discovering and measuring truth. Yet elsewhere, particularly in the opening quotation of this chapter, confession is still the discursive framework of sexuality as we know it, suggesting that modernity is closer to the Christian Middle Ages than it likes to think it is.

If we are to use Foucault to endorse queer politics and histories of sexuality, we must address some of these problematic aspects of his work, particularly his nostalgic construction of the medieval "other," his conflicted attitude towards confession, and his abdication of sexuality altogether in favor of self technologies in his later work. In a 1983 interview — the same interview in which he declared that "sex is boring" — he indicated that he would pursue the Christian ethics of the medieval volume into the sixteenth century in his fifth volume.[42] Had Foucault completed and published these two volumes, his name might be at least as evocative today of Christian ethics and "ecstatic thinking" as it is of the de-naturalization and social construction of sexuality.

For medievalists Foucault's work is likewise problematic. His homogenous description of confession, his collapse of all things sinful to sexuality, and his nostalgia for a pre-discursive, mystical sexual experience all contribute to the marginalization of medieval studies and especially its isolation from pre-modernity. Nevertheless, his insights into the discourse of confession, apart from his accounts of its relation to sexuality, are useful for reading the Middle Ages. Foucault's brief study of confession in the first volume forces us to consider how secrecy came to structure not only confession, but medieval literary texts, ideas of the individual, and power relationships, as well as how the medieval church deployed this ritual discourse. Confession became a key cultural discourse in the Middle Ages, and it spread its effects, as Foucault says, far and wide. D. A. Miller encourages us further, as I indicated in the Introduction, to examine not only what secrecy covers in confessional discourse and practice, but what cultural representations, or operations, take secrecy for their technology. In the rest of this chapter, I will explore how secrecy worked as the discourse of truth first as it was codified and promoted in confessional laws and instructions, and finally, how it was replicated in other cultural discourses. Confession represents only one path of secrecy in medieval culture, but it is one that leads to "what human beings care most to protect and to probe: the exalted, the dangerous, the shameful, the sources of power and creation, the fragile and the intimate," in the words of Sissela Bok.[43] If confession is a crucial locus of medieval secrecy, it remains to be discovered what this locus generates by way of danger, shame, power, creation, sublimity, and intimacy in the medieval culture. The final section of this chapter focuses on the Middle English poem, *Sir Gawain and the Green Knight*, to explore how the secrets of confession came to script literary texts and fund gender ideologies, not to mention pleasures.

Tongues Untied

Confession did not begin in 1215 with the Fourth Lateran Council's passing of Canon 21, *Omnis utriusque sexus*, but its regulation, codification, and formulation as a discourse did. The decree is simple enough: it required annual confession on the part of every Christian to his or her parish priest:

Every *fidelis* of either sex shall after the attainment of years of discretion separately confess his sins with all fidelity to his own priest at least once in the year: and shall endeavour to fulfil the penance imposed upon him to the best of his ability, reverently receiving the sacrament of the Eucharist at least at Easter: unless it happen that by the counsel of his own priest for some reasonable cause, he hold that he should abstain for a time from the reception of the sacrament: otherwise let him during life be repelled from entering the church, and when dead let him lack Christian burial. Wherefore let this salutary statute be frequently published in the churches, lest any assume a veil of excuse in the blindness of ignorance. But if any desire to confess his sins to an outside priest for some just reason, let him first ask and obtain permission from his own priest, since otherwise he (the outside priest) cannot loose or bind him. But let the priest be discreet and cautious, and let him after the manner of skilled physicians pour wine and oil upon the wounds of the injured man, diligently inquiring the circumstances alike of the sinner and of the sin, by which (circumstances) he may judiciously understand what counsel he ought to give him, and what sort of remedy to apply, making use of various means (*experimentis*) for the healing of the sick man. But let him give strict heed not at all to betray the sinner by word or sign or in any other way, but if he need more prudent counsel let him seek it cautiously without any indication of the person: since we decree that he who shall presume to reveal a sin discovered to him in the penitential tribunal is not only to be deposed from the priestly office, but also to be thrust into a strict monastery to do perpetual penance.[44]

Pope Innocent III (1198–1216), who called the 1215 Council, declared its goal to be "to extirpate vices and foster virtues, correct abuses and reform morals, suppress heresy and strengthen faith, settle disorders and establish peace, encourage princes and Christian peoples to aid and maintain the Holy Land." Canon 21 was one of seventy decrees designed to accomplish these goals by strengthening the doctrine of transubstantiation, condemning heresies, and requiring Jews and Muslims to wear distinctive dress. While heresy and fear of contamination by non-Christian groups clearly drives some of these canons, the agenda of the Fourth Lateran Council has more to do with the self-fashioning of the medieval church. Reflecting the "interventionist" policies of the document as a whole, the *Omnis utriusque sexus* sought to strengthen the role of the parish church, increase pastoral authority, create a mechanism of social control, and establish a program of religious instruction and education.[45]

The decree as it is quoted above provides the broad rubric for the confessional procedures that would later be inventoried, codified, and regulated. Obligatory confession, as it is described in Canon 21, is limited to persons of both genders of appropriate age and to a time which coincides with another obligatory rite of the same Council, the sacrament of communion.[46] Reception of Christ's body required previous confession, penance, and absolution.[47] The conjunction of confession and Easter not only combined the two sacraments, but it instituted the social act of eucharistic joining in the community of Christ with the private one of interrogating and confessing one's conscience. The exclusivity of these tandem sacraments was crucial to the corporate identity of medieval Christian communities as well as to the identification of the heretical threat to that community from within and without. For the enemy against Christ and his community of faithful is likely to be the one who receives the Eucharist without having first confessed or the one who neglects both. If, as Peter Comestor (c.1100–1178) had argued before the Council, "It is grave and very dangerous for a Christian to abstain from reception of that sacrament [of the Eucharist], and not to communicate at least once a year, at Easter," the *Omnis utriusque sexus* compounded that danger by attaching it to the obligation to confess.[48] The punishments are clear: not only is the sinner expelled from church, but he/she is denied Christian burial. Ignorance, as the statute notes, is no excuse. At the same time, an allowance is made for abstaining from confession "for some reasonable cause," and in later instructions, permission is given for the sinner's choosing a priest other than his/her own parish priest.

The second half of Canon 21 takes up the priest's responsibility and method in administering confession. The priest is urged to use discretion and caution after the manner of a physician, whose desire it is to heal, rather than to frighten. Inquiry into the circumstances and manner of the sin should be directed by the goals of judicious counsel and appropriate remedy. Finally, the priest is given strict warning that he must keep the confession a secret, that he not betray the sinner or the sin by word or sign on punishment of being banished to a monastery. The entire decree is phrased in language that seems designed to guide and protect the sinner for his/her own spiritual health. Contrary to Foucault's account of the unremitting interrogation required of confession, this decree commands discretion and care, presumably according to the character of the sinner and nature of the sin.[49] It also stresses the healing of the sinner's soul, rather than the exposure and punishment of the sickness. This trope of the confessor/physician healing the spiritual diseases of his patient/parishioner becomes a common one in confessional manuals and in the theology of confession.[50]

Governing all these provisions is the secrecy that binds the priest so that the penitent will be encouraged to confess without fear of loss of family, reputation, or life.[51] The levels of secrecy and privacy that came to be associated with confession go beyond the dictates of the Fourth Lateran Council. Although systems of public penance had prevailed in Europe (except Ireland) in the early Middle Ages, after the sixth century most of Europe had systems of private penance. Private confession was not created by the Council of 1215, however. From the sixth century onwards, forms of private penance had existed, especially from the ninth to the twelfth centuries. Even before 1215, according to Thomas Tentler, there was a system of confession that already recognized the importance of privacy to the forgiveness of the sinner's sins, de-emphasized the role and harshness of penance in the sinner's absolution, made contrition central to the confessional act, and increased the priest's authority. In addition, there was already a theology in place that supported this system, including the writings of Abelard, Peter Lombard, Thomas Aquinas, and Duns Scotus.[52] The emphasis on secrecy and what would be called the "seal of confession" is already familiar to the Western Church by 1215. Aquinas had argued that just as God does not reveal the sins revealed to him, so the priest, too, who conforms himself to God should be equally discreet.[53] Yet before the eleventh century, the obligation to secrecy was no more than "a sort of vague moral obligation." Burchard, bishop of Worms (1000–1025) assigns the first penalty for a priest's violation of secrecy in confession, requiring that he be deposed and sent on a pilgrimage for the rest of his life. "Above all," Burchard writes in the *Corrector Burchardi*, "let the priest give heed not to repeat to any the sins of these who make confession to him."[54] Innocent III would follow the bishop's lead by claiming that the confessor who reveals a sin is more guilty than the sinner who committed it in the first place.[55]

If the Fourth Lateran Council did not create either the system of private confession or the secrecy that governed the confession, it did constellate the act around the notion of the secret. It also created an obligatory system that "could be made to control nearly every act of external as well as of internal life and all the relations of man to his fellows."[56] The legislation of 1215 also instigated a literature of instruction for parish priests and for penitents, elaboration and popularization of the centrality of contrition to confession, and the justification for the priest's role in absolution. For if contrition — internal sorrow — had already replaced satisfaction in the form of penitential works as the key to forgiveness in confession theology in the eleventh century, the very necessity for confession was in danger of being superfluous. Why should confession to a priest be necessary, in other words, if a sinner felt sorrow in her heart for her sin? The priest's interventionist role in the process of forgiveness was at stake, and the coordination of the personal and institutional roles in confession became necessary.

Before the thirteenth century, theologians had made the remission of guilt completely dependent on the penitent's sorrow, consigning the priest to the secondary role of merely declaring God's forgiveness of the contrite sinner. Abelard, for example, had argued that contrition was the cause of forgiveness, thereby rejecting the authority of ecclesiastical intervention in forgiveness.[57] St. Thomas Aquinas provided the theology for the indispensability of the priest's role in confession. The priest's words, *Ego te absolvo*, "I absolve thee," are pronounced in the indicative mood, Aquinas argued, and therefore, have the power to absolve the sinner. The sinner's contrition thus becomes effective only by virtue of the priest's "I absolve you," which brings grace to the sinner who lacks it.[58] This understanding of the priest's role as an active, interventionist one was crucial to justifying the obligation to confess, as well as to consolidating the power of the Church, for sorrow and repentance were no longer a guarantee of forgiveness or God's grace.

Yet this very provision for the priest's authority was itself fraught with problems. The priest's role in absolution rendered him God's representative, but the human failings of clergy who heard confessions—their ignorance, their harshness, and their condition of sinfulness—mitigated that same authority. As the *Omnis utriusque sexus* stipulated, the person in need of confession could choose a confessor other than his/her parish priest (including members of the mendicant orders) under certain conditions. Laypersons were encouraged to seek alternative and subsequent confessions if they judged their confessor to be incompetent because of his ignorance or his laxness. One Middle English sermon from the *Speculum Sacerdotale* makes this option explicit:

And forthi the man that hath no preste that is sufficient for to yeve hym heleful counsel, he may lawefully aske and seche counsel of hym that is wyser. And the preste whos counsel is nedeful, he may noȝt denye hym. But it is beste, and ellis it may noȝt be done sekir, that he þat moste haue counsel of a-nother preste firste for to aske leve of his owne preste.[59]

(And therefore, the man that has no priest who is sufficient to give him helpful council may lawfully ask and seek council of someone who is wiser. And the priest whose council is needed may not deny the one who seeks it. But it is best, or else it may not be done at all surely, that he who requires council of another priest first ask permission of his own priest.)

If the layperson is permitted to seek alternative confessors because of the ineptness, ignorance, sinfulness, and "style" of his/her parish priest, the confessor's authority is at least mitigated by the power of the confessant to judge and choose. John Gerson notes that evil priests cause some parishioners to withhold some of their sins during confession, and for good reason, while another writer advised penitents simply to shut their eyes to their confessors' sins.[60]

The withholding of sins by parishioners, either in response to evil priests or out of fear, was one of the great obstacles to obligatory confession; secrecy in the form of the "seal of confession" was meant to remedy this reluctance. Not only was the priest's secrecy compared with that of God, in whom all secrets are safe, the obligation to secrecy became an indispensable part of confession for the medieval church. The primary reason for secrecy was not just to encourage parishioners to make an appearance once a year at confession, but to insure that their confessions were complete and unreserved. In spite of the clear violations of the seal, the principle of secrecy worked to extend the parish priest's power to "know as God" in confession, even as it bound him to keep what were, in effect, God's secrets, not mankind's. For if he hears and knows as God, he is also bound to keep secrets as well as God. This idea can be found in the Middle English confessional manuals and instructions to priests, serving to encourage both the penitent to talk freely and honestly and the priest to be discrete. "Shryfte ys goddys pryuyte," (confession is God's secret), warns Robert Mannyng; the priest who violates his seal violates the secrets of his parishioner and the confidence of his God. At the same time, if the priest listened as God, the parishioner found added pressure to reveal all and reveal it honestly.[61]

The extravagance of speculation on the inviolability of the seal in scholastic writing testifies to its increasing importance quite apart from its function of protecting the parishioner. Theologians go so far as to claim that the seal of confession's "violation is not permissible to save the life of the pope, or to avert the overthrow of the state, or even . . . to gain the salvation of mankind, or to prevent the conflagration of the world, or the perversion of religion, or the attempted destruction of all the sacraments."[62] The context for such hyperbolic efforts of secrecy is paradoxical. Unlike today's confession, which is secured by the physical box and technological developments in soundproofing as much as by the priest's seal, medieval confessions took place in public in the open church. John Bossy argues for a very public experience of what was already being regarded as a very private and confidential act:

Medieval confession, we need to remember, was a face-to-face encounter between two people who would probably have known each other pretty well; we may also remember that it occurred, normally speaking, once a year, in the not-so-remote presence of a large number of neighbours, and more or less at the time (Maundy Thursday) set aside for the reconciliation of the community of public penitents in the pre-scholastic sense.[63]

The custom was for a man to kneel before the priest in the front of the church to confess, while a woman was expected to be seated to the side of the priest facing the open church, so that the priest would not be tempted by the sight of her. Apparently, not all penitents showed proper obedience and recognition of the priest's authority that the kneeling was meant to convey, for one Middle English sermon scolds in exasperation that the penitent "do noȝt as is the maner of many lewde folke, *scilecet*, for to sitte euen downe bi hym [the priest] as thou were his maister or fellawe, but sitte atte his feet as man that comeþ to aske foryeuenes of God euerlastynge dampnacion" (do not in the manner of ignorant people who sit down next to the priest as if they were his master or equal, but sit at his feet as one who comes to ask forgiveness of God from eternal damnation).[64] No physical contact was supposed to occur in this public act, except in cases where the older method of absolution survived, in which case the priest would lay his hands on the parishioner to signify her absolution. Otherwise, the sign of the cross was used for the same purpose.[65] In England in the late Middle Ages, there also may have been a "shriving pew" and "shriving cloth" to formalize and structure the confessional act, as well as render it more private.[66] Nevertheless, for all the regimen of secrecy surrounding confession, it remained primarily an act conducted in public. For both men and women the very publicity of confession meant that the confidentiality of its content could never be insured by the seal of confession. There was always the danger that neighbors might overhear the confession in addition to witnessing its silent or murmured spectacle. For women this publicity was considered to be a necessary protection against the sexual desires and scandalous behavior of priests.[67] At the same time, this publicity compromised the confidentiality of confession, making it vulnerable to the gossip, speculation, and whispers of the community. Efforts to contain this threat finally led to the introduction of the confessional box in 1565 by Carlo Borromeo, cardinal and archbishop of Milan (1564–84). Evidence suggests that it was developed specifically for hearing the confessions of women and for ensuring the safety not only of their secrets but of their bodies as well. The publicity of the confessional act was thereby replaced by the privacy and intimacy of the confessional box, with its grille separating priest and penitent that barred all form of physical contact down to the squeezing of a pea through its grate.[68] The implicit danger of secret places — of sexual solicitation and of other sinful opportunities enabled by the discourse of revealing secrets itself — is dramatically characterized by Jean Gerson, the chancellor of the University of Paris and writer of several treatises on confession: "Confession should be made before the eyes of all in an open place, to prevent a rapacious wolf from sneaking into corners and causing the contemplation of shameful things."[69]

The elaborate efforts to enclose the act of confession in a seal of professional secrecy might be viewed as protective ones that attempted to compensate for its awkward publicity. Yet as I have suggested, the secrecy required of priests did not extend to the community that might overhear or conjecture about a penitent's secrets. This secrecy was originally designed not as a form of protection of parishioners but as a mechanism for encouraging them to talk, to tell those secrets that shame might otherwise prevent them from revealing. It also conferred power and authority on the priest, whose vow to secrecy superseded all others. Yet the hyperbolic prescription to secrecy exceeded any of these specific effects, and in fact, failed to serve the one function we normally assign to it, of protecting the confessant. Instead of the safe haven — the "comfort zone," courtesy of Genuflex — for the revealing of shameful secrets that it was ostensibly designed to create, the seal of confession fostered an obsession with secrecy and its violations, increased sacerdotal power, extended the reach of the Church's power in theory if not always in practice, and designed a discourse that came to define Christian subjectivity. Confession itself was neither secret nor private, but it became *the* secret of medieval culture, even as it inhabited the realm of the public and the visible. Confession is, in a sense, the secret that is manifest, the "open" secret, if you will. The seal and mechanisms of secrecy serve mainly to disclose the secrets of the individual, to bring the hidden out of hiding and into the safekeeping of a priest's discretion, notwithstanding the open church and company of neighbors. The paradoxes that structure confessional secrecy direct us to look elsewhere for its cultural currency.

As Foucault has intimated, confession was supposed to counteract the operations of shame, that refuge of Christian sin that kept it silent. Yet the objects of confessional disclosure were always less the secrets themselves than the ritualized telling and sacerdotal listening. Secrecy seems required to protect the confidences of the one who confesses, but it clearly also functions to elicit the sinner's secrets from that other human mechanism of secrecy, shame, and to empower the confessor who hears as God. It creates an intimacy between priest and confessing layperson, and yet at the same time, is curiously one-sided. For the penitent is not allowed to keep her secrets from the priest, nor is she endowed with his knowledge, discretion, or power of absolution. The obligation for the penitent to confess is part of the priest's obligation to keep her confession secret, making confession and secrecy aspects of the same discursive regime. Foucault characterizes this regime as permeated by multiple kinds of silences (or secrets), including "the things one declines to say, or is forbidden to name, the discretion that is required between different speakers," in conjunction with (not opposed to) what is said.[70] Secrecy is not simply the act of hiding or concealing what is said in confidence; rather, it is part of the "overall strategies" that include what is said and what is not, what is kept secret.

The priest, as the repository of the secrets, is indeed, as Foucault described him, "the one who questions and is not supposed to know." His secrecy in turn protects the secrets of the penitent — the one who knows and speaks, but is constrained by obstacles and resistances he/she cannot always fathom. Secrecy thus contains the act of disclosure, and the pressure to reveal is intimately associated with the obligation to conceal. Both priest and penitent are under different obligations to conceal, and this conflict haunts the obligation to tell and the truth that is finally told. As Foucault coyly puts it, "Suppose the obligation to conceal it [the sin, especially sex] was but another aspect of the duty to admit to it (concealing it all the more and with greater care as the confession of it was more important, requiring a stricter ritual and promising more decisive effects)?"[71]

The operations of secrecy are neither simple nor uniform. They presuppose as much about language, mystery, and human relationships as they do about the secret being concealed. In a discussion of secrecy that recalls Foucault, the scholar of seventeenth-century mysticism, Michel de Certeau, describes secrecy as a "web of tactics" that is woven around the secret:

Secrecy is not only the state of a thing that escapes from or reveals itself to knowledge. It designates a play between actors. It circumscribes a terrain of strategic relations between the one trying to discover the secret and the one keeping it, or between the one who is supposed to know it and the one who is assumed not to know it.[72]

The secrecy de Certeau describes here is less a function of individual secrets than it is a "social network." As such, it is hardly the thing that dare not speak its name: "The secret concerns the utterance. It is an address: it repels, attracts, or binds the interlocutors; it is addressed to someone and acts upon him."[73] Medieval confession created its own terrain of strategic relations in which the one trying to discover the secret is at the same time trying to produce an avowal. The avowal of the secret is more important than the sin disclosed. As I have already argued, confessional secrecy bound priest and confessant together in an intimate discourse, but the power of one's address to act upon the other is reserved for the priest alone. He is not supposed to react or respond to revelations made to him, and this rule confers upon him no small control of the dialogue. One Middle English manual warns the priest very explicitly that he should not give any hint of his impressions or his judgments of the sinner's words through hasty words or even through his body language. The optimal manner of the priest was to sit "stylle as ston," neither revealing his thoughts nor "wringing his thighs" in consternation, lest the penitent suppose his disapproval.[74]

The priest's "will to know" takes the form of a very elaborate protocol of interrogation. His address is primarily interrogative and indicative, in the form of absolution. The Lateran canon of 1215 urges the priest to inquire diligently "the circumstances alike of the sinner and of the sin, by which (circumstances) he may judiciously understand what counsel he ought to give him, and what sort of remedy to apply."[75] This required an extensive cataloguing and classifying of sins and a careful method of interrogation. By the early thirteenth century, books of instruction for confessors had evolved beyond tariffs of penances into manuals of pastoral instruction.[76] Among the most important post-Lateran Council confessional manuals were Robert of Flamborough's *Liber Poenitentialis* (1208–1213), Thomas of Chobham's *Summa Confessorum* (c. 1216), and Raymond of Peñaforte's *Liber Extra* (1234), which nevertheless often drew upon earlier decretals and penitentials, such as the *Decretum* of Burchard of Worms (c. 1018) and the *Decretum* of Ivo of Chartres (1091–1116). Designed to provide confessors with the knowledge necessary to the priest's role as judge, counsel, and moral theologian, these works offered a "systematic exposition of doctrine concerning the sacrament of penance and administration."[77]

The goal of confession according to these manuals was clear: a complete inventory of moral sins, including all fourteen of their "aggravating circumstances," such as place, time, person, age, condition, number, duration, motive, manner of sinning, status, and degree of resistance. Although the penitent is responsible for telling her sins, the priest is encouraged to

inquire into the circumstances and to determine the depth of the parishioner's sorrow and intention to amend.[78] Beyond the circumstances, however, a system of interrogation was developed:

The priest was . . . instructed to interrogate the sinner seriatim on each of the
precepts of the Decalogue, the seven deadly sins, the abuses of the five senses and
the thoughts and lusts of the heart. No loophole was to be left through which the
penitent could escape the searching inquisition.[79]

The priest's obligations to this elaborate system could be personal as well as
professional because if he did not push the questions into all the details of
the sin, he could be guilty of a mortal sin himself. The manuals and summas
for confessors provide unwieldy procedures for questioning on a wide
range of sins. One manual lists 700 inquiries to guide the confessor, while
another lists separate instructions for every class and occupation of sinner.[80]
Although the confessor is also encouraged to use discretion and caution, a
massive and labyrinthine literature of interrogations was produced to direct
his efforts to elicit a complete confession. The secrecy of his seal exists in
conjunction with this curiously excessive injunction to speak in the form of
inquiring after the confessant's secrets. Yet the confessant's secrets always
remain out of reach of the most erstwhile pursuits of the summa's instructions and the priest's efforts. As Robert of Flamborough warns in his immensely popular thirteenth-century *Liber Poenitentialis*, "You should not
therefore expect perfection in this matter; for the 'heart' of man 'is inscruta-
ble' and who can really know it?"[81]

But the parish priest was expected to crack the inscrutability of the
human heart as though it were possible. He needed to be skilled in tactics
for stimulating the confessant's memory and tricking him/her into admit-
ting sins that either he/she did not know were sins or did not intend to
confess. The obligation to confess itself was assumed to render confessants
more sly and deceptive, requiring ever more skillful efforts of the priest to
penetrate their cunning. In his instruction to his friars, St. Bonaventure
observes how the medieval penitent has learned all the arts of concealing,
excusing, and mitigating his sins, and how he has resorted to every kind of
subterfuge to avoid the consequences of his sin.[82] One of the more outra-
geous examples of the Church's effort to combat this subterfuge is Jean Gerson's *On the Confession of Masturbation*. Because of the reluctance of most
penitents to admit to this particular sin, Gerson lays out an explicit and
devious series of questions for tricking the sin out of the sinner: "Friend, do
you remember when you were young, about ten or twelve years old, your

rod or virile member ever stood erect?" If the confessant denies it, he is already guilty of a lie because erections are natural to young boys. Having tripped up his parishioner, the confessor pursues him:

"Friend, wasn't that thing indecent? . . . What did you do, therefore, so that it wouldn't stand erect?" And let this be said with a tranquil visage, so that it will appear that what has been asked about is not dishonorable or something to be kept quiet, but rather as a remedy against the alleged awkwardness of the aforementioned erection.

Gerson's line of questioning continues to assume the penitent's subterfuge and to adopt the manner of friendly but naive questioner:

"Friend, didn't you touch or rub your member (virgam) the way boys usually do?" If he entirely denies that he ever held it or rubbed it in that state it is not possible to proceed further except in expressing amazement and saying that it is not credible: exhorting him to remember his salvation; that he is before God; that it is most serious to lie in confession, and the like.

Once the penitent admits he masturbated, the questions do not let up; in fact, they increase in earnest:

"Friend, I well believe it; but for how long? an hour? a half hour? and for so long that the member was no longer erect?" And let this be uttered as if the confessor did not think this unusual or sinful. If the penitent answers that he did so, then there is evidence (habetur intentum) that he has truly committed the sin of masturbation, even if on account of his age pollution did not follow.[83]

The hidden sin is assumed by Gerson to be there all along throughout this sample interrogation. Every sinner comes to confession, like young boys, with something hidden in need of telling and deciphering by means of an equal skill on the part of the confessor in masking his true intention. His utterance "as if" is itself a lie, suggesting as it does that masturbation is natural and common, and therefore, not morally offensive or punishable. Not only is it designed to disclose the secret, but it leads to further inter-rogations into the details of the sin, and ultimately, to punishment.

There is a danger, however, in the confrontational style of Gerson's interrogations. Other writers warned against inquiring too deeply into such sins as sodomy or masturbation, lest the priest end up teaching the sins to his parishioner. The definitive position on this problem of the inquiry that provokes rather than elicits sins is that of Raymond of Peñaforte in his summa, the *Raymundina* (1220–45):

After he has heard the confession, let him begin to inquire distinctly and methodi-
cally. . . . Nevertheless, I advise that in his questions he not descend to special
circumstances and special sins; for many fall severely after such an interrogation who
otherwise never would have dreamt of it.[84]

Clearly, the confessant is not the only one who withholds secrets during
confession. The priest is caught between the demands of discretion, which
are aimed at protecting the confessant's ignorance of some sins, and the
requirements of interrogation, which are also designed to protect the confessant from her own confusion, forgetfulness, shame, and outright deception. The danger of provoking the penitent to sin seems only to apply to
sexual sins. Robert of Flamborough goes further than Raymond to advise
using only the most general language when alluding to unnatural sex. The
priest must ask the penitent if he has engaged in any "unusual" sins "against
nature," but if the penitent asks him what this means, the priest is not
allowed to elaborate except in the most vague and general of terms about
those things that "everyone knows to be sin."[85] Although the knowledge of
these sins is already universal, Robert implies, there is still a danger in their
verbalization in confession, where they risk being relearned through the
priest's overly conscientious interrogation.

There is another danger in confession besides that of teaching penitents the knowledge and practice of unnatural sexual acts. All confession
brings the "risk of corruption" to the priest in the form of pleasure in the
talk about sins. St. Bonaventure stipulated that a priest must repress all
pleasure at what he hears in confession. Another summa assures priests that
as long as they confess the delectation they enjoyed in the details of another's confession, they will be preserved from sin. It also warns the priest,
however, that by inquiring too specifically into the penitent's sins he risks
becoming infected himself by the sin. Finally, instructions to penitents
advise the use of language that will not excite their confessors.[86] The discourse of confession was clearly charged with the erotic for both participants, but chiefly for the priest, who after all, not only controlled the secrets
revealed but experienced pleasure in the talk and in the triumph of his will
to know over the penitent's will to conceal. The erotics of confession is, in
fact, less a function of its contents than of the secrecy and the "play between
actors," as de Certeau describes it.

If confession presumes the interrogator's will to know the sinner's
secret through complicated protocols of decipherment and disclosure, it
equally presumes the confessant's *will to conceal* at the same time that he is

telling.[87] John Mirk's Middle English *Instructions for Parish Priests* makes this presumption throughout, advising the priest to be *connynge* (clever), *slegh* (secretive), and *fel* (shrewd) so that he can grope confessants' thoughts until they have nothing left to tell.[88] To the confessant is reserved the art of hiding while pretending to show, of convincing his confessor of the truth of what he says and how he feels and, in some cases, of discovering what the confessor wants to know. The "web of tactics" here is woven around the joint effort at discernment of the confessant's secrets, but it involves a complicated mesh of seductions and manipulations on the part of both actors. This constitutes its play and its fascination, as Gerson's mock inquiry about masturbation vividly demonstrates.

The ideal of the good confession, of course, is devoid of such subterfuge, in accordance with the sincerity of the parishioner and the success of the priest. It is, in fact, transparent, unencumbered by the confessant's or the priest's desires. One verse derived from St. Thomas Aquinas presents a capsulated account of the exemplary confessional utterance:

Let the confession be simple, humble, pure, faithful,
And frequent, unadorned, discreet, willing, ashamed,
Whole, secret, tearful, prompt,
Strong, and reproachful, and showing readiness to obey.[89]

This short verse details sixteen conditions for a good confession covering all aspects of the confessional utterance and the disposition of the confessant. In an early sixteenth-century work, the *Sylvestrina* (1514) by Sylvester Prierias Mazzolini, each of these sixteen conditions is explained. The simplicity of the utterance demands, for example, that the confession focus on the sin itself and not its story; the humility, purity, and faithfulness are all properties governing the confessant's disposition, intention, and truthfulness. The confession must promptly follow the sin, and it must be frequent, that is, it must include old, already confessed sins as well as new ones. The utterance itself should be unadorned without obscurity, discreet without provocative language (which endangers himself and the priest), voluntary, and ashamed (showing proper remorse). Finally, it should be whole in the sense of complete and strong (forthright), secret on the part of both people, tearful to signify internal sorrow, accusing of the penitent alone, and it should demonstrate the penitent's willingness to obey the priest. In the *Opus tripartitum*, Jean Gerson provides a similar if somewhat shortened model for the penitent's confession: "Let the sinner accuse himself humbly, and not derisively; honestly and not deceitfully; purely, directly, and sincerely, avoiding irrelevancies; and above all discreetly, so that he does not reveal those who were his companions in sin."[90]

Versions of this model may be found throughout the Middle English manuals for parish priests and instructions for laymen. The Middle English rule for anchoresses, the *Ancrene Wisse*, stresses eight characteristics of the good confession, including shamefulness, which is considered to be a feminine characteristic to begin with.[91] Shame presents a problem in confession because, although it is the proper response to one's sins, it should not constrain one from revealing the sin, nor should it drive the confession, according to Sylvester.[92] Against this constraint of shame in women, John Mirk's *Festial* tells the story of how Christ appeared to a woman whose shame prevented her from confessing her sins. He remedied her shame by having her reach inside the wound in his side and reminding her that she should be as willing to reveal her heart as he is.[93] The trope of Christ's revealing his heart and his wounds often serves as the contrapuntal image of the penitent's proper shame. Shame thus acts in a paradoxical way as a constraint to the activity of self-exposure and as stimulus — or even effect — of proper humility. Negotiating the discursive limits and spiritual benefits of shame must have been a tricky business indeed.

One variation on the model confession includes warnings in Robert Mannyng's *Handlyng Synne* to avoid *wanhope* (despair) which, like shame, blocks a full and open confession. Other writers suggest prior preparation for the act of confession through consideration of one's sins and examination of one's conscience. Finally, all stress the importance of confessing *openliche, clyerliche,* and *nakedliche* (openly, clearly, and nakedly), neither holding anything back, nor falsifying one's sins, nor obfuscating the nature of one's guilt.[94]

The model is for unmediated exposition of one's sins without falsification, boasting, self-derision, or storytelling, which ultimately disposes one to obedience. It describes an avowal of one's sins in response both to the priest's will to know and to the terms of that knowledge. The penitent must show all and at the same time be prepared to follow the priest's counsel for penance. Chaucer's Parson defines confession in the midst of his penitential treatise at the end of the *Canterbury Tales* as the "verray shewynge of synnes to the preest" (X.318). As he further explains, in a "true showing," "al moot be seyd, and no thyng excused ne hyd ne forwrapped, and noght avaunte thee of thy goode werkes" (all must be shown, and nothing excused or hid or concealed, and do not boast of your good works, X.320).[95] The same idea appears in the Middle English *Speculum Sacerdotale*: "let him [the sinful man] putte hym alle to-geder in the dome and pouste of the preste and kepe no-thyng vnschewid but be redy in alle poyntis for to doo and perfourme as he woll consayle hym for the redempcion of his sowle and for the euitacion of euerlastyng deþe" (let the sinful man put himself completely in the judgment and power of the priest and keep nothing unshown, but be ready in all points to do and perform as the priest will council him for the redemption of his soul and for the shunning of eternal death).[96] Leaving nothing unshown is a daunting prospect, especially for the common sinner, and it probably militates against the demands of the confession to be focused and specific, not long-winded and rambling. Complete disclosure of the Christian subject is, in fact, neither possible nor really desirable, given the limitations of language, time, and human capacity for self-reflection, but the injunction to "leave nothing unshown" nevertheless governs both priest and penitent and the confessional discourse as a whole. It ensures that no matter how much is revealed, something remains unsaid — that secret of the Christian subject that is never fully verbalized and that in fact seems to go more into hiding the more it is transformed into language.

Complete confessions were governed by a systematic inventory of undesirable behavior and a categorizing and classifying of these sins so that their gravity could be assessed, measured, and finally relieved through appropriate penance. Like the system of interrogations, the categories, subcategories, and varieties of sin were complicated and extensive. While Gerson attempted to limit the investigation of conscience to the Ten Commandments and Seven Deadly Sins, most confessional manuals listed many more categories, including the twelve articles of faith, the five senses, the six sins against the Holy Spirit, and nine sins against one's neighbor.[97] In addition to the types of sin, there was the even more important classification of the sinner's culpability in sin according to whether it was mortal or venial. Although there is a stated difference between mortal sins, for which Christians are held accountable in confession, and venial sins, which are undesirable but not serious, in practice, factors such as intention, belief, knowledge, and degree vex the distinction between these two kinds of sin, as venials can turn into mortals through evil intention or repetition. Gerson sets up the most comprehensible definition of a mortal sin as a sin that violates one of the Ten Commandments and is committed with deliberation, knowledge, and consent.[98] Still, Gerson acknowledges the confusion among theologians on the issue and the impossibility of making a definite and universal distinction between the two. The slippage between the two is also apparent in the Parson's Tale where the Parson warns that when venial sins diminish a human being's love for Christ, they "skippeth into deedly sinne" (X.360).

The verbalizing of secrets, no matter how shameful, obviously represented only one measure of the confessant's truth. The priest was required to determine the state of the confessant's knowledge, consent, and especially pleasure in committing the sinful act. As I have already suggested, the confessor was also obligated to assess the penitent's intention, whether she spoke out of fear of hell or out of shame, neither of which warranted her absolution. Rather, she must speak from a heartfelt sorrow, or contrition, and remorse for her sin. The priest was also supposed to inquire delicately and cautiously into the extent of her knowledge or ignorance of the sin she committed. From her testimony of her sin, he was to gauge the nature of her consent, particularly whether in committing a sinful act, she actually consented to "the enjoyment of the pleasure of thinking about it," or in Jean Gerson's words, *consensus in delectatione*.[99] The pleasure of thinking about a sin doubles the pleasure of its commission and compounds its seriousness. Interestingly, the process of confession necessitates just such thinking, and therefore, it always risks this secondary form of pleasure described by Gerson. Confession necessarily ventured into this area of pleasure — of thinking about sin — through the act of verbalization, but this pleasure is one of the secrets and paradoxes of the confessional logic.

Foucault describes this pleasure in his general description of the Western habit of confessing as the "pleasure in the truth of pleasure, the pleasure of knowing that truth, of discovering and exposing it, the fascination of seeing it and telling it, of captivating and capturing others by it, of confiding it in secret, of luring it out in the open — the specific pleasure of the true discourse on pleasure."[100] This pleasure surrounds the self-renunciation, self-examination, and verbalization that constitutes confession. Most of all, it is structured and defined by secrecy — including the elaborate modern technologies of soundproofing confessional boxes, the scrupulous questioning designed by Gerson and others to discover and expose the sinner's secret sins, the equally intransigent secrecy of the sinner to conceal her sins, the ironclad seal that bound the priest not to reveal any secrets of his parishioners, the secret motions of thought that needed to be deciphered, tracked, and rendered up for absolution, and the notion of the medieval subject, whose peace of mind depended on the intricate system of secrets and verbalizations that confession provided. "You are as sick as your secrets," a popular wisdom of today's self-help programs, is really a modern reflex of the medieval confessional and reconciliation system. The necessity of cure through verbalization is already implicit in the idea of the disease, whether it be sinfulness, alcoholism, or any of the other dysfunctions of modern society.

Secrecy is deeply implicated not only in the ontology of sin and redemption in the Middle Ages, but in the verbalization, self-examination, subjectivity, and as Foucault reminds us, in truth itself. For the medieval subject comes into being through her acts of disclosure, through the discovery of her secrets, and through the ritual discourse that enables such discoveries. The manifestations of these secrets and the sacrifice of the self that accompanies self-disclosure — these are the requirements of the new truth technology produced by Christian confession in the Middle Ages. Pleasure was the secret and unintended effect of this technology, and it was not confined to the subject of sex and sexuality, as Foucault thought. It is true that sexual acts increasingly became organized, defined, and codified through the confessional summae and handbooks for parish priests, but sexuality itself was only one aspect of a system devoted to the surveillance of the individual, and it was not always the most verbose.[101] In Chaucer's Parson's Tale, which draws on the summa of Raymond of Peñaforte and William Peraldus, Wrath takes up the longest discussion, while Lechery comes in a close third to Pride. Yet sexuality does seem to preoccupy other summa. For example, one of the most important summae of the Middle Ages, especially in England, Thomas of Chobham's *Summa Confessorum* (c.1216), the veritable "medieval best-seller" that followed close upon the Fourth Lateran Council and influenced later summae, begins with the sins of *luxuria*, and he reserved the largest part of his discussion of the Seven Deadly Sins to this vice. In particular, he is known for his extensive discussion of nocturnal emissions among clergy.[102] Gerson, too, is known for devoting special attention to sexuality, particularly masturbation, in his treatise *On the Confession of Masturbation*.

As I hope this chapter has shown so far, however, the more important consequence of confessional theory and praxis in the Middle Ages was not the amount of talk devoted to the subject of sex but the technology of secrecy, interrogation, self-publication, and pleasure. Foucault's own analysis of confession in volume 1 of his *History of Sexuality* already points away from "sex itself" to secrecy, technologies of the self, and the systems of power and knowledge in the Middle Ages. Such a focus does not discount, dismiss, or ignore the role that sexuality came to play in confession; it merely repositions sex and sexuality back within the discourse that "made" it in conjunction with many other things. Sex was not yet bracketed off from the discourse and power relations that produced it and from the field of human sinfulness from which it derived its greatest meaning.

Foucault also alluded to the "metamorphosis in literature" that accompanied this new technology in Western culture, one that became "ordered according to the infinite task of extracting from the depths of oneself, in between the words, a truth which the very form of the confession holds out like a shimmering mirage."[103] As if to echo Foucault, Lee Patterson claims that confession was "one of the central modes of self-representation available in late-medieval England."[104] Even a superficial survey of medieval literature provides evidence to support both claims. In English literature the Wife of Bath's and Pardoner's Prologues and the Parson's Tale in Chaucer's *Canterbury Tales*, the Prologue to the *Legend of Good Women*, the Middle English penitential lyrics, Langland's confession of the Seven Deadly Sins in *Piers Plowman*, and John Gower's *Confessio Amantis* all deploy confessional structures, themes, and strategies to widely divergent ends and effects. *The Book of Margery Kempe* is a mystical treatise that broadly translates medieval confession into autobiographical narrative, although no one has explored the confessional technologies in this work. If confession was itself a hegemonic discourse of the Middle Ages, it was clearly a flexible one that could adopt various forms and adapt to various purposes in the literary texts that drew upon it.

Sir Gawain and the Green Knight is another such text that not only addresses confession thematically but inhabits a confessional structure, with all its secrecy, courtly and moral protocols, and pleasures. This poem is particularly interesting for this study of confession because it presents a crisis in the courtly and confessional codes of secrecy at the same time that it attempts to reinstall these codes. In the course of this crisis, the secret that dare not speak its name becomes the confessional subject, Sir Gawain himself, and confession is undone by its own self-parody.

Confessions of the Flesh II: *Sir Gawain and the Green Knight*

Bot in syngne of my surfet I schal se hit ofte,
When I ride in renoun remorde to myseluen
Þe faut and þe fayntyse of þe flesche crabbed,
How tender hit is to entyse teches of fylþe.

(But as a sign of my transgression I will see it often,
When I ride in renown lament to myself

The fault and the frailty of the perverse flesh,
How susceptible it is to stain through the impure suggestion.)[105]

Gawain's public confession at the end of *Sir Gawain and the Green Knight* quoted here proleptically echoes Foucault, whose unpublished fourth volume links confession to the *flesche crabbed*, with its vulnerability to the *teches of filþe*, and the enticement to speak that it engenders. If there is one quality that Gawain's shame produces, it is a talkativeness that simply will not be silenced. An interesting transformation occurs in Gawain's talent for *luf-talkyng* at the end of the poem, when it changes into a compulsion for "shrift-talking," signaled by the green girdle he wears as a sign of his shame. He is like Foucault's hypothetical penitent, who authenticates himself by proclaiming "the truth which he previously concealed." At the same time the unsettling disavowal of Gawain, voiced by the Lady in Bertilak's castle, Bertilak, and Gawain himself also proves true: Gawain is not Gawain. The poem's uncanny reiteration of this idea that Gawain the man is inconsistent with his identity and reputation as a knight echoes Foucault's summary of the effects of confession ("I am not who I am"), and it causes us to wonder, in Carolyn Dinshaw's words, "When *will* Gawain be Gawain?"[106]

An equally urgent question at the end of this poem is: How much talk can a girdle and a nick on the neck produce? Foucault's account of the secret that is dedicated to speaking its name ad infinitum can find no better representation than in this poem. If Lee Patterson is correct that confession is a central mode of self-representation in late medieval literature, then *Sir Gawain* presents both a discursive outpouring of this mode and its elusive counterpoint of self-rupture and self-disavowal. Although medieval scholars have variously commented on the role that confession plays in the spiritual restoration of Gawain and its equally trenchant exposure of the conflicts of chivalry, no one has examined how confession works as a discourse, how it *means*, and what its ideological investments are.[107] I want to look at the poem through the discourse of confession I have already outlined to suggest that the main question of the poem is not who Gawain is, but how he comes to tell his secret at the same time that the poem exerts ever more pressures towards textual secrecy. In the balance hang the "abundance of pleasurable talk" and the gender instabilities that the poem seeks to contain through its confessional imperative.[108]

J. A. Burrow constellates the third fitt of the poem around Gawain's incomplete confession as a site of his violation not just of the chivalric code of courtesy to his host but of the "whole Christian-chivalric complex" identified with the virtue of *trawþe*, or religious faith, trust, confidence, truthfulness, honesty and integrity.[109] Gawain confesses to a priest after he receives the girdle from the Lady, but in doing so he fails to mention the wrongfully acquired girdle, much less restore it to its proper owner. Two further confessions follow this failed confession, according to Burrow: the second occurs after Gawain receives his neck-wound, when he confesses again to Bertilak his cowardice, covetousness, and untruth; the third takes the form of a public confession before Arthur's court at the end of the poem from which the quotation introducing this section is taken. Invoking the Fourth Lateran Council and the church's "formidable campaign to educate laymen in the theory and practice of Confession," Burrow constructs a framework of intelligibility for the poem from this theory and practice. Interestingly, it leads to speculations about Gawain's failure to return the girdle, the contradictory judgments of Gawain's sins, and whether Gawain can be guilty of sin by omission rather than commission.[110] It is ultimately Gawain's concealment of the girdle from Bertilak and the priest to whom he confesses that Burrow, Spearing, and more recent scholars find problematic. Even scholars who are not interested in — or who explicitly resist — medieval confessional imperatives as a way of understanding the poem locate its significance in Gawain's withholding, and in the general secrecy, unintelligibility, and splitting of domains and consciousness.[111]

Indeed, the entire poem seems to be complicitous in Gawain's project of coversion, as Carolyn Dinshaw points out:

> *Sir Gawain and the Green Knight* is a poem so devoted to the surfaces of things (its lavish attention to courtly manners, occasions, and appointments is often remarked) and so preoccupied with keeping its depths and fissures from bursting forth (its narrative swerve from beheading to confession and penance is the most pointed example) that it labors to limit the significance of its signs, the nature of its characters, the meanings of their actions.[112]

Scholars curiously find in this Middle English poem a poetics of concealment, whether it is attributed to the strictures of confession, heterosexual normativity, or simply an intractability against the return of the repressed. Concealment itself becomes the method and meaning of the poem, and confession haunts both, preventing the poem's "depths and fissures from bursting forth" and dogging Gawain's efforts to reestablish his chivalric, public identity at the end of the poem.

Where there is concealment, as Foucault would remind us, there is pleasure. It is not the confessions alone that produce the "perpetual spirals of power and pleasure" that Foucault described; it is the excessive *luf-talkyng* that occupies a major focus of the third fitt of the poem and the poetics of concealment that frames the entire work — the multiform silences that limn all the talk. The spiraling of pleasure accumulates from the series of Gawain's confessions, from his sequence of seductions by the Lady, and from the poetics of the text.[113] In fact, those scholars who talk about pleasure tend to omit discussion of the confessional scenes, while those interested in the morality of Gawain's actions omit discussion of pleasure in their analysis of his confessions. What no one has noticed so far is the complicity of the two aspects of the poem — confession and love-talking — and the poet's brilliant analogizing of the discourses of penance and desire. This complicity is neither abstract nor conjectural: it is suggested in the poem by the parallels between the three confessional scenes and the three seduction scenes, between the language of love-talk and the language of confession, and between the dynamics of Lady and male lover and confessor and penitent. By collapsing these two modes of discourse, the poem implicates confession and amorous talk in the pleasure of talk about secrets, a pleasure that Foucault came to associate with the defining discourse of Western culture.

Foucault has already observed that the technology of Christian confession possessed "a whole series of methods that had much in common with an erotic art." That "pleasure in the truth of pleasure" and the pleasure of revealing and concealing a carefully hidden secret constitute the discursive resemblance of these two cultural fields. Sex and desire were the ultimate secrets circulated within both discourses, but they were not simply the goals of speech. Nor was speech simply a medium of sex and desire.[114] The *Gawain* poet's conflation of these two discourses in his poem not only allows the reader to see the complicity of this "pleasure about the truth of pleasure," but forces us to notice what this complicity might mean.

It is useful to begin an examination of the bedroom scenes in the poem by recalling Michel de Certeau's account of the "problematics of secrecy" as a "play between actors," a confrontation between the will to know and the will to conceal, between telling and not telling, that is edged with the erotic. He further characterizes the secret as an utterance, an address that "repels, attracts, or binds the interlocutors" and "acts upon" the one who is addressed.[115] The ludic aspect of the lady's seduction is apparent throughout the three instances of it in contrast to Gawain's irritable reluctance. Yet, as Geraldine Heng is surely right to point out, Gawain's wariness and discomfort should not blind us to the real attraction and pleasure that his love talk also provides. What is important about these three scenes, though, is the pleasurable talk that produces Gawain's identity crisis and the secrets that each player attempts to withhold from the other. The scenes are reminiscent of the confessional scene, in which the same elements of secrecy, withholding, pleasure, and discomfort (not to say, remorse) obtain, and the same mastery of rhetoric is required to "prevent a rapacious wolf from sneaking into corners," to borrow Gerson's apt phrase. The difference between the two that renders the one unrecognizable in the other is, of course, the relationship of power—and desire. A woman cannot easily substitute for a priest, even though critics have no difficulty substituting Bertilak for one. Nor is woman so legibly the subject of desire. The poem's co-articulation of the discourses of confession and desire serves to unsettle gender and sexuality even as it strives to repair the damage by performing its own act of coversion. Ultimately, the poem is unable to contain the erotic it unleashes through its elaborate play upon secrecy and verbosity.

The unleashing of rapacious wolves in the private corners of our lives could find no more appropriate expression than in the seduction/hunting scenes of *Sir Gawain and the Green Knight*. The alternation and alienation of public and private—of *chambre* and *halle*, of *gay bed* and *forest*—produces a distressing split both in the coherence of the public code of chivalry and in Gawain's own consciousness, as David Aers has argued.[116] This splitting not only represents the interiorization of space and consciousness but it signals a series of disjunctions in the poem: of public and private, courtesy and desire, seduction and hunting, contracts and loyalty, commodities and feminine favors, and of course, pentangles and girdles. The domestication of space and the interiorization of consciousness threaten the ethos of chivalry as a public ideal, the structure of gender relations, and the textual containment of desire.

The first day of Gawain's stay at Bertilak's castle finds him in "gay bed lygez" and fully enclosed: "Vnder couertour ful clere, cortyned aboute" (Under canopy full lovely, curtained about, 1181). Being "under coverture" carries more than merely the suggestion of Gawain's privatization; it also recalls the legal status of the married woman, the *femme coverte*, who is under the authority of—and sexually subordinated to—her husband. In fact, as I will elaborate in Chapter 4, coverture designated the wife's condition as both her husband's secret and his subject in all financial and social affairs. The sexual implication of the legal term is playfully reinforced by Gawain's predicament, as the Lady threatens to "bynde yow in your bedde" (bind you in your bed, 1211), and Gawain begs her to "deprece your prysoun" (release your prisoner, 1219). Gawain's coverture is a form of entrapment—sexual and moral—that recasts his chivalric role as abject servant into an impossible, feminized one.[117] The poem's representation of Gawain as "under coverture" elicits a serious feminizing pressure as well as a sexual objectification such as that conveyed for wives by the legal terminology. Located as he is under the canopy, Gawain is also already figured as humorously displaced, dis-integrated, de-publicized, and feminized. He resembles the Lady herself who inhabits the "comely closet" at dinner the night before, signifying her own coverture as well as her value. Yet Gawain's imprisonment in his coverture fills him with shame ("þe burne shamed," 1189)—devalues him—and he crosses himself as if to insure his protection from the demonic threat of feminization.

While this scene does not explicitly recall the confessional scene, it mimics it in several respects: it begins in Gawain's shame, although this shame is not the result of his own sinfulness; more importantly, the elements of secrecy, withholding, and pretense that penitential manuals ascribe to reluctant penitents mark this scene. The Lady enters his room secretly and stealthily ("ful dernly and stylle," 1188), and Gawain himself feigns sleep ("lay lurked") and pretends to awake in order to "discover with my discourse her desire in good time" (1199). Gawain takes his cues from the lady in a game that more and more takes on the cast of that "play between actors" described by de Certeau and associated by Foucault with the dynamics of confession. Gawain surrenders to the discourse of *luf-talkyng* in order to discover what the Lady desires at the same time that he withholds who he is and whether he desires.

When the Lady praises Gawain's reputation for his *honour* and his *hendelayk*, she also offers him her body to do with as he pleases, pledging her servitude to him. While editors and critics attribute the Lady's behavior to her "crude" and "unsophisticated" understanding of the sexual politics of romances, in fact, she is invoking the bodily within language, something that was always comprehended in confessional discourse, even if it was suppressed in the language of courtly love.[118] Later, in the passage I quoted at the beginning of this section, Gawain will recognize precisely this connection. It is because Gawain fails to acknowledge the relationship between the body (and soul) and "daynté wordez" that he is vulnerable to the Lady's seduction in the first place.

What follows in the three bedroom scenes is a kind of interrogation of Gawain by the Lady—one which precipitates the Foucaultian confessional refrain: I am not who I am. In response to the Lady's first effort to "pin

Gawain down" both figuratively and literally by imprisoning him in his bed and defining him in terms of his reputation for courtesy and "dainty discourse," Gawain simply evades her: "I be not now he þat ʒe reherce here" (I am not he of whom you speak, 1243). Like the self-splitting that underlies the confessional utterance, Gawain's posture of humility also precipitates a self-renunciation, or rather, a renunciation of the sign of himself and his *prys*, or worth. Unlike the kind of self-renunciation that constitutes the "truth about oneself" fostered by Christian confession as Foucault describes it, Gawain's act of self-disavowal is one of evasion and at the same time, of play. He uses it to avoid the suggestions of the Lady, but at the same time, to engage in her play—her *bourdez*, or jests. It is a denial that speaks volumes about Gawain himself, for it allows him to engage in the game of love-talk with all of its pleasure through self-denial. One could view this admission of Gawain's as a perversion of the discourse of Christian confession if the two were not so mutually implicated with each other.

Throughout her interrogation and seduction of Gawain, the Lady assumes that he conceals the secret to his reputation and to the art of love discourse she so eagerly desires from him. When she accuses him of not being Gawain at the end of the first bedroom scene, she implies that there is a secret to being Gawain that Gawain himself does not know: "Bot þat ʒe be Gawan hit gotz in mynde! (But whether you are Gawain is questionable! 1293). Indeed, Gawain is so flustered and fearful that he has "fayled in fourme of his castes" (failed in his form of speech) that he seems himself to doubt whether he is Gawain. But the decision of who Gawain is always rests with the Lady, who continues to use this self-rupture to humble him and render him in her power to define him. He can only be restored to "Gawain" by observing the protocols of courtesy as the Lady defines them and demanding a kiss of her, however grudgingly. In doing so, he concedes that only she knows the secret of Gawain, even as her idea of Gawain more and more paradoxically defines him as "not-Gawain." His self-sacrifice ironically is pressed into the service of his chivalric courtesy rather than his salvation or redemption, as it would be in confession. But this is also the point, since Gawain is preoccupied with the "forms of speech" and not with any type of self-examination.

In the midst of Gawain's apparent distress is an equal measure of pleasure. On the second day, the Lady becomes more persistent, scolding Gawain for his lack of courtesy and reiterating her doubt that he is Gawain because of his failure to recall her instructions in kissing from the day before: "Sir, ʒif ʒe be Wawen, wonder me þynkkez" (Sir, if you be Gawain, it is a wonder to me, 1481). Gawain is scolded not only for forgetting to kiss her but later for refusing the "tokenez of trweluf craftes" (tokens of true love's crafts, 1527) that she requests. In spite of her persistent attempts to "bring him to sin" (1550), Gawain is not as distressed and fearful as some scholars think. While he guards himself, Gawain also clearly takes pleasure in his narrow escapes and her taunts. Even though the poem frames her efforts as sinister, Gawain continues to enjoy himself, "ne non euel on nawþer halue, nawþer þay wysten / Bot blysse. / Þay laȝed and layked longe" (nor did either find any unpleasantness in the other / But bliss. / They laughed and sported for a long time, 1552–54). Gawain's pleasure clearly resists the poet's own displeasure in the Lady's temptations to "harm" (woȝe). This is one of the crucial moments in the poem where the taciturnity of the narrative breaks with the contrary, obstreperous pleasures that Gawain experiences in spite of the dangers.[119] This same split occurs again during the third visitation before the Lady gives Gawain the green girdle, when their "blis" and "bonchef" (happiness) is once again severely checked with the reminder of their "great peril" (1768).

Elsewhere the text attempts to contain the pleasurable effects of their love-talk by reducing it to summary, or report. Just as in the quotation above, dalliance is truncated in narrative vagueness, leaving the reader to guess at the sport (1554), "much wele" (much delight, 1767), "muchquat" (many things, 1280), and "much speche" (1506) that signal the narrative withholding. The persistent narrative foreclosure of pleasure in the three seduction scenes is directed at regulating the reader's pleasure and resisting the sexual tension of the artful interrogations and negotiations played out between the Lady and Gawain. In the end, however, this monitory voice of the text fails to prevent the pleasure of the discourse from having its way in the poem with both Gawain and the Lady. Critics have been too eager to adopt this same narrative taciturnity in their own readings of the Gawain's distress and the Lady's "temptation" of him. While this narrative effort of containment does assert itself at the end of the poem, it is not without unleashing the endless circuit of desire and pleasure that all confession-cum-love-talking risks. Foucault's description of the transformation of confession into psychiatric investigation, etc., might have been written of this circuit of desire, pleasure, and sheer talk in *Sir Gawain and the Green Knight*:

The pleasure that comes of exercising a power that questions, monitors, watches, spies, searches out, palpates, brings to light; and on the other hand, the pleasure that kindles at having to evade this power, flee from it, fool it, or travesty it.[120]

The Lady who questions, searches out, brings to light Gawain's chivalric flaws, and palpates his courtesy with kisses, and Gawain, who evades her by deferring to her or by his own "flirtatious wit" (*luf-laȝyng*, 1778), fools her, and flees her ruses — reenact the confessional scene where interrogation prompts similar spirals of pleasure through talk and evasion.

The relations of power in both confession and these three seduction scenes rest with the one who knows but who also interrogates. Like the priest, the Lady always seems already to know Gawain better than he himself does, and her questions aim at disclosing who he really is. Over and over again, she elicits from him disavowals of his own identity, including his reputation for love discourse, *prys*, and *prowes*. While these disavowals are mere tactics in his effort to evade the Lady's lines of questioning, they accrue to his own self-fragmentation. By the end of his third seduction, he is incapable of drawing upon his worth, prowess, or courtesy because it has been dismantled through the successive interrogations of the Lady. As long as Gawain is the one who does not know who he is — as long as she is in the position to know what his worth is — he is incapable of *being* Gawain.

Each of the bedroom scenes is doubled by the exchange of winnings with Bertilak. As a type of commodified version of the bedroom play, these scenes translate the self-knowledge that usually accompanies confession into a commercial exchange of *cheuysaunce* (1406), *chaffer* (1647, 1939), merchandise acquired at cheap cost. This exchange of winnings serves a similar function, that is, to measure and interrogate Gawain's *trawpe* and his courtesy. At the same time, this series implicates confession in a larger arena of social meaning beyond the confessional or the bedroom. The medieval codes of masculine hospitality, fellowship, and courtesy all circumscribe the agreement that Bertilak and Gawain make to exchange their winnings at the end of each day. Yet the commodification of these same values along with confession through the symbolic exchange of winnings surely mystifies the risks and dangers of their confessional pact. The homosociality and pleasure of Bertilak's court and Gawain's Camelot are here reduced to a commercial transaction that bears untold moral consequences for Gawain. He fails to see the truth for the *chaffer*; at the same time, the conversion of the Lady's kisses and sexual seduction into a rendering up of winnings to Bertilak dangerously produces a homosexual erotics in the poem.[121] Like the seduction scenes in the bedroom, this one is *technically* never consummated, but as in the heterosexual version, this technicality is irrelevant, for the desires and pleasures lie in the discursive (and commercial) exchanges. Not only does Gawain drink to this *layke*, or sport, he engages in it with apparent pleasure.

He delivers his kisses to Bertilak with courtesy, saying he offers everything to Bertilak, "even if it were more" than it is (1391). The same kind of tantalizing suggestion that forms the game of love-talk is reproduced here in these brief physical and discursive exchanges. Gawain's withholding is implied in both, as he here says he gives only what he received, though he would give more if he were required to do so. This is especially true of the last exchange, where Gawain delivers his most passionate kisses to Bertilak — "as sauerly and sadly as he hem sette coupe" (as feelingly and firmly as ever he could, 1937). Not since Absalon kissed Alisoun's ass "ful savoury" (I.3735) has a kiss been delivered with the relish with which Gawain gives one to Bertilak. This kiss is as filled with "savour" or relish as that other kiss that Absalon gives to Alisoun's ass, which he mistakes for her mouth. Gawain's is no perfunctory kiss, nor is it the "semely" kiss of the Lady. The exchange here exceeds the agreement, for Gawain's kiss is his own, and Bertilak is left wanting more. He jokes about having only a fox pelt to give for "suche prys þinges" (such precious things) and teases Gawain just as the Lady did, as if asking for more, until Gawain cries "enough!"

The replication of seduction in the exchange scenes between Gawain and Bertilak in the name of courtesy and truth implicates confession in the homosocial and homoerotic world of the poem. Pleasure in the sheer talk and game of seduction dangerously veers on the dislocations in masculine and heterosexual identity that are crucial to the chivalric / Christian ethos of the poem. The poem itself unleashes the very pleasures it seeks to contain and finally remonstrate at the end when Gawain performs his series of public confessions. The paradox is, of course, as the poem already knows, that confessional talk is endless and so are its pleasures. While Gawain's self-renunciation at the end seems to put to rest any errant pleasures still circulating from the love-talk and exchanges with Bertilak, it in fact does not. For it's all in the telling, the poem has shown, and so it continues in the proliferation and contestations of lessons at the end of the poem.

In contrast to the Green Knight's interpretation that Gawain's lack of loyalty arises from his fear for his life, Gawain produces a riff of confessional declarations ranging from shame and a denunciation of his own cowardice, covetousness of life, treachery, and dishonesty (2372, 2375, 2383) to his blaming of the "wyles of wymmen" through which many a great man has been beguiled. In contradiction of the Green Knight's declaration that Gawain is fully confessed, pardoned, and atoned for his sin, Gawain insists on wearing the green girdle as a badge of the frailty of the flesh, his pride, sign of his surfeit, and mark of his disloyalty (2433, 2437, 2433, 2500).

Gawain's confession before the court when he returns ends with yet another moral, that "mon may hyden his harme bot vnhap ne may hit, / For þer hit onez is tachched twynne wil hit neuer"(a person may hide his harm/affliction but he cannot get rid of it, / For where it is once attached, never will it be separated, 2511–12). This last message is often overlooked in favor of the more moralistic one of Gawain's self-incrimination and rumination on the frailties of the flesh. Although the two public confessions are not incompatible, neither are they identical. Here Gawain focuses on the consequences of concealment, of failing to tell the secret that then becomes his wound, but he also seems to suggest that such harms finally cannot be expunged, though this goes against the lessons of his own experience. What exactly is Gawain saying here, and is it any more important than any of the other confessional declarations that he makes?

First of all, this statement does not erase Gawain's previous statements, which are significant, too, in their very proliferation and confusion, for they render that split that Foucault observes between self-publication and self-renunciation. They also seem to render almost symptomatically Foucault's notion of the proliferation and sheer inexhaustibility of confessional discourse and its obligations to tell. Even the Green Knight's absolution does not diminish Gawain's need to tell his secrets, to search out that truth that he lacks, and finally to confess to more than the actual sin itself can bear. We must not forget that pleasure is part of the mechanism that induces this proliferation—"pleasure in the truth of pleasure, the pleasure of knowing that truth, of discovering and exposing it, the fascination of seeing it and telling it."

The poem is both interested in and worried about this very pleasure. In the two enigmatic lines quoted above, Gawain dismisses the powers of absolution and penance to release human beings from those harms they conceal; instead, he fixes on the concealment itself as the real point. Secrecy makes sins and harms cleave to us, and it finally prevents us from ever being free of them. Nevertheless, Gawain tells, and tells, and tells, and this is also the point: his telling is but another reflex of the secrecy that conditions all sin; it too, as we have seen, is endless. The only truth to be said about Gawain is the one that he and other characters have uttered throughout, that he is not Gawain. Being Gawain finally means confessing that he is not and knowing what that means. The absolution—even the sin itself—are lost in this surfeit of talk and the pleasure of Gawain's confidences, pleasures even the poem is unable and finally unwilling to contain.[122]

Nevertheless, Gawain verbalizes the central paradox of the confessional technology of secrecy as Foucault, de Certeau, and others have characterized it: that secrecy is the precondition for endless talk, confession, and disclosure and that the dis-covery of the secret does not end the process of verbalization. The lodging of the secrets of the individual in the frailty of the flesh insures that the process of self-examination and individuation must go on indefinitely, just as Gawain's public confessions are recapitulated in the poem. The secret about Gawain is finally not so important as the confession of the secret; in fact, the issue is the telling of the fault, not the fault itself. At the same time, the issue of telling allows the poem to engage in its own kind of secrecy, that of concealing the homosexual erotics disguised beneath the covenant that Bertilak and Gawain make to exchange their winnings. The kisses that Gawain and Bertilak exchange, with all their savor, are displaced by the green girdle, which is safer in spite of its connotations of female sexuality. Finally, it is not even the green girdle itself that is the problem, but the concealment of it that incriminates Gawain — his failure to place this object, too, into safe circulation between men. Or is it? The Green Knight accuses Gawain not of concealing it but of taking it out of fear for his own life and of lacking in loyalty. Gawain blames that unyielding secret of all Christians — the frailty of the flesh — and makes the green girdle its sign. In this way, he places the secret back where it is safe, that is, in the realm where feminine sexuality and the flesh are one, and men are safely outside rather than inside.[123] The secrets of the poem remain intact and safely mystified under the plethora of messages, Gawain's shame and theologizing, and his confessions. The talk goes on, and so does the pleasure.

Gawain's solemn pronouncement on his own shame and on the dangers of concealment are met with laughter from King Arthur's court and the adoption of his "sign of surfeit" as a sign of the "renoun of þe Rounde Table" and a tribute to Gawain. Their laughter echoes Bertilak's laughter at Gawain's earlier confession of his cowardice. Whether the court's laughter signifies their admiration for Gawain and their own courtesy, an affirmation of fellowship, the "sound of Camelot's fall," or the poet's abandonment of the issues raised in the poem, it adds one more meaning to the confusion of meanings in the poem.[124] Another meaning, another concealment. Dismissing Gawain's shame and self-awareness and adopting his girdle to make it resignify renown of the Round Table rather than the multitude of personal meanings Gawain attaches to it, the court laughs, pointing the reader elsewhere for the poem's meaning.

The poem has shown the complicity of courtly love and confessional operations as "games between players" involving elaborate games of secrecy and their pleasures. In spite of the poem's efforts at containment and moralization, it offers a radical and unsettling glimpse of this complicity. The confessional preoccupations of the poem cannot be separated from the bedroom seduction scenes, nor from the games that seem to structure each. By co-articulating courtly love and confessional discourse, the poem investigates the delicate interrelationships of what Foucault called the "West's most highly valued techniques for producing truth," and, I would add, identity. Chivalric identity and Christian subjectivity depend upon the creation and circulation of secrets, upon concealment and verbalization; yet this same system threatens the coherence of the Christian subject, the chivalric ideal as it is represented in the pentangle on Gawain's shield and as it composes community identity and religious morality itself. By placing disclosure at the heart of Gawain's predicament, the poem exposes the problem of the Western technique for producing truth: its "immense verbosity." Gawain dedicates his life to the recapitulation of his confession and to its proliferation. The pleasures of such verbal acts of self-renunciation are only implied in the poem and in the laughing response of Bertilak and Arthur's court. Gawain has become Foucault's "confessing animal" at the end of the poem, just as he was a "love-talking" animal in the beginning. The difference is that Gawain is no longer Gawain, for all his confessions, and the act of confession itself has been revealed to be tricky, at the very least.

"Tricky and treacherous, like all confessions," writes Margo Jefferson of the *New York Times* about a contemporary memoir of incest, *The Kiss*. For the very technology that was designed to produce the truth becomes impossible to tell from lies: "It plays fast and loose with every kind of truth . . . and it never stops questioning the nature and purpose of lies."[125] The irony of confession is that it plays fast and loose with the truth, rather than producing or discovering *the* truth. Gawain's riff on Bertilak's analysis of his lack of loyalty and love of life is finally gratuitous, and it becomes caught in its own questioning of the nature of all flesh, which is to be frail and secretive. But literary confessions are also tricky and treacherous because, as Foucault has put it, they are "ordered according to the infinite task of extracting from the depths of oneself, in between the words, a truth which the very form of the confession holds out like a shimmering mirage." The shimmering mirage that Gawain's confession holds out is as elusive as it is deceptive, for the truth is in the telling, not in the flesh. In the medieval equivalent of the contemporary memoir, Gawain dedicates himself to persistent remembrance of the frailty of his flesh as he rides in renown.

Whether this is a sign of his remorse or his narcissism is the kind of question that plagues contemporary memoirs as well.

The poem seems cognizant, too, of the trickiness and treachery of confession, both in its narcissistically fashioned truths and in its verbosity; yet for all the poem's exposure of the problems of confessional subjectivity, it too depends upon the play of secrecy for its narrative art and suspense. It too is bound by the system of telling that binds Gawain as the paradigm for medieval truths. It too, finally, enlists the reader in its confessions and its secrets to produce the pleasures of reading in the web of tactics woven around the elaborate dynamics of telling and not telling, desiring to know and desiring to conceal, publicizing and renouncing the self. To the reader are given all the pleasures of surveillance — of the one who wishes to know, who wrestles with the furtive text and Gawain's own self-ignorance, and who hears its secrets involuntarily rendered up for our judgment.

2

Tongues Wagging

Gossip, Women, and Indiscreet Secrets

Gossip will not be suppressed. It thrives in secret, it speaks what needs to be said.
— Patricia Meyer Spacks[1]

No one understands and exploits the pleasures of keeping and speaking the secret more than Chaucer's Wife of Bath. The Prologue to her tale is usually identified generically as a literary confession, defined as "a dramatic monologue in which the speaker explains, and often defends, his or her sinful way of life."[2] Yet her Prologue is nothing so much as it is gossip transformed from an oral to a written mode of discourse, from a private, covert utterance to public declaration. The slippage from confession to gossip is also tricky and treacherous, as we saw in Chapter 1. By its very proliferations, Gawain's threefold confession — to the priest, to Bertilak, and to Arthur's court at the end of the poem — threatens dangerously to devolve into gossip. The laughter with which the poem ends is suggestive of just such a slippage, and it makes reading the text a tricky and unsettling endeavor. For confession and gossip are closer in nature than the medieval church would have liked, in spite of the elaborate system of regulations it devised for the sacrament following the Fourth Lateran Council. Both "thrive in secret," as Spacks writes of gossip; both arguably speak what "needs to be said"; and both types of discourse are irrepressible even as they insist upon secrecy and containment, making them each treacherous and tricky in different ways.

It is the different cultural status assigned to the two and the stigmatization of gossip that makes all the difference. Gossiping was considered in the Middle Ages to be a vice, while confession, of course, was not. The moral opprobrium attached to gossip was not neutral because this particular vice was usually associated with women, particularly their loquaciousness, bodiliness, secrecy, and their susceptibility to deception. Gossip was also associated with a kind of insurrectionary discourse on the part of women as a marginalized medieval community, one that existed alongside — but also in resistance to — a variety of institutionalized, written discourses. This function of gossip as a resistant oral discourse of marginalized groups is one that persists in the twentieth century, as some socio-linguistic studies have shown.[3] At the same time, the equation of femininity with gossip serves in medieval and modern cultures to reinforce gender ideology and valorize traditional institutional forms of discourse and authority. No one knows this better than Chaucer's Wife of Bath. Her Prologue offers a telling introduction to the workings of gossip, including its potential for miming dominant medieval discourses, and thereby rivaling them, as well as being contained by those same discourses.

The Wife's opening distinction between experience and authority sets up a sequence of differentiations between the lived text of her marriages and clerical writings about marriage and virginity, between her voice and written authority, between interpretive communities of wives and clerics. She argues for her right to marry as often as she likes and to choose marriage over virginity by miming clerical discourse on both topics — citing authorities like Sts. Paul and Jerome, creating the false detachment that lends authoritative discourses their authority, and constructing an argument based on medieval religious precepts and principles, such as "that man shal yelde to his wyf hire dette" (that man shall yield his marital debt to his wife, III.130). Later in her Prologue, the Wife of Bath actually converts the arguments of clerics and church fathers about the evils of women and marriage into a form of gossip that she inflicts upon her first three husbands.

While it is common to view the Wife's Prologue as an appropriation of clerical discourse, or in earlier criticism, as a distortion of it, few scholars have noticed the Wife's primary identification of herself as a gossip, or of her Prologue, as the translation of antifeminist discourse into gossip by which she creates her own speech community as well as her own authority. The Wife of Bath's famous assertion of her own experience is meaningless without her implicit assertion of gossip as the discursive mode that frames, interprets, and even authorizes that experience. At the same time, it is experience as gossip that signals her own wanton transgression of the codes and discourses within which she operates. Several features of the Wife's gossip as a rival discourse emerge in the course of her Prologue.

First, her claims to experience, beyond simply asserting the authority of her life over clerical representations of women, succeed in multiplying the authorities she cites and thereby appropriates for her own use and abuse. As Jan Gordon has argued about gossips in nineteenth-century British literature, "the gossip thus mimes the absentee authority of infirm patriarchal 'men of letters' by surreptitiously multiplying authorship. Authority becomes plural rather than silently distant, but the attempt to trace it, to make it directly 'respons-ible' is equally difficult."[4] The Wife of Bath is a master at multiplying her sources, from Jerome to St. Paul to Ovid to her five marriages, which has the ingenious effect of indirectly guaranteeing her own "absentee authority" by obfuscating authority itself. Making authority untraceable is most effectively achieved through the Wife's parroting of clerical misogyny and her deliberate misattribution of her diatribe to the husbands themselves. By recasting clerical misogyny as a husband's drunken blather, which the Wife in turn angrily mimics, she succeeds in diminishing it, distancing it, and setting herself up as its mouthpiece. Her humorous way of disarming clerical discourse and authority is to consign it to a drunken blackout, rendering it not only silent but forgotten.

What distinguishes the Wife's gossipy version of authority from the "real thing" is its openness, its surplicity, its excess, and of course, its bodiliness. The Wife's openness as it is expressed in her willing disclosure of her strategies for gaining sovereignty over her husbands, however, should not be confused with confession. For the Wife of Bath never really reveals much about herself. She does declare the intentions of her marriages, the strategies and deceptions she practices on her husbands, and the sheer scope of her desires, but she never reveals herself in the Prologue. She is as much a creation of her own gossip as her five marriages are, and this allows the Wife a great deal of freedom and disguise at the same time. The fact that students and scholars think they "know" the Wife of Bath more than any other pilgrim in Chaucer's *Canterbury Tales* is a testament to the success of her gossiping narrative. For it is one of the key components of gossip as a discursive mode that it is always secondhand and always roving. Although we may recognize the Wife's voice, it is difficult to trace her speech back to its source in the self.

The Wife of Bath as a gossip insists upon a surplus speech that allows her to dominate her husbands but also to counter clerical culture and to create a web of secrecy that she shares with other wives. Her talkativeness, with its repetitiveness and relentlessness, constitutes not only her identity but her power, and it is this that she shares with other women — with "every womman that is wys" (III.524) and knows how to manage her bodily *chaffare*, or wares, and with her own *godsib*, Alisoun, who alone "knew myn herte, and eek my privetee / Bet than oure parisshe preest, so moot I thee!"

(knew my heart and also, my secret / Better than our parish priest, so might I thrive! III.530–31). The Wife allows us a brief glimpse of the network of secrecy that she maintains under cover of her verbosity and apparent openness. More importantly, she makes explicit the way in which gossip mimics confessional secrecy, ultimately surpassing it to the point where her priest is left out of the loop.

It is in the Wife of Bath's Tale that she elevates women's gossip to the level of oracle. The Knight of the story, who is given the task of discovering what it is that women most desire, is required to enter the secret network the Wife inhabits. First, he is assigned the task by Guenevere and the women at court in opposition to Arthur's legal recourse to the death sentence. The nightmare of the Knight's quest is the very indeterminacy of the answer to the riddle of what women most desire because the answer depends on his asking individual women. Some say women love wealth, others say happiness, others say satisfaction in bed, some say flattery, some say freedom, and so on (III.924–48). The multiplicity of answers given the Knight by the women does not solve the Knight's problem because he, like the cleric, must reduce the plurality of answers down to a single, universal truth. He is vexed by the surplus of speech until the Hag provides the solution to the riddle. Yet the Wife of Bath uses this fable of the Knight's search for the secret of women's desire to pose gossip as a rival interpretive community to that of conventional medieval *auctoritas*, a community authored and authorized by women. Although the secret of women's desire becomes revealed in the tale, the secret network of women's gossip that the Knight consulted for a year recedes behind the Knight's surrender to the Hag's sovereignty at the end of the tale. Yet if this tale is somewhat too conveniently resolved with the Knight's surrender, the Hag's transformation into a beautiful woman, and her mutual obedience to the Knight, the specter of the gossip's power to unsettle patriarchal discourse and to resolve the Knight's dilemma still haunts the end of the tale.

This admittedly sweeping and yet selective overview of the Wife of Bath's Prologue and Tale is not meant to be a definitive analysis. Instead, I am using her Prologue and Tale to sketch out some of the ways in which gossip resembles confessional practices of secrecy, to illustrate some of its features as a discourse that rivals authorized medieval discourses, and to suggest the gendered nature of gossip as a secret discourse tailored to medieval ideas about femininity. Just as women's bodies and sexuality were commonly associated with secrecy (and deception), as we shall see in Chapter 3, so their speech was conceived as occult and transgressive. It is, paradoxically, a secret discourse that is already indiscreet for its verbosity and its penchant for revealing the secrets of others. The Wife's attempts to appropriate medieval discourse about marriage and women by translating it into gossip are very suggestive of the way secrecy can be used as a strategy of resistance for marginalized groups. The problem in this case, of course, is that the Wife is herself the product of a kind of literary gossip that trades in its own masculine pastiche of the gossip — a parody of a parody.

The Wife of Bath cannot be understood outside the persistent concern in medieval texts with the dangers of gossip as a corrosive discourse associated almost exclusively with women. Not only did it represent an oral textual community that was separate from traditional written culture, but it also represented a feminine appropriation of masculine language that posed a threat to masculine culture. The pervasiveness of the discourse against women and gossips in medieval texts suggests that gossip was taken very seriously, that it was not trivialized in the Middle Ages the way that it is today. If we tend to associate gossip with irresponsible tabloid journalism, prurient talk, and the stuff of "wives' tales," the Middle Ages assigned gossip its place among the Seven Deadly Sins and generally elevated it as a female vice of extraordinary power.

In spite of the pervasiveness of gossip in medieval and modern cultures, it is a relatively unstudied phenomenon in either context. Partly because of its trivialized status and partly because of its obviousness, which makes it invisible, gossip is often ignored by sociolinguists, sociologists, and ethnographers.[5] In contrast to contemporary silence on the subject, gossip provoked a lot of talk in the Middle Ages, making it as much discoursed about as it was discursive. Medieval scholars need to be more aware of gossip as a discourse if we are to recognize alternative literary discursive modes and strategies of resistance to normative cultural forms of conversation and textualization.

As a discourse governed by secrecy, gossip could be described in many of the same ways that Foucault defined confession. Both presume that the individual possesses an endless reservoir of secrets that must be verbalized, though the effects of this verbalization were judged differently. While one leads to the Christian subject's spiritual health, the other leads to that subject's demise because the secret of gossip was almost always someone else's rather than one's own. Yet it is probably because medieval confession was such a central discourse of medieval culture that gossip was so seriously criticized. What becomes interesting in medieval literary texts, as we saw very sketchily in the Wife of Bath's Prologue and Tale, is how gossip becomes a discursive mode as significant to medieval literature as Patterson argued that confession was. After first examining the place and meaning of gossip in medieval culture, I will turn to Chaucer's *House of Fame* to see the pressures of gossip on medieval literary discourse, especially as it whispers gender ideology along with its secrets.

The Serious Business of Gossip

Gossip is a discourse of secrecy that claims to "speak in the world's voice." Its site is the "intersection of the social and individual," according to Spacks, and it bespeaks a relationship and an interpretation more than it does any information that it circulates. Because it intersects the public and the private in complicated ways, it often blurs their boundaries and in the process creates that anxiety that is one of gossip's chief (public) effects. This faculty for intersection produces what Spacks views as gossip's epistemological problematic: "Gossip as a phenomenon raises questions about boundaries, authority, distance, the nature of knowledge; it demands answers quite at odds with what we assume as our culture's dominant values."[6] Such questions, however, can reinforce the dominant values of culture in addition to being at odds with them. Gossip as a subversive mechanism, in other words, occupies a place — an "elsewhere" — in the interstices of the "power-knowledge apparati" expressed also through gossip.[7] Gossip is allied with the "power-knowledge apparati" in its own consolidations and use of social power within communities and in its effects, its "illusion of mastery gained through taking imaginative possession of another's experience."[8]

A contemporary example of the way gossip functions as a voice of the "power-knowledge apparati" even as it provides the mechanism for subversion is the military policy governing gays in the military. The affectionate title "don't ask, don't tell" already names gossip as the policy's chief principle and the regime of the policy's enforcement. Gay identity and conduct are placed under heterosexual interdiction, in the form of the "rebuttable presumption": gays and lesbians must not tell their homosexuality unless they are faced with an accusation derived from their conduct, in which case they *must* rebut the presumption with the truth. In effect, homosexuality is thus regulated within the regime of heterosexual gossip, rendering homosexual "telling" gossip to be policed by heterosexual knowing. Gossip here (as elsewhere) serves as the discourse of the closet as it is constructed in a heterosexist society. The knowledge-power apparatus of this military policy acts as a safeguard against knowledge, or more accurately, against the "knowledge of a knowledge," that is, of a particular person's homosexuality. The military/heterosexual community protects itself from the threat of homosexuality by forbidding it to speak, while the community itself adopts a position of "privileged unknowing."[9]

Gay speech and conduct are always gossip within such a regime because "not telling" conditions all gay speech-acts and behavior. This can provide, as Spacks argues in a different context, "a resource for the subordinated . . . , a crucial means of self-expression, a crucial form of solidarity."[10] Gossip becomes necessarily a queer code of behavior and speech allied with camp, creating anxiety for the heterosexual apparati that attempts to control it.[11] This particular gossip represents a form of solidarity in all gay and lesbian communities, but as a mechanism for subversion, it is limited. While gossip seems to offer that mechanism—for resistance, at least, because of its secrecy—it does so only at the cost of the gay subject's construal as an open secret: "The paradox of the open secret registers the subject's accommodation to a totalizing system that has obliterated the difference he would make—the difference he does make, in the imaginary denial of this system, 'even so.'"[12] The regime of heterosexual gossip enforces such a denial even as it creates that dangerous condition of open secrets—epistemological transparency—for a class of people. The difference gays and lesbians make is obliterated in the process in favor of heterosexual unknowing, an unknowing which is privileged because it is protected from the knowledge of a particular knowledge.[13]

Secrecy as a regime thus takes gossip as one of the discursive modes by which it structures such cultural fields as knowledge, authority, identity, and community. Gossip establishes boundaries of outside and inside, public and private, and it draws distinctions between insiders and others. As such, it performs a crucial cultural function of constructing social identity and exclusion. As a particular social formation, however, gossip is nearly always identified with anti-social behavior, excluded groups of people, and a diminished form of social expression. When it becomes a "resource for the subordinated" as "a crucial means of self-expression, a crucial form of solidarity," in Spacks's words, it does so as a parody, pastiche, and excessive iteration of dominant culture. If "the gossip" and "gossiping" are primary cultural representations of women and their speech in the Middle Ages, then the adoption of these positions and modes by actual women is necessarily limited. The power of gossip to raise "questions about boundaries, authority, distance, the nature of knowledge" is an oblique one—one that never directly repudiates the dominant culture or institutions it iterates.

The representation of feminine discourse as gossip derives in part from the medieval construction of women as secrets, as we shall see in Chapter 3. This representation in turn underwrites other crucial sites of meaning in medieval culture, such as the differentiation between oral and written transmission, knowledge and ignorance, masculine and feminine, and authority and experience. Spacks has located gossip at "the intersection of the social and individual," where it causes anxiety precisely because it blurs the line between public and private. She also claims that its power to solidify communities by designating an insider- and outsidership in its dynamics "matters more than the information it promulgates."[14] Its position at the intersection of social and individual derives from its peculiar dynamics: it at once announces a private, dyadic relationship yet always threatens to "spill over, sometimes dangerously, into the real world."[15] Gossip's excess—its tendency to "spill over"—allows it to cross cultural boundaries of public and private observed by other kinds of discourse. This is one reason why gossip is always indiscreet, for in spite of its secrecy, it publicizes the private, personal, and secret affairs of others, disregarding the boundaries of public and private when it comes to others.

In its dynamics as well as its "content," gossip crosses other cultural boundaries as well. Heidegger's discussion of "idle talk" in *Being and Time* offers some distinctions between gossip and legitimate forms of oral and written discourse. One of gossip's most dangerous and persistent properties is its rootlessness, its groundlessness, and paradoxically, the authority it constitutes through this rootlessness:

What is said-in-the-talk as such, spreads in wider circles and takes on an authoritative character. Things are so because one says so. Idle talk is constituted by just such gossiping and passing the word along—a process by which its initial lack of grounds to stand on [*Bodenständigkeit*] becomes aggravated to complete groundlessness [*Bodenlosigkeit*].[16]

The authoritative character of this groundless speech derives from its sheer circulation, in other words, "because one says so." What Heidegger does not say, though, is that the rootlessness of the circulated gossip belies its origins in a particular contextual situation and that gossip follows clear patterns of progression and self-authentication, including an implicit moral framework.[17] The real crisis that Heidegger sees in gossip is its rootlessness and its unearned authority, which even in written discourse threaten to confuse the "average" reader. Gossip "feeds upon superficial reading," and in turn, creates a false sense of understanding:

The average understanding of the reader will *never be able* to decide what has been drawn from primordial sources with a struggle and how much is just gossip. The average understanding, moreover, will not want any such distinction, and does not need it, because, of course, it understands everything. . . . Idle talk is the possibility of understanding everything without previously making the thing one's own. . . . Idle talk is something which anyone can rake up; it not only releases one from the task of genuinely understanding, but develops an undifferentiated kind of intelligibility, for which nothing is closed off any longer.[18]

Several negative formulations of gossip are suggested in this passage. The most prominent objection to gossip implied here is its failure to distinguish between types of intelligibility, one achieved with struggle through the weighing of sources and making the subject matter "one's own" and the other hardly "achieved" at all because it is gotten with ease and without "genuine understanding," possession, or authority. What seems to be at stake here is discursive authority, the nature of knowledge, and the hierarchy of intelligences. The "undifferentiated" kind of intelligibility is one for which "nothing is closed off any longer." The illusion of unlimited access to knowledge that idle talk produces constitutes part of its danger. The limitless trajectory of this talk is another: nothing is closed off any longer.

Throughout Heidegger's description of idle talk runs the depth/surface distinction between kinds of discourse. Gossip circulates only the surfaces of things, people, and events and elicits therefore only a superficial understanding.[19] Its danger lies in its trivialization of profound modes of discourse and understanding through its delight in surface. In this respect, too, gossip seems to be inveterately amoral because of its unwillingness to "close anything off" or to make distinctions of intelligibility or intention. Gossip is thus defined by its failure to respect discursive, social, and intellectual boundaries and by its consequent excess, superfluity, and lack of substance.

As Spacks maintains, "Gossip insists on its own frivolity" — in spite of the range of intents and functions it serves.[20] Regardless too of its sometimes serious consequences, gossip refuses and repudiates authentic speech, that is, speech that is consistent with intention and behavior. This is because, while gossip clearly does originate with individual speakers, it always announces itself as already circulated, as speech not of speakers but of intermediaries. Its frivolity consists in its detachment from the ordinary contingencies of discourse. This is also what makes it slightly dangerous because it threatens to reduce the presumed moral and ethical dimensions of language to mere surface, to words that can be proliferated without end: nothing is closed off any longer. Such medieval commonplaces about language and human responsibility, that "the words must be cousin to the deed" or that language should be true to its intention and its meaning, as Chaucer would have it, are jeopardized by gossip.[21]

In its detachment from origins, institutions, and contingencies, gossip is always a residual speech — language that is left over from the human experiences, interactions, and discourses of daily life. As a residue, gossip often claims to contain the essential secret, otherwise unexpressed truths of those experiences, interactions, and discourses, but its mode is necessarily fragmentary. Of uncertain origins and with no clear *telos*, gossip derives its material and mode from the world and official culture to create "its own territory" and "a new oral artifact."[22] This new artifact presents itself as the residue of social activity — as language that merely repeats what is not said in public forums, as the truth about experiences, as the narratives of people's lives. It always pretends to be a report and a revelation at the same time. As we shall see in its medieval constructions, women's gossip in particular is thought to be a kind of residual masculine speech that circulates men's secrets. According to this formulation, the residual nature of gossip derives from the fact that it is a *stolen*, proliferated, and finally indiscreet speech.

Unlike other forms of discourse, gossip is not associated with its sources, institutions, or moral principles; its primary distinguishing feature is exchange. It is no coincidence that the economy of gossip resembles gender economics as well. Women, who are themselves marked and desired in terms of their exchangeability and use value, are the chief purveyors of gossip, whose value is likewise defined by its exchange but whose danger of *unlimited use* is always present.[23] The difference is that instead of women being the exchanged goods according to the patriarchal economy, they are the exchangers of gossip, which circulates endlessly without any value necessarily accruing to it although it proliferates its subject without end. This is because the exchange allegedly takes place among women rather than men. As such it parodies the commodification of women, their exchange, and the investments of men in them through its senseless repetition and its lack of meaningful outcome. Worse, it stands to render men the objects of exchange, a meaningful outcome to which I shall return later.

Even more dangerous is the association of gossip with a private form of pleasure, an erotics.[24] Because gossip usually deals in the secrets of others, it occupies the position of the voyeur. Pleasure in the sheer exchange is part of gossip's allure; another part is its power to objectify the subject of gossip; and a third aspect is its paradigmatic gesture of revealing what is hidden. Freud's account of sexual voyeurism identifies as a primary feature its tendency to "*linger* over the intermediate relations to the sexual object which should normally be traversed rapidly on the path towards the final sexual aim."[25] This definition might be adjusted slightly to distinguish gossip from normal discourse by its lingering over *intermediate relations* to its subject without pursuing any "final" discursive aim. If scopophilia characterizes the voyeur's pleasure, logophilia might be said to characterize the gossip's intermediate relations to her subject and the source of her pleasure.[26] Logophilia takes pleasure not in the achievement of understanding, truth, or affective relations but in the "talking about"—the intermediacy (as opposed to immediacy) of its relations. Like the voyeur, then, the gossip enjoys an illicit—because intermediate—pleasure.

The Middle Ages recognized the dangers and pleasures of gossip, particularly as it was thought to have been practiced by women, and it earnestly sought to analyze gossip's workings, create a taxonomy of its varieties and features, and catalogue its harmful effects. The next part of this chapter sketches out the medieval understanding of gossip both as an especially violent form of speech that thrives in secrecy among marginal social groups and as a discourse particularly characteristic of femininity. Medieval discourse about women's gossip is, like gossip itself, voluble, even verbose, and it crosses textual genres from sermons to literary texts. A survey of some of the words and semantic fields of Middle English words for gossip along with sermon literature will help to flesh out the medieval ideology governing the representation of women's gossip. Then I will focus on a fifteenth-century masculine fantasy of women's gossip as a site for elaborating some of the discursive and ideological aspects of the discourse that I have just described. Finally, I will turn to Chaucer's *House of Fame* to examine how gossip becomes a contested site of masculine representation, anxiety, and power.

Murder By Language

He [is] . . . the nastiest word in the language: pronoun of the nonperson, it annuls and mortifies its referent; saying "he" about someone, I always envision a kind of murder by language, whose entire scene, sometimes sumptuous, even ceremonial, is *gossip*.[27]

Roland Barthes here expresses an anxious view of gossip as a "murder by language." Using the third-person pronoun "he," the gossip commits an "annulment" of the subject of discussion by converting "him" to an object. It is appropriate for this study that Barthes limits this kind of discursive murder to men: "he" who is objectified by the use of the third-person pronoun. Objectification through the use of "she" is, perhaps, less mortifying because it bolsters male subjectivity. The passage reveals masculine anxiety over the objectification that is gossip's chief mode and pleasure. Neither trivial nor superficial in its effects, gossip has the "nasty" power to mortify its referent under the disguise of the "sumptuous" or "ceremonial."

This view of gossip coincides with the medieval view in two ways: first, in its implicit formulation of the masculine subject as the referent (and victim) of gossip, and second, in its equally implicit moral condemnation of gossip as a kind of murder by language. As an example of just how close Barthes is to medieval sermon literature on the subject, compare this description of male gossipers with Barthes's comment, in which *iangling* and *bacbiting* are the two offending activities corresponding to our modern notion of gossip:

And somme gon abouʒt here neyʒeboris fro hous to hous and tellen sleveles talis and apposyn her neyʒboris sutely and undirgropyn hem slili, and comyn in with a flateryng and seyn — "I aske not this for hindring of ony man, and that that thu tellist me schal be conseile"; and al this is to seche ont sum yvel tale of hem that thei [the gossipers] haten. And whanne that thei drawen out of hem a yvel tale, a-noon be the backe turned, thei sclatren out to alle that wolen here hem so fer forth that, if thei myʒtten do her neiʒboris to hange and to drawen with oo fals lesing, it schulde be blowen out a-non. And here-of comyn mony debatis and stryvyngis, foule chiding, eche man to wrangle with othere as were houndis and cattis. *Suche men, in as myche as in hem is, sleen all tho of the whiche thei tellen suche bacbitingis.* (my emphasis)[28]

(And some go among their neighbors from house to house and tell profitless tales and subtly raise objections to their neighbors, and interrogate them slyly, and come in with flattery and say: "I don't ask this to injure any man, and what you tell me shall be kept secret"; and all this in order to seek out some evil tale about those they hate. And when they have drawn out an evil tale, as soon as their back is turned, they chatter it out to all who will hear them to such an extent that if they can cause their neighbors to be hanged and drawn by one false lie, it should be spread around immediately. And from this comes many debates and strivings, foul chiding, each man fighting with the other like cats and dogs. *Such men, as much as they can, slay all those about whom they tell such gossip.*)

The murder by language described in this sermon goes beyond Barthes's annihilation of the referent to disrupt the entire community. Malicious intent lurks beneath both formulations of gossip, and the morally reprehensible consequence — death by language — prevails.

The number and array of Middle English words for this murderous activity testifies to "a proliferation of discourses" about gossip.[29] The word gossip did not mean "idle talk, trifling or groundless rumour," according to the *Oxford English Dictionary* until 1811. In the Middle Ages, the word retained its etymologically construed meaning, "god-sibb" or "god-related," to refer to a "spiritual relative (of a sponsor at baptism in relation to child or its parents)." A second, gender-specific meaning was already being invoked in Middle English texts by Chaucer's time: "woman companion."[30] The word was not used as a verb, however, as we most often use it today. The verbs designating the activity of gossip in Middle English include *janglen*, *bakbiten*, and *clateren* and the purveyors of these activities are called *jangleres* and *jangleresses*, *bakbiters*, and *claterers*. These words are used interchangeably even though slight distinctions are sometimes made among them. *Janglen* means "to chatter, talk idly, gossip" and "to grumble or complain," and it is linked to the indistinct chatter of birds as well as the gaggling of geese. It also carries the less pejorative sense of debating, discussing, or arguing.[31] It is the only word of the three that attaches specifically to women to produce *jangleresses*, talkative, nagging, and/or lying women. The Wife of Bath, for example, boasts that "I was . . . of my tonge a verray jangleresse" (III.637–38). It is interesting that the *janglere*, by contrast, could be an eloquent person, as well as a gossiper, backbiter, idle talker, and raconteur of dirty stories. The term attaching to women, *jangleresse*, is much more specific in its meaning. Chaucer's Parson classifies *jangling* under the sin of Wrath following idle words, double tongues, wicked counsel, chiding, flattery, lying, swearing, and other sins of discursive discord. If idle words are a "venial sin," so is *jangling*, which the Parson defines after Solomon as "a sygne of apert folye" (a sign of manifest [public] folly, X.649).

Akin to *jangling* is the idle and noisy activity of *clatering*. Babbling, uttering noisily or foolishly, and prating are synonyms for *clatering*. Its main distinction from *jangling* seems to be its volume, which makes it a particular distraction in church. In addition, the word carries a meaning that *jangling* does not: to betray secrets. A *claterer* is therefore not only a "noisy talker" but a "betrayer of secrets." The *Middle English Dictionary* cites an interesting illustration of this term from the late medieval *Five Puzzles*, which lists three claterers — a magpie, a jay, and a woman.[32] Although there is not a gender-specific term for female claterers, the term often applies to women when it means a betrayer of secrets. Otherwise, men and women are both guilty of the venial sin of clattering, particularly at mass.

The most dangerous form of gossip is designated by the term *bakbiten*, meaning "to detract from the good name of someone behind his back; to defame, traduce, slander, disparage, criticize."[33] Like Barthes and the medieval sermon quoted above, Chaucer's Parson considers it a form of homicide, or *spiritueel manslaughtre* (X.564). The backbiter's talk is not idle, for it springs from an evil intent to "turne al thilke goodness [of others] upsodoun to his shrewed entente" (turn all that goodness [of others] upside down to his evil intent, X.495). The Parson identifies five species of backbiting in his elaboration of the sin of Envy, including praising with wicked intent, exploiting the goodness of others, diminishing the generosity of neighbors, "dispraising" those deserving of praise, and consenting to harmful speech about others (X.492–97).

The distinctions between forms of gossip suggested by the *Middle English Dictionary* are in fact not so clear in the words' uses. The sermon quoted above, for example, uses all three in its evocation of the murder by language that results from gossip. Using the Parson's categories of linguistic homicide, however, we can observe two theological distinctions between those inspired by Wrath (*jangling*) and those committed out of Envy (*bacbitynge*). Even the more idle of the two kinds of talk, *jangling*, proceeds from the hostile motivation of Anger, and its consequences can be serious breeches of social decorum and cohesion. The more serious, however, is the sin of backbiting, which intends harm to others. It also derives from the sin of Envy, "the worste synne that is," according to the Parson, because it opposes all virtues and goodness and because it is the only sin that offers no delight (X.487–89).

Langland's portraits of Wrath and Envy in *Piers Plowman* concur with the Parson's analysis, relegating *jangling* to the first mortal sin and *bacbitynge* to the second with an interesting twist. In the confession of the Seven Deadly Sins of passus 5, Envy's livelihood is gained from *chidynge* and *chalangynge, bakbitynge, bismere* (scorn), and "berynge of fals witnesse."[34] Envy describes his efforts to flatter those who are stronger than he and to destroy those whom he hates (B 5.93–121). He is an example of backbiting and the ill will it produces. He has lived, he says, among the burgesses of London "and made backbiting a broker to blame men's wares" (B 5.130–31), and among households, where he creates discord unto death.

Wrath by comparison with Envy is more humorous and benign in his brand of murder by language. His province of activity is almost exclusively female religious houses because he finds male monastics hostile to him. In fact, the entire portrait seems to have an argument about women as its subtext. First, Wrath announces himself as cook for his aunt, the abbess, and he recounts the culinary delights of *jangling* among the nuns:

I was þe Prioresse potager and oþere pouere ladies,
And maad hem Ioutes of Ianglyng þat dame Iohane was a bastard,
And dame Clarice a Kny3tes dou3ter ac a cokewold was hir sire,
And dame Pernele a preestes fyle; Prioresse worþ she neuere
For she hadde child in chirietyme; al oure Chapitre it wiste.
Of wikkede wordes I, wraþe, hire wortes made
Til "þow lixt!" and "þow lixt!" lopen out at ones
And eiþer hitte ooþer vnder þe cheke.
Hadde þei had knyues, by crist! eiþer hadde kild ooþer (B 5.157–65)

(I was cook for the Prioress and other poor ladies,
And I made them stews of gossip — that Dame Joan was a bastard,
And Dame Clarice a knight's daughter, but her father was a cuckold,
And Dame Parnel a priest's wench; she will never be a Prioress
For she had a child in cherry-time; our whole chapter knows it!
I, Wrath, cooked their vegetables out of wicked words
Till "You lie!" and "You lie!" leapt out at once
And each hit the other under the cheek.
Had they had knives, by Christ, they'd have killed each other.)

The stew of *ianglyng* cooked up by Wrath consists mostly of tales of illegitimate birth and sex committed by nuns. Lacking knives, the nuns are unable to commit murder, and gossip instead reduces them to blows in a medieval version of a cat fight.

This portrait of Wrath not only dramatizes the effects of gossip and links them to women exclusively, but at least in the B version of *Piers Plowman*, it leads Langland to a significant aside:

Seint Gregory was a good pope and hadde a good forwit:
That no Prioress were preest, for þat he purueiede;
They hadde þanne been *Infamis*, þei kan so yuele hele counseil (B 5.166–68).

(St. Gregory was a good pope and had good foresight
When he provided that the priesthood should be closed to prioresses.
They would have been *infamis* (infamous) then and there, they keep secrets so
   badly.)[35]

Women would have been "infamous" in the sense that they would certainly have violated the priestly office of confession. The gossiping prioress and nuns here become essentialized in Langland's aside in order to indict women's nature in general for their inability to keep secrets and to support the Church's exclusion of them from the priesthood. This is perhaps why Wrath finds no support for his gossip in male monastic houses because the male prerogative of confession and sacerdotal privilege rests upon the distinction between the essential natures of men and women. Wrath's aside mystifies the true source of women's gossip, causing it to slip from anger to a gendered inability to keep counsel. While men "jangle" elsewhere in the company of the Seven Deadly Sins — such as with Gluttony in the taverns (2.93–95) — their gossip is never so essentialized nor their masculinity so insinuated. When Repentance counsels Wrath to repent and never to reveal secrets by look or speech, he speaks to men implicitly, not to women who "keep secrets so badly."

The essentializing of women and gossip extends to Mary Magdelene's announcement of Christ's resurrection in passus 19. Conscience attributes Magdelene's witness and report that "Christus resurgens" to all she met on the road to Galilee to the fact that "what a woman knows may not well remain secret" (19.162).[36] No longer courtesy of Wrath, the Magdelene's announcement of the resurrection is reduced to women's gossip, though it hardly leads to discord and cat fights in this case.

In Langland's representation of the venial form of gossip, *iangling*, Wrath serves more as a witness than a cause of linguistic violence. The real cause is women's natures. Although women are also capable of wrath, their anger seems to be merely the function of their fundamental inability to keep secrets. Most of the murderousness of women's gossip is self-directed, although Wrath takes revenge against inhospitable monks by spreading rumors about them among the nuns (5.181). They experience no pleasure or frivolity as exchangers of gossip; only the murderousness prevails among them. It is important to see how Wrath's speech is itself a bit of *iangling* for the reader's pleasure, making gossip out of gossip for our delight. The representation ultimately renders the nuns objects of Wrath's (and the text's) gossip, rather than delighted subjects of logophilic pleasure. Readers are the beneficiaries of gossip's pleasures, as we witness religious women engaged in mutual accusation and fisticuffs. The entire scene is one of gossip about the gossip of religious women.

The pleasure women derive from gossip is represented elsewhere in medieval sermons and manuals for lay instruction. The sumptuous, ceremonial scene of such gossip is usually the church, a "hous of dadull [house of Daedalus], and of whisperyng and rownyng, and of spekyng of vanyte and of oðer fylthe." The fifteenth-century collection of sermons, John Mirk's *Festial*, recounts a typical story in which a holy bishop at mass sees two women whispering together unaware of a fiend sitting on their shoulders and writing down everything they say. When the bishop later asks the women what they were saying, they lie to him by replying that they were saying their Pater Noster. The bishop then calls the fiend to read his notes of their whisperings aloud, and the women are chagrined as they beg the bishop for mercy.[37]

The medieval topos of the fiend taking notes as women gossip in church is a common one with many variations.[38] The fiend, Tutivillus, supposedly collected fragments of words of the divine service skipped or mumbled by parishioners as well as gossip.[39] Yet the gossip of women often defies Tutivillus's powers of dictation. In two accounts, Robert Mannyng of Brunne's *Handlyng Synne* (c. 1303) and *The Book of the Knight of the Tower* (1484), the fiend writes furiously as two women whisper (*iangle*) during mass. Barely able to unwind enough parchment from his scroll as he writes, he pulls it with his teeth and ends up humorously smacking his head against the wall because the roll has become so long.[40]

The recording of women's excessive speech is likewise humorous, especially in the context of the Last Judgment. In the Wakefield play of the Last Judgment, two fiends compare their registers of sins. "Has thou oght writen there of the feminine gendere?" asks one fiend of the other. In keeping with the theme of women's gossip as excess, the other fiend responds, "Yei, mo then I may bere, of rolles for to render!"[41] Tutivillus later enters and enumerates a range of female vices, including vain array and deception. Nothing renders better Heidegger's idea of that "undifferentiated kind of intelligibility, for which nothing is closed off any longer" than Tutivillus' inability to keep pace with women's gossip or fiends' difficulty in finding rolls enough to record it.

By comparison with wrath and gossip, envy too produces its own language, according to medieval sermons, but its effects are more murderous. One sermon places the backbiting species of gossip under prohibition of the eighth commandment against bearing false witness. The power of envious speech to slay the soul is at issue. The envious man's speech is characterized in another sermon as the "language of hell" with its "slaundur and detraccion of þer neyȝbore owt of charite."[42] It is filled with "trechery" and "bytter wordes" that cause the destruction of his neighbors' reputations. Envious speech renders the tongue of man "a penne to the deuell."[43] Nowhere in the sermons against envy is gender implicated the way it is in sermons about the sin of wrath and its attendant speech forms, jangling and chattering.

Two fifteenth-century handbooks of instruction elaborate on the social consequences of women's gossip. Caxton's English translation of Geoffrey de La Tour's instruction for his daughters (ca. 1371) addresses the inability of wives to keep their husbands' secrets. In one story on the subject, a squire decides to test his wife's ability to keep a secret by confiding in her that he has laid two eggs. His wife agrees not to reveal his secret but, finding the night too long with this burden, she runs to her "godsep" to tell her that her husband has laid *three* eggs. Her gossip, in turn, violates her vow of secrecy and multiplies the story and the husband's hatchings to four. By the time the gossip gets back to the squire, he has laid five eggs. The husband calls his wife on her broken confidence and lie, and Geoffrey advises his daughters: "And therfor by thys ensample al good wymmen ought to kepe secrete the secrete & counceylle of theyr lord and not discouere it for nothyng to ony body" (and therefore, by this example, all good women ought to keep secret the secret and counsel of their lord and not reveal it for anything to anyone).[44]

Here gossip is specifically construed as a residual masculine speech, that is, as the fragments of masculine confidence entrusted to wives. Women's gossip consists of men's secrets exchanged and, worse, enlarged upon and proliferated by women's indiscreet speech. The secrets women tell are not their own, nor are they the achievement of a special knowledge. The inability of women to keep their husbands' secrets is the result of their logophilia, the sheer pleasure they take in the intermediary delights of gossip. The woman is kept awake all night by her husband's secret like a lovesick lover suffering the effects of desire. In fact, gossip is the outcome of the wife's desire to reveal without concern for the objectification of her husband and the defamation that results from it. Elsewhere in Geoffrey's counsel to his daughters, he provides a metaphor for the dangers of women's gossip about their husbands:

And in lyke wyse as the shafte is departed fro the bowe must take her flyght and cours and neuer cometh ageyne to the bowe tyll it haue smyte somme thynge. Soo is the word whiche yssued oute of the mouthe lyke it. For after that he is put out of the mouth it may neuer be put in to the mouthe ageyne but that it shal be herd be it good or euylle.[45]

(And just as the shaft which is shot from the bow must take flight and never come again to the bow until has hit something, so is the word which issues out of the mouth. For after the word is released from the mouth it may never be put back in again, but it shall be heard whether it be good or evil.)

As the arrow is released from the bow and "smites" something, so wives' language smites its object without regard for its target. Neither may be retracted or recalled: nothing is closed off any longer.

Peter Idley's Instructions to His Son concludes with advice on proper behavior in holy places. After warning not to *iangyll* with Jankyn, Janet, or Jane, Idley becomes sidetracked on the subject of women's gossip in church:

And specially þeis women, as I dare sey,
Haue besy talkyng of huswyffreye;
Gaggle as a goose and Iangyll as a Iey,
And how þeir husbandes be full off Ielosye.
Sum set þeir myndes galentes to asspye,
Beholdyng þe schort garmentes round all abouȝt
And how þe stuffyng off þe codpece berys ouȝt.[46]

(And especially these women, I daresay,
Who are busy talking of housewifery,
Gaggle as a goose and chatter as a jay,
About how their husbands are full of jealousy,
And some set their minds to spy on gallants,
Beholding the shortness of their garments,
And how the stuffing of the codpiece stands out.)

The slippage from women's jangling about their husbands to their "beholding" of the bulging of men's codpieces is an interesting one, suggesting the allied erotic and intermediary pleasures of these two activities. Although Peter Idley later concedes that men too are guilty of not paying attention in church, he does not accuse them of the sins of gossip and loose looking described here. The gossip here depicted is not limited to the subject of husbands, as it seems to be in Geoffrey de La Tour's accounts. It includes the mysterious subject of housewifery, too.

From the moral condemnation of *iangling* as a sin of wrath to the social representations of the dangers of women's gossip, there is a continuity of masculine anxiety. The endlessness, proliferation, and sheer pleasure of women's gossip is placed under prohibition in all the accounts I have examined. While women's gossip is represented as trivial and even humorous, it is also dangerous in its effects of objectifying men and appropriating and proliferating their secrets. Masculine fantasies of women's gossip are laden with anxiety not about women circulating some hidden knowledge about them but about the sumptuous, ceremonial exchange economy of it. At stake is not only the murder by language, as Barthes would have it, but the troubling disregard for authority, institutions, and masculine reputations. Trifling with men, normative values, and gender hierarchy is part of the performance and the ceremony of women's gossip, at least according to masculine fantasies of it.

The readiness of women to reveal men's secrets is replicated in major literary texts as well, from Andreas Capellanus's discussion of their inability to keep secrets to Genius's condemnation of disclosing masculine secrets to women in the *Roman de la Rose* to Chaucer's Wife of Bath, who takes particular delight in her own revision of the Midas story, which attributes the disclosure of his ass's ears to his wife, rather than his servant, as the Ovidian version has it.[47] While some readers might cite this last example as evidence of the Wife's internalization of masculine antifeminist discourse, we should not forget the power of this story to invoke the very masculine anxiety about women's gossip that produced it.

One fascinating lesser-known literary representation of women's gossip from the late fifteenth century is a poem entitled "The Gossips," which purports to tell the "full good sport / How gossyps gather them on a sort."[48] Yet this topic of women's gossip is also freighted with danger, compelling the speaker to withhold the full story:

But I dare not, fore ther displesaunce,
Tell off thes maters half the substaunce;
But yet sum whatt off their governaunce,
As fare as I dare, I wyll declare.[49]

(But I dare not, for fear of their displeasure,
Tell half the substance of these matters;
But yet somewhat of their conduct,
I will declare, as far as I dare.)

The threat of "their" displeasure polices the speaker's sport, forcing him to confine himself to their behavior rather than the content of their gossip. By invoking the taboo of the gossip's displeasure, the speaker creates the sumptuous, ceremonial scene of gossip between himself and his reader. He thus renders this poem about gossip into a gossiping text. He enacts through his withholding the gossip's sport, the creation of what Derrida calls a *secret capital*. Derrida describes this secrecy value according to Foucault:

This value would come down, in the end, to a *technique* of the secret, and of the secret without knowledge. Wherever knowledge can only be supposed, wherever, as a result, one knows that supposition cannot give rise to knowledge, wherever no knowledge could ever be disputed, there is the production of a *secrecy effect*, of what we might be able to call a *speculation on the capital secret or on the capital of the secret*.[50]

In the poem a secret is set up by the gossips' silent interdiction, which renders the knowledge the speaker claims to withhold unavailable even through its revelation. Instead of the secrets of women's gossip, then, the poem invests gossip with a secret capital by withholding its "substaunce." At the same time, the speaker mimics the activity of gossip in an effort to appropriate the secret capital for his masculine audience. Both the speaker's gender and that of his audience are revealed only at the end of the poem, where the secret's capital is finally made manifest.

This secret capital exists in spite of — or, most likely, because of — the mundane substance the poem actually reveals. What follows is an overheard conversation of gossips in the streets calling each other by name — Eleanor, Joan, Margery, Margaret, Alice, and Cecily — to bring a dish to the tavern. One gossip advises the others that they not let themselves be seen because she will suffer a beating if her husband sees her, but Alice defiantly declares, "She that is aferd, lett her fle, / . . . I dred no man" (She who is afraid, let her flee, / . . . I dread no man, p. 6). The scene that follows at the tavern includes an exchange of food and wine with commentary. The main "substance," however, occurs when one gossip notices another's sad countenance. When the sad one is encouraged to be merry, she confesses that her husband beats her. This inspires Alice to pray in a loud voice that God shorten the lives of such husbands, while Margaret vows that any man who gives her two strokes shall receive five in return: "I ame not aferd, though I have no berd" (I am not afraid, though I lack a beard, p. 8).

The conversation is interrupted by the departure of one of the gossips, who fails to leave enough money to cover her share of the tab. The others vow never to invite her again, as they all pay up and leave the tavern. In the streets Anne declares that "What so ever ony man thynk, / Whe cum fore nowght but fore good drynk" (Whatever any man thinks, / We come together naught but for good drink, p. 9), and the overheard scene ends. The narrator returns to sum up that gossips meet once a week or more to drink the best wine. He then addresses his reader:

Who sey yow, women, is it not soo?
Yes, suerly, and that ye wyll know;
And therfore lat us drynk all a row,
And off owr syngyng mak a good endyng.

Now fyll the cupe, and drynk to me;
And than shal we good felows be.
And off thys talkyng leve wyll we,
And speak then good off women (p. 10).

(What say you, women, is it not so?
Yes, surely, and that you well know;
And therefore let us drink all together,
And of our singing make a good ending.

Now fill the cup, and drink to me;
And then shall we good fellows be.
And off this talking leave will we,
And speak then good of women).

The creation of a dispute between women and the narrator along with his fellows at the end of the poem pits women against men. It also suggests that the narrator has revealed their secret. We might wonder what they object to: *what* exactly is "not so"? The fact that women slip off to the taverns on a daily or weekly basis to drink the best of wines seems to be the speaker's point. The united stand Alice and Margaret take against spouse abuse seems not to be the speaker's point, nor is it the bad reflection on husbands in their brief conversation. His larger point seems to be the deception gossips practice on their husbands through their tavern escapes.

But a more important secrecy effect is achieved through the poem as a whole. The secret capital of the poem lies in its pretense of a secret knowledge shared by men in spite of women's protestations. While the women's gossip about their husbands might be seen as another example of "murder by language," it is neutralized by the larger, ceremonial scene of masculine gossip about women. The tavern community of men (and women) drinking revealed at the end of the poem asserts itself over the supposed protest of women, claiming its truth and notoriety at the same time. All of this constitutes the technique of the secret — the assertion of the masculine community, the pretense of revealing a secret knowledge without actually doing so, and the implicit gesture to a masculine tradition the opposite of which is "speaking good of women."

While the ballad ends in the triumph of masculine gossip, it also sug-

gests a secrecy capital in women's gossip that exceeds the speaker's account of it.[51] The ceremony of it—the gathering of food, discussion of the
wine, and the prayer to God to get their husbands out of debt so that they
can spend their money in taverns—is part of its mystery. Yet for all the
poem's detail, we are left with only "half the substaunce" and the possibility
of women's retaliation. The celebratory ending and facetious gesture to
"speaking good of women" merely mystifies the uneasy awareness that the
secret of women's gossip cannot be found in the poem. The masculine
fantasy of women's gossip raises the very problem it pretends to solve, the
risk to men of "being deceived less by a secret than by the awareness that
there is secrecy," in the words of Foucault.[52] Women's gossip is never really
closed off by this playful discussion of it, but instead, its secrecy lies in wait
for the masculine speaker, who never finally "gets" it.

Contrary to the representations of medieval sermons and lay instructional guides, the women of this poem do not gossip because they cannot
keep secrets, rather it is because they can, and do, and with great pleasure
and celebration. What does this particular masculine fantasy have to tell
about the cultural representation of women, secrecy, and gossips? It reveals
some of the anxiety behind this representation; more importantly, it demonstrates the way in which, even under the auspices of a masculine narrator,
gossip can exceed and threaten the interests of its own representation..
Masculine speculation in and on the secrecy capital of women's gossip
creates the community at the end of the poem, but it does not contain
masculine anxiety. At the same time, the poem raises the distinct possibility
that men are deceived by the awareness of secrecy and that the physical
violence the women discuss may be returned in kind. Ironically, the most
significant secrecy effect of women's gossip is that men cannot stop talking
about it.

Finally, I want to argue—tentatively at this point—that the representation of women's gossip, like that found in the rest of the examples I have
cited—takes place within a particular epistemological regime, that of igno-
rance/knowledge. Women's language as gossip is always elucidated within
the context of masculine privilege of knowing female secrets, but at the end
of the poem "The Gossips," there is a repudiation of this knowledge in the
gesture towards a more benign and favorable talk about women. Women's
gossip thus occurs within the contradictory realm of masculine knowing
and repudiation of that knowledge—"and of thys talkyng leve wyll we, /
And speak then good off women." Masculine ignorance of women's secret
talk defines the terms of the ballad and of the final gesture of "leaving off"

further revelation. "You" women, the narrator claims, "wyll know" that "it is so." Women who know the "truth" of what the ballad reports about their gossip deny it, pretending ignorance of the "sport." While the narrator pretends to know more than he tells, the "women" he addresses pretend "it is not so." What is at stake in this dynamic created by the narrator?

The epistemological enforcement of women as secrets whose speech is likewise covert is the project of this poem. It is not possible, however, without first feigning masculine innocence of women's gossip, which in turn makes possible the enforcement of women's secret talk in the poem.[53] The real violence of it consists in rupturing the secret circle that is the (masculine fantasized) domain of gossip. It is no coincidence that the content of the women's talk is masculine physical violence against them, for it haunts the "sport" of masculine insurgency into their "scene." Masculine discovery of women's secrets retreats back into the domain of ignorance, where men will speak "good of women," thereby both distancing the narrator from his subject and recuperating the women from their dangerous, fringe domain into his own ostensibly benign tavern revelry.[54] The masculine community of the tavern is safe once again, and women's gossip finally defers to masculine poetics and play.

The representations of gossip depend upon the structure of masculine ignorance and feminine secret knowing. Masculine interrogation renders women and their discourse open secrets to masculine knowledge. Its effect is, once again, to create an intimate masculine exchange through the pretense of exchanging and discovering women's secrets, as well as differentiating masculine discourse and knowledge from its feminine "other." The unintended and ironic effect is, of course, masculine gossip. This poem offers a lighthearted glimpse into this larger cultural activity surrounding the gender dynamic of ignorance and knowledge.

Chaucer's Wife of Bath allegorizes this same gender dynamic in her tale, as the Knight desperately searches among England's women, infiltrating the gossip networks in order to discover what it is that women most desire. To save his life he must somehow become privy to women's gossip and the secrets of their desire. Once he publicly discloses that the object of women's desire is sovereignty, he assumes his quest is finished. But while he lives happily ever after by surrendering sovereignty to the Hag who saved his life, the suggestion that something vital is circulated in women's gossip lingers at the end. The mystery of women's desire is but one of the secrets contained in women's covert network of conversation; the power of that network, however invisible it is to the Knight until he is forced to consult it, is palpable in the tale. Its danger and potential violence for the Knight — his death if he fails to discover its secrets — is also present in the tale. For the Wife of Bath, who uses gossip to mimic clerics, manage husbands, and satisfy her own desires, the triumph of women's gossip in her tale is surely one of her agendas. While Chaucer creates the Wife straight out of the medieval misogynist tradition, he allows her a resistance of the very tradition that made her possible through her strategic use of gossip.

In fact, Chaucer was very interested in — and even anxious about — the relationship of gossip to poetry. The Wife of Bath's performance raises the unsettling possibility that tale-telling — even masculine storytelling — is really not significantly different from women's gossip. Perhaps, like Heidegger, he worried whether the "average understanding" would be able to discern the difference between the Wife's mimicry of authorial *auctoritas* and the real thing, between the poet's art and the gossip's skill, and between literature's truths and gossip's groundless and endless spinning of tales. Perhaps he also worried about the trajectory of his own reputation as a writer because it was entrusted to Fame, who, like the Wife of Bath, uses rumor, falsehood, and gossip to make and break poets, lovers, and women. In Chaucer's unfinished poem, *House of Fame,* he attempts to discover the difference between art and gossip.

House of Fame and the Secrets of Poetry

Ignorance is as potent and as multiple a thing there is as knowledge [is]. Knowledge, after all, is not itself power, although it is the magnetic field of power. Ignorance and opacity collude or compete with knowledge in mobilizing the flows of energy, desire, goods, meanings, persons.[55]

If masculine ignorance structures the representations of women's gossip in the Wife of Bath's Tale, Langland's scenarios of Wrath, Middle English sermons, and the anonymous late Middle English poem "The Gossips," it remains to be seen how this ignorance "colludes," in Sedgwick's words, with knowledge to mobilize power, desire, goods, meanings, and persons. In the passage quoted above, Sedgwick analogizes Foucault's idea that silences are "an integral part of the strategies that underlie and permeate discourses" to say that ignorances, too, crucially structure knowledge.[56] In medieval discourse about women's gossip, the idea that women are unable to keep secrets depends upon a pretense of masculine innocence / ignorance, like the Knight's in the Wife of Bath's Tale. The whole "sumptuous, ceremonial scene" of gossip that Barthes described is charged not only with the violence of language but with a kind of "epistemological pressure" generated by the masculine desire to know—what it is that women most desire, or at the very least, what they talk about when they meet in secret at the tavern. What is mobilized in medieval representations of women's gossip is a "labor-intensive" masculine ignorance of women's secrets that serves to enforce disparate ideologies—from Langland's aside about women in the priesthood to the charges of women's excess in medieval sermons to the indictment of wives for compromising their husband's confidences.[57]

The twin themes of masculine ignorance and feminine gossip are at the center of Chaucer's wonderfully enigmatic poem *House of Fame*. Critics traditionally view the poem as Chaucer's exploration of poetry and development of "an ars poetica of his own."[58] Although I would not necessarily argue with this, I would like to examine how the poem locates this meta-literary end within the field of women's gossip. Because I am primarily interested in the way in which masculine ignorance, feminine secrecy, and gossip function in the poem, I will be confining my reading to a few instances of these things. In particular, I want to investigate the figures of Dido in Book I and Fame in Book II and their relationship to the "house of rumors" in Book III. My purpose is to explore how this poem "mobilizes" masculine ignorance in conjunction with feminine gossip in the service of its "ars poetica."

Of the many critical readings of the poem, Elaine Tuttle Hansen's is the first to raise the important ideological function of the Dido story in Book I in connection with the poem's larger philosophical and literary concerns. Implicating gender politics in Chaucer's "ars poetica," Hansen raises the simple question: "Why does a poem that turns out to be about the illusory nature of fame, truth, and interpretive authority start as the story of a woman's response to a man's sexual betrayal?"[59] I agree that this question, which implicates gender in the art of poetry making, is an important one that others have overlooked. But I want to begin before Dido with Chaucer's narrator, who is an exemplary case of "labor-intensive ignorance" if there ever was one. I would add to Hansen's question the related question: How does masculine ignorance collude with the poem's "story" of the "illusory nature of fame, truth, and interpretive authority" and what desire, goods, meanings, and persons does it mobilize?

Noght wot I—"I know not"—is the narrator's repeated response to the ideas and events he describes, beginning with the theories of dreams and their causes that he invokes in his Proem and proceeding through his visit

to the Temple of Venus in Book I, his foray into the science of sound with
the eagle in Book II, and finally, his visit to the house of rumors in Book III.
While his various ignorances are protested throughout the poem, they seem
to derive from his primary ignorance of love. His ignorance of this "faculty,"
as he calls it, is so great that it exceeds the portraits of love he "reads" in
Venus's Temple. He is able to read/see the story of Troy's destruction, the
flight of Aeneas, Venus's intervention in Aeneas's flight, and the ill-fated
love of Dido and Aeneas, but he stops short of describing the sexual con-
summation of their love. After "reading" that Dido became Aeneas's love
and "let him doo / Al that weddynge longeth too," the narrator interrupts
his own reading:

What shulde I speke more queynte,
Or peyne me my wordes peynte
To speke of love? Hyt wol not be;
I kan not of that faculte (I.245–48).

(Why should I speak more elaborately,
Or struggle to use circumlocutions
In order to speak of love? It will not be;
I know not of that field of learning.)

The narrator's lack of knowledge about the faculty of love is reiterated in
the eagle's mocking of his bookishness in Book II. "Geffrey's" visit to the
House of Fame is proposed as a compensation for his fruitless, scholarly
labour and devocion to Cupid. In place of his *studye* and *endityng* of love, the
eagle promises *tydynges* of Love's folk (II.614–75). The narrator's ignorance of love and just about everything else he encounters becomes the
condition under which the poem explores the "illusory nature of fame,
truth, and interpretive authority." Most readings focus on the radical indeterminacy of the things the narrator claims not to know, such as the re-
liability of authority and experience.[60] Some readers also discern in the
narrator's unknowing a sympathy with Dido.[61]

　　Geffrey the narrator cloaks his dream in his own unknowing, but this
gesture might say something about *his* project rather than the nature of his
subject. What knowledge does his labor-intensive ignorance protect or forbid? How is his unknowing implicated in the representations of Dido in the
Temple of Venus, Fame in the House of Fame, and language in the house of
rumors? Finally, how does gossip as a gendered discourse shape his project?

　　I would like to suggest tentatively at this point that the poem is less

Chaucer's ars poetica than an anxious exclusion of gossip from the domain of art even though that art is everywhere revealed to be no more than gossip or "tydinges." The labor-intensive ignorance that structures the dream vision is meant to misrecognize gossip as the source of art, to insist on distinctions between the search for Fame and the practice of art and between Dido's lament and authority as the source of myth. In fact, the series of misrecognitions that are meant to exclude fame, rumor, gossip, and women's sexual misconduct end up reinforcing their power instead. The domain of Geffrey's art is ultimately subject to the "tydings" he has come to the House of Fame and the house of rumors to hear, where "the elevation of gossip to an expression of communal myth-making pays tribute to speech's unpredictability."[62] The man of "gret auctoritee" is finally irrelevant to the myth-making powers of gossip, whose *auctor* is neither Virgil nor Ovid, but Dido herself.

Dido's lament and the narrator's "sympathy" in Book I are often linked to competing reputations of her in Virgil's *Aeneid* and Ovid's *Heroides*. I would like to argue, however, that these "traditions" are rendered irrelevant by Dido's own speculative gossip about herself, which the narrator extends in his lament about the *untrouthe* of men. In her lament Dido complains about the untruth of Aeneas, who seeks women for their capital in increasing his fame, *singuler profit* (personal pleasure), and friendship. Her lament centers around the falseness of men's speech by contrast with women's, for while "ye men [have] such godlyhede / In speche, and never a del of trouthe," "we wrechched wymmen konne noon art" (you men have excellence / In speech, and never a speck of truth, we wretched women know no art, I.330–31, 335). The duplicity of men and what Hansen appropriately calls the "rhetorical innocence" of women seem to structure her complaint.[63] Chaucer heightens this innocence by suppressing Virgil's excuses for Aeneas and his judgment of Dido's own duplicity when she calls her "secret love" a marriage.[64] Yet what besides sympathy does this representation of Dido's ignorance mobilize?

First of all, Dido's rhetorical innocence is meaningful only in the context of her sexual knowledge. In fact, I would argue that her sexual knowledge, like that of all "wrechched wymmen," is the condition of her lack of knowledge of art and her betrayal, of course. More importantly, though, it is her lack of knowledge that signals her sexual misconduct and, interestingly enough, allows her to be converted into masculine gossip — into that epistemological enforcement described by Sedgwick and exemplified in "The Gossips."

The narrator does not share Dido's epistemological ignorance about men or about sex in spite of his pretenses. Nor does he sympathize or identify with her. His increased role inventing the narrative that began with his reading of Virgil's account is one not of the self-reliant poet but of the masculine gossip who has little interest in the accounts of Virgilian and Ovidian authority. His venture into Dido's shame reveals the mythologizing power of gossip, but more importantly, it separates the myth of Dido from the masculine world of authorities and the narrator. Dido herself initiates the gossip that Fame and Geffrey circulate about her:

O wel-awey that I was born!
For thorgh yow is my name lorn,
And alle myn actes red and songe
Over al thys lond, on every tonge.
O wikke Fame! — for ther nys
Nothing so swift, lo, as she is!
O, soth ys, every thing ys wyst,
Though hit be kevered with the myst.
Eke, though I myghte duren ever,
That I have don rekever I never,
That I ne shal be seyd, allas,
Yshamed be thourgh Eneas,
And that I shal thus juged be:
"Loo, ryght as she hath don, now she
Wol doo eft-sones hardely" —
Thus seyth the peple prively (I.345–60).

(O wellaway that I was born!
For through you is my name lost,
And all my acts read and sung
Over all this land, on every tonge.
O wicked Fame! — for there is
Nothing so swift, lo, as she is!
O, it is true, everything is known,
Though it be covered in a mist.
Also, though I might endure ever,
What I have done will I never recover,
Nor that I shall be said, allas,
To be shamed through Aeneas,
And that I shall thus be judged:
"Lo, right as she has done, now she
Will do again, certainly" —
Thus will the people say privately.)

Dido here implies her own innocence in the face of Fame's rampant dispersal of her acts and reputation, yet she acknowledges the lesson of it by alluding to Christ's speech to his disciples: "For there is nothing covered, that shall not be revealed: nor hidden, that shall not be known" (Luke 12: 2). She laments that "everything is known though it be covered in a mist" through the tongues of slander, and alluding to the conjunction of lost chastity and loose speech, she mourns that "what I have done I will never recover." Dido imagines the gossip about her, the speculation in her name and her sexual guilt "on every tongue."

While this complaint might seem sympathetic, it reads like an exemplum from the Knight of La Tour Landry's instructions to his daughters. Not only does he link women's sexual knowledge and practice with slander about them, but he also berates the "fals and deceyuable" men who exploit women.[65] The Knight's warning about the falseness of women does not indicate his sympathy with women, including his daughters; instead, it bespeaks his sympathy with a morality based on women's "rhetorical innocence" conjoined with their sexual vice as women. The arrow of women's gossip that cannot be retrieved in the Knight's exemplum of wives who should keep their husband's secrets is tipped by charges of their sexual guilt as well.

Dido's lament creates sympathy for her — from readers and the narrator — only within the context of the specific gender ideology that links women as secrets for masculine "interrogation" with their rhetorical innocence and sexual guilt. The narrator's proliferation of examples of men's *untrouthe*, far from vindicating Dido, performs the function of Fame, swiftly delivering her story to every tongue. As others have pointed out, this is one of the few places in Book I where Geffrey leaves off his *reading* of the story of Aeneas ("tho sawgh I") with a performance of Dido's lament that takes its cue from her prediction of the gossip about her. While Aeneas's search for fame is left to the authorities, Ovid and Virgil, Dido's fame is played out as gossip, or rumor.[66] The story of Aeneas comes to a rapid end soon after, and the narrator is left confused and disoriented.

Dido dies twice, both times by her own hand, first through her physical suicide and second through the "murder by language" she herself foretells. Her death signifies a coming to know: "everything is known, / Though it be covered with mist." The epistemological enforcement summoned by her rhetorical ignorance constitutes the pleasure of the narrative. The narrator's own pretense at ignorance allows him to engage in this fantasy of Dido's ruin, to enlarge upon it in the manner of a gossip but without responsibility to himself: "rede Virgile in Eneydos / Or the Epistel of Ovyde" (I.378–79).

At the same time, what "people say privately" becomes indistinguishable from what authoritative tradition says. Much as the narrator tries to shore up Dido's lament with examples from the *Heroides* of the betrayals of Phyllis, Oenone, Breseyde, Hypsipyle, and Medea, his efforts fail, and the primal scene of gossip based on the fact that "wrechched wymmen konne noon art" veers dangerously close to the art Geffrey seeks to protect. His dream has not allayed his fears of the Proem that people will "mysdemen in her thoght / Thorgh malicious entencion" his own work (I.92–93). At the same time, that "delyt" for which women are used and abandoned, according to Dido, haunts Geffrey's telling of her story. When he abandons his reading of the *Aeneid*, he no longer knows where he is, and the provinces of men's art lies in seamless contiguity with what "seyth the people prively."

Book I prepares for Geffrey's initiation not into the tradition of Ovid and Virgil, but into the world of "tydynges" in Book III, where he attempts to repudiate Dido's unknowing and lack of art. After listening to the petitions of Fame by nine groups, Geffrey denies his own dependence on her in favor of his knowledge of his own art:

Sufficeth me, as I were ded,
That no wight have my name in honde.
I wot myself best how y stonde;
For what I drye, or what I thynke,
I wil myselven al hyt drynke,
Certeyn, for the more part,
As fer forth as I kan myn art (III.876–82).

(It is enough for me, when I am dead,
That no man have my name in hand.
I know myself best how I stand;
For what I experience, or what I think,
I will myself all of it drink,
Certainly, for the most part,
In so far as I know my art.)

This assertion of his independence from fame, control over his own reputation, and knowledge of his art is ridiculous in the context of the House of Fame. The denial in this passage is deafening, though critics seem willing to support it.[67] The lesson of Dido and of the nine groups of supplicants proves that he does not control his own reputation, that self-knowledge also has its limits, and that knowledge of his art is tenuous at best for the man who claims everywhere to "wot naught." More importantly, the fact that he visits the House of Fame to hear "tydynges . . . of love or suche thynges glade" suggests that he is more dependent on the gossip that Fame generates than he pretends.

As in Book I, Book III "attacks oral transmission and sides with writing," although ultimately writing loses out to the sheer "noyse" of gossip.[68] The ceremonial scene of oral transmission, it turns out, is Fame's court and her ruling feminine principle is inconstancy. Like the figure of Lady Meed in *Piers Plowman*, who is "fikel of hire speche" and attempts to marry False Fickle-Tongue, Fame is wedded to the principle of gossip, slander, unmeasured speech, and incommensurate reward.[69] Fame's very body, as it is witnessed by the narrator, "speaks" her nature: changeable, hyperbolic, and murderous:

Y saugh, perpetually ystalled,
A femynyne creature,
That never formed by Nature
Nas such another thing yseye.
For alther-first, soth for to seye,
Me thoughte that she was so lyte
That the lengthe of a cubite
Was lengere than she semed be.
But thus sone in a whyle she
Hir tho so wonderliche streighte
That with hir fet she erthe reighte,
And with hir hed she touched hevene (III.1364–75).

(I saw, perpetually enthroned,
A feminine creature,
That never formed by Nature
Was such another thing seen,
For first of all, truth to say,
It seemed that she was so little
That the length of a cubit
Was longer than she seemed to be.
But thus soon in a while she
Stretched herself then so wonderously
That with her feet she reached the earth,
And with her head she touched heaven.)

Fame's modulation in size from less than a cubit to the span between heaven and earth is suggestive not only of the excesses of her discourse but of her unnatural femininity as well. In spite of her numerous eyes and ears, Fame is the object of men's desire in Book III, just as Dido was the object of Aeneas's search for Fame. At the same time, like Meed in Clare Lees's excellent analysis, Fame is the object of exchange as well, serving the heroic-chivalric ethos, poetry, and mythology.[70] Unlike Meed, though, Fame has the power to name and to revoke names, in the case of Dido, by placing them on the tips of "every tongue." It is this power that makes her dangerous, for she threatens to upset the system of social relations upon which medieval culture is built. By denying good reputation (*loos*) and praise (*laude*) to those who have devoted themselves to good deeds, *gentilesse*, and God's love, and granting it to pretenders who seek only the "name" of renown, Fame repudiates the principle of commensurate reward for deeds. In the process she wreaks havoc with the literary systems of authority as well as social systems of justice and morality.

There is an uncanny parallel between Fame and Dido, who "visualises herself shrinking to the two-dimensional figure of gossip and literary exemplum."[71] Fame is as subject as Dido is to the tidings that constitute her and to the people who exchange her. Fame, like Dido, is that which is "yronge . . . on every tonge (III.1655–56). As objects of masculine desire, both feminine creatures, the natural and the unnatural, shrink (and grow) through their appropriation by the world's gossip. Throughout the poem the workings of gossip are thus feminized and made tangible expressions of displaced masculine desire. Both exhibit a circulation of names, reputations, and worldly reward that is dangerous because it is arbitrary. The principle of oral transmission elaborated in both Dido's lament and Fame's day in court is that of excess, undifferentiated whisperings, and unlimited circulation, like Aeneas's use of women. It is this principle that is reinforced in Geffrey's list of examples of women defrauded by men. While Fame and Dido both originate slander, neither can control its voicing abroad on every tongue, an activity parallel to the dilation and shrinking of feminine bodies.

The instability and feminization of oral transmission as gossip is further explored in the house of rumors. Chaucer's description of it as a "Domus Dedaly," a House of Daedalus, curiously echoes Mirk's description of the corruption of the church, rendering the "hous of oresons" into "an hous of dadull [Daedalus] and of whisperyng and rownyng."[72] The gossip that funds Fame, like that which disrupts mass, perverts the ends of language/prayer in endless circulation:

Ne never rest is in that place
That hit nys fild ful of tydynges,
Other loude or of whisprynges;
And over alle the houses angles
Ys ful of rounynges and of jangles (III.1956–60).

(Nor is there any resting place there
That is not filled full of rumors,
Either loud or softly whispered;
And throughout, every corner of the house
Is full of whisperings and of gossip.)

The content of these whispered tidings is listed in the next sixteen lines—war, peace, marriage, love and hate, illness, death, social upheavals, jealousy, business, and accidents. The source of tidings lies, according to the eagle, in the principles of sound, not in Heidegger's "primordial sources," and their nature lies in sheer "multiplicacioun."

Geffrey's entrance into the house of gossip immediately unsettles him. He finds everyone whispering in each other's ear "a newe tydynge prively, / Or elles tolde al openly" (III.2045–46). The tags of gossip—"didn't you hear what just happened? then I heard . . . you wait and see . . . I'll bet on it"—are all that Geffrey actually hears, the visible and audible diminution of Fame's activity. Each person adds "to this tydynge in this speche / More than hit ever was" (III.2066–67), without regard for truth or falsehood. The tiding spreads from mouth to mouth like the burning of a great city, until its escapes through one of the numerous holes in the wicker structure. When a true and false tiding collide, they agree to intermingle: "Thus saugh I fals and soth compouned / Togeder fle for oo tydynge" (III.2108–9). Fame then assigns to each tiding a name and a duration. In the midst of all the noise in one corner of the hall, Geffrey locates the men who "told of love-tidings," only to find them clambering on top of each other to glimpse someone Geffrey is unable to identify: "But he semed for to be / A man of gret auctorite . . . (III.2157–58).

Given the essentializing of Fame's femininity in this same book and the medieval feminizing of gossip generally, it is interesting that this house of rumors is the domain of *masculine* gossip. The gossips are male, and they are spreading rumors about other men: "'thus he hath sayd,' and 'thus he doth'" (III.2052). The two tidings, one true and the other false, are also gendered masculine, becoming "sworn brothers" when they unite as one.

Among all the shipmen, pilgrims, pardoners, couriers, messengers, Geffrey seeks out specifically men who tell "of love-tydynges," which leads him to the man of great authority. Men are figuratively placed into circulation under the auspices of Fame, and the masculine is the site of the true and the false compounded. At the same time, men are the authors of love-tidings and the reputations of other men, such as Aeneas.

Dido's lament leads to this realm of masculine intimacy and power where a "man of great authority" defers the truth. But the truth has already been revealed, and it reduces the credibility of Geffrey's "art" and of masculine pretensions to authority. The construction of this search for authority and art on the reputation of Dido is no different than Aeneas's search for fame by abandoning her. Both are compounded with the true and the false; masculine desire itself becomes the troubling condition for gossip. As Bennett puts it: "In each of these abodes [Venus's Temple, Fame's Palace, and the house of rumors], as in men's passion for women, for renown, for story, the true and false are intermingled."[73]

As seeker after love tidings, Geffrey is as much an active participant in Fame's project as are the nine groups of petitioners. If his poem presents an ars poetica, it is of the author as voyeur of other men's love-tidings, even those of Aeneas. It is an art that is practiced in the company of shipmen, pilgrims, and pardoners bearing bags full of lies, documents of institutional duplicity, and equally suspect masculine love-tidings. Geffrey has already done Fame's work by retelling the Dido story, proliferating those stories told on every tongue and the lessons for women they are meant to contain. While his ignorance has allowed Geffrey his own pretense of being independent of Fame in the name of his art, his search for solace from men's tales of love-tidings suggests his own duplicity, complicity, and, perhaps, even his desire.

Masculine gossip occupies its own place in the scheme of authority according to oral rather than written cultural transmission. It constitutes its own "unlocated but insistent authority."[74] Geffrey's attempt to dissociate himself from the world's talk only leads him to this corner in the house of rumors where men whisper love-tidings to each other in queer fashion. As a writer of love poems himself, he should be able to participate; no experience seems to be necessary. What need have they of the man of great authority? How meaningful is his authority in this corner of Fame's domain?

From Dido's story to this masculine sport of "love-tidings told," Chaucer's poem reaches the unsettling conclusion that oral and written transmission are indistinguishable. Worse, as Spacks notes of gossip and fiction,

"Perhaps the truth is not that gossip mythologizes . . . but that [poetry] mythologizes gossip.[75] The attempt to separate masculine written authority from feminine mythologizing effects of gossip breaks down in the poem, and Geffrey seeks rescue in the man of great authority. Yet this provides little direction out of the impasse.

A troubling impossibility haunts Geffrey's enterprise of rescuing his art from gossip, even as the Dido story reaches an ideological impasse. Writing disappears in the whisperings of men and feminine dispersal at Fame's hand. Written authority ultimately does little more than attempt to fix speech by elevating gossip to the level of communal myth.[76] This attempt is always doomed to fail not only because of the compounding of true and false in speech but because of the power of gossip to circulate language, exceed the boundaries of written texts, and represent its own authority — that of the society. The entrance of the man of great authority is a humorous and desperate attempt to resolve this impasse. The author writing from authority is reduced to the gossip who is straining to overhear the whisperings of others and scrambling to get the final word from the "man of great authority." The poem breaks off at just this point, as if to join the secret world of the house of rumors and to suggest the endlessness of the gossip's text. Chaucer's poem keeps its own secrets by breaking off into silence.

Meanwhile, the Dido story funds the impossibility of Chaucer's text to rescue art from gossip with its own secret: that of heterosexual love. Because of the nature of masculine speech, which like gossip is always one part lie, and feminine lack of art, "thus be we [women] served everychone" (I.337), heterosexual love is necessarily doomed from the outset. The moral of the story is, as Dido says, that every woman is thus "served" because all masculine speech is false — a theme that is repeated endlessly in another gossipy text by Chaucer, *The Legend of Good Women*. Women are not only served thus by lovers but by the tongues that wag and the authorities that mythologize them, in other words, by the literature and culture that represent them. The resulting impossibility of heterosexual love is subsumed under Dido's rage against Fame and the narrator's seeming sympathy with her. Gossip serves to mystify the inadvertent moral of Dido's tale.

The narrator's ignorance of love does not prevent him from writing extensively about it, but it does permit him to dissociate himself from the murderous effects of gossip, Fame's handmaiden. It structures his enterprise of differentiating masculine authority from feminine hearsay, art from fame, and writing from speech — an enterprise that ultimately fails. Just as the narrator of "The Gossips" and Langland are caught up in the very gossip they portray, so Geffrey's vision degenerates into the gossip he seeks to repudiate in his art. The ghost of Dido haunts this final scene where men gather to spread love stories, to circulate women, to mix the false with the true, and finally, to create art. The man of great authority offers nothing more than another tiding for Fame's corrupt fashioning.

Women *become* the secrets of Chaucer's vision in the process — the names whispered by men engaged in the telling of love-tidings. They are the medium of homosocial masculine intimacy and the consolatory object of Geffrey's own desire, displacing the real object — the "fruit of all thyn hertys reste" (III.2017). Yet they are absent from the scene, where masculine desire is permitted to circulate without interruption or disruption within earshot of men of great authority: poetry in the making.

Perhaps in an age when confession was being established and regulated as the primary technology for expressing the Christian subject, it is no coincidence that gossip came under increasing speculation and censure. If Foucault is right that confession instigated an almost unlimited obligation to talk under the most elaborate strictures of secrecy, gossip came to represent that obligation gone awry. The structures of privacy and silence that confessional practices sought to enforce were violated by this other kind of talk. Worse, the relations of power and authority that confession was partly responsible for were undone by a gossip that mimicked and trivialized both. Undone, too, were the other cultural practices, such as poetry, that depended upon confessional ideas about the Christian subject, the public and the private, and legitimate modes and contexts for concealment and revelation. The assignment of gossip and its secrets to women, though, was not an isolated practice in medieval culture. As we shall see in Chapter 3, secrecy was the domain of the feminine itself, including women's bodies, sexualities, and reproductive faculties in some medieval treatises. It was also the domain of the excluded — the non-Western, non-masculine, and non-Christian. The covert operations of the Middle Ages extended from its sacrament of confession, through its censure of confession's evil twin, gossip, and to its esoteric books of secrets, which claimed to contain all knowledge about the secrets of nature, art, and science, not to mention the East and women. The appeal of secrets, as we are beginning to see, lies not in the secrets themselves but in their "promise of virtually unlimited power: over nature, over one's enemies, over the uncertainties of chance."[77] And, as the Wife of Bath seemed to be aware, it is always better to *have* the secret than to *be* it.

3

Men's Ways of Knowing

The *Secret of Secrets* and the
Secrets of Women

What I know, that you ought to know but do not know, makes me powerful.
— Tribal elder from Ghana[1]

What the tribal elder from Ghana knows and keeps hidden becomes powerful only through his withholding of it and holding it over those who are ignorant. Without revealing what he knows, the Ghanaian elder asserts the currency of his power, that is secrecy itself. The act of secrecy, his bald claim suggests, is a social one that draws boundaries between "those who ought to know but do not" and those who know and distributes power between them. In the words of Michel de Certeau, "the hidden organizes a social network" around the acts of withholding and revealing, as well as the desiring to find out. As the previous chapter has argued with respect to gossip, ignorance is as crucial in this interaction as knowledge is: both have the power to galvanize and to charge human relations. Secrecy is thus not so much a matter of secrets as it is a manner of rhetoric, and its power lies less in what is kept hidden than in the dynamic between the "knows" and the "know-nots." It is worth recalling from Chapter 1 de Certeau's description of secrecy as a rhetorical principle in sixteenth-century mysticism:

Secrecy is not only the state of a thing that escapes from or reveals itself to knowledge. It designates a play between actors. It circumscribes the terrain of strategic relations between the one trying to discover the secret and the one keeping it, or between the one who is supposed to know it and the one who is assumed not to know it (the "vulgar").[2]

Knowledge, ignorance, and authority are only a few of the cultural categories located in the "terrain of strategic relations" circumscribed by secrecy. Chapter 2 showed how gossip is defined as women's language that thrives in secrecy. In addition, I argued that the covert operations required to designate gossip as a secret are at least as important as the secret these operations keep. De Certeau likewise stresses the necessity of examining not only "what escapes or reveals itself to knowledge," but the performance of secrecy itself—the play between actors—to map the cultural terrains of knowledge, ignorance, authority, and in the case of gossip and books of secrets, gender.

Before examining specific rhetorical instances of secrecy, I want to explore the theoretical scaffolding of this type of concealment as a specifically masculine form of acquiring and transmitting knowledge. As the words of the Ghanaian elder reflect, secrecy is often an implicit dialogue constructed between the one who knows and the one who is presumed to *want* to know. "What you ought to know, but do not" is as crucial to the dialogue as "what I know." The Ghanaian elder provokes our desire to know what we were, perhaps, previously unaware we did not know, at the same time that he asserts his authority by "imagining" our collective ignorance. He creates, in effect, a dynamic that was not already there between the will to know and the will to conceal.[3] This declarative act goes no further. It does not offer to instruct, nor does it invite "you" to solicit the revelation of his knowledge. It shuts down further dialogue by implying that we/"you" *ought* already to know what he knows. Herein lies the discursive enactment of power contained in "what he says." He accuses us/ "you" of willful self-ignorance. We contain the secret and do not know it; only he possesses the knowledge we ought to know, and thus, our/"your" very selves. His claim differs from that of the confessor in that he presupposes our ignorance, while the confessor insisted on the subject's knowledge, which she was earnestly and consciously attempting to conceal but which the confessor must trick into speech.

In fact, the kind of dynamic that this type of secrecy produces is more akin to the ars erotica as Foucault describes it in contradistinction to confession. Instead of an imperative to examine the self and convert everything down to the last, most subtle stirrings of the flesh and desire into talk, this type of knowledge technology configures the secret around a particular knowledge, which is then kept and transmitted only from master to student. Before he focuses on the confessional uses of secrecy, Foucault summarizes the workings of this alternative type of secrecy:

In this way, there is formed a knowledge that must remain secret, not because of an element of infamy that might attach to its object, but because of the need to hold it in the greatest reserve, since, according to tradition, it would lose its effectiveness and its virtue by being divulged. Consequently, the relationship to the master who holds the secrets is of paramount importance; only he, working alone, can transmit this art in an esoteric manner and as the culmination of an initiation in which he guides the disciple's progress with unfailing skill and severity. The effects of this masterful art, which are considerably more generous than the spareness of its prescriptions would lead one to imagine, are said to transfigure the one fortunate enough to receive its privileges: an absolute mastery of the body, a singular bliss, obliviousness to time and limits, the elixir of life, the exile of death and its threats.[4]

The protection of knowledge in this truth technology is only one of the functions that secrecy serves. It also preserves the master's mastery, excludes the ignorant/student from knowledge except through an elaborate process of initiation, and organizes the master's technique of guiding the disciple and revealing his knowledge. Perhaps most importantly, the elaborate secrecy of the master in the know functions to ensure the value — the capital — of his knowledge, rendering it esoteric, dangerous, and desirable because it is secret. What else is this circumscription of knowledge with secrecy but a form of recognizing intellectual property and asserting the master's proprietorship of that property? The secrecy itself promises, as Foucault writes, not only mastery of a particular knowledge but considerable power and privilege that comes to anyone who is privy to the secrets of life and death.

This particular model of coversion is, like that of confession, a masculine one, but with a difference. This model of secrecy tailored to the transmission of knowledge was exclusively a masculine model, and it served to exclude women disciples as well as to circulate knowledge about women among men. It also functioned to develop a particular kind of homosocial network among masters and disciples that depended on intimacy, power relations, and even the hint of sexual energy. While confession could certainly create sexual and homosocial effects, as we saw in *Sir Gawain and the Green Knight*, its effects were more broad in that it affected the Christian subject as a whole. The power relations were primarily between the individual and the medieval church, although it is certainly true that parish priests were able to exploit this power relation to reinforce gender and sexual hierarchies as well. This truth technology of the master and disciple is a discourse between men almost exclusively, and one that produces its own specific pleasures. At the same time, as I will argue, this particular technology is often deployed to appropriate, if only fictionally, the secrets of the "other," including the secrets of nature, the East, and women.

    The game of secrecy in this case enables a range of pedagogical moves between the master and his disciple. The holder of secrets can also refuse to reveal secrets that he has received from elsewhere, from divine revelation or occult sources, because "you" are not worthy or capable of understanding. He can refuse to reveal a secret because to do so would transgress a divine law. Or he can claim to be withholding a secret even as he is in fact revealing it. The holder of secrets can, alternatively, offer to reveal a secret even as he pronounces the inadequacy of human language to do so, and hence, his secret must remain hidden in language. Or he can offer to reveal secrets but only in a highly figurative language, so that the secret remains protected from unworthy persons, who nevertheless desire to know, and from the ruthlessly ambitious. All of these rhetorical scenarios are fraught with danger because the potential for deception is everywhere present. Those who are denied the secrets they "ought to know" are already self-deceived, while those who are granted the knower's arcana may lose them to the crude limitations of human language or in the "labyrinthian fictions" of the concealer's art.[5] The secret and the concealer remain suspect, while the beneficiary of the secret knowledge can never be certain he/she is not deceived. "Thus the endless task of 'discernment,' the struggle against deception," notes de Certeau, is one of the challenges and frustrations of this type of coversion.[6]

Whatever the strategies of discovery and concealment, the "play" of secrecy always involves a complicated web of desires between those who know and those who do not. The ostensible desire — to know what we do not or, on the other hand, to reveal or conceal what we know — represents merely the occasion for a nexus of other, unstated desires. Dialogic acts of secrecy do not take place without a seduction between those who know and those who do not. We have already seen how the Ghanaian elder's claim of a secret knowledge is an assertion of his power (and your powerlessness), a statement that acts upon "you."[7] In addition to the desire for the power that secret knowledge confers on its keepers, the uttering and withholding of secrets produces a desire between the knowers and the seekers of knowledge: "The secret introduces an erotic element into the field of knowledge. It impassions the discourse of knowledge."[8] It likewise impassions the acts of writing and reading, where authority once again coyly engages the reader's desire to know.

The two actors engaged in the eroticized discourse of knowledge are themselves captivated with each other. The Ghanaian elder invites our captivation from the other side of a secret knowledge. The social network thus begins with the principle of exclusion, and this principle, in turn, charges the discourse and its participants as they hunt, demand, or defer secret knowledge. It produces, in effect, the desire for knowledge so that we may pass from our collective ignorance to the elder's singular knowledge, there to bask in a more exclusive community. It also promises intimacy in the process of coming to know and union, ultimately, between knowers.

What about the secrets? They are as lost in the ineffabilities of language as seekers after them are in their own self-deception. Ironically, "the secret" stands for a reality beneath appearances, but the production and circulation of secrets throws such a reality into doubt. Secrets are trapped in the artifice and inadequacy of language, the human desire for power, the equally human capacity for self-deception, and defective hermeneutics. As often as not, the secret itself proves to be the fiction: there was never a secret in the first place, only this play between actors. The secret's reality has the power, however, to reassert itself and to distance itself from our search by recourse to authority, divine and textual.[9] We are once again reassigned to the status of those who ought to know but do not.

There is one more aspect to the play between actors that is crucial: the tension between disclosure and concealment and the conflict between desires for self-revelation and self-protection that that tension bespeaks. The revealing of a secret always risks self-betrayal and the transgression of divine or epistemological laws. This constitutes the fascination of the secret for those who know, the "fascination of the abyss, of giving oneself [or someone else] away."[10] Yet the power accrues to the speaker who withholds, who infuses his speech with silence.[11] In effect, the Ghanaian elder says, "What I know *but do not say* . . . makes me powerful." Knowledge is construed through silence in the midst of speech.

The dynamic I have just described is not a universal one; since I know little about Ghanaian culture, I cannot presume to represent the practice of secrecy in that culture. Nevertheless, the words of the Ghanaian elder do speak to a medieval practice of secrecy that was popular enough during the Middle Ages and afterwards to be called a genre, the so-called "secrets" literature. Two sets of texts in particular, the *Secretum Secretorum*, the *Secret of Secrets*, and *De secretis mulieribus*, *On the Secrets of Women*, offer striking examples of medieval and early modern uses of secrecy, ostensibly in the service of transmitting and at the same time circumscribing knowledge as a form of intellectual property. In these texts we can find the rhetorical effects of secrecy already described, as well as their circumscription of certain cultural functions. Further, these texts make visible the gendered interests of these dialogic acts of secrecy that always take place between two men in the

form already described. In spite of the range of subject matter represented in
these texts, I want to argue that their epistemological projects are bound up
with the coversion of women and other feminized subjects, such as the East
and nature. The play between actors described by de Certeau represents a
"defining structure of oppression" by which the secrets of women — women
and their sexuality — are translated into secrets to be exchanged by men.[12]
This structure is defining in the sense that secrecy determines what women
and their sexuality come to *mean* in the Middle Ages. The structure is thus
not simply the context or the activity within which "women" and "female
sexuality" are found. The structure itself is not limited to gender or sexual
ideologies; instead it represents a governing paradigm that crosses the spec-
trums of discourse — medical, political, scientific, even literary. Nor is this
paradigm of secrecy exclusive to women and their sexuality: it depends on
the interchangeability and displacement of its terms, so that in the case of
the *Secret of Secrets*, the Persians — the East — become the secret, and by the
rules of the paradigm, the feminine. As Foucault says of *scientia sexualis*, "we
are dealing . . . with the operation of a subtle network of discourses, special
knowledges, pleasures, and powers."[13] Such a network depends, in
Foucault's words, on the "proliferation of discourses, carefully tailored to
the requirements of power." Secrecy provides the paradigm for this proliferation to satisfy not only the "requirements of power" but the production of pleasure. The "interplay of knowledge and pleasure" is maintained
through the play of secrecy. What I know that you ought to know but don't
not only makes me powerful, it gives us both pleasure. What happens to the
secret — the East, the feminine, female sexuality — in the process?

Aristotle's Best Kept Secret: The *Secret of Secrets*

The wise have always been divided from the multitude, and they have veiled the
secrets of wisdom not only from the world at large but also from the rank and file of
those devoting themselves to philosophy. . . . Aristotle also says in his books of
Secrets that he would break the celestial seal if he made public the secrets of nature.
For this reason the wise although giving in their writings the roots of the mysteries
of science have not given the branches, flowers, and fruits to the rank and file of
philosophers. For they have either omitted these topics from their writings, or have
veiled them in figurative language or in other ways, of which I need not speak at
present. Hence according to the view of Aristotle in his book of secrets, of his
master, Socrates, the secrets of the sciences are not written on the skins of goats and
sheep so that they may be discovered by the multitude.[14]

Roger Bacon (ca.1220–ca.1292), a Franciscan friar and philosopher, characterized the secrecy of the Pseudo-Aristotelian work the *Secret of Secrets* and its function, to divide the wise from the multitude and to protect the divine seal that governed all scientific knowledge. Like the secrets of nature that the treatise imparts, the knowledge contained in Aristotle's treatise, and for Bacon in all philosophy, was under strict obligations of secrecy. Even other philosophers must be content with receiving only the roots of Aristotle's knowledge, while the full truth — the flowers, fruits, and branches of philosophical knowledge — is either denied them or couched in figurative language, or in Bacon's own cryptic expression, "in other ways, of which I need not speak at present." Contrasting the learning of Pseudo-Aristotle's treatise and all true science with the fraudulence of magi, jugglers, and women, Bacon asserts the necessity of securing the secrets of natural philosophy from corruption and from the ignorance of the multitudes. Even the preservation of such knowledge in the form of manuscripts endangers their discovery and abuse by readers. Bacon justifies Pseudo-Aristotle's elaborate stratagems of secrecy as being necessary to protect knowledge and the elite coterie of wise men who truly and responsibly possess that knowledge and to exclude the vulgar readers who might use the knowledge for evil or foolish ends. The hidden text of Bacon's statement and the *Secret of Secrets* is that knowledge is power and knowledge is property.[15]

Knowledge is not only power, it is divine revelation, and Bacon situates the *Secret of Secrets* in the company of the received visions of Adam, the prophets, and saints:

And especially was this wisdom granted to the world through the first men, namely, through Adam and his sons, who received from God himself special knowledge on this subject, in order that they might prolong their life. We can learn the same through Aristotle in the book of Secrets, where he says that God most high and glorious had . . . revealed these things to his saints and prophets and to certain others, as the patriarch, whom he chose and enlightened with the spirit of divine wisdom, etc.[16]

Considering the comparison that Bacon makes here, one might expect the scientific equivalent of Isaiah's prophecies or John's Book of Revelations. Roger Bacon not only edited the Latin text of the *Secretum Secretorum*, but he wrote an extensive commentary on it.[17] He was clearly not alone in his enthusiasm for the work, for as William Eamon has shown, it "aroused passionate interest among intellectuals" and was "far more popular and more widely known than any of the genuine works of Aristotle." In its various versions, the *Secret of Secrets* could be said to be "among the most widely read works of the medieval and Renaissance periods."[18] This popularity is evident from the more than 600 Latin and vernacular manuscripts and numerous printed editions dating from the twelfth through the seventeenth centuries. Among the translations into the vernacular are manuscripts in English, Italian, French, German, Hebrew, Turkish, Russian, Czech, Croatian, Icelandic, Castillian, and Catalan.[19] The prose treatise was also translated across genres into poetry.[20]

Bacon might have attributed the enormous popularity of the *Secret of Secrets* to its contents, that is, the secrets themselves, which he himself considered to be "the greatest natural secrets to which man or human invention can attain to in this life."[21] No wonder he insisted on the concealment of the branches, flowers, and fruits of the mysteries of science because they constituted the highest truths to which a human being could attain. Even he was bound by the philosophical code of secrecy not to go into their methods of coversion, lest he allow the wrong readers to crack the code. The irony is that the contents of the treatise are anything but mysterious or occult; instead, they include conventional treatments of subjects currently in vogue not among philosophers or scientists but among the "middle-brow" readers, such as discussions of the different branches of science and medicine, political advice on kingship and justice, and information about health regimens, alchemy, astrology, physiognomy, and the calendar. A more pertinent reason for the treatise's popularity among medieval readers has been suggested by Eamon. It was not the contents of the *Secrets of Secrets* that made it such a good read so much as it was the "promise of virtually unlimited power: over nature, over one's enemies, over the uncertainties of chance." Such a promise both of power and of elite knowledge furthered the "exclusiveness of scholastic culture" and promoted the interests of the university masters.[22] Beyond its value to the institutions of scholastic culture and the university, the hyperbolic efforts of secrecy in the *Secret of Secrets* that Bacon described configure a crucial cultural dynamic for the masculine transmission of knowledge and a notion of intellectual property.

Interestingly enough, the secrets tradition as a model of cultural transmission is not a Western one. Like much of the scientific literature of the Middle Ages, the literature of secrets that began in the twelfth century in the West was acquired from the esotericist tradition of Arab culture, in particular, the Islamic esoteric sciences.[23] The secretive traditions of Islamic sciences became available to the West following the conquest of al-Andalus, or

Muslim Spain, in the eleventh century. The *Secretum Secretorum* was influenced by this very tradition that had been appropriated from Spain through conquest. The conquest of Islamic territory in Spain and the Middle East led Western intellectuals to seek out the "arcana of lost antiquity" concealed in Arabic science and philosophy. The treatise comes to be affiliated with medieval science through Roger Bacon and others, Western science in the Middle Ages tended to minimize its debt to Islamic science.[24]

The twelfth-century Latin texts of the *Secret of Secrets* and later translations were based on a tenth-century Arabic version, *Kitāb Sirr al-Asrār* (Book of the Secret of Secrets), which the ninth-century translator, Yahyā ibn-al-Bitrīq (John son of the Patrician or of Patrick), claims to have translated from a lost Greek original to Syriac and then into Arabic. While the Arabic version survives in 50 manuscripts, the Greek and Syriac versions do not.[25] Long and short Arabic versions of the *Sirr* produced the two main Latin recensions of the treatise from which both Latin manuscript editions and translations were made. The earlier and shorter one from the middle of the twelfth century is the work of John of Spain, while the longer and more popular version from the first half of the thirteenth century is attributed to Philip of Tripoli.[26] In keeping with the secrecy of the treatise, Phillip the translator claims to have discovered this treatise in his pursuit of secrets.

The *Secret of Secrets* adapted Arabic esoteric methods to a fictional epistolary dialogue between Aristotle and Alexander. Purporting to reveal the secret doctrines of Aristotle during a time when Aristotelian translations were becoming plentiful, the attribution of the *Secret of Secrets* was strategic. It gained credibility, legitimacy, and authority from the already extant body of Latin apocryphal letters from Aristotle to Alexander, particularly Alexander's letter to Aristotle informing him of the wonders of the East, such as the Anglo-Saxon prose translation found in the *Beowulf* codex.[27] Medieval readers could assume the authenticity of the *Secret of Secrets*, in spite of its divergence from the rest of Aristotelian philosophy. Beyond guaranteeing the treatise's authenticity, this tradition of letters also sets up a rhetorical appropriation of Eastern wisdom that duplicates the textual incorporation of Arabic esotericist methods.

The exchange of letters is inspired by Alexander's conquest of Persia, which has left him uncertain as to the best way to govern his conquered nation. Alexander reports to Aristotle that there are certain people of this region of "sound judgment and powerful understanding, who are ambitious to rule."[28] In the Latin version, Alexander wonders whether he should have them all slain because of their penetrating intellect. In his response to

Alexander's dilemma, Aristotle explains by means of a riddle that Alexander should go ahead with his plan only if he thinks he can also change the air, water, and cities of that land. If he cannot, then he should practice good government instead in order to foster the Persians' obedience to him. Alexander follows the philosopher's advice with good results. This part of the *Secret of Secrets*, in conjunction with some of the subsequent sections, coincides with the medieval genre of advice to rulers, or a mirror for princes.

The next letter is from Aristotle in apparent response to a request from Alexander for the revelation of certain secrets, although the ruler's letter is not included. The philosopher agrees to divulge these secrets after first protesting the difficulty of complying with his prince's request:

Furthermore what you ask and desire to know is so great a secret that the human breast is hardly able to survive it; in what manner then is it possible for such a secret to be depicted on dead skin [of parchment]? Therefore to that which it is fitting for you to inquire and it is lawful for me to discuss, I am duly bound and obligated to respond, just as you are duly obligated not to require from me more of this secret than I have treated it in this book.[29]

In the passage to which Bacon refers in his discussion of secrecy, Aristotle asserts that the sheer magnitude of his secret knowledge is incapable for either human breast or manuscript parchment to sustain. Aristotle's claims here are the stuff not only of good advertising, with its inflated promises, but also of his logic of withholding the very secrets he agrees to reveal. His next move is to cloak his knowledge in divine mystery. He reluctantly agrees to share his secrets (*occulta* and *arcana*) with his leader, but only in enigmas, to protect them from unworthy men and to avoid transgressing divine law:

The reason that I reveal my secret [*secretum*] to you figuratively, speaking to you by enigmatic examples and signs, is because I fear greatly that this book should come into the hands of untrue men [*infidelium*] or to the power of arrogant men, and so should they gain access to the last good and God's mystery [*archanum*], to which the high God judged them undeserving and unworthy.[30]

One might well wonder whether Aristotle is even agreeing to reveal any secrets at all if he is routing those secrets through enigmas and elaborate stratagems of concealment. He justifies his secrecy by saying that in order not to offend divine grace or betray heavenly secrets, he writes in *figura*, and he assures Alexander that he will be able to find the meaning if he reads and understands well. Any reader — including Alexander — is left to wonder how he will know if he has read well or not. The unstated effect of Aristotle's secrecy, of course, is to protect the master's knowledge and at the same time, to limit the disciple's inquiry. It also increases the intellectual capital of the treatise's contents, while excluding the undeserving and unworthy readers, none of whom, presumably, are those of us actually reading it. Secrecy asserts intellectual property and expresses Aristotle's proprietariness.

What this hyperbolic secrecy is intended to safeguard is never explicitly identified. The real secret of this opening exchange is what Alexander requested in his letter to Aristotle. His letter is suppressed in the narrative, leaving us to interpolate from Aristotle's reply what secrets Alexander asked him to divulge. The play of secrecy, apparently, has begun, and it is not limited to Alexander and Aristotle. *We* do not know what Alexander asked of Aristotle, nor what boundaries separate this secret (or secrets) from those that Aristotle considers too sacred to reveal even to his sovereign. Only the full title of the Arabic version gives us a clue to the nature of the secret being discussed in Aristotle's letter: *The Book of the Science of Government, on the Good Ordering of Statecraft.*[31] What began as a guide to statecraft became through compilation an encyclopedia of political, moral, medical, and pseudo-scientific subjects, such as astrology, physiognomy, alchemy, and magic. Aristotle's warning to Alexander not to inquire further after secrets beyond what he has written apparently went unheeded by later compilers.

Before looking at the contents of the *Secret of Secrets*, I want to comment upon the epistolary play I have just summarized. If Aristotle were to speak the Ghanaian elder's language in his letters to Alexander, he would say, in effect, "What I know and you do not I will reveal, but not openly, that is, I will do so in a concealed way, so that what I know doesn't fall into unworthy hands, and so that I don't transgress God's grace; nevertheless you ought to be able to find what you want to know, unless you are unworthy, in which case you won't; and besides, I forbid you from inquiring further." Aristotle implies his own unwillingness to reveal secrets that are so dangerous that the human breast could not endure them, while at the same time cleverly, if only technically, fulfilling his obligation to his sovereign. Duty compels him to reveal these secrets, but the reader's duty not to desire to know more allows Aristotle to remain silent. Aristotle's power is doubly invoked even as he seems to be relinquishing it in his cautious promise to reveal the very mysteries of God. He justifies the concealment of these precious secrets under figural language and signs (*examplis enigmaticis atque signis*) to prevent their indiscriminate disclosure to unworthy and ruthlessly ambitious men.

At the same time Aristotle defines the "strategic relations" of his discourse, creating an insidership through a system of signs and a gesture of simultaneous concealment and revelation. In essence, he creates further secrets through language of "things" that were already secret. His text is as much an activity of creating and inventing secrets as it is one of revealing preexisting and long-kept secrets. Secrets thus become "secrecy-effects," that is, the effects of Aristotle's double duty translated through *enigmata* and *signi*. Whether the *occulta et archana* really exist separately from and previously to this collection of secrecy effects becomes a problem for the reader who desires to know. Secrets become indistinguishable from the "labyrinthian fictions" they require for their disclosure. Aristotle's power consists not in the secrets he holds, but in his activity of creating of his knowledge a field of pleasure. Part of this pleasure results from his reluctance to reveal the secrets in the first place. Yet this reluctance is converted into an economy of desire by which the philosopher cajoles and rebuffs the reader's desire to know. Under the guise of an "obligatory act of speech," Aristotle tailors the confession of his knowledge to an equally incumbent obligation to conceal. The obligation to conceal is in fact proportional to the obligation to reveal.[32] The play between these two obligations and between Aristotle and Alexander's (or the reader's) desire to know circumscribes the economy of pleasure in the introduction to the treatise.

By swearing the reader and Alexander to secrecy, Aristotle further binds us to him even though he remains apart from us. He creates that "social network" described by de Certeau mainly by exclusion of the unworthy (*indignos*), but also by the insidership he constructs. If secrets produce fictions and even lies in the course of their disclosure, secrecy as an activity produces a rhetorical intimacy between those who desire to know and those who agree (and refuse at the same time) to deliver on that desire.[33] Aristotle is in fact the manufacturer of the reader's desire to know (remember that Alexander's letter requesting the philosopher's secrets is not included in any edition of the treatise). The intimacy he creates and performs under the guise of deference to his sovereign actually asserts his own mastery and authority over both reader and prince. The social network depends upon the regulation of desire and the eroticizing of knowledge. Secrecy, in turn, is the principle of the eroticizing of knowledge and of intellectual property.

In their important study of *Sexuality and Medicine in the Middle Ages*, Danielle Jacquart and Claude Thomasset locate the *Secret of Secrets*' eroticization of knowledge within a broader tradition of pseudo-scientific discourse:

In fact, what we have here [in the *Secret of Secrets*] is another treatise of scientific popularization, in a form which, whatever the field envisaged may be, allow[s] the person in possession of knowledge — or pseudo-knowledge — to be placed in a situation of domination with respect to the person in possession of political power. This literary mechanism, which is that of a narrative fiction, in other words a dialogue between a venerable philosopher and his disciple, functions in reality as a message from author to author, with the added effectiveness created by didactic scruple and the tone of confidentiality. The knowledge transmitted is often of little value, even by the standards of medieval thought, but the fields of enquiry are well chosen.[34]

Echoing Foucault's analysis of this type of secrecy, Jacquart and Thomasset are among the only scholars I know of besides Eamon who comment upon the rhetoric and politics of this literary format for the transmission of scientific knowledge. As a narrative fiction, the master's secrecy creates a sense of confidentiality and scruple that belies his dominance. Aristotle's cagey explanation for his concealment of the very mysteries he has been commanded by Alexander to reveal both speaks and denies his intellectual superiority to his ruler. As for the knowledge imparted, as Jacquart and Thomasset are right to point out, it was common even by medieval standards, causing one to wonder why Bacon regarded it so highly. At the same time, the fields of inquiry are not arbitrarily chosen. Under the guise of offering personal and political advice to Alexander, they frequently assert subtextually the master's superior powers of discernment, as in the segment on physiognomy or the advice to kings on taking good counsel.

The longer version of the *Secret of Secrets* consists of four main topics: the proper conduct and comportment of a king, the practices of good health; the properties of herbs and stones; and physiognomy.[35] Within each of these broad topics, a range of subjects is addressed. For example, the first section includes a brief discussion of astronomy, in addition to the principles of royal justice, wisdom, goodness, and mercy. Here the king is given a guide to maintaining the obedience of his people through his wisdom, prudence, mercy, providence, faith, the promotion of education in his realm, and the proper maintenance of his bodily health. The section on good health that follows in the second part includes a discourse on the four seasons and four parts of the body, as well as information about balancing the humors, the secrets of good sleep, the importance of regular meals, medicines, laxatives, bloodletting, and the constellations. The unit on the properties of herbs and stones includes a section on justice in addition to a segment on the philosopher's stone. The last section is the most consistent of all, with its detailed indexing of the significations of outward attributes, from foreheads, eyelids, and eyes down to the feet and ankles, of individual character and temperament. For example, red eyebrows suggest a dull and wrathful character, black eyebrows belong to persons with a highly developed sense of justice, and blond eyebrows signify an unteachable and wild nature. On the matter of chins, the small-chinned person is impatient and envious, while the round-chinned man is effeminate. As much popular magic as medicine, science, philosophy, and the principles of statecraft are combined in this treatise.[36] The treatise also reads like the wide-ranging compilation that it is.

Intriguing as some of this material may be to the modern reader, there is little in the treatise as a whole to justify the elaborate secrecy that Aristotle proclaims in the introductory letters. Moreover, there is not even any evidence of the cryptic signs and figures necessary to "veil the secrets of wisdom," in Bacon's words, that Aristotle cautioned Alexander he must use. The treatise is straightforward, as far as I can tell, unless, of course, I am among those *indignos* who are incapable of reading them. But this is exactly how Aristotle's elaborate secrecy is supposed to work, to assert the power of the master's knowledge, exclude the reader, and, at the same time, always defer the text's meaning. The reader never knows when he or she is finished reading because a deciphering of the signs and figures to the truth is endless. The trick of Aristotle's secrecy is that, like the self-examination of confession, it withholds the object of the secrecy indefinitely. Just as Foucault's Christian subject is bound to an interminable process of self-examination in order to plumb the depths of his own unconscious concealment, so the reader of the Pseudo-Aristotelian *Secret of Secrets* is seduced into another kind of imperative that demands an infinite task of reading to uncover the secrets of the text. There is no way of telling when one has reached the truths that belong to God's mystery and wise men's secret lore. There is no way of determining whether one has harvested merely the roots of the mysteries of science, politics, and medicine, to use Bacon's metaphor, or the very branches, flowers, and fruits that constitute the essence of the secrets of nature reserved to the likes of Adam, saints, prophets, and certain wise men. To conclude as I have that there is "nothing" here is to consign myself to the rank and file who have not begun to penetrate the secrets with which Aristotle has riddled his text. What I know and you don't makes me powerful, is the subtextual refrain of Pseudo-Aristotle's text.[37]

The hyperbolic secrecy in the beginning of the *Secret of Secrets* is tailored to the subject matter of the treatise, the secrets of nature, and to popular scientific discourse in the Middle Ages as a whole. Evelyn Fox Keller argues that modern scientific discourse is based on two main motifs, the secrets of life and the secrets of death. She links these motifs to the notion of nature's secrets, which were in turn always associated with the feminine as well. Thus the goal of science becomes one of revealing, unveiling, even undoing the secrets of nature. Keller explains how the masculine secrecy of science responds to a conceptualization of nature and femininity as secrets:

> Well-kept secrets . . . pose a predictable challenge to those who are not privy. Secrets function to articulate a boundary: an interior not visible to outsiders, the demarcation of a separate domain, a sphere of autonomous power. And if we ask, whose secret life has historically been, and from whom has it been secret, the answer is clear: Life has traditionally been seen as the secret of women, a secret *from* men . Indeed, throughout most cultural traditions, the secrets of women, like the secrets of nature, are and have traditionally been seen by men as potentially either threatening — or alluring — simply by virtue of the fact that they articulate a boundary that excludes them.[38]

If secrecy becomes the governing trope of modern science, according to Keller, one could argue that the *Secret of Secrets* text was instrumental in its establishment.[39] Eamon agrees with Keller, although he fails to recognize the resulting gender implications: "The message implicit in the literature of secrets was that nature was power-laden, and that this power could be exploited by those who knew, by experience, its secrets."[40] Nature was figured in the Middle Ages as a goddess who covered herself in a veil with an air of feminine modesty and mystery so that no man could discern her secrets, and this figuration sets up the gendered economy of this rhetoric, which becomes extended through a masculine play of secrets.[41]

The uses of secrecy found in the *Secret of Secrets* are not limited to the rhetoric of scientific discourse that developed during the Renaissance. This kind of covert operation with its ideology of secrecy came to govern other kinds of technical secrets particularly in craft guilds. The close guarding of craft secrets may have been in part a result of economic pressures, but as in Pseudo-Aristotle, the air of secrecy surrounding craft technologies also increases the value of the material that is placed under its veil. At the same time, the coversion of craft secrets helped to protect guild monopolies over specialized crafts and to initiate the idea of intellectual property.[42] Men's ways of knowing were clearly exportable to different groups of people, not just the intellectual elite, and they could serve a multitude of functions. The practice of corporate secrecy found in both intellectual and craft communities relied on the master-disciple model of secrecy described by Foucault and Bacon and found in Pseudo-Aristotle's treatise.

As I have already suggested, the treatise itself is equally wide-ranging, its secrets adapted to a range of topics. Its title, the *Secret of Secrets*, is thus misleading because the topics covered in the treatise are not limited to a single, monolithic idea — *the* secret of all the secrets. The treatise does rely, however, upon a primary set of boundaries, as Keller calls them, that frames the various and diverse topics covered. In the beginning of the treatise, as we have seen, Aristotle and Alexander together use secrecy to articulate a boundary not between the masculine and feminine as Keller has it, but between the East and West, the Persian and the Greek, and this provides the initial, foundational distinction for what follows. The masculine boundary of knowledge coincides with this distinction, as Keller suggests for later scientific discourse, and both indeed derive from the perception of a threat from the Persian intellect and feminine mystery, though the latter is not immediately apparent in the opening letters from which I have quoted. As I shall show in the next segment of this chapter, however, the feminine was allied with the secret, just as nature came to be in the Middle Ages, and the identification of the two even in this treatise is unmistakable. It is against this culturally marked domain of secrets — of women and nature — that Aristotle establishes his own domain of secret knowledge, which he claims possesses (and hence, dispossesses) the truth of the Persians, of science, of government, and subtextually, of women too. In turn, he uses this secrecy to set up an intimate masculine system for exchanging these secrets by revealing them and keeping them at the same time. For the prohibition against revealing the secrets of the pseudo-Aristotelian treatise, like the "obligation to conceal" in confession, is but another aspect of the duty to reveal these secrets.[43] Masculine verbosity is the result, only it is called science and philosophy, in contradistinction to feminine verbosity, which is gossip. Not only masculine verbosity, but the sensualization of intellectual mastery through the demarcation of a secrecy domain and the appropriation of the other's secrets — these constitute the particular pleasures of masculine ways of knowing à la Pseudo-Aristotle.

Three parables in the *Secret of Secrets* offer interesting examples of the way this masculine secrecy works, both as part of the whole rhetoric of masculine knowledge and as a technique for dispossessing those areas marked as secret of their secrets and hence their threat. The first is the story of the venomous maiden. In Chapter 21 after Aristotle warns his prince against women, venoms, and physicians, he reminds Alexander of the following incident:

O Alexander, recall the case of the Indian queen, when she sent to you out of friendship many presents and fine gifts, and among others she had sent that fairest of maidens who from infancy was tainted and nourished with the venom of serpents, until her nature had become the nature of the serpents. And if I had not at that hour diligently inspected her and assessed by my art how the girl boldly and horribly and incessantly and shamelessly fixed her gaze in the face of men, I would not have determined that she would have slain men merely by means of her bite or look, which you proved by experiment afterwards.[44]

Aristotle concludes with a reminder to Alexander to preserve his soul's purity. The variations on this story highlight certain of its features. The Arabic version concludes with Aristotle's warning that Alexander guard his soul's purity but adds, "And do not be like the ignorant people of the temples who follow the letter without understanding the meaning."[45] The Latin and Middle English versions omit this warning and proceed to advise Alexander not to sit, eat, drink, or do anything without an astronomer's counsel.[46] The story with its different warnings suggests a number of readings — that rulers need to rely on their philosophers / astronomers, that they need to preserve their souls from earthly (feminine) pursuits, and that they need to read figuratively.[47] The Arabic version is the only one to point to a meaning concealed in the story and to threaten death by literal reading. I will return to this point shortly.

A second major variation that occurs in some versions of the story is the element of the deadly female gaze.[48] In the original Arabic the woman's poison is spread through her bite, while in a Hebrew translation she kills by means of her embrace and her perspiration.[49] Although these texts convey the same danger of the feminine through images of contagion, only the Latin texts and translations derived from them include the feature of the deadly female gaze that looks boldly, shamelessly, incessantly, and horribly on men. Claude Thomasset suggests it is no coincidence that this Latin version of the deadly female gaze appears at the same time that a pseudo-medical idea was being established: "It is precisely in the thirteenth century that a tradition seemed to be established which attributed an evil look to old women. The retention of menstrual blood infects the body, conveying to the eyes and their communication a mortal power."[50] This idea of the power of women's gaze during menstruation to stain mirrors, sour wine, and cause death is an old one dating back to Aristotle and Pliny the Elder.[51] Albertus

Magnus explained the principle of women's contagion in this way: the woman's eye receives the menstrual blood and infects the surrounding air with its poison.[52]

In light of contemporary theorizing about the masculine gaze, this medieval inversion in the form of the female gaze is interesting.[53] The woman's boldness, her "horrible and incessant" stare, reverses the usual function of the feminine as mirror of the masculine gaze. The Indian maiden seems to appropriate masculine subjectivity, as does the menstruating woman, both of whom have the power to objectify by means of infection and death. Strangely enough, though, Alexander does not notice her gaze or the danger he is in. Only Aristotle is able to perceive her secret by means of his art and save Alexander's life. This is clearly a valuable lesson for princes in the importance of deferring to their philosophers. In the Arabic text it is a signal of the need to read beyond the letter to the spirit of the text. Here (in the Arabic version at least) Aristotle's opening injunction to secrecy and to careful reading finds its curious analogue, the warning to beware of women's poisonous gaze.

Before addressing that riddle further, I want to turn to the second parable, which is found in the third section of the *Secret of Secrets* on the properties of herbs and stones, where the text diverges into a discussion of the selection of counselors and secretaries.[54] In a segment devoted entirely to the advice "never trust the man who does not believe in your law," a rather lengthy story once again illustrates Aristotle's secret lore. A Christian magus and a Jew are traveling; the Christian is adequately supplied and rides upon a mule, but the Jew lacks food and other necessities and is on foot. The two enter into conversation about their laws and faiths. The Jew espouses his belief in God, who tends to the health of his soul and rewards him for his faith. He adds: "And it is lawful for me when I find someone contrary to my faith and law to shed his blood, bereave him of his goods, wife, children, father and mother. Also I am accursed if I . . . do mercy to him or spare him."[55] The Jew then inquires after the Christian's law and belief. The Christian man vows not to do harm even to those who do not keep his law because he believes that every living creature deserves mercy and fairness. He concludes by saying he desires prosperity, health, and happiness to all men universally. The Jew asks him whether this includes those who wrong him. The Christian replies that God rewards all good and punishes all trespasses. The Jew then accuses the Christian of not following his own law because he is not aiding the Jew, who is on foot, hungry and tired, while the Christian goes satisfied and at ease riding on a mule. When the Christian agrees and attempts to remedy the situation by giving his mule to the Jew, the Jew races off, vowing to confirm the Jewish law, presumably, of showing no mercy to those not of his faith. The Christian begs the Jew not to leave him to die in the desert, but the Jew refuses to turn back.

The Christian prays to God for confirmation of his law before the Jew. Soon he finds the Jew who has broken his neck and shin in a fall from the mule. The Christian prepares to take his mule back and leave the Jew to die, until the Jew reminds him of his Christian law of mercy. When the Christian protests about the Jew's abandonment of him, the Jew says that he is blameless because he told the Christian of the law he followed. The Christian takes mercy on the Jew once again and takes him into safekeeping. The Jew dies soon afterward, while the Christian is rewarded by the king for "the goodness of his law" with a counselorship.

The last story appears in the final section on physiognomy as a testimony to its powers as an aid to discernment. The disciples of the physician Hippocrates draw his picture on a piece of parchment and present it to the master of physiognomy, Philemon.[56] They ask him to tell them of the figure's character. Philemon considers the image and pronounces the man represented to be a lecherous liar who enjoys venereal acts above everything else. The disciples, thinking they have disproved Philemon's abilities, assure him that the picture represents the most worthy of men. When they report the incident to Hippocrates, however, he concurs with Philemon's judgment and says that he has endeavored to resist his own concupiscence, for "philosophy is nothing else but abstinence and victory over concupiscence."[57]

These three stories are dispersed through the three main sections (following the introductory one) of the treatise. I want to argue that, together with the introductory exchange between Aristotle and Alexander, they constitute an ideological scaffolding behind both the narrative of secrecy and the body of knowledge imparted in the treatise. The first story of the poisonous maiden posits the feminine as the locus of the secret and the mortal. The young woman is a gift of the conquered Indian queen (in some accounts, the king) to Alexander. The girl's beauty hides her nature, with its sinister source in the venom of serpents. The only sign of her evil nature is the bold gaze she directs at men. Her power lies in her gaze and in her menacing ability to provoke male desire. The conquered East and the feminine coincide in this story as threats to masculine subjectivity and power. The evil of the Indian maid coincides with the feminine evil of menstruation, both of which are viewed as contagions. When Aristotle warns Alexander to keep his soul pure, he is not merely promoting a Christian ideal; he invokes a social taboo against pollution as well. R. I. Moore explains how the imagery of contagion underlies "rhetorics of persecution" and bespeaks fear:

> The threat which the victims present is omnipresent, and so highly contagious as to be virtually irresistable [sic]. It is contained especially in sexual menace and represented most vividly by it. . . . This is the language of fear, and of the fear of social change. The fear of pollution protects boundaries, and the fear of sexual pollution, social boundaries in particular.[58]

Fear of sexual pollution in particular, as Moore notes, suggests that social and racial boundaries are being threatened. What is being threatened in this story is, ironically, Alexander's "knowledge" of women and of the Indian race. Only the Indian maiden and her people are privy to the secret deadliness of the feminine because of their very natures—and Aristotle, who is privy to this knowledge through his "art." He is, in effect, able to read her gaze and forcibly reveal her nature without evidence. In the Arabic version Aristotle's remonstration that the prince guard his purity is accompanied by a caution that he read beyond the letter for the meaning. The fear of pollution resonates throughout the boundaries between masculine and feminine and the literal and figurative. The two binary sets are analogous here.[59]

What Alexander finally discovers "by experiment," Aristotle already knows through art: the secret of women and the East that resides in their natures. Only through the uncovering of feminine and Persian secrets, their circulation between men, and their reinscription within the masculine (as opposed to the feminine, sexual, and Eastern) economy of secrecy will masculine society be restored to health. The play between actors begins with the projection of secrecy on the Indian girl and her culture: they are withholding the venomous secret, presumably in order to kill Alexander and nullify his conquest. Their secrecy is exposed by Aristotle's knowledge, then appropriated to that knowledge and re-presented under the secret narrative of the treatise. The threatening gaze of the feminine is removed once her secret is exposed and entrusted to the system of knowledge predicated on the Western masculine economy of Alexander's rule. She is now *their* (Alexander and Aristotle's) secret, not her own or her culture's. Thus the moral and social purity are restored to masculine society, as long as masculine reading does not fail to "discover" its figural meaning. In the process, Aristotle's mastery is further confirmed and rendered indispensable to Alexander.

The second story of the Jew and the Christian magician serves the general principle that introduces it, namely, that one should not trust the man who follows another law, or religion. The political lesson is that kings should not adopt non-Christian counselors because the story appears following advice regarding the manners and virtues of true counselors.[60] The anti-Semitism of the story coincides with the rise in cultural anti-Semitism in the Middle Ages.[61] Like the story of the poisonous maiden, however, this tale serves the larger ideological ends of the treatise as a whole, extending to the introductory letters of Aristotle and Alexander. The Jew, like the maiden, poses a threat to the community because of his alternative, hostile law. He is an outsider who, unlike the maiden, does not conceal the aggression and violence of his law. His danger lies in the alterity of his law and his nature, which capitalizes on Christian compassion for selfish ends. He poses a crisis in the Christian law of mercy, for there can be no retribution against the Jew without contamination by his law of revenge. The story resolves this crisis by divine intervention, violence against the Jew ending finally in death and the political promotion of the Christian. In contrast to the poisonous maiden, the Jew is the other who is no secret, who is openly hostile and exploitative of Christian mercy.

Yet there is a hidden principle of secrecy in the tale. When the Jew asks the Christian what his recourse is when he has been wronged, the Christian replies that God, unto whom no thing is secret, hidden, or unknown, punishes trespasses and rewards the good. When the Christian is left alone in the desert, he prays to the God from whom no things are hidden. When the Jew is being left to die in the desert, he reminds the Christian that he told him of his law, that is, he did not keep it a secret. This convinces the Christian to grant him mercy a second time. Why then does the Jew die in the end? Because God, from whom no secrets are hid, demands justice. The Jew, in spite of his open declaration of his beliefs, has a secret that only God knows and judges. The Christian is forced by the Jew's reasoning to show him mercy. He has no choice. A necessary corollary to that doctrine of mercy is the doctrine of God's secrets. Why should the Jew be punished by death? Only God knows. For the Christian, the Jew is the open secret, with unfathomable malice and explicit designs on Christian mercy, and hence, the Christian community. The story justifies the exclusion of Jews and others who obviously have secrets that only God knows.

The story of Philemon and Hippocrates concerns a more general anxiety, the difference between being and appearing. Hippocrates is both the most worthy man in the world and the most lecherous of men. The science of physiognomy allows the interpreter to force the other's body to give him away, to reveal the being beneath the appearance. It is a science of reading the signs of the body—of hair color and texture, size and settings of eyes, configuration of nose and nostrils, shape of mouths and qualities of voice, shapes of limbs, shoulders, thighs, knees, and feet, and carriage — and the significance of each sign. In this way, the interpreter renders up the body's secrets, the secrets of the soul and character, which no amount of worldly fame or power can hide from him. All secrets are open, but only to Philemon and his disciples.

In these three stories, as well as the opening letters of Aristotle to Alexander, secrecy is the place of the "other" and the condition of otherness. The Persians, with their store of secret knowledge and penetrating intellects, resist Alexander's political control. Women's sexuality, like the condition of femininity itself, occupies this zone of the secret, capitalizing on male desire. The non-Christian occupies it as well, only openly, to use Christianity against itself. Finally, the body itself is a withholder of secrets, even as language is. While all three threaten the community of Christianity, conquest, masculinity, and interpretation, secrecy offers Alexander and Aristotle a means of converting threats to the service of Western, masculine knowledge and community. First, by designating women, female sexuality, Jews and Jewish laws, and bodies as secrets to be interpreted, Aristotle places them in interpretive circulation. Second, by doing so through hypertrophied acts of secrecy, the philosopher creates a system of exclusion and appropriation, a "play between actors" that is infinitely reproducible. Secrecy is an ideological mechanism that can be replicated in other discourses of medieval culture.

One interesting example of this replication occurs in a late medieval English translation of the *Secret of Secrets*. Johannes de Caritate, the English translator, compares Aristotle's secretive method with the contemporary practices of physicians, who use abbreviations and figures in their bills to apothecaries. The physician's purpose, John comments, is "þat no man can vndyrstonde ner rede but physycienis, to kepe þe craft clos [closed, secret]." Just so, he concludes, Aristotle and other philosophers wrote in a style limited to "clerkys stodying in þe same syens." Secrecy not only protects the physician's and philosopher's crafts but protects the ignorant from the dangerous poisons used in medicine. Finally, he adds a second professional justification for the use of secrecy:

for if þei [physician's instructions] had be wrytyn opynly, so þat gramaryens myght vndyrstonde ther bokes, þe most part of þe pepyll schuld a ben physyciounis, and so þe syens noȝt schuld a ben had in reputacion, þat philisophris for a specialté labourryd.[62]

(for if physicians' bills had been written openly, so that grammarians might understand their books, the majority of the people could have been physicians, and so the science over which philosophers had labored would not have been held in high repute.)

The irony of the translator's statement is that the publication of this text along with the burgeoning industry of books of secrets in the sixteenth and seventeenth centuries did precisely the opposite, making craft secrets of physicians and others available to lay people.[63]

Even the phrase "secret of secrets" assumes a life of its own in diverse contexts in the Middle Ages. Its most immediate and idiomatic reference is to the science of alchemy because of the alchemical additions to the Latin treatise.[64] Thus in the Canon Yeoman's Tale of Geoffrey Chaucer's *Canterbury Tales* the "secret of secrets" acts as a code phrase to designate the philosopher's stone in particular and alchemy in general. The Canon Yeoman warns unlearned men such as himself to shun the practice of alchemical science, invoking both the phrase and system of secrecy found in Aristotle's epistles:

"Lat no man bisye hym this art for to seche,
But if that he th'entencioun and speche
Of philosophres understonde kan;
And if he do, he is a lewed man.
For this science and this konnyng," quod he,
"Is of the secree of secretes, pardee."[65]

("Let no man labor in search of this art,
Unless he can understand
The intention and language of philosophers;
And if he does, he is a foolish man.
For this science and this knowledge," said he,
"Is of the most secret of secrets.")

In addition to learning, the key to this great secret is the *privee stoon*, "secret stone," the elixir that transforms lead into gold. The phrase "secret of secrets," however, is not limited in this story to alchemical allusions: it broadly signifies the exclusive world of learning and the secrecy that safeguards it. As the author of an alchemical treatise, Petrus Bonus, writes, the *Secret of Secrets* is not simply a book about alchemy: "Imo totus ille liber est mysticus" (Indeed, the whole book is mystical).[66]

The manuscript history of the *Secret of Secrets* also suggests the proliferation and adaptations of the discourse of secrecy throughout medieval culture. The *Secretum* is found in volumes of the works of Aristotle, mirrors for princes, alchemical treatises, and physiognomic texts. In England the treatise appears three times alongside treatises on the coronation of kings, including the coronations of Richard II and Edward IV.[67] These manuscript affiliations are presumably tied to the diverse subject matter of the treatise. The discourse of secrecy found in the Pseudo-Aristotelian treatise is not limited, however, to the subjects found in it. The *Secret of Secrets* is found in compilations of moral treatises, histories, chronicles, and political prose and verse.[68] In addition, literary manuscripts contain partial or entire texts of the *Secret of Secrets*. One mid-fifteenth-century English translation of the *Secrets* appears in a manuscript along with works of Chaucer, Gower, and Lydgate.[69] Each of these authors, in turn, incorporated the treatise in some way into their work. In addition to Chaucer's use of it in the Canon Yeoman's Tale, John Gower includes part of the *Secret of Secrets* in his *Confessio Amantis*, while John Lydgate (with Benedict Burgh) translated the treatise into verse, *Secrees of the Old Philosoffres*.[70] Thomas Hoccleve also translated the first part of the *Secret of Secrets* in his *Regiment of Princes*.[71]

These manuscript anthologies suggest an intersection of the literature of secrets with other cultural discourses, while the literary translations of the *Secret of Secrets* argue for specific literary affiliations. The two Middle English adaptations of the *Secret of Secrets* material by Gower and Chaucer offer interesting glimpses into the sheer range of adaptation of which this text was capable in the Middle Ages. John Gower's *Confessio Amantis* frames its own discourse on the Seven Deadly Sins of secular love broadly according to the same master-disciple rhetoric of the *Secret of Secrets* and utilizes its own rhetoric of secrecy. In the notoriously digressive Book VII, Genius suddenly departs from his discussion of love at Amans's request to address the wisdom of Aristotle "though it be nought in the registre / Of Venus" (though it be not in the register of Venus).[72] Genius embarks on a discussion of kingship seemingly as a diversion from the erotic subject of the rest of his treatise, though his effort ultimately fails. Amans confesses throughout the discussion that "my herte is elleswhere" and begs Genius to return to the matter of love.[73] While the excursion into Pseudo-Aristotle does indeed seem to be deliberate diversion for the purpose of "tranquilizing" the erotic subject with an intellectual one, the play between actors in each provides the overriding discursive parallel between the two.[74] The dialogue of Genius and Amans is analogous to that "narrative fiction" described by Jacquart and Thomasset in connection with the *Secret of Secrets*. In addition, some scholars have argued that the advice to kings functions in the poem as a whole to offer a model of self-governance that counters the doctrine of courtly love that Genius supposedly advocates.[75]

As we have already seen, Chaucer uses the subject of alchemy as well as Aristotle's mystification of his subject in the Canon Yeoman's Tale. The Canon Yeoman repeats very nearly Aristotle's warning to Alexander about the dangers of this material falling into the hands of "lewed" men. Yet the Canon Yeoman breaks the contractual arrangement of secrecy that Aristotle so carefully constructs. His own master, the canon who exploits the greed of others through alchemy, uses Aristotle's very words in most Middle English editions when he begs the priest he has tricked to keep his craft a secret. The Canon Yeoman's lesson, that the secret of secrets should be left to the philosophers, merely perpetuates Aristotle's own mystification and enables the fraudulence such mystification protects. Further, the Canon Yeoman uses his own revelation of the canon's secrets to bind himself to the host and the Canterbury pilgrims, creating that social network usually reserved for those "in the know." He plays the Aristotelian game of revealing trade secrets, while pronouncing them better left to the philosophers.

These brief examples, along with the manuscript evidence, suggest the infinite adaptability of the discourse of secrecy in medieval culture. The purposes it serves are likewise manifold: it can protect professions, elevate the authority of philosophers, erotically charge the transmission of knowledge, and mystify the commonplace. The stories of the poisonous maiden, the Jew and the Christian, and Philemon disclose, however, the wider mappings of secrecy in the treatise as a whole. What is reserved for scrutiny — the East, women's sexuality, Jewish exploitation of Christian charity, and the body's visible duplicity — are those things that threaten the masculine, Western, Christian community circumscribed by the play of secrecy. By making each of these topics a secret that Aristotle reveals to Alexander, their threats and power are neutralized. In the process, the scientific code likewise conceals its Arabic origins, except for the single voice of the Arabic translator, John, son of Patrick.

Furthermore, the very structure of secrecy implies a power structure, as we have seen with the Ghanaian elder's statement. This power structure implies others. According to D. A. Miller, secrecy is

a subjective practice in which the oppositions of private/public, inside/outside, subject/object are established, and the sanctity of their first term kept inviolate. And the phenomenon of the "open secret" does not, as one might think, bring about the collapse of those binarisms and their ideological effects, but rather attests to their fantasmatic recovery.[76]

As I already argued in Chapter 2 regarding the relationship of women and gossip to men and legitimate cultural discourses, knowledge/ignorance is another one of the binarisms based on the subjective practice of secrecy. What Aristotle protects through the elaboration of secrecy is not only knowledge *and* ignorance, but the multiple binarisms dependent on them both, such as masculine/feminine, Greeks/Persians, philosophers/vulgar readers, and figurative/literal reading. Having observed some of the ideological effects of secrecy in the Pseudo-Aristotelian treatise, the *Secret of Secrets*, I want to turn to another treatise, *De secretis mulierum*, *On the Secrets of Women*, to see how the practice specifically affects the representation of gender and women's sexuality in medieval culture.

Just Between Men: *On the Secrets of Women*

In 1322 a woman named Jacquéline Félicie was accused of illegally practicing medicine in Paris; the 1271 statute invoked against her prohibited unlicensed persons from practicing medicine. The medical faculty at the University of Paris were responsible for "concerted efforts" to restrict the practice of medicine to university-trained physicians.[77] In her defense, Félicie argued that women were under no special prohibition, as the prosecution had argued, and that furthermore, her knowledge and training excluded her from the prohibition.[78] In addition to arguing for the legitimacy of her practice, Félicie made the case that where "women's secrets" are concerned, women and not men are the best physicians:

> It is more fitting and honest that a wise woman, experienced in the art of medicine, should visit a sick woman, to examine her and to inquire into the hidden secrets of her nature, than that a man, who is not permitted to examine her, nor to investigate or feel women's hands, breasts, stomach and feet, etc. should do so; on the contrary a man should avoid the secrets of women and flee their intimate society as much as he is able. Also a woman would allow herself to die rather than reveal the secrets of her illness to a man because of the virtue of the female sex and because of the shame she would be exposed to by revealing them.[79]

What is interesting in Félicie's formulation is the convergence of fantasies — legal, social, moral, and medical — she employs to mystify women's secrets. First, she asserts that it is more fitting that a wise woman "inquire into the hidden secrets of her [woman's] nature," suggesting that women's natures conceal these hidden secrets *naturally*. Yet she also implies in the same sentence that women's hands, breasts, stomach, and feet are secrets that are protected by social taboos and protocols of medical procedure. She then advises men to avoid the "secrets of women" and their "intimate society," implicating the feminine nature itself in a larger social danger to men. Here she implicitly invokes the misogynist convention of the moral and physical danger represented by the feminine, quite apart from the social taboo governing inquiry into the female body. Finally, she appeals to that feminine nature, not in its masculine representative capacity as physical and moral danger, but as shame and discretion. The defense as a whole thus proliferates the referents of women's secrets from nature to bodies to illnesses to female society; it also makes everything dependent on women telling (or withholding), rather than on masculine inquiry. By restricting the telling of women's secrets to female physicians and by mystifying those secrets, Félicie exploits (to her own and women's advantage) the incoherence within masculine representations of women's natures as secret(ive), necessitating flight and inquiry at the same time, just as the poisonous Indian maiden did.

"Silence and secrecy are a shelter for power, anchoring its prohibitions," notes Foucault.[80] The discourse of women's secrets is a shelter for masculine power, anchoring its prohibitions against feminine secrets, including their natures, bodies, and sexuality. Félicie's defense assumes meaning within the practice of secrecy found elsewhere in medieval medicine — a practice that likewise obscures (for different reasons) the relationship between women and secrets/secrecy and among the activities of inquiring into, knowing, and telling those secrets. Secrecy represents a discourse and ideology that includes those virtues associated with femininity — particularly shame — and the physiological code of femininity in medieval gynecological texts.

One of the most popular of these texts was *De secretis mulierum* (*Concerning the Secrets of Women*, hereafter called the *Secrets of Women*), which was attributed to Albertus Magnus, though it was probably composed by a student of Albert's in the late thirteenth or early fourteenth centuries. Its popularity is attested by the 83 manuscripts and 120 printed editions of it dating from the fifteenth and sixteenth centuries.[81] The treatise's field of inquiry includes the topics found in its chapter headings: the generation of the embryo, the formation of the fetus, the influence of the planets on the fetus, the exit of the fetus from the uterus, the signs of conception, features distinguishing male and female fetuses, chastity and its corruption, the defects of the womb, the impediments to conception, and the generation of sperm.[82] While the nature of the material included in the treatise seems commonplace by medieval standards, the author claims that it "bring[s] to light certain hidden, secret things about the nature of women."[83] Like Félicie herself, Pseudo-Albert implies that these "secret things" — specifically, embryology, fetal development, female reproductive functions and dysfunctions, and female sexual behavior — are "hidden" by women and therefore require masculine inquiry.

The author's pretext for disclosing these secrets is the request of his male reader, his "dear friend and companion in Christ." Written within and for a male monastic community, the *Secrets of Women* eventually included among its readership aristocratic and bourgeois men outside the cloister. [84] Although some gynecological texts were written by women, this genre was primarily male-authored and was intended for a male audience. [85] Interestingly enough, medieval gynecological literature was transmitted chiefly through male monastic culture, presumably for medical purposes. Monica Green observes, however, that we do not really know how these treatises were used, whether they were intended "to satiate monkish curiosity about the female nature or to serve as the basis of real medical practice."[86]

Whatever the actual utility of the *Secrets of Women*, the 1353 commentator of the treatise provides a rationale for the urgency of the disciple's request of Albert to be informed of women's secrets. First, he notes that the book was written so that "we might be able to provide a remedy for their infirmities, and so that in confessing them we might know how to give suitable penances for their sins." The revealing of women's secrets serves the ends of pastoral care, so that religious men might be able to prescribe remedies for "female problems" and also determine the appropriate female penances. The latter suggestion is tantalizing, for it suggests the need to incorporate the female subject into a penitential system that was more explicitly designed for male penitents. There is little in the contents of the treatise, however, that would provide such penitential guidance, nor does the treatise offer a system of remedies for treating gynecological disorders, leading Green to claim that, strictly speaking, the *Secrets of Women* is not a gynecological treatise.[87] The commentator proceeds to mystify the reason for bringing to light women's hidden nature:

The reason for this is that women are so full of venom in the time of their menstruation that they poison animals by their glance; they infect children in the cradle; they spot the cleanest mirror; and whenever men have sexual intercourse with them they are made leprous and sometimes cancerous. And because an evil cannot be avoided unless it is known, those who wish to avoid it must abstain from this unclean coitus, and from many other things which are taught in this book.[88]

Félicie's warning to men to flee women's secrets could find no stronger support than this rationale for the *Secrets of Women*. Nor could the slippage of "the" secret in her defense find a more apt elaboration. The discrepancies registered in Félicie's testimony and this commentary alert us to the radical indeterminacy surrounding the contents of the treatise and, not coincidentally, the representation and location of female sexuality. Such indeterminacy, finally, points us to an "elsewhere" of masculine secrecy. The dangers of menstruation and sexual intercourse for men constitute women's secrets, even though the majority of the treatise is not taken up with these dangers. Yet this commentary is not meant to mislead the reader, for although Pseudo-Albert never directly states this purpose, the activity of secrecy, exposure, and exclusion are critical to the masculine social network benignly signaled by the author's address to "my friends and companions in Christ." I will return to this activity after a survey of the text's audience and intellectual affiliations.

Nature, female bodies, embryos, astrological inflection of embryos, menses, conception, and sexual intercourse are all collapsed in this treatise under the rubric of "women's secrets," while masculine fears of their danger also erupt into the text. Although the contents themselves are cultural clichés, the representation of the topics as secrets that Nature forbids women to tell charges them with danger and excitement. Further, the opposition between the masculine "desire to know" and the feminine refusal to tell constructs a "regime . . . of epistemological enforcement" throughout the treatise.[89] Men, by definition, are not secrets, but they must protect themselves against dangerous feminine secrets by *knowing* them. The priest's desire to know the nature of women derives from his own "natural appetite," notes the commentator, "for men naturally desire to know."[90] Knowledge/ignorance, in conjunction with masculine/feminine, thus precipitates the regime of epistemological enforcement in the treatise. Women's bodies and their bodily functions, such as menses, must be forced to render up their secret dangers through masculine interrogation and exposure, by which women are dispossessed of their secrets. It is crucial to note that this formulation does not grant the secrets, that is, women (or their bodies), the *possession* of any knowledge about those secrets. In fact, women are ignorant of the very secrets that they are. To masculine knowledge belongs the possession of women's secrets, just as the Indian maiden's secret poison belonged to Aristotle's art of reading her gaze in the *Secret of Secrets*.

Although women do not *know*, they manage to work harm from the secrets of their nature. The *Secrets of Women* explicitly warns men against women who conceal iron in their vaginas to damage the penis during intercourse: "O my companions you should be aware that although certain women do not know the secret cause of what I shall describe, many women are familiar with the effect, and many evils result from this."[91] In addition to harming men with their intravaginal weapons, women are supposedly able to exploit the effects of the moon on intercourse, choosing times when it is known to be dangerous to men. It is at this critical point that the author of the treatise suddenly reverts to silence, refusing to divulge any more of women's secret evils. "And if it were right to talk about this," writes Pseudo-Albert, "I would say something about them, but because I fear my creator I shall say nothing more about these secrets at present." Ironically, his coy silence here does not prevent him from revealing elsewhere that women conceal pregnancies and abortions from men, counterfeit virginity, and secretly infect others with their glances because of retained menses.[92] Pseudo-Albert's task is thus not only to enlighten men about the secrets of women but to appropriate the secrets of women's bodies into masculine texts and create from that appropriation a masculine intimacy, which one can observe in the gesture of withholding just quoted.

An incoherence surfaces through Pseudo-Albert's concealment, or silence. The boundary between masculine and feminine so clearly drawn in the preface and commentary to the treatise is here obscured. Men's desire to know justifies their disclosure: knowledge is disclosure. Women's desire to conceal is similarly constitutive of their femininity. In Pseudo-Albert's act of disclosing women's secrets, the male author becomes the one who conceals and at the same time *keeps* women's secrets. The incoherence is twofold: first, the author suggests that women don't know their own secrets, but they must in order to hide them so successfully from men. Second, the author's ultimate refusal to divulge these secrets leads to the uncomfortable paradox that, though men deserve to know women's secrets, the process of coming to know cannot occur without some withholding of their own. So the author interrupts the treatise to withhold indefinitely the secrets of women from his reader. In the process he creates an intimacy, much like that of Aristotle in the *Secret of Secrets*, that depends on men keeping the Other's secrets from each other.

One of Pseudo-Albert's methods of authorizing this appropriation is to claim privileged access to women's testimony. In describing the different positions of the fetus during childbirth, the author both critiques the practices of midwives and authorizes his own text with their reports: "I have heard from many women that when the fetus presents the head during birth, then the operation goes well, and the other members follow easily."[93] In a French version of the treatise, the author claims that "we" know about the secret nature of women from two sources, Trotula and Hermaphrodites, who obtained information about women by disguising himself as one.[94] Trotula is usually identified with an eleventh-century physician from Salerno and credited with authoring an important gynecological treatise.[95] Both gestures to Trotula and to female experience rely on the format of rumor, which ultimately lies outside the masculine circuit of secrecy in the text.

The difference between masculine secrecy and feminine secrecy lies in the elements of control and dispossession. Masculine secrets are secrets of knowledge, while feminine secrets are secrets of nature. Masculine secrecy controls the representation of women, while feminine secrecy is often inadvertent and where it is not, it merely deceives men. The circulation and exchange of women's secrets between men creates a masculine bond at the same time that it dispossesses women of their secrets (which were not, paradoxically, theirs in the first place). Pseudo-Albert *has* the feminine secret, while woman *is* the secret that men know. Through their exchange, women become the "open secret," a product and object of masculine ways of knowing. As open secret, the feminine is confined to masculine performances of secrecy and transmission of knowledge. Because she does not share in the processes of knowing, woman does not have the power to withhold her secret or to possess it discursively.

The value of masculine secrecy lies in the performance itself, with women as the pretext for the eroticization of knowledge. The performance can reveal its own duplicity without violating the terms of its play. In fact, such revelation constitutes a display of the power of the master of secrets and an erotic discourse at play with its own exclusionary tactics. *Placides et Timéo*, one text in the genre of the *Secrets of Women*, illustrates the performative nature of this masculine rhetoric of secrecy. Written in the last quarter of the thirteenth century, this treatise combines the *Secret of Secrets* and *Secrets of Women* formats with its discussion of reproduction and female sexuality between a philosopher, Timéo, and the son of a king, Placides. In one section of the text, Timéo instructs Placides on the physiological symptoms accompanying coitus. One of these symptoms is that during coitus the woman, who is cold and moist naturally, begins to steal the man's heat, for men are naturally hot and dry. At this critical juncture in the narrative, Timéo's instruction breaks off abruptly, and he turns from women's desire to that of Placides and his reader:

And the more she feels [the man's heat during intercourse], the more she desires, and in this matter, when you have been more obedient, when I have received from you more marks of affection, then I will tell you the deep secrets that must not be revealed to anyone, except to one's dearest friend: it is the essence of the secrets of nature which should not be written, the philosophers say, except in slender, small, and feeble letters, that are hard to make out, and on poor quality parchment that is hard to read and does not last long, and in hidden meanings, because that which is surrendered easily is vile and that which is discovered with difficulty is dear and precious.[96]

Timéo's reluctance to entrust his secrets to the manuscript page recalls the same fear of Aristotle in the *Secret of Secrets*. Here the master's desire to render his knowledge illegible through a crabbed script on feeble parchment is belied by the manuscript in which it is actually preserved. Not only are his words legible and the parchment intact, but the two surviving manuscripts are actually resplendent examples of late medieval book production, which ironically calls attention to the author's fiction.[97] The master's fiction is based partly on the principle of Augustinian poets alluded to in the last few lines of the passage, that understanding is only precious when it is achieved with difficulty.

There is more going on in the passage, though, than a mere conventional allusion to the necessity of achieving truth through struggle. The elaborate artifice of secrecy contains within it a crucial transaction between master and student that is implicated in the representation of women during coitus. The woman's body is appropriating heat from the man's body, signifying the increase of her desire. Woman's desire, which proceeds from her physiological deficiency of being cold and moist in humor, nevertheless poses a threat just at the point of orgasm, where Timéo breaks off. The textual *coitus interruptus* marks the point where the master withholds, demanding more *samblant d'amours*, "show of love or affection," from his student before proceeding. The concealment of the ultimate effects of women's desire presumably increases Placides's desire for more knowledge, particularly that precious knowledge that is fraught with difficulty. The woman's increased desire for the man's heat is displaced through Timéo's secrecy by the reader/student's desire for knowledge. More specifically, though, the circuit of masculine desire replaces coital passion, with the master "turning up the heat" on the student's affection. The transmission of knowledge becomes the condition of homoerotic desire in this passage, while the concealment of women's desire becomes its site. The master withholds the woman's desire and sexuality so that the student will increase his desire. This is, Timéo says, the secret of secrets, and it must not survive or be discovered easily. Women's desire is thus created as a secret, so that it may be withheld, destroyed, and revived for the sake of masculine intimacy — to stimulate man's natural desire to know and reverence, his *samblant d'amours*, for the philosopher. In the process, the danger of man's refrigeration from the female humors is averted, or rather, deferred. The rhetoric of mastery in the text is thus eroticized through the deferral of female desire by masculine intimacy, perhaps even masculine desire. The example of *discursus interruptus* suggests that the secrecy of these medical treatises is as much about the master-student relationship as it is about feminine nature, bodies, and dangers.

What happens to female desire, female pleasure in the process? Both *Placides et Timéo* and *Secrets of Women* defer or avoid the issue entirely, which is strange in light of the fact that it was the subject of much scholastic debate in the Middle Ages. The burning question was: who received the greater pleasure during intercourse, men or women? One answer provided by Albert the Great used Aristotle to argue that "pleasure is greatest and desire is greatest in woman" because of her greater lack.[98] Yet Albert, like other scholastic authors, also made qualitative distinctions between male and female pleasure. Given the extensive discussion on the topic of female desire, it is odd that the *Secrets of Women* is silent about it. Nevertheless, where the author is silent, Commentator B is not. He picks up Albert's argument about the qualitative difference between male and female pleasure:

A question arises as to whether the male or female experiences greater delectation in coitus. Aristotle discusses this question in his first book on the *Generation of Animals*. After dealing with the arguments on both sides, he replies that the statement that one delectation is greater than the other in the venereal act can be taken two ways. We can understand it intensively, and in this sense the male's pleasure is greater, because his semen is hotter. We can also understand it extensively, and in this way the female would have greater enjoyment, because she has a double delight: one because she receives seed, and another because she emits it.[99]

The measure of pleasure, according to this commentator, depends upon its quality, and the popular view that women experienced greater pleasure and desire is here compromised. Likewise, the second commentator attenuates the popular view of female desire, rendering it "mutual" with male pleasure, but in his own secretive gesture, refuses to say anything more about it.[100] Discussions of female desire in the text proper confine it to pregnant women, in whom increased desire for coitus is a sign of conception, and in women who retain menses.[101] The author's indefinite deferral of the question of female pleasure and his reduction of the sphere of female desire from its usual treatment in medical literature neutralizes the dangerous agency of the female body and female desire. Both become subsumed under performances of masculine secrecy.

An interesting example of this neutralization occurs in the author's discussion of female hysteria. Citing a case study of Galen's on hysteria, Pseudo-Albert actually conceals Galen's analysis of the disease and its cure:

> The great doctor Galen tells about a certain woman who was suffering a suffocation of the womb so serious that it prevented her from talking, and she fell down as if she were dead, with no sign of life. Many doctors were called who looked at her and, not knowing the cause of these symptoms, pronounced her dead. Galen then came on the scene, considered the cause, and freed the woman from this illness.[102]

What did Galen actually do to cure the woman? Nothing, by Galen's account. He reports how a midwife told him the story in the first place and how she cured the woman by applying heat and stimulating the woman's genitals to orgasm.[103] Galen never came on the scene, according to his version of the story, nor did he free the woman from her illness. Instead, what Pseudo-Albert conceals is the sexual cure Galen indirectly prescribes to be administered by the female midwife to the afflicted woman.[104] Pseudo-Albert recommends in place of Galen's solution that women not be prevented "from having sex with the man they choose" even though this "goes against custom." Apparently, this solution goes less against custom than the midwife's stimulation of the afflicted woman's genitals.

By attributing the hidden solution to the "great doctor" Galen without revealing that solution, Pseudo-Albert places this women's secret securely back into the domain of masculine medicine. As a result, the dangerous cure of the professional female midwife stimulating the hysterical woman to orgasm is suppressed. Female desire itself is reinscribed within the heterosexual framework, albeit one that "goes against custom." Even though female desire is not quite neutralized in this passage, it is appropriated by masculine authority and medicine and rendered safely heterosexual. Female pleasure is thus safely returned to the domain of masculine secrecy and authority.

Like the audience of the *Secret of Secrets*, the readership of the *Secrets of*

Women extended beyond the monastic community that is thought to have produced it. Its appeal is explained by Joan Cadden: "*The Secrets of Women* illustrates the authenticity of late medieval curiosity within and beyond universities about sexuality and sex difference, as well as the ambiguity of university-style formality, which lent cool legitimacy to topics fraught with danger."[105] Not only is some of the subject matter the stuff of medieval science, but the format of the question-and-answer between student and master was one that was emerging in medieval universities, particularly in connection with medical and scientific subjects. The pedagogical practice in the medical schools of Salerno contributed to the genre that consisted of a compilation of questions and answers on topics of natural philosophy and human generation. The so-called prose Salernitan questions "acquired a life of their own in their later form as prominent components of widely distributed question-and-answer literature."[106] Later developments in university practice benefited from the Salernitan questions. In the thirteenth and fourteenth centuries, university lectures took the form of *questiones*, or a set of problems and disputations on a particular subject.[107] Like the Salernitan questions, this highly structured format eventually traveled outside the university forum, where its literary value as authorizing fictions proved popular.[108] Thus, while the author of the *Secrets of Women* was not a member of the university community, he was familiar with its discussions and able to imitate them.[109]

A number of works addressing the subjects of human reproduction and female sexuality form another context for the *Secrets of Women*. Constantine the African imported and translated Arabic medical works on human reproduction, introducing them to secular communities in the West. His treatise *On Coitus* in particular addresses the subjects of intercourse and reproduction, though it gives little attention to women.[110] William of Conches's *On the Philosophy of the World* explores sexuality and reproduction in the course of a treatise on natural philosophy, using the Salernitan format.[111] Other treatises, such as Michael Scot's *On the Secrets of Nature*, combine medicine, natural philosophy, and physiognomy, including a description of the dangers of menstruating women and the astrological effects on the fetus.[112] Albert the Great also contributed to the discussion of human generation in his *Quaestiones super De animalibus*.[113] This is not by any means an exhaustive list of works on topics related to those found in the *Secrets of Women*.[114] It demonstrates, however, the currency and urgency of what Cadden calls "topics fraught with danger."

The charging of medical subjects with an air of danger is achieved in part by the related activities of secrecy, disclosure, and exclusion. The passage in the treatise commentary quoted earlier points to the dangerous effects of women's menses and intercourse on men as the inspiration for the treatise. In addition, the commentator goes on to say that the priest who asked for the information was inspired to investigate women's nature because "men naturally desire to know." This natural, gendered desire for knowledge is placed in opposition in the commentary with women's poisonous bodies — those "secret things" that constitute their natures. Men's "natural appetite" to know is distinguished from women's natural condition to conceal the powerful dangers of their bodies. By naturalizing these two activities as appetites and by equating women's bodies (along with their sexualities) with *the* secret, the commentary on the *Secrets of Women* interprets the terms of the masculine intimacy and feminine exclusion.

This exclusion is implicit everywhere in the treatise. The author warns the priest/inquisitor "not to permit any child to peruse it, nor anyone of childlike disposition."[115] Women are not explicitly named here under the category of those with childlike dispositions, but the principle of exclusion does extend to them. Since the "secrets of women's nature" — or their nature as a secret — is the subject of the treatise, they are logically excluded as readers. Lady Reason in Christine de Pizan's *Book of the City of Ladies* alludes to a French translation of the *Secrets of Women* in which "some pope — I don't know which one — excommunicated every man who read the work to a woman or gave it to a woman to read." Clearly, Christine and other female readers were aware of the implicit and explicit masculine community circumscribed by secrecy, for Reason goes on to offer her own reason for masculine secrecy in the treatise:

> It was done so that women would not know about the book and its contents, because the man who wrote it knew that if women read it or heard it read aloud, they would know it was lies, would contradict it, and make fun of it. With this pretense the author wanted to trick and deceive the men who read it.[116]

Christine de Pizan characterizes the book as the product of masculine secrecy and fear, not the scientific "bringing to light" of feminine secrets, as it claims. This masculine plot guards the contents of the treatise — as Christine understands it, a discussion of "the constitution of [women's] natural bodies and especially their defects" — and it prompts her to defend Nature and the perfection of women's bodies. Her reading of the *Secrets of Women* construes Nature and women's natural bodies as the secret of the hostile masculine treatise, while modern scholars of the texts see female sexuality as the secret.[117] This slippage of secrecy's reference is likewise characteristic of the treatise and its commentaries, and it is indispensable to the deliberate mystification of its contents. It also points to the fact, as I have stressed throughout this book, that the activity of secrecy is always more important than the secrets themselves. Christine de Pizan understood not only this but also that secrecy was a masculine discursive strategy for excluding and deceiving women.

The real exclusion of women, as Christine knew, occurs through their representation as *the* secret. The female body, as Marie-Christine Pouchelle has argued, belonged "to the domain of trickery, of seeming, of lies" in the Middle Ages, and nowhere is this more true than in the *Secrets of Women*.[118] Seeming, lies, duplicity define the woman's body and warrant masculine efforts to know and to appropriate those secrets. The larger end of this masculine secrecy, however, was masculine community. Both this text and the *Secret of Secrets* are concerned with articulating that boundary, as Evelyn Fox Keller put it, around an "interior not visible to outsiders," "a sphere of autonomous power." I have also suggested that secrecy forms a circuit of exchange among the "secret sharers" and that in both texts, a homosocial network is the result. This network establishes its boundaries between those who know and those who don't, between those who possess the secret and those who are the secret. And this network is a cultural template for the transmission of knowledge at least in these two extremely popular genres of medieval discourse.

Jacquéline Félicie never challenged the equation of women's sexual and reproductive functions with secrecy; instead she used it to argue for the necessity of female physicians to whom women could comfortably reveal their secrets. Whether it was true or not that women preferred to reveal their secrets to other women rather than to men, this argument was used again in a fifteenth-century English translation of Trotula's gynecological treatise:

Because there are many women who have numerous diverse illnesses — some of them almost fatal — and because they are also ashamed to reveal and tell their distress to any man, I therefore intend to write about curing their illnesses. . . . And although women have various maladies and more terrible sicknesses than any man knows, as I said, they are ashamed for fear of reproof in times to come of exposure by discourteous men who love women only for physical pleasure and for evil gratification. And if women are sick, such men despise them and fail to realize how much sickness women have before they bring them into this world. And so, to assist women, I intend to write of how to help their secret maladies so that one woman may aid another in her illness and not divulge her secrets to such discourteous men.[119]

Women's secret illnesses are connected to their secrets, that is, their sexual and reproductive faculties, as the author implies. The exploitation of male physicians together with women's shame prevents the successful treatment of women's secret illnesses. The argument as a whole, like Félicie's, is for the professional control of women's secrets.

The popularity of the *Secrets of Women* must be seen in terms of the professional rivalry so evident in the University of Paris prosecution of Félicie. The masculine rhetoric of secrecy in the Pseudo-Albert treatise was popularized during a time when male physicians were engaged in circumscribing and insulating their practice. Félicie was not the only woman to be cited under new licensing laws that sought to exclude women practitioners, as well as Jews and Saracens.[120] In addition to the enforcement of licensing of physicians, medical practitioners formed guilds and protective societies as the rivalry between university-trained physicians and nonuniversity practitioners (barbers, surgeons, and apothecaries) emerged.[121] The effect of the coterie reader created in the *Secrets of Women* coincides with this professionalization of a masculine, university-trained, Christian physicianry.

Jacquéline Félicie lost her case, was forbidden to practice medicine, and was excommunicated.[122] Her attempt to turn the masculine representation of women as secrets and rhetoric of secrecy against the physicians at the University of Paris failed. Beyond this case's significance for the history of the professionalization of medicine, what does it say about women's appropriation of the rhetoric of shame and secrecy found in *Secret of Secrets* and some versions of the Trotula treatises?

Jean Renart's lai, *Galerent de Bretagne*, offers one fictional example of what happens when women appropriate masculine language. The story tells about two neighboring knights of great worth who were both married. One wife soon becomes pregnant and gives birth to twins, to her husband's great delight. When his neighbor is given the good news, the knight is likewise happy for the new father. The neighbor's wife, however, is scornful. She expresses great surprise at the father's delight, since she says that "clerks and priests" tell us that two children means two fathers. Her husband is immediately ashamed at his wife's foolishness and intervenes, saying:

Lords, my wife is dreaming.
I could tell you much of this incident,
If she knew the nature
Of the things which clerks have learned,
Which they have written about in their studies,

Who know the secrets of women
Better than women do. It is no lie [*diffames*].[123]

The jealous wife uses the secret knowledge of priests against other women, but she does not get away with it. It is interesting that the word for slander, *diffames,* is rhymed with *femmes*: the wife uses slander to "defeminize" the mother of the twins, in other words, to undo her reputation and with it, the masculine representation of *femmes*. But the final sentence might be read another way to say, "it [the knowledge, secret] is not for women to know." Her husband invokes the *Secrets of Women* to dispossess his wife of the knowledge she claims, averring that clerks know *better than women do* the nature of women's secrets. When women speak their secrets, they speak slander (*diffame*) and the de-feminization of all women. It is thus no coincidence that in a similar version of this tale, Marie de France's *Fresne*, all women become angry at the scornful wife for slandering them.[124] Women's appropriation of the *knowledge* of their own secrets always defames and de-feminizes all women because it undoes the masculine representation of women as secrets who nevertheless do not *know* — and cannot *possess* — them.

His Master's Voice

Both the *Secret of Secrets* and the *Secrets of Women* deploy a rhetoric of secrecy that simultaneously excludes the "other" and affirms masculine mastery. Before Aristotle's exaggerated efforts to protect the secrets from unworthy manuscript pages and readers, there was the secret. The secret precedes the secrecy; secrets are designated culturally as secrets, and the entire apparatus of secrecy is then pressed into service. The narrative fiction of secrecy thus performs a deception, or rather, a decoy from its ideological intent. It is not what Aristotle knows that is important in the *Secret of Secrets*, nor is it women's secret plots against men that drive the dialogue of the *Secrets of Women*. It is, rather, what gets designated as a secret in the first place in order to be fixed, controlled, neutralized, and ultimately recuperated by masculine authority, or mastery.[125]

The power of secrecy lies not only in the system of mastery that it creates but in the consignment of things and people — nature, Persians, wisdom, female bodies — to the realm of the secret. It becomes the task and duty of masculine knowledge to penetrate these secrets in order to neutralize their threat and to recuperate them for masculine use and the maintenance of patriarchal social and textual order. Like Galen in Pseudo-Albert's version of the story, the master who appears on the scene of the woman suffering from the defective womb to solve the riddle of her illness, the master of the book of secrets draws upon his secret wisdom to perform a miraculous cure; or like Aristotle, he penetrates the beauty of the Indian maiden to the fatal poison within, thus displaying his discerning wisdom in the service of political and social order.

A complicated gesture of revealing and concealing characterizes the master's secrecy. One of the chief paradoxes of the secret that is responsible for this gesture is that making something a secret requires it to be told. As Ross Chambers observes, "only divulgence makes a secret . . . because a secret exists only as discourse . . . the discourse which 'realizes' the secret is that which destroys it as a 'secret' (something unspoken)."[126] To put it simply, discourse makes and breaks the secret. It also makes the master. Concealment is at least as important to the system of mastery as disclosure is.

So is masculine pleasure. The charged intimacy that results from the master's esoteric discourse is one of secrecy's main effects, and it is crucial to the entire transaction of transmitting knowledge in the *Secret of Secrets* and the *Secrets of Women*. In fact, it is more important than the actual secrets themselves, which are hardly the "treasure of wisdom" or "secrets of nature" that Bacon claimed for the *Secrets of Secrets*. The masculine "desire to know" sets in motion a bond between master and student that seeks erotic pleasure in the multiple gestures of revealing and concealing that constitute the master's art. Further, this masculine pleasure is rendered through the penetration or transgression of those domains of secrecy that Keller argues designate cultural spheres of taboo and hence, of power — like nature, life, and the feminine. This masculine intimacy is not unlike the gossip of the male narrator as voyeur in the poem "The Gossips" or in masculine poetics in Chaucer's *House of Fame*, as we saw in Chapter 2. Masculine pleasure comes from repairing the fear of masculine exclusion — in other words, of "avenging the excluded male" — and of appropriating the secrets and coyly exchanging them among men.[127]

The difference between having and being the secret is a vast one indeed, for it is the master who possesses the secret. Being the secret is of little value — to women, nature, wise Persians — until it is incorporated into Aristotle's esoteric discourse or Pseudo-Albert's instruction to his dear companions. Part of the function of secrecy, then, is to dispossess secrets of their power and accrue power to the master and the master's knowledge. If there were no secrets to tell, masters would have had to create them for their own survival and as a defense of what they are claiming to be a kind of intellectual property.

Medieval habits of secrecy as they are exemplified in these two treatises can be found elsewhere in medieval literature. The entire discourse of courtly love makes similar use of the secret and of the master/disciple structure, dynamic, and erotics. The insistence on the secret in courtly love romances in particular depends on the association of the feminine with the secret that the masculine lover must keep.[128] The treatise of Andreas Capellanus on *The Art of Courtly Love* adopts the masculine erotics of the master/disciple relationship for the ostensible purpose of transmitting the secrets of love. In different ways, John Gower's *Confessio Amantis* and Jeun de Meun's *Roman de la Rose* incorporate this same dynamic. Chaucer's trope of the failed student of love in his early poems also might be viewed in light of the same secretive technology belonging to the master/student.

The most apt modern analogy, if Evelyn Fox Keller's analysis is correct, is science, with its inquiry into the secrets of life and the secrets of death, whether in the rise of molecular biology or the development of the atomic bomb. The so-called scientific method ends up being a "drama between visibility and invisibility, between light and dark, and also between female procreativity and male productivity—a drama in need of constant reenactment at ever-receding recesses of nature's secrets."[129] The history of gynecology, as Terri Kapsalis has recently shown, is even more clearly the history of a performance of masculine knowledge unveiling the secrets of female reproductive health and pathology—one that is staged with the notorious sheet to protect the doctor's authority and women's shame.[130] Echoes of Jacquéline Félicie . . .

Academic discourse, too, might be legitimately accused of Aristotle's esotericism and of what Bacon recognized as the practice of insulating the elite from the rank-and-file purveyors of knowledge. Just as it was never clear beyond the benefits of mastery what the secrets that were being kept actually were, so in today's academic technologies of knowledge, there is more secretiveness than actual secrets. The clear sense of exclusivity and entitlement that contemporary theoretical mastery displays also engenders an equal sense of exclusion among students and members of the general public. Whether it is real or imagined, the Ghanaian's cryptic statement reverberates throughout contemporary discontent about academic discourse and theoretical discourse in particular: "What I know, that you ought to know but do not know, makes me powerful."

From confession to books of secrets, the Middle Ages produced two truth technologies, not one, as Foucault thought. Each depended upon an elaborate system of secrecy, and each exploited the secret as a means of power. Vastly different though their methods and effects were, we must finally see them as peculiarly akin to one another and wonder at the medieval culture that produced both. While one made the secret the key to Christian subjectivity, the other discourse made the secret the boundary of knowledge, truth, and power. One set up an endless process of self-examination before the ever-receding secret of individual sinfulness, while the other manufactured an equally interminable inquiry into the recesses of nature, women, and linguistic enigmas. That the Middle Ages produced two such complementary discourses must be testimony to something more than a penchant for secrecy. That contemporary culture continues to farm these discourses is testimony to the power of secrecy to transform, adapt, and proliferate itself to changing times and needs even as it continues to mark its boundaries of power, identity, knowledge, and unworthiness.

4

Covert Women and
Their Mysteries

Privacy is everything women as women have never been allowed to be or have; at the same time the private is everything women have been equated with and defined in terms of men's *ability to have.*

—Catharine A. MacKinnon[1]

The discourse of confession established a site of privacy in the depths of the Christian subject, and it devoted itself to the refinement of the task of interrogating and publicizing this site. The private sphere so carved out by confessional interrogation and presumption of human sinfulness was also the sphere of the secret, the hidden, the deliberately covert. It was the silence that was obligated through confessional rules and practices to speak, to do so endlessly because the extent of the individual's private sinfulness was limitless, or rather, it was limited only by the individual's self-deception and deliberate concealment. While the discourse itself was not a gendered one, it did have consequences for gender, mainly in its twin notions of the concupiscence of the flesh and its moralization of the secret. The discourse of confession, too, as we saw in *Sir Gawain and the Green Knight*, was easily adaptable to medieval gender ideology that associated the feminine with the private, secret, and immoral and depended crucially on the power relations that confession sponsored, both between the medieval church and the culture generally and between the one who asked and the one who told.

Gossip represented the perverse analogue to confession and its gendered effect. Like confession, gossip assumed that each individual concealed secrets that constituted the key to his or her identity, but unlike confession, gossip violated (or was perceived to violate) the very secrecy and privacy that had made both discourses possible. The association of gossip with communities of women and the nature of the feminine further identified the realm of the secret and the private with women, even if, paradoxically, it was women's failure to keep secrets or respect privacy that marked their gender. It was also the association of women and women's talk with secrets that invited masculine insurgency and exposure. At the same time, the designation of women's speech as gossip allowed masculine medieval culture to recuperate the threat of women's secret and diminish their power.

Books of secrets show us how knowledge in the Middle Ages could be constructed around the mysteries and pleasures of the secret. Not only does secrecy assume a mode of cultural transmission, but it functions to create masculine communities of writers/narrators and readers and to exclude the feminine. The hyperbolic rhetoric of both the *Secret of Secrets* and the *Secrets of Women* calls attention to the way in which secrecy itself always serves to mark cultural boundaries, establishing a privileged interior and excluded "rank and file," as well as lending cultural capital to what is marked "secret." The secret seems to circumscribe a private space that, in the case of the books of secrets, promotes science, the transmission of knowledge, and perhaps most importantly, masculine pleasure.

In the Middle Ages the secret and the private were more synonymous than they are today. Georges Duby points out, for example, that in courtly French the adjectives, *privé*, *privance*, and *priveté* shifted in meaning from affectionate intimacy and family to the clandestine, secret, and therefore suspect.[2] The Middle English word for privacy, *privete*, designated both the condition of being private and concealment, or secrecy. Because it carried its Latin *privatus* meaning, "secluded from the public life," and the Old French meaning of "secret," the Middle English word could refer to that which is private or personal, as well as that which is concealed. As we shall see later in this chapter, the semantic field of the Middle English word also ranges vastly from its primary sense of God's mystery to its secondary meanings of intimate fellowship and, in a different register, the genitals. This allows for some interesting play in the word that is no longer available to us in modern English. If today the private has come to designate crucial spaces of personal subjectivity and property that are secured from publicity but are not necessarily secret, in the Middle Ages the association of the secret with divine mystery and Christian subjectivity (as we saw in medieval confession) rendered medieval privacy something more covert and charged than its modern version is. If I do not have the evidence or the space to support this admittedly large claim, the evidence of medieval English words and their etymologies at least argues for the possibility that medieval secrecy and privacy were more mutually defining than they are today.

The secret and the private may no longer be synonymous concepts, but they are related operations of coversion. Sissela Bok distinguishes contemporary secrecy as "intentional concealment" from privacy as "protection from unwanted access" (physical access, personal information or attention).[3] And yet, the two realms are not so clearly differentiated in Ariès and Duby's *History of the Private Life*, where the private is that which is opposed to the public, including the realm of the hidden, secret, or reserved.[4] As the first three chapters have shown, the domain of secrecy articulates cultural boundaries that include and exclude, protect and mystify, empower and disempower, exalt and dispossess, ward off and recuperate, shame and threaten. While medieval privacies and secrecies surely performed different cultural functions than modern ones do, MacKinnon's observation about the equation of privacy with the feminine and the modern liberal state already has recognizable medieval analogues — in the masculine representations of women's gossip, in the power relations between priest and confessant, and in the whole "domain of strategic relations," in de Certeau's words, that accompanies the master/disciple relationship and the transmission of knowledge as secrets.

I would like to expand MacKinnon's statement to include the secret with the private because what is protected often overlaps in medieval discourses of secrecy with what is intentionally concealed, the activity of protecting overlapping with the practice of concealment. Like privacy, secrecy functions to define women in terms of men's ability to have. At the same time, our legal and social understanding of privacy has excluded women: women are not allowed to be or to have it, but privacy "has" women as a function of men's ability to have, own, or possess. There is an important connection here between the guarantee of personal identity, autonomy, and control that privacy signifies in the liberal state and the propertied sense of the word. MacKinnon is primarily concerned with the former sense of the word, but as this study has already shown, secrecy (if not privacy) always implies possession in terms of concealment. If secrecy is "everything women as women have never been allowed to be or to have," nevertheless, the secret "is everything women have been equated with and defined in terms of *men's* ability to have." As we have seen, the secret is equated with women's gossip, women's sexuality, and the Persian's knowledge so that these same things may be converted into masculine science, knowledge, and intimacy. Women and nature are the secrets that justify masculine insurgency in the name of science and knowledge, and at the same time, rival masculine secret technologies. The function of this masculine secrecy is to recuperate the already secret feminine, or "other," and to dispossess it of its secrets. Men's "ability to have" depends upon this doubled secrecy and privacy, whereby the feminine is first constituted as a secret so that masculine secrecy may set about probing, revealing, and recovering the secrets. Masculine authority and intellectual property are the cultural beneficiaries of this technology of secrecy and privacy.

The paradox of these twin ideologies of secrecy and privacy is that women are everywhere keeping secrets in medieval texts, from the Wife of Bath's Tale, where the Hag "holds" the secret to what women most desire, to Morgan le Fay and Bertilak's wife in *Sir Gawain and the Green Knight*, where women's secrets force Gawain to violate his code of honor and courtesy, to Andreas Capellanus's *The Art of Courtly Love*, and to French romances, where women's honor depends upon their ability to keep their love secret.[5] At the same time misogynistic literature of the Middle Ages continually essentializes women according to their natural inability to keep secrets, such as when Genius asserts: "No man born of woman, unless he is drunk or demented, should reveal anything to a woman that should be kept hidden, if he doesn't want to hear it from someone else."[6] What accounts for this seeming contradiction between women's inveterate secret-keeping and their chronic inability to keep secrets?

MacKinnon's distinction between *being* or *having* privacy and *being equated with the private* makes all the difference. Not only is "men's ability to have" at stake, but other cultural formations — of knowledge, poetics, authority, the truth of the individual — are also dependent on these equations and practices of secrecy. According to misogynistic logic, women's inability to keep men's secrets explains their deficiency and defends the terrain of masculine subjectivity as one of masculine secrets. Within this terrain women might indeed *be* secrets, but their ability to be secret allows them no subjectivity because it is only within the masculine economy of secrecy that women's secrecy signifies. What female secrecy signifies depends on the masculine efforts to dispossess, contain, and recuperate it. Already dispossessed of the very secrets women are, any "keeping" of secrets is necessarily attenuated from the start.

The first three chapters have shown how masculine secrecy functions rhetorically to define and contain the feminine, to frame crucial power relationships and the notion of the medieval subject, and to foster masculine textual community, authority, and intimacy. This chapter turns to the legal and social site of secrecy that practices the kind of equations of women and secrecy that MacKinnon describes for privacy. The "covert women" of my title is a loose translation of medieval legal terminology governing married women. The allusion extends this legal terminology to suggest the larger social and political implications of a class of women who are de-subjectivated by their legal designation. These are not women who *have* secrets, as gossipers and the subject of the *Secrets of Women* are; they are women who *are* already secrets belonging to others. Their "mysteries" is a pun on the medieval term for craft. This chapter explores the coversion of women's work, along with their legal, social, and political subjectivity. It also invokes the mystification of women, their "mysteries" that men seek to recuperate, which necessitates their coversion in the first place. The second part of this chapter explores one example of the way in which the cultural representation of women as covert is transposed and translated into literary discourse in Chaucer's Miller's Tale and the tales which follow it in the *Canterbury Tales*.

Much of the legal and social information that I will elaborate is neither new nor contested. My argument, however, construes this information in a new and, I hope, contestable way by placing it in the context of the ideological formulation of women as secrets governed by masculine individual, institutional, and ultimately literary coversion. My purpose is not to reduce the topics under discussion to MacKinnon's formulaic assertion of the gender dynamic governing our political notions of privacy. Instead I want to open her formulation up to suggest the range of cultural work that secrecy performs in the service of gender ideology. In other words, I am interested in the flexibility and adaptability of the alliance between gender construction and secrecy rather than its stigmatic reduction. As I hope to show, the terrain of secrecy and gender relations is never so stable as MacKinnon suggests it is for privacy. Indeed, the terrain is continually being negotiated, as we will see in the Miller's Tale. In addition, all disclosure is, as Michel Foucault and Eve Sedgwick argue, lined with secrecy, with opacity, complicating the terrain of secrecy and gender relations even further.[7] Far from wishing to produce a static equation of women and secrecy, I am interested in the powerful proliferation and cultural reach of the medieval construction of women as secrets, beginning with the married woman.

Women Undercover: Marriage and Coversion

English common law borrowed a curious term for married women from French legal terminology. While the widow and singlewoman were designated by the French term, *femme sole* ("independent women"), married women were commonly referred to in English law as *femmes coverts*, which literally means "hidden/secret woman," but was loosely translated to mean "married woman." The term is actually a shortened from of the longer legal description of the wife as *covert de baron*, usually translated to mean "under the protection of a husband."[8] In fact, this idea of protection that is metaphorically linked to the married woman's definition in medieval England is often lost in translation, so that the phrase "coverte de" comes simply to mean "married to," even though the phrase would *never* be used for a man's marriage to a woman. The legal term for the condition of marriage for medieval women was coverture, that is, the period during which the wife is subject to the medieval laws of marriage. The death of the husband ended her period of coverture. The same term does not apply to husbands in their legal capacity as married men unless it is used in a humorous sense.

Legal historians and medievalists generally have elided the etymological meaning of the legal phrases *femme covert* and *covert de baron* with their conventional medieval meaning, "married to," and coverture with "marriage." In the process we have lost one of the indices of what marriage meant for women in medieval society, that is, how it was culturally construed and institutionally elaborated. More importantly, we have ignored the fact that, even in its legal construction, marriage signified something different for men and women according to the common law of medieval England. This very terminology makes an important gendered distinction between the position, status, and powers of wives and husbands — a distinction that is lost in the translation "married to." I want to argue here that it is not enough to examine marriage in terms of medieval laws and customs. We need to consider the language that articulates and represents those laws and customs as well.

The connotations of the legal phrase derived from Norman French law, "coverte de baron," are suggested in the standard *History of English Law Before the Time of Edward I* by Frederick Pollock and Frederic Maitland. Pollock and Maitland note that the "the disabilities of the woman who is *coverte de baron* . . . are often contrasted in the charters with the liege power, the mere, unconditional power, . . . of the widow or the maid to do what she likes with her own."[9] The contrast found in charters between women who possess *ligia potestas*, "liege power," as *femmes soles* and the condition of being *covert*, or "protected," limits the wife's legal and social capacities as a woman. The protection suggested by the legal terminology is conferred on the wife only at the cost of that power that women — widows and single women — otherwise have in their capacities as *femmes soles*. This protection also serves to distinguish wives legally from all other adults in terms of their surrender of that "liege power" accorded not-married women in exchange for the legal protection of marriage, and specifically of a husband.[10]

While protection is the ostensible meaning of the terminology *covert de baron* for "wife," Pollock and Maitland speculate that in French medieval law, it "seems to point, at least primarily, to the sexual union, and does not imply protection."[11] If this is true, the terminology enfolds the notion of the wife's protection in the suggestion not just of "sexual union" but specifically of her sexual sub-position "underneath" her husband in marital sex. Before its legal codification, then, coverture already construes the wife's existence "primarily" in terms of her supposed physical position in the sexual act, a position that conceals her. Whether women actually assumed this position or thought of themselves as "covered" in the sexual act is immaterial. The legal term in effect frames the social and legal condition of women in terms of their perceived sexual domination by a "baron." Even if such a connotation did convey "protection," it was a protection that relied fundamentally on wives' sexual subordination. Chaucer's Wife of Bath seems to exploit this duplicitous equivalence of a wife's social subordination and her assigned sexual sub-positioning, for her arguments in favor of women's sovereignty and mastery in her Prologue rely on an inversion of this logic. She promotes female mastery in marriage by implying female super-positioning in sex, if not literally in women's assumption of the "top" role, at least figuratively, in women's control and manipulation of the sexual act. The Wife of Bath's Prologue could, in a sense, be viewed as a riff on medieval coverture that exposes the sexual subtext of its social, economic, and theological ideologies of marriage.

Coverture carries a number of other connotations through the Middle English senses of the word *covert*. The adjective *covert* derives from the verb *covrir*, meaning to cover, hide, conceal, protect, or to pretend, hide one's intentions, or misrepresent. The noun *covert* could thus refer to a roof or cover, such as a lid, or to armor. Aside from its reference to the marital status of women, the word *covert* could function as an adjective to mean hidden, secret, sly, cryptic, or obscure. It could also imply disguise or dissemblance as a variation on the activity of covering and protecting. The adverb *covertement* could mean secretively or covertly in the modern sense of the word. Finally, in addition to its legal designation of marriage for women, coverture referred to any type of protective covering, including roof, shelter, cover, blanket, and veil. The metaphorical equivalent of this protective covering carried more sinister implications of concealment, disguise, and deception.[12]

From the notion of covering derived from the French verb *covrir*, all of these words imply by way of metaphorical transfer medieval concepts of secrecy and concealment. Their connotative valences range from the positive, suggesting protection and shelter, to the neutral, conveying the obscure or cryptic, to the negative, signifying deception, pretense, disguise, veiled motives, and deliberate efforts to mislead. While none of these related words is a legal term, all of them do exist within the semantic range of the legal definition of married woman and the gendered designation of marriage for women. Legal terms are no more exempt from semantic fields than are other types of terms or language. If we are to gauge their cultural significance, we need to account for the semantic company they keep, as well as their specific relationship to medieval laws and customs.

Middle English cognates of the word *covert* map some of the same semantic domain as the legal term occupies. The ideas of protection and coverage, for example, are conveyed by the Middle English verb *coveren*, "to cover." In addition to its various literal uses, the Middle English verb also invokes metaphorically the action of shielding from harm by means of armor or an instrument. It is from this verb that the French legal term becomes translated into the Middle English "wommen kevered baroun" or "women covered under husband."[13] One of the meanings of the legal term is clearly that of protection, but the question is, whose protection is it? In all other examples of the verb's meaning of protection, that protection is extended to its *agent*. Knights, for example, cover themselves with their shields or suits of armor. In fact, this particular definition is specifically assigned in the *Middle English Dictionary* to agents. Yet the wife is not the agent of her own coverage. The baron and the medieval legal system are. Those who cover, like those who conceal, assume agency through the activity, while those who are covered — are concealed — are thereby deprived of agency. Women *become* covered in marriage, thereby losing their agency. The verb in its legal usage does not apply to them as agents; rather, it applies to men as agents and to wives as abdicators of agency. In addition to signifying agency through the act of protecting, this Middle English verb — when it is applied to wives — signifies the absence of agency as well, and this split signification is bounded by gender and marital status.

The Middle English adjective *covert* carries many of the same connotations that the corresponding French word has. Concealed, obscure, secret, furtive, sly, reserved, guarded, and crafty are among the definitions of the word. It also takes on specific associations with speech that is false and insidious and people who are secretive in their manner. The adverb *covertli* likewise suggests the furtive, stealthy, insidious, and artful manner of serpents. It is also applied to metaphorical speech, including the prophecies of Merlin and the fables of poets.[14]

The condition of coverture, too, is one that is exploited by poets in their craft as well as by others skilled in the sleight-of-hand. According to John Gower in the *Confessio Amantis*, religious hypocrisy "hath his pourpos ofte achieved . . . be stelthe, / Thurgh coverture of his fallas" (has often achieved his purpose . . . by stealth, / Through disguise of his fraud).[15] *Coverture* is also the companion of Faus Semblant in affairs of the heart, as Gower's Confessor explains to the lover.[16] The "covertures of soth" can be used both to edify, in the case of poets, or to serve deceitful projects. "Under honest couerture / Offte ys hyd ful gret ordure" (Under honest fable / Often is hidden great filth), we read in John Lydgate's *The Pilgrimage of the Life of Man*, suggesting a duplicity in the nature even of honest coverture.[17] The measure of good coverture is divine mystery after which the soul burns with the desire to know in spite of its own epistemological limitations. It seeks "thilke notificatiouns that been ihid undir the covertures of soth" (those signs that are hidden under the secrets of truth).[18] The coverture of truth and *ordure* (filth) — of concealment and stealth — thus converge in the works of poets, the designs of human beings, the figures of speech, and the parables of divine providence.

Using this sketchy mapping of the semantic fields of the French and English words, covert and coverture, we can ask what happens when we situate the legal terminology for marriage (for women only) and married women within its general linguistic context. What did marriage *mean* as it applied to women and what did woman *mean* as marriage was applied to her? Coverture, in both its good and bad senses, means secrecy, disguise, concealment, and protection. Marriage as coverture is protection of women by means of their concealment. It is a system of laws and customs that makes a veritable secret of the wife and that guarantees to the husband the proprietorship of that secret. To be a married woman is to be a secret belonging to a husband and to society. Coverture grants women economic protection in exchange for their virtual erasure.

Beyond the term's practical usefulness for insuring a system of marriage that supported patriarchal privilege, it is simply very curious and significant that the legal terminology that defined marriage from the Middle Ages until the nineteenth century was primarily associated with deception, duplicity, disguise, and secrecy. Protection may have been the intended meaning of the word in its legal capacity to describe marriage, but the word was loaded with other senses of furtiveness, concealment, and falseness that may have also figured into its legal sense. The implication of sexual "covering" is the most obvious case in point. It is ironic that coverture, a word that often means stealth or secretiveness, signified women's protection in marriage. Perhaps it was also appropriate because the legal ramification of this term was both duplicitous and insidious.

Married women are thus covert women, *femmes coverts*, who are "covered." They are secrets created by the legal system in the name of protection. Their status is defined by their lack of agency, their surrender of their rights as a *femme sole*, an independent woman. A woman who is *covert de baron* is not simply a woman who has surrendered her independent, single status as *femme sole* to join her husband in marriage: she is a woman who is no longer. She is a woman in disguise, or if you will, a baron with a secret. Her subjectivity evacuated, her identity merges — or submerges — into that of her husband. The marital union thereby created elides the woman entirely and substitutes for her the secret she must become. The medieval married woman cannot be defined simply as a secret, however, for she has no power over coverture: she is always someone else's secret. If *lieu covert* referred to a "hiding place" in medieval French, marriage could be said to be that hiding place, at least for women, where the *femme covert*, by analogy, referred to the "hidden (not hiding) woman."

The chief difference between the hiding place and the hidden woman is that the latter is a manifest secret. Coverture announces the gender category of married woman, distinguishing her from single women, widowed and unmarried, and from married men. This open secret — the married woman — is secluded from all other categories of adults by the legal system of medieval England and from the category of her gender. At the same time, the term *covert de baron* defines a particular category of gender, a kind of third gender that exists only under the baron's cover and his covers. She is not in the same class, however, as those other secrets of divine providence, poetic *figura*, and human dissemblance because her concealment is not meant to safeguard knowledge about her. Instead, as an open secret, the married woman is marked and qualified by her concealment and by her husband's possession. In turn, the husband's legal power is increased by his wife's conversion into his secret: not only is he the sole possessor and articulator of her person and property, but he is the virtual guarantor of her very existence. In fact, there is no real designation of the wife apart from her husband's possession of her as a secret. The name for wife and husband is, curiously, one and the same: a baron with a secret. A secret without a baron is nothing at all.

The semantic relationships of words derived from the French verb *covrir*, including the legal terms for married woman and marriage for women, constitute one set of indicators of the cultural construction of women in the Middle Ages. This excursion into the semantic field of the legal terminology is merely suggestive of MacKinnon's axiom that women are equated with the private/secret so that men may have and women, ultimately, have not. It is not, however, the whole story. It is merely one part of the story of the medieval legal and social organization of women and wives under marriage. What legal terminology could merely suggest, medieval common law elaborated and encoded in multifarious ways.

Under English common law, the husband was granted sole possession of land and chattels acquired through marriage. There was not a concept of a "community of goods" shared by husband and wife in England, such as there was in other parts of Europe in the Middle Ages.[19] The wife's property and movables became the property of her husband during the period of her marriage, or coverture. A husband had the power not only to alienate his own property without his wife's consent, but he could also alienate his wife's property without her consent. The one protection a wife had against her husband's power of alienation was her right to one-third of his property as dower set aside for widowhood.[20] This protection of dower was meant to compensate for the fact that, according to the twelfth-century treatise of Glanvill, "she could not contradict him in any matter nor act against his will, and thus could not, if her husband were unwilling, take care for her own right."[21] In theory the wife's consent was required for the alienation of her lands, but this consent was limited by the requirement that she obey her husband's will in everything.[22]

In addition to property the husband had exclusive control over conjugal chattels, his wife's and his own, for the duration of their marriage. He could dispose of her possessions while he was alive, and he was entitled to them if she died, including any debts owed to her.[23] The wife, by contrast, had no claim on her husband's goods either during their marriage or upon his death, unless he died intestate. Husband and wife were, with respect to property, regarded and treated as a single person.[24] The wife was relegated, in Judith Bennett's words, to "a condition of virtual non-existence (especially in economic matters)."[25] As Glanvill reasoned, "since legally a woman is completely in the power of her husband [*plene in potestate uiri sui*], it is not surprising that her dower and all her other property are clearly deemed to be at his disposal."[26] The husband maintained a profitable guardianship over his wife and her property.[27]

The restrictions against wives' control of property extended into other legal areas. The husband's role as guardian of conjugal possessions entitled him to all the legal rights and responsibilities attendant to them. Husbands were most often the litigants in suits of debt or contract. Because wives held no chattels, they were prevented from entering into contractual agreements and from making loans. English common law forbade married women from making wills or testaments because that right, too, was reserved for those who owned property, unless they had the permission of their husbands. Glanvill makes this point quite clearly:

A woman of full capacity [*sui iuris*, i.e., unmarried, of full age, or under no other disability] may make a testament; but if she is in the power of her husband she may not, without her husband's authority, dispose of chattels which are her husband's, even in her last will.[28]

At the same time, wives escaped the liabilities associated with ownership. "During the marriage the husband is in effect liable to the whole extent of his property for debts incurred or wrongs committed by his wife before the marriage, also for wrongs committed during the marriage."[29] This meant that husbands were usually litigants in suits brought against debts or contracts. Wives could pursue joint litigation with their husbands, but this option merely underscores their status as dependents. In fact, it was sometimes the case that a joint litigation could proceed without the wife's involvement. The same was not true of joint litigation in the absence of the husband.[30]

The only loophole for a married woman from her invisible status as *covert de baron* was to register as a *femme sole*, thereby achieving economic independence from her husband and assuming responsibility for her economic transactions. According to the London rules, "where a married woman follows any craft in the City by herself, with which the husband in no way interferes, she shall be bound as a single woman as to all that concerns her craft, and shall plead and have her 'law' as single."[31] If this *femme sole* was found guilty of a crime, neither her husband nor his property was in danger because she was viewed as independent of him. Yet this option was not generally available, nor did it necessarily translate into a woman's advantage. Only urban women could avail themselves of this option, and only in some towns. Furthermore, as Bennett reminds us, we do not know much about the activities and lives of these *femmes soles*, nor how much of a liberation this actually represented for married women.[32]

The wife's legal protection under English common law is rendered in terms of her legal invisibility. Her protection differs significantly from the various protections available to husbands who, as sole proprietors of conjugal possessions, have recourse to legal grievances against those possessions. The same "protection" extended to any other medieval woman, widow, daughter, or single woman. These other categories of woman in the Middle Ages were also protected, but through their access to—rather than exemption from—the legal system. Coverture thus signified a gendered legal distinction as well as a category that set married women apart from all other categories of women. Compared to those other categories, coverture amounted to a divestiture of legal viability and ultimately, a submergence of woman's gender in the husband's legal status. *Covert de baron*, women became invisible and were newly defined by that invisibility. Hidden, covered, and protected, married women became part of a gendered economy that defined their protection differently than it did for any other category of person.

The famous eighteenth-century jurist Sir William Blackstone summarized the status of married women under English common law:

By marriage the very being or legal existence of woman is suspended, or at least it is incorporated or consolidated into that of the husband, under whose wing, protection and cover she performs everything, and she is therefore called in our law a *feme covert*.[33]

Blackstone articulates the meaning of this law, namely that the woman's very being is "suspended" indefinitely. Her activities performed under her husband's coverage belong to him, and thus they are not identified with her. A popular saying ascribed to Blackstone confirms this status and the semantic evidence of the legal terminology for wife: "In law husband and wife are one person, and the husband is that person."[34] Such a definition of conjugal relationships extends beyond the legal boundaries it is intended to define. As we shall see, it affects the very identity of women and their activities performed during marriage. Whereas men are identified in medieval society by their work, women are not defined by their work. Chaucer's Wife of Bath is a good example. Although she is skilled in the trade of cloth-making, she is the only figure in the *Canterbury Tales* who is not identified either by her occupation or her social position. She is simply the "wife" of Bath, and as such, as much "covert de baron" under the law as more conventional wives were.

If protection was the ostensible reason for the legal status of wives, there is evidence that this protection might have actually been designed for husbands, particularly in laws governing violence in marriage. While hus-

bands could be punished for exceeding the boundaries of "reasonable chastisement" by killing or maiming their wives, wives were tried according to
the statutes of petty treason if they killed their husbands.[35] The 1352 statute
of treason extended the definition of treason to three categories of persons
and acts, including "when a servant kills his master, a woman kills her
husband, when a secular man or man in religious orders kills his prelate, to
whom he owes faith and obedience."[36] Paul Strohm argues that this extension reflects a fear of women's increasing economic opportunities after the
plague, as well as insurance against the only real option for married women
to gain control of their possessions: through widowhood.[37] Whatever the
motivation behind this statute, it does invest women's coverture with a
larger social and political significance outside the household economy a
woman inhabited. Her relationship to her husband is here rendered analogous to servant/master and secular man/prelate relationship, implicating
the gender hierarchy of medieval marriage in the other hierarchies of medieval culture. It also marks women's coverture with danger because it is a
crucial site of patriarchal self-definition and power.

An important distinction that both the terminology and the laws and
customs serve is that of the public and the private. Women's coverture not
only limited their ability to own property, but it established a realm of privacy around their household identities and activities. Their economic re-
striction translated into what Bennett has called "public disabilities," that is,
exclusion from socially significant action, political power, and public prestige. Compared to the publicity of widows and daughters — those women
who were not disabled by marriage — the coverture of women meant the
contraction of their legitimate sphere of action and influence. It is this
difference that medieval patriarchy was concerned to protect, even if it
meant giving only one of a married woman's actions public meaning and
power, the murder of her husband. What Bennett finds to be true of marriage for women in the town of Brigstock before the plague is true for many
medieval married women in the fourteenth century:

In Brigstock before the plague, the rules that shaped the lives of all women and men
were supported by the conjugal household and its ideal dichotomy of public men
and private women. Even though that ideal was regularly contradicted by the activities of men who were not householders and women who were not wives, it
nevertheless structured the social relation of the sexes in the community.[38]

The privacy entailed by women's condition of coverture was hardly the
entitlement we so vigilantly guard today. It did not mean controlled access

to one's person and freedom from public scrutiny, as it often does in contemporary legal debates. Neither women nor men were protected by this modern kind of privacy. It was a privacy that signified dependence, lack of personal responsibility, and public disability. In this way coverture not only distinguished the experiences of marriage for men and women, it structured social relationships along the axis of private women and public men. If women were becoming private, men's ability to have was being defined by their publicity and the system of coverture that entitled them to privacy, including wives who were equated with the private.

Placing the legal terminology alongside this brief analysis of the laws governing coverture, we can observe an appropriateness of the choice of covert to describe married women. In his discussion of the woman's dower, Glanvill identifies the key premise of women's coverture, namely, that she is "completely in the power of her husband," as compared with the woman "of full capacity," the unmarried woman. For Glanvill, the issue is power and its material effects, including ownership of property and the right to sue in court and to make wills. Secrecy as a concept contributes to this premise, for it invests the holder of the secret — the baron — with more power than he had as a single man at the same time that it divests the one who *is* the secret — the wife — of power, publicity, and self-determination. A married woman is, as I have already claimed, a baron with a secret, a third gender if you will, and nothing (without a baron). Yet it is this very privacy, this very secrecy, that relegates her to the feminine in her social world.

The legal status of married women did not, in spite of its other restrictions on ownership and publicity, prevent women from working. Indeed, work might be considered the one activity that allowed married women to escape the limitations of coverture and to recover a sense of personal power and agency as well as public viability. Given the medieval legal construction of marriage for women, we must wonder how work was incorporated into it. It is more likely, after all, that women's labor in the household economy benefited medieval patriarchy rather than thrived in opposition to its legal systems and gendered hierarchy of power.

When Work Disappears

The Book of Margery Kempe begins with the conversion of fifteenth-century housewife from pride and worldly desire to the spiritual life. Kempe's pride, covetousness, and desire for worldly recognition are presented in two representative aspects of her life: her dress and her work. Vain attire, by Kempe's own account, was meant to make men desire her and the world admire her by reflecting what she considered to be her elevated status in the society of King's Lynn. The other manifestation of her excessive pride is her attempt to establish a business of her own. Kempe's narrative recounts her two unsuccessful business ventures, one at brewing ale and the other at milling corn, as mysterious failures. There is no logical explanation or technological recourse for the fact that, in the first case, her ale goes flat, and in the second, the horses refuse to draw in the mill. While Kempe's neighbors speculate that she is cursed or that God is punishing her, her post-conversion narrative explains the mystery of her failed "housewifery" as God's chastisement for "her pride, her covetousness, and her desire for worldly adulation."[39]

Pride of dress was a common theme of medieval sermons, and it was more often than not a sin attributed to women.[40] Women's work, however, was usually condemned for other reasons. Alewives and brewsters in particular were excoriated and caricatured in popular representations as "sinful, tempting, disgusting, and untrustworthy women," as Judith Bennett has shown.[41] Not only were they often found swarming hell, as in the Chester *Harrowing of Hell*, but they were unregenerate in their corrupt adulteration of the ale and in their promiscuity. Given the general unsavory image of the medieval alewife in popular culture, it is interesting that Kempe uses her experience of brewing at all, even as an example of her inordinate pride.

Although Kempe's account of the mysterious failure of her brewing venture is humorous, she uses it to make a serious moral comment on her character before she became a mystic. She attributes her entrepreneurial efforts at brewing and milling to her covetous pride, which she maintains against her husband's advice, reminding him that she is of a higher social station than he. God's miraculous tinkering with her beer and her horses causes Kempe to acknowledge her selfish motives and abandon her business ventures altogether (in spite of earlier success brewing for three to four years). Given the fact that neither brewing nor milling were particularly high-status or unusual occupations for women, it is important to consider what Kempe's use of the incidents suggests about the cultural meaning of women's work.

Kempe's pride is identified in her autobiography with her entrepreneurship because she uses it to augment her public stature and to assert her superior economic status in the household, defying the gender hierarchy prescribed by medieval religious and social mores. Interestingly enough, the chastening of her ambition fails to modify Kempe's insistence on her own publicity as a mystic rather than as a businesswoman. What does the divine chastisement for her work mean in the context of her autobiography? How much is Kempe herself relying on medieval attitudes towards women's work in order to construe her own conversion?

In spite of its seeming rejection of women's work, Kempe's conversion narrative does not rely on fifteenth-century antipathy toward women's work for its drama and moral conviction. After all, later in the autobiography when she is being accused of Lollardy, the men of Beverley urge her out of concern for her welfare to quit this dangerous life of hers: "Damsel, forsake þis lyfe þat þu hast, & go spynne & carde as oþer women don, & suffyr not so meche schame & so meche wo" (Woman, forsake this life which you lead, and go spin and card wool as other women do, and do not suffer so much shame and woe).[42] The typical work of married women is here a metaphor for safety and security, and it is offered by the men of the town as sympathetic advice to Kempe. The difference between what they recommend and what Kempe attempts to do in her milling and brewing ventures is that the activities they suggest are more "safely" positioned within the household economy than are her business ventures. Considering the annoyance that Kempe causes many of the men in the book, mostly public figures such as archbishops, monks, and mayors, one wonders whose safety is really at issue in their recommendation.

Whatever their motives, the issue in Kempe's autobiography is not women's work per se, but women's work outside the parameters of the household economy. As long as she serves in the capacity of carder or spinner of wool — two traditionally female occupations that were regarded as low-skilled and low-status in the trade of cloth-making — Kempe would be regarded as suitably performing both her roles as worker and as wife.[43] Although brewing was also traditionally a woman's occupation, Kempe's experimentation with it and milling is characterized by the desire for public approbation and power. It is this desire that defies the laws of the household economy because it threatens to define a woman's work outside of her marriage and in a public way. That is, one of the key elements defining married women's work was marriage; marriage and women's work were mutually intelligible terms, and women's work outside the parameters of marriage, such as Kempe aspires to against her husband's objections, is either unintelligible or symptomatic of her pride. Her pride and covetousness in turn are marked by her conscious effort to exceed the confines of domestic respectability and earn the respectful admiration of her neighbors, obtaining clear publicity for her efforts. Her desire, moreover, is for power—economic and social—and this damns her business from the outset.

This is a danger of women's work that is explicitly to be avoided, according to the late medieval poem "How the Good Wijf Tauȝte Hir Douȝtir." Here the mother instructs her daughter in how to maintain her household, including running her husband's business while he is away, correcting the faults of her workers, setting things in order at the end of each day, paying wages, and carrying out her tasks with a "housewifely" comportment: "Houswijfli þou schalt goon on þe worke day [iwis], / Pride, reste, & ydilnes, makiþ on-þriftines (Honestly shall you go on the work day, / Pride, rest, and idleness makes for unthriftiness.)[44] Kempe's error is not in desiring to set up a respectable business venture but in her motives for doing so, to earn the respect, admiration, and envy of her fellow townspeople, as well as to heighten her own social status.

If Margery Kempe's account of her two disastrous ventures in housewifery implies a restrictive moral code that applied to women's work, the laws and customs governing the work of women in the medieval household were likewise restrictive. Kempe's business endeavors violate one of the principal customs of the household economy, namely, that the husband's work was the defining work of the household, with the wife's work being either secondary to his or supplementary to it. Women could assist their husbands in their work, for example, by helping their weaver-husbands in the production of cloth or their butcher-husbands with the cleaning of animals. At the same time that they participated in their husbands' work, wives could also supplement their husbands' work and income by brewing and selling ale or other kinds of food.[45] Kempe's business ventures recklessly disregard her husband's role in the economy and her own obligations to him. In fact, we never even learn from her narrative what work her husband does. In an interesting reversal of the submergence of women's work in the male-identified household economy of poll tax records, Kempe features her own work as the defining enterprise of her household. Her husband comes off more as her adjunct than as the master of a trade even after she gives up her business enterprises for a new mystical enterprise.

Kempe's exception to the rule and custom of work in the medieval household ultimately relies upon those rules and custom for the ethos of her narrative and conversion. As readers we are expected to apply the medieval custom in order to see her error. Her pride is reflected in her inversion and transgression of the medieval codes—moral, social, and economic—for women. In the course of exceeding these cultural codes, Kempe identifies herself too completely with her trade. Her pride thus derives from a strong work identity, a quality that was reserved for men in the medieval household. She makes the spiritually fatal mistake of substituting work for marriage as the source of her identification. Kempe thus characterizes her moral failings that preceded and precipitated her conversion in terms of a failure to observe her proper role in the household economy. She implicates the ethos of this economy in the spiritual direction of her book.

Maryanne Kowaleski summarizes five characteristics of female employment in fourteenth-century Exeter that are true of women's work generally in medieval England: 1) Women rarely benefited from formal training through apprenticeship in the workplace; 2) even when women did find some training in skilled labor, they tended to hold low-status, marginal positions in the trades for which they were trained; 3) marital status and position in the household dictated the kind of work women undertook; 4) women's work was intermittent and inconsistent, as compared with the work of men; and 5) women tended to practice more than one trade.[46] The legal status of married women as *covert de baron* makes it difficult to trace their work. As helpers to husbands in their occupations, women are virtually invisible. Even where wives established independent brewing trades out of the sexual division of labor in the household, their work is submerged under their husband's name because he is the head of the household. Thus, one of the few ways in which we can determine the woman's contribution to the household economy or her independent trade is by the death of the husband. The widow would either continue in her trade or assume her husband's trade, suggesting an earlier partnership with her husband.

Married women in the Middle Ages experienced several restrictions — besides a remonstrative husband — against attempting the bold business ventures Kempe tried. First of all, the kind of trades available to women was circumscribed. Studies of women's work in the fourteenth century reveal that women resorted to a few clusters of occupations, including domestic service, making and mending clothes, providing victuals, manufacturing textiles, and retailing. The majority of single women in London in 1381 are found in two main areas: domestic service and textiles and cloth-making.[47] Except in the area of domestic service, married women supplemented their family incomes by pursuing some of the same trades that single women sought.

Women are most visible in the urban economy as alewives, or brewsters. Wives often supplemented their work brewing for the household by

producing extra ale for retailing, probably on a much smaller scale than
Kempe envisioned doing. While other women's work in textiles and clothing might not appear in poll tax records, women brewers appear in court
records because of ale fines imposed on retailers as a way of regulating
commercial brewing.[48] Although it drew a large sector of working married
women, brewing was not a highly profitable trade, nor did it guarantee the
kind of social position Kempe sought. Instead, as Bennett argues, "brewing
was a localised, small-scale industry that required little capital investment
and yielded small profits; it was, therefore, a classic sector of women's work,
characterised by low status, low skill, and low remuneration, and suitable
for intermittent work patterns."[49] Because of the wives' lack of capital (since
their property was controlled by their husbands) and their lack of access
to other financial resources, they were confined to such trades as brewing, which were piecework and brought little wealth, prestige, or political
power.[50] Moreover, the domination of working wives as brewers did not
translate into public or political power. Female brewers, like other women,
were excluded from manorial and borough courts, and thus from many of
the rights men enjoyed and litigated. For example, they were unable to
secure cash or credit to set up more secure and profitable enterprises.[51]
Excluded from the networks of retail and mercantile power, women had no
access to political offices or positions. Their work, unlike that of men (including male brewers), did not translate into public and political prestige.[52]

The same restrictions apply to the other main areas of married women's
work, textile production, cloth-making, and victualing. In the textile trade,
women usually worked in the early stages of production as spinsters, kemp-
sters, carders, washers, and sewers. Their work was less skilled than men's, it
was usually done in the home, and it was usually meant to support the
husband's income.[53] As dressmakers, tailors, lacemakers, and glovers in the
cloth-making trade, women were engaged in work already associated with
the household. They were unable to expand their work into the mercantile
sector of the medieval economy. The trade of victualing follows the same
pattern. Female brewers, tapsters, cooks, and hostlers encountered the same
restrictions that their sisters in the textile and cloth-making trades faced.

Medieval women were restricted not only by the nature of the work
available to them but by their exclusion from the systems of apprenticeship
and the civic privileges accorded men in craft and trade guilds. Although
women could apprentice, their apprenticeships were limited to certain
types of trades such as textiling, and their apprenticeships failed to gain for
them the public and political status that men gained from theirs.[54] I will

return to guild restrictions later, but for the moment, it is important to recognize that women's work was defined less in terms of one specific craft organized around an urban franchise, such as men's work often was. Instead, women's work was defined by its household origins and status, its low level of skill and hence, its irrelevance to the system of apprenticeship, and by its eclecticism.

In 1363 a statute was issued stipulating that male craftsmen practice only one craft, while it permitted women to engage in several trades.[55] This statute legitimized what was already the practice in medieval England of men becoming specialized in one craft or trade and women assembling different kinds of work to supplement their household income. The effect of both the practice and the regulation was to condemn women's work to the amateur level and indirectly to define married women's work in terms of their household duties. Thus married women tended to practice trades associated with their household chores, such as brewing, making butter, and mending clothes, and to organize their work around those chores. In turn, because married women's work was piecemeal, informal, and sporadic, it was valued less by comparison with the "one man, one trade" ethos of the Middle Ages.[56]

A late medieval satirical poem, "Ballad of a Tyrannical Husband," exploits this distinction within the household economy between the husband's single labor of plowing and the wife's multiple tasks. In this poem the husband, an "angry man" given to chiding and brawling, demands dinner at the end of a day of plowing, though the poem notes that his wife "hade meche to doo," including caring for "many smale chyldern to kepe besyd hyrselfe alone." When the husband returns home where there is no dinner waiting, he berates his wife and swears that he wishes she could follow him through a day's work so that she would appreciate it and, presumably, have dinner ready. His wife counters that she has more work to do in a day than she has time to do it and that she is very weary. She complains of milking the cows, taking them to pasture, making butter and cheese, feeding the poultry, baking and brewing every fortnight, carding, spinning and beating flax, watching the children, and being up at night nursing the baby. To her protests of weariness, her husband scoffs:

"Wery! yn the devylles nam!" seyd the goodman,
"What hast thou to doo, but syttes her at hame?
Thou goyst to thi neybores howse, be on and be one,
And syttes ther janglynge with Jake an with John."[57]

("Weary! In the devil's name!" said the good man,
"What have you to do but sit here at home?
You go to your neighbor's house, one by one,
And sit there gossiping with Jake and with John.")

The good man's version of a wife's work is gossiping. He does not see what
constitutes her work because it is not a single occupation as his is. In
response to her litany of tasks, the husband says that other housewives
could accomplish all of her tasks before prime and vows that she should
work for half "the good that we have." As a way of more evenly dividing the
labor, the husband proposes a swap: he "will be the housewife" and she
shall plow. She readily accepts, and the test begins. The manuscript breaks
off as the housewife leaves parting instructions to her husband to take care
of the children, finish making the butter, attend to the malt, and feed the
geese. He, in turn, sends her off to her plow: "Teche me no more howse-
wyfre, for I can i-nowe" (Teach me no more housewifery, for I know
enough). All we know of the outcome is that they were busy all day.

Yet the sexual division of labor depicted in this poem was not the rule
in the medieval peasant economy, according to Bennett: "Although many
tasks were loosely associated with either men or women, few were actually
proscribed for one sex."[58] Perhaps what is at stake in the poem is not the
sexual division of tasks per se but the gendered ethos of work. The poem
calls attention to the invisibility of women's work compared to the single
occupations of men, according to the husband's admittedly irascible logic.
The multiplicity of tasks involved in housewifery to his way of thinking
does not amount to a day's worth of plowing by medieval standards, which
are derived from the gendered division of labor — the "one man, one trade"
ethos.[59] Although the poem predicts the husband's defeat — because he is
"angry" while she is "curteys and heynd" (courteous and gracious) — the
humor of it depends on the recognition of the categorical difference between men and women's work raised by the experiment in "cross-laboring."

Married, widowed, and single women resorted to alternative kinds of
work on the margins of society that escaped the usual restrictions, such as
huckstering and regrating. Both of these trades were condemned by medieval society in spite of the fact that they were a necessary part of medieval
commerce.[60] Hucksters were simply retailers who sold their goods on the
street, while regrators bought up goods in the town market and resold
them later in the day for a higher price.[61] Although the word huckster
originally applied to a retailer, the -ster ending implied a female retailer,

and the word took on pejorative associations. The main complaint against hucksters and regrators was that they drove up market prices and that the hucksters often sold goods that were inferior to those they reserved for their families.

Female hucksters were admonished not to wash cheese to make it appear fresh, not to adulterate or water down ale, and not to scrimp on thread in their weaving.[62] In medieval literature, hucksters and brewsters are singled out for their promiscuity, deceit, avarice, and fraud. Gower criticizes hucksters generally in his *Mirour de l'Omme*, but he reserves a pointed remark about female regrators, who employ more treachery and deceit than men.[63] In Langland's *Piers Plowman*, Rose the Regrator is suitably married to Covetousness, who boasts of his wife's ability to cheat her customers by spinning her yarn loosely to make it go farther and by stretching her ale by diluting it and saving the best for her husband and herself. Rose's skill comes from eleven years of practice in the wiles and exchange of wares of "hokkerye," or fraudulent retail trade.[64] Even though her husband is equally guilty of greed, lying, and cheating, Rose represents the feminization of those vices through the identification of women with huckstering.

If women's work was dictated by their marital status, perhaps one of the most obvious and simplistic conclusions to be drawn from this brief summary of their work is that it, too, was "covert." Ironically, because of the restrictions governing women's work, many resorted to covert activities in the pejorative sense of the word instead of its legal sense of "protected." Secrecy, trickery, and deception all characterize the literary and popular views of women's alternative trades, including huckstering, regrating, and prostitution. The range of meanings suggested for the word "covert" is curiously appropriate to both types of women's work, that "protected" within the household economy and that which strays into those marginal, covert areas condemned by Langland and Gower. The one legal definition thus implies the illegal one because the "protection" of women's work under the law led them to seek less regulated and restricted means of livelihood. Ironically, too, the second form of coversion was less invisible than the first, for there is documentation of suits and fines against petty traders like Rose the Regrator. This covert work is more visible than women's work in the household economy is.

Beyond the observation that women's legal status in marriage affected the kinds of work they were allowed and sought, we need to consider how the legal status of wives as secrets affected the meaning of their work, and vice versa. We should also consider what this legal status meant for medieval husbands and, by extension, medieval patriarchy. For Margery Kempe the desire to work without the restrictions of marriage was a perverse one she confesses on the path to her narrative conversion. In an echo of Covetousness's boasts about Rose, Kempe admits her own greed and desire for worldly fame as the source of her business ventures. Both literary texts implicitly draw moral and spiritual lines along the lines separating legitimate women's work — that is, covert in the sense of hidden and protected — from illegitimate women's work — covert in the sense of being outside legal and social boundaries. The private women/public men binarism defining marriage and work thus reinforced and was reinforced by the moral pair of covert work/covert women deployed by Kempe, Gower, and Langland. Women's privacy came to be synonymous with their corruption, both spiritually and professionally in their business practice.

At the same time, this coversion or privatizing of women and their work in marriage contributed to the power of men in marriage, particularly their power of possession. Their possession was defined in terms of the coversion of women, women's work, and women's possessions. Their own publicity depended on the privacy of women and women's work, not only because it ensured that women did not compete with them but because privacy (and secrecy) constituted what men owned in the Middle Ages. The ethos of coverture also managed to tarnish women's privacy with the same brush, equating it with moral turpitude and ethical depravity. In the process women's work not only often disappeared from public view under the auspices of husbandly coversion, but it was culturally abjected as the "other" against which true work — one man, one trade — was rendered visible and legible.

But medieval work was not simply a matter of possession, independence, and identity. It was also a matter of community through guild membership. I would extend Hilton's "one man, one trade" ethos to include "one man, one trade, one partnership (*societas*)," which describes the larger ethos governing men's work and distinguishing it from women's. Without the sense of community, fraternity, partnership, and moral obligation attached to guilds, the craft or work one pursued did not achieve a corporate status or recognition. In fact, guilds were important in defining the nature of a craft, its status as skilled, and the work identity associated with it. Antony Black analyzes the ethos of the guild, including its values of community, brotherhood, morality, and even friendship, concluding that membership in a guild was a crucial psychological component of working a craft or trade:

Membership of a craft-guild was important both psychologically and practically. One incurred serious and enduring obligations and benefits, affecting one's self-perception and moral identity. . . . It gave one position in society. It enabled one to ply a trade, and so crucially affected one's economic status. Sometimes even political rights depended on guild membership.[65]

In addition to providing a ready community for apprenticing, financing, and practicing one's trade, the guild lent status to the trade and its practitioner. One's very self-perception, as Black argues, was shaped and validated in the guild societies. At the same time the guild offered status and power through enfranchisement and office as well as civic privileges. If it is true, as Herlihy claims, that guilds "dominated the town economies, . . . their governments and even the ritual life of the cities," then guild membership was a crucial index of power, identity, and publicity in the larger community.[66]

How did guild membership affect the work of married women, which I have so far characterized as lacking in identity (for themselves as well as for tyrannical husbands), publicity, and power? Women were members of guilds in England and Europe in a variety of industries, including brewing, weaving, cloth dying, silk making, gold spinning, yarn making, saddle making, metal working, and bread selling. In Rouen, Paris, and Cologne, there were even all-female guilds connected with the craft of cloth making.[67] The incidence of women's membership in guilds has led some historians to claim that they shared with men access to the various privileges and to the esteem accorded crafts and trades protected by guild organizations.[68]

The circumstances of women's membership, however, tell a different story. First of all, most women were admitted into guilds as wives of husbands, and their activities were restricted. Even widows, who enjoyed the most extensive privileges in guilds, were restricted by their gender from enfranchisement and some social rituals.[69] In urban craft guilds, women were admitted, but they were "excluded from office and had no voice in gild affairs."[70] Women were members of petty merchant guilds, but not the major merchant guilds.[71] Some guilds even excluded women as members, the most notorious example being offered by the 1461 statute in Bristol forbidding weavers to employ wives, daughters, or maids in their craft. Bristol was not alone in its restrictions, however. Bans and regulations governing women's work in the guild can be found elsewhere in England and Europe throughout the Middle Ages and in the Early Modern period.[72]

The medieval guild established a fellowship, ethos, and work identity for each craft, encoding these values in its rules and regulations. In fact, the three traditions were mutually defining. Fellowship determined the social, moral, and religious ethos of the guild. The notions of duty, honor, voca-tion, and social responsibility were inseparable in guilds from their concept of craft. The intimate connection between the *misterium artis* "skill of the craft" and the *mysteria* or "secrets" of the guild fostered a sense of commu-nity founded on secrecy.[73] The guild of tailors in Exeter, for example, in-cluded among the oaths belonging to its members a strict prohibition: "Ye shal not dyscouer þe counsell of þe bretherynhod or of þe crafte, þat ye have knowlych of, þat shold be sekret withyn ouer-selfe" (you shall not reveal the counsel of the brotherhood or the craft which you have knowledge of, it should be kept secret among ourselves).[74] Brotherhood, secrecy, and craft integrity were mutually dependent in the tailors' guild. They were linked in the document of tailors' oaths with the obligation of guild members to exclude foreigners from the franchise of the guild. While foreigners and others might as easily practice a craft as guild members, the latter were distinguished by their knowledge of the craft secrets, and this, in turn, guaranteed them the security of the fellowship.

Guilds circumscribed the fellowship of practitioners of crafts by re-stricting membership and ensuring the transmission of craft knowledge through the apprenticeship system. Reinforcing the corporate structure of the medieval craft guild was its developing notion of corporate ownership of trade secrets. Pamela Long views this as one of the chief contributions of medieval craft guilds:

The significance of the medieval craft guilds includes their role in the development of proprietary attitudes toward craft knowledge. In promoting attitudes of owner-ship toward intangible property — craft knowledge and processes as distinct from material products — the guilds developed the concept of "intellectual property" without ever calling it that. . . . "Intellectual property" became an aspect of corporate ownership — whether the corporation was more or less autonomous, or was closely tied to the government of the commune.[75]

While women could have practiced the crafts of brewing or cloth making without belonging to the urban guild, they were prevented from owning the knowledge of their craft, and thus they were excluded from the power that issues from this proprietary claim.

Women's access to such a fellowship ensured by craft regulation and se-crecy was, as I have already maintained, limited. The medieval notion of fel-lowship associated with guilds was masculine in conception. It was meant to sustain and protect masculine work identity from foreign competition, including competition by women.[76] "For most medieval townswomen," Kowaleski and Bennett generalize, "gilds were male communities in which women had little or no role."[77] Where women dominated a skilled trade, as did the English silkworkers, they did not form a guild. More than any other indicator, this pursuit of a craft by women without the attendant corporate recognition or organization suggests that the Middle Ages defined work on the basis of gender, as I have already argued.

Unlike most women who undertook low-skilled jobs, the London silkworkers of the fifteenth century described by Marian K. Dale practiced a true craft.[78] This meant that their work was skilled and that it required training in its *misterium artis* through apprenticeship. In addition, the women bought their own raw materials and traded their goods. They even organized collectively six different times between 1368 and 1504 in order to gain protection of their craft through petitions to Parliament. And, unlike most female workers, women silkworkers occupied their trade for life.[79] In spite of their accomplishments as skilled workers, their work "was not recognized as a regular craft gild," nor did they organize themselves into a guild. As a result, "they have left little trace of the craft consciousness that is obvious in the gilds of male workers," according to Dale.[80] It is interesting that, when men eventually took over the craft of silkworking by 1555, they incorporated it into the Weaver's guild, a guild that explicitly forbade the apprenticeship of women. In later ordinances, the guild excluded women from silkweaving altogether, unless they were widows of guild members. The new craft of silkweaving protected itself with secrecy and complained when immigrant weavers disclosed trade secrets to women.[81]

This example of the female London silkworkers is a reminder that true craft was only visible in the Middle Ages under the aegis of the guild and as it was practiced by men.[82] Work was defined not simply by what one did but by guild fellowship with others who did the same thing. Community, in turn, was viewed and eventually regulated in masculine terms, thus limiting what was called craft or trade to that which was practiced by men. Crafts that were practiced by women were rendered invisible because of the women's secondary status as wives of male guild members and by their exclusion from medieval masculine notions of community (or fellowship). Their work was recognizable only as a part of the household economy, a very restricted kind of community that entailed for women none of the civic enfranchisement that guilds allowed men.

Although this survey of women in guilds is necessarily restricted both by a lack of information and by my overriding interest in secrecy, it nevertheless permits a number of general observations. We saw in the legal definition of wife as *femme covert* the validity of MacKinnon's claim that privacy (in this case, secrecy) defines women and represents them in terms of what they lack. Along with the cultural equation of women with secrecy comes a lack of agency or power. The medieval construction of women as "covert" belies their actual dispossession of the benefits of *having the power* to make, keep, and exchange secrets. The coversion attributed to women's natures does not translate into any of the kinds of power or legitimacy that masculine coversion enjoys. *Being* a secret amounts to belonging to someone or something else. It does not give one license to have or to work or to be a part of a larger socio-political community.

In the three areas of medieval culture that I have reviewed — conjugal laws, women's work, and women's participation in guilds — secrecy defines and organizes relationships of men and women, and hence of power. Under the name of protection, the married woman in the Middle Ages gave up her status as *femme sole* with all her rights to possession and personal responsibilities for status as her husband's secret. In the process she surrendered her rights to possess and often to represent herself in court. Women's work in the household economy is likewise inflected by their legal status. "Disabled" in the words of Glanvill, wives were limited in the kind of work they did and the meaning/value it held in their communities. The tyrannical husband quoted earlier dismisses his wife's litany of tasks she performs daily, not because he does not believe her but because he does not recognize those tasks as work. The one man, one work ethos was reserved for men and some widows who continued their husbands' trades. In addition, the restrictions on women's work forced them into such marginal trades as huckstering and regrating. Although these trades were indispensable to the medieval urban economy, they failed to earn respect, status, or recognition in medieval society.[83]

Women's work, like their membership in guilds, was always mediated by marriage, and marriage defined women as secrets. If marriage under medieval law defined women as disabled, "protected," and dispossessed, marriage under medieval customs relegated women's work to the status of surplus. Men worked the essential tasks, such as the tyrannical husband's plowing, while women produced surplus from their household tasks. This surplus was also viewed as supplemental rather than primary. Women's work in the medieval household remained "covered" by the defining occupation of the household, that is, the husband's work. In spite of their membership in the guilds, women did not enjoy the civic enfranchisement or power through their craft that men did. They did not assume public or guild offices. Their work was circumscribed by their status as married women.

The close association in medieval guilds between the concepts of *misterium*, "mystery" or craft, and *mysterium*, the "secrets" of the craft, gave work some of its value and gave the men who plied their craft a "comradely ethos" and even a moral identity.[84] Secrecy helped to define the community of the guild as well as the status of particular crafts. By the early modern period, the "connotations of secrecy" increasingly distinguished masculine, and hence skilled, work from unskilled and often feminine work.[85] That the London silkworkers practiced a skilled craft that was never recognized as such is evidence of this crucial alliance between the medieval concepts of craft (*mysterium*) and of secrets (*mysterium*). Only in the cases of the all-female guilds of Rouen, Paris, and Cologne do we find women in control of their craft secrets. Nevertheless, this power did not extend to administration of the guild or to participation in civic affairs.[86]

Being a secret and keeping a secret are two mutually intelligible forms that gender relations took in the Middle Ages. Possession and power for men was construed in terms of their keeping of secrets, including wives and craft secrets. The implication of this secrecy for women was tacit: they could be secrets but not have them. They were defined by a paradox: though women's natures were "covert" and wives "protected," both lacked the capacity for secrecy, and hence, agency, power, possession.

If secrecy/privacy are twin representative principles by which men's *ability to have* and women's *inability* to have are culturally signified, the medieval system of concealing women, their legal subjectivity, and their work operates upon a corollary exchange economy. The economy at work within the relations of feudalism, the household, and the medieval institution of marriage is one that circulates women by rendering them exchangeable as secrets, valuable as a sign of men's ability to have, and usable as a principle of social and economic intercourse. We can glimpse the ideological underpinnings of the coversion of women, as well as the fear that this practice disguises, in such literary texts as the "Ballad of the Tyrannical Husband," in Langland's twin figures of Lady Meed and Rose the Regrator, and Chaucer's Wife of Bath. In the final section of this chapter, I want to investigate how this economy of coversion works to circulate women in literary texts, specifically, in Chaucer's fabliau sequence in the *Canterbury*

Tales that begins with the Miller's Tale. The selection of this tale provides an experimental rather than a representative one for the reading of cultural practices of coversion in medieval literature.

From Women's "Pryvetees" to Literary Coverture

The medieval system of coverture established a domain of the secret and the private that women were made to inhabit and that came to be identified with the feminine and domestic spheres of daily life in opposition to the masculine domain of publicity. While coverture guaranteed masculine regulation and containment of the feminine and domestic, it also produced its own anxieties — anxieties that were reinforced by other cultural gender associations of women's bodies with the private and the secret as well. The emergent notion of privacy that this system of coverture entailed corresponded to larger cultural distinctions between the public and private, particularly evident in architectural changes. The development of private rooms in addition to hall and chamber in the fifteenth century are suggestive of an increasingly materialized demarcation of the domestic, and hence, of the private and secret.[87] The increasing privatization of domestic space in more affluent medieval households spacialized the already current medieval gender ideology that associated women with the secret and private, and men with secrecy and privacy. The potential for subverting this system was very real, and it resided in the nature of secrecy and privacy themselves. Both invite violation, or as Peter Brooks puts it, "we know privacy by way of its invasion," to which we might add its corollary, "we know secrecy by way of its revelation."[88] The domain of coverture, as the domain of covert women and the private sphere of men, was always in danger of the violation that secrecy and privacy entailed. And the fate of women became the one described by MacKinnon.

Chaucer's Miller's Tale explores the complex intersections of the various notions of privacy and secrecy in the Middle Ages, including their identification with women. The masculine anxiety surrounding these domains is of particular interest in the tale. Among the sites of privacy that converge in the poem are Nicholas's private knowledge and skill in the art of "derne love," John's coverture of his wife that is represented by his jealous containment of her, and Absolon's all-too-public courtly wooing of Alisoun. Most importantly, Alisoun herself is the site of privacy and secrecy in the poem, the object of the three men's desire and also of the subversion of their desire.[89]

The name of the game in this fabliau is clearly privacy, or *pryvetee*, as the excessive use of this particular word in the tale suggests.[90] The tale virtually reverberates with the word and its cognates. Nicholas, who is described as sly and "ful privee" (I.3201), makes his moves on Alisoun by catching her "prively" (I.3276) by the crotch. He then concocts a ruse to fool John and bed Alisoun by predicting Noah's flood from his astronomical calculations and telling John "in pryvetee" (I.3493). John fears inquiring too deeply into "Goddes pryvetee" (I.3454), and Nicholas reveals everything but "Goddes pryvetee" (I.3558). John in turn tells his wife his "pryvetee" (I.3603), but she already knows it better than he. Even Absolon inquires "prively" (I.3662) into the whereabouts of John the Carpenter before he makes his move on Alisoun. Nicholas makes the fateful mistake of putting his "ars" out the window "pryvely" (I.3802) for Absolon's kiss and gets a hot coulter instead.

The emphasis on privacy and secret plots, whether God's or man's, calls attention to itself in the poem, suggesting a site of inordinate anxiety, instability, and compromise, at least among the men in the poem. It is interesting that the adjectives and nouns suggesting the private are used only with regard to the men in the poem and are never used in conjunction with Alisoun's thoughts or actions. Privacy is what each of the men in the poem seeks in the person of Alisoun, but like God's mystery, it proves to be dangerous and disillusioning.

In his Prologue, the Miller provides a riddle for the tale in which he reveals the connections between masculine anxiety, privacy, and women. When the Miller first announces that he will tell a tale about a carpenter, his wife, and a clerk who tricks the carpenter, the Reeve becomes incensed. He cautions the Miller not to defame any man or woman with his story. Already, there is an interesting problem, for one might wonder what it is in the Miller's summary that leads the Reeve to expect the denigration of men and women. The fact that the Reeve is a carpenter is the usual explanation for his resentment of the Miller, but it does not explain the Reeve's assumption that the Miller's tale will be about cuckoldry. It is true that the Miller's own character might predict such a topic, but it does not quite explain the subtext of the rest of the exchanges between Reeve and Miller, that is, that the issue is cuckoldry. How does the Reeve know this?

This is where coversion operates metaphorically to predict the story.

The Reeve is not simply overly sensitive and irascible when he accuses the Miller of trying to defame men and wives. He has read the subtext of the Miller's simple statement. A carpenter, his wife, and a clerk already sets up a logic of its own based on the coverture, or privacy, or even secrecy, of the woman. In the threesome, she is the secret that belongs to the husband, the *femme covert*, the secret that implies its own transgression. This is the logic of the covert woman, and the Reeve knows it implicitly. The offense he takes is not really at the kind of the story the Miller plans to tell but at the prospect of a carpenter being cuckolded and made a fool of. He is certainly overly sensitive on this point, but it doesn't matter: he and the Miller understand each other.

The Miller's response is to reassure the Reeve by saying, "Who hath no wyf, he is no cokewold" (I.3152). If men who have no wives are not cuckolds, the Miller's statement implies, then all husbands are cuckolds and all wives are covert in the negative moral sense of the word. Although the Miller goes on to protest too much the goodness of wives, he returns to the conditions of husbands, including his own. After all, the Miller says, he has a wife just as the Reeve does, but he would not think himself a cuckold: "I wol bileve wel that I am noon" (I.3162). Under the guise of comforting the Reeve even to the point of identification, he once again intimates that all husbands are cuckolds, including himself. The only difference is that he believes he is not a cuckold. Cuckoldry is, in a sense, every husband's secret, just as sure as his wife is *covert de baron*. The Miller's statement about marriage gives new meaning to the idea of a baron with a secret.

The Miller concludes his retort to the Reeve with a sly and brilliant equivocation on the subject of the relationship of husbands to the "privacies" of their wives:

An housbonde shal nat been inquisityf
Of Goddes pryvetee, nor of his wyf.
So he may fynde Goddes foyson there,
Of the remenant nedeth nat enquere. (I.3163–66)

(A husband should not be too inquisitive
About God's mystery or his wife's.
As long as he may find God's plenty there,
Of the remnant he need not inquire.)

This passage is rich in puns and play. Most scholars have already pointed out the crucial pun on the word *pryvetee* in the second line of this passage.

The word is made to split its reference between that which belongs to God and that which belongs to wives. God's *pryvetee* refers to God's mystery, or even secrets, and especially in this context, His providence.[91] This is the meaning John gives to it when he tells Nicholas to desist from his astronomical predictions, warning him that man is not meant to know of "Goddes pryvetee." This sense of the word is found in Middle English mystical and theological texts almost exclusively, designating those sacred mysteries, divine secrets, and revelations that are reserved for mystics and prophets. John's Book of Revelations, for example, was usually rendered into the Middle English "bok of privetees," according to the *MED*.

Chaucer is alone in pairing this exalted meaning of the word *pryvetee* as divine secrets and mysteries with the debased, popular meaning of "private parts," as he does in this passage. The Miller borrows the popular adage that "man should not inquire too deeply into God's mystery," humorously extending it to husbands and wives, so that husbands, too, should not inquire after their wives' "pryvetees." The Miller's pun conflates the word's various senses of "secrets," "privacy," and "private parts" into one and elevates the lot of them to the status of sacred mysteries, or conversely, demystifies the divine in the obscene, that is, the wife's "privates."

The wife's privacy, however, is also at stake in the Miller's axiom of husbandry. The husband's right to his wife's privacy is, as we have already seen, guaranteed through the system of coverture. At the same time, à la MacKinnon, the wife's privacy is the measure of the husband's right to ownership and status. In a crucial gesture to the ideology of cuckoldry itself, the Miller identifies the struggle between the three men in the tale as not only a contest for the possession of Alisoun's "pryvetee" in the sense of private parts, but as a competition for control of that privacy that women are equated with and that accrues to masculine subjectivity. The plenty that husbands and others find there is not restricted to sexual abundance or the supply of pleasure, but instead, it extends to the very expression of masculinity itself in terms of coversion, whether as a husband who "covers" the wife or as the undercover paramour who invades the husband's privacy. The very privatization of the wife, the Miller suggests, invites her — and privacy's — violation.

The rest of the Miller's axiom for husbands exploits this conflation, creating an economy of plenty and "remnants" for each. As long as the husband finds God's plenty "there," of the rest he need not inquire. The remnants of plenty, in the Miller's formulation, are the wife's surplus exercise of her private parts, and it is that issue that the husband should resist interrogating as long as he has plenty of privacy and privates. God's plenty still hangs in the balance, even if it has become depreciated by association with the plenty of women's private parts. The deep mysteries that elude human beings are, like the remnants of women's "pryvetees" that elude husbands, to be deliberately unsought. The leftovers of female privacy are thus presumably circulated endlessly among men.

The Miller understands the ideology he plays with, and his joke works because it recognizes the ideological complicity of different kinds of covert operations. As we saw in Chapter 3, the coversion of knowledge of the secrets of nature is crucial to the ideology that informs books of secrets and the transmission of scientific knowledge, as Bacon envisioned it. The branches, flowers, and fruits of scientific knowledge that philosophers were supposed to conceal from the rank and file belonged to the secrets of nature and ultimately, to divine mystery. The Miller routes medieval gender ideology that equates women also with secrecy, privacy, and mystery through their theological analogue, that is, God's impenetrable mystery. The difference between God's secrets and women's, of course, is that few are privy to the former, while multitudes of men are treated to the infinite plenty of the latter. Women's remnants are a mystery only to husbands, while God's remnants are vast and elusive.

The Miller's little joke on the Reeve exploits overlapping ideologies that use secrecy as their chief mode of operation; it also humorously evokes masculine anxiety about the collusion of the feminine and private that is so crucial to medieval gender and power relations. It is the straying of the private, its invitation to violation, and the capacity of women to exercise the secrecy with which their culture defines them that worries medieval men. The Miller's joke gives voice to this anxiety, while projecting it onto the irascible and abject Reeve at the same time that it recuperates the secret for masculine use. The recuperation works through the logic of cuckoldry by means of which the private — as feminine "privates" — is violated. But it is also recuperated at the level of the Miller's text, for he manages to assuage masculine anxiety by "knowing" (and making known) the secrets of wives and by converting women in the story into *pryvetees* (secrets and genitals) for use, laughter, and circulation by his masculine readership. In effect, the Miller creates wives as secrets for the purposes of his story, and in this way, he creates a narrative technology that I will call literary coverture (by analogy with the legal condition of medieval women). Like the husband and the cuckold, the Miller engages in the secret activity of inquiring into, penetrating, and revealing the secrets of women for laughter, pleasure, and

enjoyment of his reader. Just as Nicholas will later mystify his own transgression of Alisoun's (and John's) "pryvetee" with an elaborate ruse, so too,
the Miller uses his elaborate joke to convert wives into their "pryvetees" not
only for masculine use in the story, but for the narrative satisfaction of his
reader. The logic of the fabliau as a work of literary coversion is first to
equate women with their genitals, their privacy, and all that is secret and
then to expose them to public laughter, both in the world of the tale at the
end and in the reading public.

Chaucer compounds this strategy of literary coversion with his dis-
claimer immediately following the Miller's advice to husbands. While he
distances himself from the Miller's Prologue and Tale, he also mimics his
methods. Chaucer the pilgrim apologizes for the Miller in advance and begs
his reader not to blame him, but rather to choose another tale of "gen-
tillesse," "moralitee," or "hoolynesse" more suitable to the reader's gentle
values and tastes. He is obligated, as he has stated elsewhere, to "reherce" all
their tales, or else he will "falsen some of my matiere" (be unfaithful to
some of my material, I.3175). Chaucer here plays literary husband to an
unfaithful text that strays into the degraded realm of "harlotrie," at the same
time that he is obligated to be true to it by narrating it faithfully without
editorial suppression. By so distancing himself, Chaucer is able to maintain
his own authority and faithfulness as literary husband to his text at the same
time that he, like the Miller, admits the feminine text's cuckoldry of him.[92]
This rhetorical move on Chaucer's part superficially removes him from
responsibility for the tale, but more slyly, it mystifies his complicity in the
Miller's project. In effect, he displaces the gendered strategy of the Miller's
comments to the Reeve for a class technology that replaces women's promiscuous private parts and privacies with the Miller's churlish intentions
over which he, like the blissfully ignorant husband, has no control. Further,
he sets himself apart from the Miller's "harlotrye" by disapproving of his
"cherles tale," inviting the gentle audience in on the secret that the Miller
becomes in the telling. In a sense, then, the Miller (and the text) becomes
feminized by the very "pryvetee" he seeks to divulge. Chaucer thus shields
himself from the threat of the secret's feminizing effects by joining his
complicitous (masculine) reader in ridiculing the Miller for his churlish
story, while concealing his own role in the divulgence of the secret.

Both the Miller and Chaucer want to create the secret in order to reveal
it and allay masculine fears that surround the feminized secret in medieval
culture generally. As readers we no more believe the Miller's speech in favor
of "goode wyves" and husbands' innocence than we do Chaucer's embar-

rassed apology for the Miller. In fact, these elaborate apologies constitute the rhetorical pleasure of the ruse each man is constructing. Chaucer has more in common with the Miller than some readers think. The sober authorial denials of each serve to elevate their own complicity in the game of pursuing the "pryvetee" that the men in the tale play to the level of sport. The transactions of secrets between men are thus played out in the tale and textually in the Miller's and Chaucer's disclaimers.

Secrets are everywhere in the Miller's Tale, and they mostly belong to the men, beginning with the character and preoccupations of "hende Nicholas." The young clerk's desire for privacy and things secret is apparent in his dwelling place itself, a private room to himself instead of the cohabitational living that was the rule for most clerks — "allone, withouten any compaignye" (alone without any company, I.3204).[93] Nicholas's unusually private living arrangements are not so suggestive of his sexual prowess as they are of his intellectual pursuits. I have already shown in Chapter 3 how the books of secrets tradition construed intellectual and scientific knowledge as vast secrets to be penetrated only by the most worthy and devoted scholars. Nicholas's study, with its books on astrology, its astrolabe, and its abacus stones, materializes that arcane realm of the scholar's knowledge and mastery. Nicholas brings his own suitably "sleigh and ful privee" (sly and discreet, or secretive, I.3201) character to his secretive scholarly pursuits and his mastery of "secret love," as he demonstrates in his wooing of Alisoun.

John the Carpenter and Absolon are also devoted to secrecy, but their devotion is less intellectual. For John, the husband who observes the laws of coverture literally with his narrow confinement of Alisoun, secrecy is the anxious recourse of a man who is not assured of his possession. The Miller blames John's jealousy on the age discrepancy between husband and wife, but as the Miller himself has suggested already in his Prologue, this accounts for only part of the anxiety of husbands generally about women's "pryvetees," an anxiety that is most dramatically expressed in the fabliau's preoccupation with cuckoldry. Masculine anxiety about cuckoldry is based, as I have already argued, on a medieval gender ideology that makes women the secret that men possess and that is most visible in the legal system of coverture. In the fabliau the privacy that the wife represents in her body and especially her private parts is literally the husband's secret, and this secret demands its own violation in the form of masculine desire. It is not only because John is old that he will lose control of his wife, or because he is jealous. The reason for cuckoldry is axiomatic by the Miller's own joking declaration to the Reeve: husbands are excluded from their wives' secrets. It is the Miller's job to remedy this condition by recuperating the feminine secret through his own secretive storytelling and exchange of Alisoun.

Finally, there is Absolon, the ridiculous parody of the courtly lover who should, like Nicholas, be skilled in the art of secret lovemaking. Instead, he is public in his exploits—his loud singing, playing of the rebeck and guitar, tripping and dancing after the fashions at Oxford, and his general devotion to the common entertainment: "In al the toun nas brewhous ne taverne / That he ne visited with his solas" (In all the town there wasn't an alehouse or tavern / that he hadn't visited with his entertainment, I.3334–35). The only qualification of Absolon's irrepressible publicity is his sqeamishness of farting and his fastidiousness of speech. While these might seem like narrative-driven qualities designed to predict Absolon's downfall, they also assign a feminine privacy to him. His "daungerous" speech and squeamishness of farting are expressive of his feminine nature, recoiling from all public discourse and bodily grotesqueness. The conventional identification of the feminine with the bodily grotesque and indiscreet speech (as we saw in Chapter 2) is contained by the cultural representation of the privatized, virtuous, disembodied, and silent feminine. This ideal is transferred to Absolon as courtly lover, making him grotesque through his own feminization. At the same time, Absolon is necessary to the tale's exposure of the feminine secret that is kept pretty well concealed by all the hyperbolic machinations of Nicholas's and John's jealousy. Absolon's squeamishness is a humorous formulation of his masculine horror of the female body, a horror that the Miller implies in his characterization of him. The famous misplaced kiss is a displacement of this masculine horror and distancing of it through Absolon's disgrace.

Alisoun is not simply the object of three men's desire, she is privacy itself, and this privacy determines masculine subjectivity in the tale. The anxiety that Alisoun's private body creates—for John, of course, but also for the Miller—is resolved through the conversion of that body for masculine use, or invasion.[94] The Miller's description of Alisoun, as scholars have sufficiently pointed out, emphasizes her physicality and sexuality especially by troping it in animal and natural metaphors.[95] I do not wish to replicate these analyses or revisit them here. Instead I wish to focus on the conversion the Miller makes of her body for his reader's use through a kind of literary coverture that culminates in his speculation on her "elusive promise"[96]:

She was a prymerole, a piggesnye,
For any lord to leggen in his bedde,
Or yet for any good yeman to wedde (I.3268–70)

(She was a primrose, a "pig's eye,"
For any lord to lay in his bed,
Or yet for any good yeoman to wed)

The setup for this conversion of Alisoun into speculation about her sexual capital is the description's gesture throughout to the private space and private parts that Alisoun represents. From her belt lined in silk to her embroidered smock to the silken purse that hangs in the middle of her body and occupies the center of the Miller's description, the portrait invites the reader's gaze to the inner space — the slim loins and body, as lithe as a weasel's, the "bihynde" that her embroidered smock covers, and her softness like the wool of a sheep. Her private body invites lords to desire and yeoman to marry, as well as the Miller to express his appreciation in response to her "likerous ye," which metonymically welcomes masculine lust. She is the incarnation of that privacy that implies its own invasion and the secret that invites its own transgression. She is, in effect, the masculine fantasy of the covert women, a woman whose privacy both conceals her "pryvetees" and signifies her femininity, the object of masculine fear and anxiety. But the Miller assuages masculine fears by transgressing the private space that is Alisoun in his portrait of her. His triumphant conclusion, that she is a good lay for a lord and wife for a yeoman, completes her conversion into the "femme privee," if you will, placed at masculine disposal both within the tale and between teller and reader.

What is legal coverture for the yeoman is sexual coversion for the lord, and Alisoun's privacy is appropriated for masculine approval, desire, and the Miller's high praise: "There nys no man so wys that koude thenche / So gay a popelote or swich a wenche" (There is no man anywhere who could imagine / So gay a little doll or such a wench, I.3253–54). The Miller arrogates to himself that ability, and he creates for his own pleasure and use the gayest little thing any man ever fantasized. The Miller's fantasy resembles Absolon's more than we might expect, for it is just as idealized in its effects, however sexual the portrait may be. That is, Alisoun's body is rendered an abstraction for the purposes of its exchange. As Luce Irigaray writes, "When women are exchanged, woman's body must be treated as an *abstraction*. . . . It is thus not as 'women' that they are exchanged, but as women reduced to some common feature — their current price in gold, or phalluses — and of

which they represent a plus or minus quantity." [97] Alisoun renders her
secrets up to any man—lord, churl, or reader—who is willing to put his
labor where his desire is, and this is what gives her value. Masculine labor—
whether it is the Miller's labor of love in his description of her, Nicholas's
ruse to bed her, or Absolon's ineffective labor of courtship—gives Alisoun
her value. As long as the Miller, Nicholas, and the masculine reader find
"God's plenty" in this portrait, they need not inquire about the remnants.

But remnants have a way of straying outside the transactions of masculine desire, as the Miller has already warned. In the famous "misdirected
kiss" scene at the end of the tale, Alisoun's "pryvetee" emerges from masculine phantasmatic efforts to secret it away for individual use, precipitating
masculine hysteria and physical injury on a grand scale.[98] It is appropriate,
given the Miller's introductory remarks on the subject, that all this confusion, disillusionment, and violence should come of a woman's "pryvetee"
exposed, but the Miller never said what would happen when those "remnants" take their own initiative and escape from masculine strategies of
coversion. The first consequence of Alisoun's substitution of her "nether
ye" for her mouth at the window where Absolon waits to be kissed is masculine horror and havoc. Accompanied by Alisoun's triumphant "tehee,"
the "pryvetee" confounds as much as it repulses Absolon:

Abak he stirte, and thoughte it was amys,
For wel he wiste a womman hath no berd.
He felte a thyng al rough and long yherd,
And seyde, "Fy! allas! what have I do?" (I.3736–39)

(Back he started, and thought it was amiss,
For he knew well a woman has no beard.
He felt a thing all rough and hard,
And said: "Fy! allas! what have I done?")

While the Miller identifies the "thyng" only as her "hole," Chaucer scholars
have associated this Absolonian horror with the "unsavory bearded female
fact" and with the metaphorical "dirt" in which Absolon unwittingly rubs
his nose.[99] Yet their certainty resolves that which is genuinely "amys" in the
tale. The reduction of woman to thing, "pryvetee," hole, has been the sport
and logic of the story up till now. Absolon kisses the creation of male fantasy
in the fabliau—the synecdochic woman—and he is confounded by it. A
riddle is set into motion with the confusion of orifices and genders, and the
homosocial economy of cuckoldry suddenly becomes sexualized in the pro-

cess. Absolon applies the logic of sexual difference to lead him to the disturbing conclusion that what he has kissed is not a woman at all. It is a "thyng" with all the features of a man, that is, with a beard. The humor comes with the substitution of a sign of gender difference for one of sexual difference, or a man's beard for a woman's "thing." Is Absolon horrified that he has kissed Alisoun's genitals or that he has kissed a man?

Nicholas plays this riddle out, yelling "A berd! a berd!" The Middle English word *berd* could mean both "beard" and "prank." Woman's "pryvetee" is the prank men play on each other, Nicholas on Absolon and John, and later, Absolon on Nicholas. It is also the "thyng" that unsettles masculine representations of woman, ambiguous as a gender marker and slightly repulsive to masculine sensibilities, including those of Chaucerians as well as squeamish parish clerks. In fact, the "thyng" as "berd" is horrifying partly because of its seeming (and unseemly) mimicry or even appropriation of a masculine gender characteristic. It is also a reminder—a remnant, perhaps—of the homosocial investments that these men have in the prank of cuckoldry to begin with.

Absolon's kiss is truly misdirected because it stumbles on the homosocial origins of masculine pranks, gender/genital confusion caused by the reduction of women to "pryvetees," and the horror of woman's sexuality concealed in cuckoldry. Absolon's vow of revenge, "I shal thee quyte," is ambiguous as a result of these confusions. To whom does he address his threat? The "berd" or the "thyng"? Alisoun laughs during the incident and Nicholas cries out, so that both are implicated in the prank. The confusion persists as Absolon vigorously tries to wipe the offending kiss off his lips and swears off love altogether. The Miller's narrative knows which it is that Absolon has kissed, setting his aversion to love to the "tyme that he hadde kist hir ers" (I.3755). Yet this knowledge does not resolve Absolon's confusion, nor does it restore women's genitals and men's beards to their "rightful" places.

Absolon's retaliation is thus directed at both Alisoun and Nicholas, both genitals and mouths, and ultimately, anuses. His attack with the hot colter is aimed blindly at whatever "thing" appears at the window. The "hint of sexual violence" underlying Absolon's attack is both homosexual and heterosexual at the same time because Absolon does not know the object of his hatred. Nicholas's attempt to improve on Alisoun's joke backfires, but in the process the homosexual subtext of the game of cuckoldry is briefly displayed and woman's "pryvetee" disappears as the pretext for it.

Masculine madness, rather than God's plenty, is the result of this sport in women's "pryvetees." Absolon's love-sickness is turned into vengeful rage; Nicholas's effort to duplicate Alisoun's trick leaves him "scalded in the tout" and crying for water "as he were wood" (as if he were mad, 1.3814); John breaks his arm in the fall from the tubs and is judged "wood" by the townspeople for his fantasy about Noah's second flood. Only the remnant knows the secret of all this masculine disarray, and it is keeping its secret.

The disappearance of Alisoun at the end of the tale is sometimes read as her triumph, as her escaping unscathed from the justice of the poem. The Miller reports her last appearance in the tale, where she and Nicholas are telling all the townspeople that John is crazy (I.3832–33). The end of the Miller's Tale places Alisoun where it has wanted her all along, in the private rivalry between men that causes their disillusionment, confusion, and physical harm. The Miller humorously exposes the risks of privacy's plenitude in the interest of asserting masculine rivalry in the tale and masculine coverture as a textual strategy. In the world of female "pryvetee" on the loose, the three men of the tale are identified in relationship to it—whether like Nicholas, they succeeded in "swyving" it through false prophecy and getting scalded in the ass for it, whether they guarded it so closely that they were robbed, discredited, and injured, or whether, like Absolon, they finally saw women's true nature—their *pryvetee*—not through a glass darkly but face to face and disbelieved in love thereafter. The disillusioning of masculine fantasy and vanity is at work in all three cases, though the Miller is careful not to disrupt the economy of coverture upon which his tale depends. The laughter he invites at the end of the tale celebrates the secrets it has exposed: that female sexuality is in fact no more than a rough, hard, beard, that masculine ingenuity is madness, and that masculine storytelling is the trickiest of husbandries, for the remnants of the very secrets its endeavors to control, exchange, and enjoy are as elusive and as dangerous as God's mysteries.

The problem with literary coverture is that there is no end to it. Those pesky remnants will return another day to try husbands' efforts to contain them and lovers' efforts to penetrate their veil of privacy and mystery. The Reeve, taking his cue from the Miller, offers a stripped-down, harsh version of this same economy of coversion, whereby men's "quiting" gets ugly and women's "pryvetees" are vulgarly taken and traded for a half a busshel of cake. This is the disabused Absolon's vision of men in love, post-kiss of the "pryvetee." While the world of the Reeve's Tale might seem far removed from the lighthearted and sportive world of the Miller, the economy that drives it is one and the same. Only the narrative position differs, as the Reeve brings all the peevish humor that he can muster to take revenge on the Miller with his tale. Clearly, the economy of coversion is a highly adaptable one.

Like the legal system of coverture, the masculine literary strategy of coverture first designates women as secrets in order to constitute a masculine community of exchange within the tale and extratextually between the Miller, Chaucer, and their listeners/readers. Although one might discern in the tale a radical demystifying of divine mysteries and the knowledges that are designed to protect them for the select few, this gesture is possible only through the correlative mystifiying of women as secrets and the dependence of male subjectivity and eroticism on that mystification. It is interesting that at the end of the tale Nicholas's ass is substituted for Alisoun's *pryvetee* because he thought he could "amenden al the jape" (improve upon the joke, I.3799). Women's *pryvetees*, it seems, are as easily displaced by men's asses as textual secrets are displaced by the Miller's joke. The mitigating conversion of the tale is thus the translation of women's secrets into masculine "japes" (jokes) or "berds" (pranks), whereby men are relieved of the phantasmatic fear of the feminine remnant. One need inquire no further, or in Chaucer's formulation of the same idea, "men shal nat maken ernest of game" (I.3186), for the game is, after all, the most serious of businesses.

So are cultural uses of secrecy. If women and their work could be legally and socially rendered secrets for masculine use and profit — if this system then replicated itself in certain literary strategies for pleasure as well — secrecy was an extremely productive mechanism of gender ideology in medieval culture. But it did not end with the coversion of women and women's bodies, speech, and sexualities, as we have seen in the last three chapters. One of the greatest feats of medieval secrecy was to designate a class of sexual acts too horrible to be named, marking the beginning of the secret that would become the homosexual. For even if modern identities are the recent creation of medical science and psychoanalysis, they bear the traces of other, earlier secrets. If there is ultimately no neat historical continuum to be mapped for the uses of secrecy over time, nevertheless there is a comparison to be made between medieval habits of secrecy and contemporary closets. According to one scholar of secrecy, "the trails in memory that secrets leave reveal the distances they have traveled, the force of their passage, the gashes they have left in the ongoing order of things."[100] They also reveal, I would add, the intersections among those things that get designated as secrets, including women and sodomites, privacy and sexual aberration, desire and disease.

5

Sodomy and Other Female Perversions

In the 1997 film *Female Perversions*, directed by Susan Streitfeld and based on a book of the same title by Louise J. Kaplan, perversions are everywhere. The central character, whose name is not coincidentally Eve (played by Tilda Swinton), is by day a highly successful lawyer who has just been recommended for a judgeship. By night she engages in a multitude of sexual fantasies, dreams, and activities, including an affair with a female doctor. Her sister, Matty (played by Amy Madigan), is defending her dissertation for a Ph.D. in anthropology on the matriarchal tribe of women wrestlers in between bouts of kleptomania—stealing a garter from an upscale clothing store as she prepares for her thesis defense. The other female parts in the movie include a rural Emma Bovary (named Emma) who desperately and slavishly adores a man who casually rejects her; her daughter Edwina, whose nocturnal journeys, self-cutting, and strange behavior remain mysterious and vaguely threatening until the end of the film, and a stripper who instructs all the others in how to "become" feminine and powerful, saying, "It's not something that comes natural. You gotta work at it."

What becomes immediately apparent in the film is that these perversions are not perversions as we know them: the sex is missing. Like the book on which it is based, the film attempts both to redefine perversion itself and to make female perversion more visible. Instead of the customary idea from psychoanalysis that perversion is the "irresistible attraction toward some abnormal or bizarre sexual behavior," Kaplan and the writers of the screenplay, Streitfeld and Julie Hebert, redirect our attention to gender—to the feminine itself—as the source of perversity.[1] Quotations from Kaplan's book such as "Perversions are never what they seem to be" and "Perverse scenarios are always about desperate need" appear elusively throughout the film. On embroidered pillows near Eve engaged in sex with her lover, scrawled as graffiti on street pay phones, and blazoned like advertising on benches at bus stops, they reinforce the twin ideas of the film that perversion is a form of bondage and that this bondage represents "pathologies of gender role identity" as much as "pathologies of sexuality."[2] As Eve pauses in her Saab convertible at a stoplight to apply her new lipstick, *la minie rouge* (the red pussycat), behind her an old woman sits down on a bus stop bench and applies her lipstick in humorous sync with Eve, each oblivious to the other. On the back of the bench is painted a bright red pair of lips and another quotation from Kaplan: "In a perversion, there is no freedom; there is only bondage to a stereotype." This last quote sums up Kaplan's main argument that perversions of sexuality and gender are always conservative, that is, that they "actually preserve and memorialize whatever is most conservative and reactionary" in the social order. She is particularly critical of the move to appropriate sexual perversions as a way of rebelling against convention or undoing the very social structure that makes them possible. For all of its bizarre humor, the movie also emphasizes the pain and self-destructiveness that female perversions always signify.

I wish to make a similar argument for medieval sexuality, including its perversions, and that is that gender pathology is always both the manifestation and the organization of the medieval perverse, particularly as it is construed in theology, penitentials, and confessional manuals. Furthermore, I agree that these perversions *as they are represented* (rather than experienced as in the film) are also conservative in their effects: they maintain and subvent medieval gender ideology even though they may also appear to be subversive. Finally, I want to argue beyond Kaplan that female perversions are (perversely) the norm for medieval sexuality, destabilizing both "natural" (what we might call heterosexual) sexuality and unnatural sexualities alike. Like Kaplan, I am trying to make the feminine perversion more visible, especially as the perverse is already identified with the feminine. My analysis of medieval sodomy in particular as a female perversion will suggest that histories of sexuality need to look elsewhere than specific sexual acts or the heteronormative/sodomitic binary to understand the larger connections between sexuality and power in the Middle Ages.

Cultural secrets have a way of reinforcing one another, as we have already seen. The operations of secrecy define social and political relations and groups, such as those groups that are "protected" by husbands, those social communities whose idiolect is characterized by materiality, promiscuity, and danger to social order; those seekers after secrets, the included as

well as the excluded; and ultimately, all Christian subjects (and their contemporary descendants) for whom self-knowledge is inseparable from the
obligation to confess. But secrecy also articulates boundaries of cultural
anxiety, prohibition, fantasy, and devotion, securing and framing the sexual
along with the divine, the medieval wife along with the gossip, the sinner's
deepest truth with the most frivolous of husbandly ignorances, and the
knowledges that crucially structure masculine power and textual relations.
It is not surprising that sodomy should find itself among those secrets that
the Middle Ages cared most to protect, control, and most of all, *tell* in the
covert language of prohibition. It is even less surprising, if sodomy was
culturally associated with the feminine, that it was singled out for particular
strategies of coversion and discursivity.

Secrets have a way of persisting or, at least, of reinventing themselves
historically, of leaving "trails in memory" and "gashes in the ongoing order
of things."[3] Without returning to transhistorical, continuous histories, we
might wonder about the distances that sodomitic secrets have traveled from
the Middle Ages to the present and wonder at the sheer force of this particular secret's historical passage, as well as the scars visible in the contemporary "order of things." In spite of the difference that modernity and
postmodernity make in the conversion of sexual acts to identities, there
is nevertheless a mapping of secrecy technologies and effects to be made
across historical difference. What secrets sodomy might tell us about contemporary sexual categories depends upon the willingness of scholarship
and queer theory to listen rather than to collaborate in the secret.

Sodomitic Secrets and Misplaced Secretions

The fifthe spece is thilke abhomynable synne, of which that no man unnethe oghte
speke ne write; nathelees it is openly reherced in holy writ. This cursednesse doon
men and women in diverse entente and in diverse manere. . . .[4]

(The fifth specie [of fornication] is that abominable sin, about which no man ought
scarcely to speak or to write; nevertheless it is openly narrated in holy writ. Men and
women do this cursedness with diverse intentions and in diverse ways . . .)

The sin that dare not speak its name except in Holy Writ marks the
secret space of the seventh deadly sin, *luxuria*, or lechery, in the Parson's
treatise on penance that ends the *Canterbury Tales*. In spite of the Parson's
refusal to name the abominable sin of which he speaks — or rather, *because*

he refuses to name it—it is recognizable as *the* secret sin, that is, the sin of sodomy. Technically, the sins singled out for excoriation are probably all vices against nature, but the Parson's allusion to scripture narrows the field to those vices practiced in Sodom. The only clues the Parson gives are that the sin is described in scripture and that it is obviously not a single act but a classification of acts performed by both men and women in diverse and multitudinous ways and according to a plurality of intentions. Suddenly, "this cursedness" loses the singularity of its reference, becoming a "them" instead of an "it," as medieval scholarship is inclined to regard "it."

This brief and passing allusion to the secret abominable vice offers a caution to modern historians of sexuality seeking to reclaim and make visible as well as speakable the vice of sodomy. It is not limited to sexual activity between men, nor is it limited to a clearly defined category of acts. There is a danger in taking the Parson's own secrecy on the topic to mean what we think he means, that is, same-sex acts generally, and acts between men in particular. Although recent studies of sodomy acknowledge the medieval confusion of the term, the diversity of its references, and the instability of its usage, sodomy continues to be associated almost exclusively in scholarship with sex between men, and even more specifically, with anal sex.[5] One reason for this narrow emphasis is that there is simply more theological discussion of sodomy as the vice of male-male sex acts and more literary examples and representations of this type of sodomy. Yet the nature of the evidence, in conjunction with the desire of scholars of sexuality and queer theory to recuperate sodomy, sometimes obscures the complex ideological structure of the term. The bracketing of sodomy as a category of erotic and sexual activity not only sets it apart from the category in which it usually appears, the vices against nature, but it contributes to the assumption of a heterosexual or heteronormative/sodomitic divide for the Middle Ages that may not have existed. What is lost in this narrative of medieval sexuality that lodges sodomitic acts between men at the center of queering is the crucial function that medieval gender ideas served in the formation of medieval ideas about unnatural vices, the vice between men in particular. I want to argue that the secret of the unmentionable vice is gender and that there would have been no medieval sodomite without certain medieval pathologies of femininity. In addition, I think it is dangerously misleading to detach sodomy from its theologically created kinship to certain heterosexual forms of desire and sexual activity. This bracketing off of sodomy from its location in heterosexual vices divests it of its subversive potential in medieval discourse. Finally, I will argue that it is the conceptualization of sodomy as a gender pathology that threatens to disclose the impossibility of heterosexuality itself. My project here is to expose the "secrets" of the secret sin, including its foundation in medieval gender ideology and its uncanny reminder of the errant, even impossible, nature of heterosexuality itself. I also want to insist that medieval scholars not collude with the medieval coversion of the sins against nature by assuming without question or critique the absence of discussion about female-female desire and sex, by isolating the study of sexuality from considerations of gender, and by assuming a medieval heteronormativity that is questionable.

First, let us return to the Parson's excoriation of the secret vice that can be named overtly only in scripture without corruption to the speaker/ writer: "But though that hooly writ speke of horrible synne, certes hooly writ may not been defouled, namoore than the sonne that shyneth on the mixne" (but although holy writ speaks of horrible sin, certainly holy scripture may not be polluted any more than the sun that shines on the dunghill is defiled by it, X.911). While the story of Sodom appears in Genesis 19, St. Paul's Letter to the Romans is the scripture to which the Parson refers.[6] Here St. Paul describes God's wrath against those who abandoned the glory of God: "For this cause God delivered them up to shameful affections. For their women have changed the natural use into that use which is against nature. And, in like manner, the men also, leaving the natural use of the women, have burned in their lusts one towards another, men with men working that which is filthy, and receiving in themselves the recompense which is due to their error" (1:26–27). The sexual departure from the "natural use" into "that use which is against nature" is first attributed to the women, and secondarily to the men, although it is described more fully in the case of the men. The Parson follows St. Paul in including women among those who were guilty of abandoning natural sexual relations, or, in his words, practicing the "abominable vice" "in diverse ways and with diverse intentions."

Before exploring what the Parson means by this, I want to look at its context. The abominable vice of men and women is the fifth species of lechery in a series of six, including fornication, rape, adultery (of which there are three subspecies), incest, and nocturnal pollution (X.865–914). Unlike some penitentials that separate the vices against nature from other natural vices, such as incest, fornication, and adultery, the Parson includes all in the same general category of lechery, or *luxuria*. In a strange departure from most accounts of lechery, the Parson designates fornication between a man and a woman a "deadly sin and against nature," the only one so designated. Without the clear distinction between natural and unnatural categories of lechery so important to the penitentials, the Parson's treatise offers a confused discussion that sets adrift the theology of medieval sins. The only thing that differentiates the fifth specie of lechery in the Parson's discussion is its unspeakability, a feature to which I will return later.

In contrast to the contemporary matrix of nature versus culture that dominates much debate in feminist and sexuality studies, the Middle Ages understood sexuality and gender in terms of the categories of natural and unnatural.[7] Beyond this categorical distinction, however, writings on the sins against nature from the thirteenth century onward are notoriously inexplicit when it comes to defining what sins against nature, including sodomy, are. The phrase was, according to John T. Noonan, a "catch-all phrase" that often included anal intercourse, oral intercourse, coitus interruptus, and abnormal sexual positions. The very language of theological discussion, however, suggests a much broader category than can be delineated by a taxonomy of specific acts. When Bernard of Pavia writes about "extraordinary pollution" or Alexander of Hales condemns marital coitus "beyond the natural mode," there is a discernable confusion about the very conception of unnatural acts in the first place.[8] This confusion derives in part from the very convention of concealing specific vices from the innocent, but it also reflects the medieval habit of including sodomy among the marital unnatural acts, rather than making a heterosex-act/same-sex-act distinction.

Although definitions of unnatural sex varied, the broad formula governing most penitential treatments was the "use [of] a bodily member (or vessel) not granted by nature for such use."[9] One of the principles behind this definition seems to be to limit natural sex to the function of procreation, and the writings of Albert the Great and Thomas Aquinas confirm this.[10] This is not, however, the extent of the agenda behind the medieval understanding of sins against nature. As Pierre Payer has shown, there was often a further distinction operating in the category of unnatural acts between form and position. The natural form of sexual relations was vaginal intercourse, while the natural position was what is called the missionary position, with the woman on her back and the man on top.[11] This distinction, like the reproductive one, has the effect of further segregating vices against nature from natural ones, but it also explicitly introduces gender roles into the definition of what is natural in sexual relations. The importance of sexual position is meant to exclude not only the sodomitic and the bestial but any heterosexual sex in which gender roles are not observed.

Medical and theological ideas about gender were based on the foundational binary categories of active and passive, with activity constituting masculinity and passivity femininity. The physiology of the humors, sexual and reproductive functions, and gender difference reinforced the theological distinction between activity and passivity as the primary terms that governed other hierarchies as well. The analogizing in theological and mystical literature of women to flesh, body, humoral coldness, matter, and appetites and men to soul, spirit, humoral heat, form, and reason represented an extension of the physiological hierarchy, and its principle was the binary, activity/passivity.[12] Acts contrary to nature, including sodomy, were thus disruptive not only of the teleological definition of sex as appropriate only for reproduction, but what was even more troubling, of medieval gender categories based on philosophical and physiological rationales.

While the Parson fails to name the diverse ways and intentions of those who practice the abominable vice, his sources are more explicit, pointing to the gendered nature of this particular medieval perversion. Raymond of Peñaforte's immensely popular *Summa de poenitentia* (1222–29) served as the source for other portions of the Parson's Tale, though not the section on the abominable vice. His comments and his hesitation to speak of the vice offer one context for understanding the Parson's subtext. Unlike the Parson, Raymond actually defines natural sex as "between men and women in an orderly way in the appropriate vessel." Unnatural sex is everything else, especially sodomy. Raymond goes on to make the surprising claim that this sin of sodomy is worse than the crime of incest with one's mother. Presumably because incest with one's mother, much as it violates the bonds of kinship and a cultural taboo, still satisfies the definition of natural sex, it is less heinous a crime than sodomy. It does not violate gender roles or the misuse of vessels. Finally, he cautions that "among all crimes, I believe that this one needs inquiries with caution and speaking with fear" because the dangers of sodomy were not limited to acts: even the speaking and hearing of it could pollute the mouths of its speakers and ears of its listeners.[13]

The Parson's discussion of the abominable vices is probably more closely based on William Peraldus's *Summa vitiorum* (1236).[14] Peraldus's taxonomy of the sins of lechery is quirky in that it includes five types of sin ranging from soft clothing and bedding to the generative sins, which are the same ones found in the Parson's Tale. The association of the sin of lechery, and especially sodomy, with luxuriousness, delicacy, and opulence is an old one that can be found in Patristic writing, including texts of Jerome and Ambrose.[15] At the same time, there is already a distinct suggestion in the

general category of lechery of an effeminacy associated with the soft bedding and clothing conducive to lecherous desire. Although this connection
between softness, excessive delicacy, and luxury is not carried over into the
Parson's text, it is implicit in St. Paul, who after all, points to a general
disordered desire that precedes the turning of the people who have abandoned God to "shameful affections." Jerome makes the connection explicitly between the sodomitic sin and "bloatedness (*saturitas*), the abundance
of all things, leisure and delicacies."[16] Soft bedding and clothing are signs of
the self-indulgence that is responsible for sodomy as much as the commission of specific sexual acts is.

The five "generative" sins in Peraldus's discussion of lechery corre-
spond to the Parson's five sins of lechery (except for nocturnal pollution):
simple fornication, deflowering of virgins, adultery, incest, and the sins
against nature. Like the Parson, Peraldus includes the sins against nature as
merely a subset, not a distinct species, of lechery, placing them in the company of simple fornication, rape, adultery, and incest. More striking, however, is what Peraldus has to say about the sins against nature, that very
category about which the Parson refuses to speak for fear of pollution.
Peraldus establishes two ways of acting contrary to nature sexually, one
according to form and the other according to manner. The nature and
purpose of his distinction are revealing for the treatment of sodomy as well:

The fifth species [of lechery] is the sin against nature, which occurs in two ways. For
sometimes it is against nature in terms of the manner as when a woman mounts or
when this act is done in a bestial manner but in the correct vessel. But sometimes it is
against nature in terms of the substance when someone procures and consents to
semen being spilled elsewhere than in the place deputed by nature.[17]

The sexual sin against nature according to manner is primarily one of sexual
position, and this in turn is both a gendered and a human category. Sex in a
bestial manner usually connotes intercourse from behind, inverting the
appropriate face-to-face encounter and dehumanizing the participants because of the act's mimicry of animal sexual positioning. The other example,
which seems to be on a par with the bestial manner of sex, is where, in
Peraldus's words, "a woman mounts." The sin here is analogous to sex of the
bestial variety in its inversion of positions and by implication the roles that
go with those prescribed positions. Just as human beings exchange their
humanity for bestiality in all sodomitic and heterosexual intercourse from
behind, according to the morality of sexual relations offered in most medi-

eval penitentials and theological texts, so too, in the case of the woman mounting the man, is a hierarchy threatened, the hierarchy of gender roles.

The second distinction of sins against nature according to substance — the spilling of semen in places not prescribed by nature — suggests a larger procreative logic for both types. Indeed, Peraldus justifies the prohibition of sexual sins of position on the grounds that they are not conducive to the proper emission or reception of semen.[18] Others, however, argued that the woman on top position did not prevent conception because "the uterus draws the semen to itself even if the virile member does not penetrate the vagina."[19] Whether the position of the woman on top does in fact prevent conception or not, Pierre Payer is surely right to point out that Peraldus's reasoning does not explain the particular hostility of theologians to "the woman who mounts."

Peraldus does allude to an alternative explanation — or authority, at least — for the problem of the "woman who mounts." Peter Comestor notes that one of the reasons for the Flood was that God was angry with the sexual sins of human beings, including those women who "in their madness abused men by mounting them."[20] Peraldus's use of Comestor and his pairing of women on top and the bestial manner as two examples of positional irregularities within the sins against nature suggest that heterosexuality is not what is at stake in the definition of sins against nature. Procreative sex and gender are, and these are the categories that come to condemn sodomy. The abomination that the Parson never names includes men and women and what we would call heterosexuals as well as sodomites. The crime of sodomy itself, a sin too dangerous and contagious even to name, represents a disorder in nature generally, and a disorder in gender position in sex specifically. In men, it constitutes an exchange of masculinity for femininity and an abuse of the natural superiority of masculinity. Women can also be guilty of the sin against nature if they are married and mount their husbands or if they engage in sex with other women, thereby assuming a masculine role. What is unwritten and unspoken in these discussions of sins against nature — besides the name of the sin itself — is the principle that makes it so horrifying: an insurrection of gender categories and hierarchies that occurs when men occupy the passive position sexually and women occupy the active position, whether they are sodomites in the technical sense or not. Worry about the procreative potential of specific sexual acts and positions is secondary to this primary cultural fear of the exchange of gender roles during sex.

Immediately following Peraldus's distinction between the sins of position and of substance, he delivers a caution that the Parson clearly heeded: "There is to be great caution in speaking and preaching about this vice and in asking questions about it in confession so that nothing is revealed to men that might provide them an occasion for sinning."[21] While the Parson seems more concerned with the threat of pollution from speaking or writing about this vice, Peraldus fears the suggestibility of those who confess and even the attractiveness of the vice itself, for there would be no danger of men sinning if they were as horrified by the vice as Peraldus and the Parson are. Finally, Peraldus must have included women among those from whom this particular sin must be kept secret, for he includes them in its definition. The lure of the "woman on top" must have been as dangerous as the lure of the "bestial manner" of intercourse not only for its suggestion of sexual pleasure apart from procreation, but for its fantasy of gender appropriation and, of course, power.[22]

The Parson's cryptic allusion to the abominable thus embeds in its very secrecy a fear of contagion from merely naming the abominable sin, a concern over its seductiveness, a recognition of its alliance with other sexual sins and with excessive desires in general, and a particular horror at the gender insurrection it enacts. At the heart of all the proscriptions about moral sexual relations is first and foremost a fear of gender perversion in the form of an abandonment of the positions and roles that make feminine and masculine *mean* in the Middle Ages. The fear of same-sex sexual activity cannot be separated from this prevailing agenda of ensuring the separation, difference, and hierarchy of masculine and feminine. The concern for procreation is of secondary importance, since it was still possible to procreate (or desire to procreate) and yet commit a crime against nature. Or, to put it another way, because the only reason for gender differences in the first place, according to Albert and Aquinas, was for the purpose of procreation, there is no threat to procreation that is not also already a threat to gender difference and divinely ordered asymmetry.[23] When desire is detached from procreation, the whole reason for gender difference itself disappears, along with the difference itself.

Ultimately, it was not only the unnatural sex act itself that worried the Parson and his predecessors, but the nature of the desire, which must be traced, mapped, and exposed in confessional self-reflection without being incited. What also goes unmentioned in most discussions of this desire for unnatural sex was that it was fundamentally and inexorably a feminine one. The association of *luxuria* in the first place with delicacy, luxury, and excess is suggestive of the feminine in women and effeminacy in men. But beyond this, concupiscence and *libido* were always located in the flesh, and the flesh for the Middle Ages, was always feminine.[24] Concupiscence was a condition of the flesh arising from the Fall that manifested itself, according to Peter Lombard, as "a certain diseased affection or sluggishness that moves unlawful desire." *Libido* (also known as cupidity or lust) was the desire that arose from this condition, unless it was restrained by reason. Augustine's account of pleasure focuses on the desire that precedes it — "a certain craving that is felt in the flesh as its own desire, such as hunger, thirst, and the desire that is mostly called lust when it affects the sex organs, though this is a general term applicable to any kind of desire."[25]

It is no coincidence that St. Paul's account of the disordered desire begins with the betrayal by women of "natural" for "shameful" affections. The perceived suggestibility of women and the resultant gender confusion leads men onto the same errant path "in like manner," and this manner is characterized by an unbridled desire. Medieval writers on sodomy who write primarily about male-male sexual activity often represent it as being derived from a wanton, libidinous, essentially *feminine* (because unchecked by masculine reason) desire. While no one — man or woman — can escape concupiscence, men can escape lust by channeling it towards procreation or monitoring it with reason — by in effect, *being* masculine; to fail to do so is to be guilty of disordered desire, in other words, to be guilty of femininity itself.

Joan Cadden cites an example of how the perceived nature of desire as already gendered influenced one medical analysis of what theologians called sodomy. Peter of Abano writes in the early fourteenth century about men who derive pleasure from anal intercourse because of a physiological irregularity. He prescribes a dietary and medicinal regimen in order to correct their condition, which if it were to go unchecked, would cause them to become insatiable like women. Insatiability here is not so much a moral deficiency in women as it is a physical property owing to their deficiency of moisture.[26] Women's insatiable appetite for sex was located in her womb with its appetitive faculty that served the purpose of drawing male seed to it.

Perverse masculine desire is analogized to feminine desire in treatises on sodomy that are devoted exclusively to the male version. Probably the most notorious polemic against male sodomy among the clergy is Peter Damian's *Book of Gomorrah* (1049). In this excoriation on the various manifestations of this vice, Damian figures sodomy allegorically as female — as the "most pestilential queen of the sodomists," who lures men into her service, deprives soldiers of virtues, defiles and humiliates her servants, infects their consciences, condemns them to secrecy, and ever "pants to satisfy her desire for pleasure." Her modus operandi is secrecy, for she "fears lest she become exposed and come out in public and become known to men."[27] Damian's feminizing of the entire sodomitic category is consistent with his feminizing of the sodomist, whom he refers to as "unmanned man" and "effeminate man." " 'To be unmanly,' " asserts Damian, "is to relinquish the strong deeds of a virile life and to exhibit the seductive weakness [*mollitiem*] of feminine conversation." He exhorts his audience to act like a man, meaning to "tame manfully the lascivious pimping of lust, to repress the petulant incentive of the flesh," and finally, to "collect your strength, act manfully, presume to try brave things."[28] The feminizing of sodomites is clearly manifested in Damian's treatise by their surrender to lust, excess, seductive weakness, even conversation as opposed to virile deeds. The pestilential queen who reigns over this breed of man and sin signifies her very femininity through that "petulant incentive of the flesh" and contagion that defiles in secret, seducing men to become women.

Early in his treatise Damian cites four types of the sodomitic vice arranged in ascending order of seriousness: 1) masturbation, 2) mutual masturbation, 3) femoral fornication, and 4) the "complete act against nature."[29] Yet the clarity of Damian's distinctions here is blurred throughout the rest of his treatise, as the passage about the pestilential queen shows. The true source of all these different forms seems to be a raging feminine lust that works according to a principle of contagion as much as it does through the regular medieval channels of sin, that is, through disobedience and willful abandonment of reason. What distinguishes the sodomist, then, is not so much the four types of acts but his raving feminine lust that contaminates even without any particular commission of acts. After insisting that the four types of sodomy form a four-headed serpent that infects the entire person equally, Damian adds: "Nor do we read that the inhabitants of Sodom corrupted others only by the consummated act. We should rather believe that under the impulse of unbridled lust they acted shamefully alone and with others in different ways."[30] Echoing the Parson, Damian seems to open up the category of sodomy here to include the nebulous designator of the sodomite's "different ways," all driven by the unbridled lust of the sodomite, who is capable of corrupting others merely through association. The pestilential queen can only be overthrown, says Damian just after this passage, by "tam[ing] manfully the lascivious pimping of lust." The feminine threat that is the main source of Damian's polemic includes both the substance of the sodomitic vice — its voracious libido — and its manner of corruption, through feminizing acts *and* contagion.

The other major treatise against sodomy is Alan of Lille's *The Plaint of Nature*, written in the second half of the twelfth century. Like Damian, Alan of Lille is exclusively concerned with the vice of male sodomy, though his treatment is broader, implicating sodomy in all that is amiss in the world and in grammar. A "Venus turned monster" is responsible not only for turning " 'hes into shes' " and the "active sex" into the "passive sex" but subjects into predicates, as man abandons his manhood for feminine predication. The perversion of the active / passive gender categories is echoed throughout the treatise using grammatical metaphors, but the most characteristic image Alan uses is a sexual one: the conversion of hammers into anvils:

That man, in whose case a simple conversion in an Art causes Nature's laws to come to naught, is pushing logic too far. He hammers on an anvil which issues no seeds. The very hammer itself shudders in horror of its anvil. He imprints on no matter the stamp of a parent-stem: rather his ploughshare scores a barren strand.[31]

The prescription for procreation is meaningless in Alan's analogy without the gender prescription of activity to the male and passivity to the female, of stamp and wax impression, of emitting and receiving seed, not to mention the violence that gives meaning to the relationship of the sexes and the sex act itself. Alan also expresses vicariously the hammer's "shudder of horror" at its inappropriate anvil — inappropriate because it does not receive the stamp of the parent-stem. Ironically, Alan bases his appeal to his reader on their shared horror of the gender inversion and perversion that makes for unnatural sex acts. Like Damian, Alan clearly attributes the sodomitic vice to a gender pathology, that is, to an infection by femininity, a "degenera[tion] into the passive sex," and degrading conversion of hammers into anvils in the sex act. But also like Damian, Alan implies that the source of this gendered disorder is the nature of female desire itself, which dangerously veers off course from its assigned passivity to a perverse and often murderous activity.

Although he says nothing of the nature of the pseudo-anvil's desire in this passage, elsewhere in his treatise Alan locates the disorder of sodomy among Venus's misfits. Nature condemns those who deface Venus through their unnatural desires, and for illustrations of venereal dysfunction, she turns not to sodomites, but to examples of women who have abandoned their natures — women such as Helen of Troy, who sullied the marriage bed by forming "a disgraceful alliance with Paris"; Pasiphae, who under the appearance of a heifer entered a bestial marriage with an animal"; Myrrha, who was "goaded by the sting" of Venus into exchanging her role as daughter for her mother's role by tricking her father into sleeping with her; and Medea, who violated her role as mother when she murdered her sons, thereby "turning stepmother" to them.[32] All these examples precede the story of Narcissus and the plague of youths who convert Venus's hammers into anvils. Narcissus's exchange of his masculinity through inordinate self-love is here contextualized by the waywardness of female desire and female gender pathology. As in St. Paul's account of the unnatural practices in Romans 1:26–27, Alan associates the source of male gender and sexual perversion with the errancy of female desire.

Later in the treatise, Alan lists examples of how Desire changes the shape of human beings. In women Desire takes the form of a horrifying madness:

> If this madness sickens a woman's mind, she rushes into any and every crime and on her own initiative, too. Anticipating the hand of fate, a daughter treacherously slays a father, a sister slays a brother, or a wife, a husband. . . . The mother herself is forced to forget the name of mother and, while she is giving birth, is laying snares for her offspring.[33]

Medea is invoked once again as an example of the mother who actively practices treachery instead of loyalty and murder instead of affection. She is followed by Byblis, who fell in love with her brother, and Myrrha (again), who slept with her father. As Cadden points out, the disorder of female desire in Alan's work "comes primarily in the forms that attack the integrity of the family" and undermines "not so much the gender roles associated with sexual expression as the gender roles associated with social integration."[34] The origin of this social disorder, however, is a sexual desire that usurps masculine activity and leads to domestic and social tragedy.

The work of Alan of Lille and others points to a central paradox that informs medieval representations of femininity: the physiological sign of the feminine is its passivity derived from woman's humoral composition and her genital structure (as anvil, to use Alan of Lille's favorite metaphor). At the same time, the feminine nature is also equated with a debased, unnatural moral condition of insatiable, unfettered appetite. The physiological contradiction results from competing Aristotelian and Galenic accounts of the female sexual organs. Aristotle considered the female to be the anatomical inversion of the male and therefore passive. Galen, however, located the female seat of desire in the uterus, an active and dangerous component of the female body.[35] The moral equivalent of this physiological paradox has been widely documented and is perhaps best captured in the Eve/Mary antithesis. It is not so surprising, then, that when theologians turned to sodomy, they located its sinfulness and its horror in its most deeply conflicted gender attributes: its passivity and its insatiability. Worse than the feminine itself is the masculine adoption of the feminine, exchanging activity and reason for passivity and unrestrained desire, an "abominable" state that could not be named without danger of contamination and corruption.

Jean Gerson and, later, Egidio Bossi both used St. Paul's account of the progression of the shameful affections to argue that women's behavior was the primary cause of male sodomy. Bossi called the women of Sodom the "mothers of lust," and he blamed them for abandoning intercourse with men for novel perversions to satisfy their desires. Men merely imitated these "womanly perversions," and sodomy was born. Similarly, Jean Gerson attributes male sodomy to the straying of women.[36] Both accounts make explicit the clear gender inversion at stake in medieval discussions of male sodomy; more importantly, they manifest what is only implicit in many of the works cited here: that sodomy is essentially a female perversion.

Although sodomy as a social practice in the Middle Ages is beyond the range of this study, one example from fourteenth-century London reinforces my own evidence that sodomy was primarily conceived of as a gender disorder. Ruth Karras and David Lorenzo Boyd analyze the intriguing case of one John Rykener, who was apprehended dressed as a woman (calling himself "Eleanor") and having sex with a man in a London street.[37] Throughout the document the sexual act is phrased in the characteristic cues of sodomy, as "that detestable, unmentionable, and ignominious vice"; equally marked in the transcript of Rykener's confession, however, is reference to his imitation of femininity in the sexual act in his cross-dressing and even in his employment as an embroideress. He claims to have learned the feminine ways from two women, one named Anna, who taught him how to "practice this detestable vice in the manner of a woman," and another named Elizabeth Brouderer, who dressed him in women's clothing. The sexual acts he performs with men echo the language of Alan of Lille and Peter Damian: he engages in sex *"modo muliebri"* (in a womanish manner), while his male partners have sex with him *"ut cum muliere"* (as with a woman) and *"ut cum femina"* (as with a female). In contrast, when he has sex with women, he performs "as a man," though one wonders whether he was still dressed as a woman.[38] There is no record of how Eleanor's case was treated by London authorities, but the document confirms the medieval genealogy of sodomy that replicates St. Paul's account of the turning from natural to unnatural sexual practice by tracing it to women and femininity, whether of Sodom or of London, and it intriguingly mirrors both the secrecy and the gendering of the vice found in theological discussions.

What happens, then, when women practice this gender pathology? How does the discourse of sodomy treat the straying of women from their already pathologized gender?

Sodom's Women, or Women on Top

The sins against nature and gender, including sodomy, are not limited to men, according to St. Paul as well as Chaucer's Parson. Yet medieval medical and penitential literature on the subject is weighted much more heavily on the side of male same-sex acts than it is on female same-sex activity, and this asymmetrical treatment is now being reproduced in scholarship on sodomy. Sodomy in most recent discussions is assumed to mean male same-sex relations, often anal intercourse specifically, despite the Parson's proliferation of the category. This narrowing of the medieval conception of sodomy to men and anal intercourse, excluding women and certain types of what we now call heterosexual sex, seriously distorts our own understanding. Not only does it obscure the gender ideology of much of sodomitic discourse but it reproduces some of the misogyny embedded in that discourse. Taking their cue from the relative silence of medieval canonists, medical writers, and penitential manualists on female same-sex relations, most modern studies of sodomy effectively ignore female sodomy entirely or dismiss it as relatively insignificant. One of the foremost authorities on medieval sexuality, James Brundage, can be taken as an example because his work is a key resource for contemporary studies on the subject:

> Writers of this period rarely mentioned lesbianism. The few references that do occur indicate that sexual relationships between women were thought more shocking than male homosexual relationships. Despite this, however, canonists apparently did not perceive lesbian practices as a major problem or as a serious threat to the social order.[39]

This is an extremely puzzling passage. How could lesbian sexuality have been considered at once more shocking than male homosexuality and less serious a threat or problem? The question of why the Middle Ages might have been silent about female sodomy, even though it recognized it conceptually and even found it more shocking than male sodomy, is rarely even considered. Instead, sodomy in early modern and medieval scholarship is almost exclusively concerned with male homosexual acts, and the Middle Ages is blamed for its silence on the subject.

But the Middle Ages was not silent on the subject of female sodomites. As I have already pointed out, sodomy was consistently seen in terms of other kinds of female perversions, and it was, in fact, conceived of *as* a female perversion. This renders the question why medieval writers were silent about female same-sex acts even more puzzling. We need to remember, too, that silences are not self-explanatory, nor do they necessarily signify the opposite of what is said. As Foucault writes,

> Silence itself—the things one declines to say, or is forbidden to name, the discretion that is required between different speakers—is less the absolute limit of discourse, the other side from which it is separated by a strict boundary, than an element that functions alongside the things said, with them and in relation to them within overall strategies.[40]

The category of sodomy itself is subjected to this kind of silence that functions alongside the discourse about Lechery in the Parson's treatise and others like it. It is part of the strategy of medieval discourse about confession and about *luxuria* in particular, and as I have been arguing, it is also part of the medieval gender ideology. The explicit silence about sins against nature is usually taken to signify their greater threat to heterosexual norms and religious moral authority. Could the same be true of female same-sex contact? If not, what is the range of possible reasons for the silence and the functions that this silence performs? Before addressing this question, I want to look first at exactly what is said about this sin against nature in order to discern some of the overall strategies that the silence might be said to permeate.

First of all, as I have already suggested, most definitions of vices against nature echo the Parson in including female perpetrators. Patristic commentary on St. Paul's Letter to the Romans is not silent about the vices of the women who practice unnatural sex. In his homily on Romans 1:26–27, John Chrysostom describes how first women and then men did not merely become enamored of one another, but burned with lust, and he attributes this to the fact that "the whole of desire comes of an exhorbitancy which endureth not to abide within its proper limits." Although both men and women were equally guilty of this exorbitancy, he judges the women's to be more serious: "And a yet more disgraceful thing than these is it, when even the women seek after these intercourses, who ought to have more sense of shame than men."[41] Chrysostom sees this gender disorder as contributing to a larger social confusion that pitted the sexes against each other and against themselves.

Most other commentaries on St. Paul simply include women with men among those guilty of the vice against nature. Ambrose expands upon St. Paul's meaning in Romans 1:26, saying that "a woman would desire a woman for the use of foul lust." Although he is less explicit than Ambrose, Anselm of Canterbury also interprets St. Paul to mean that "women themselves committed shameful deeds with women." Peter Abelard is perhaps the most explicit and most vehement of the three regarding the meaning of women's acts against nature referred to in Romans 1:26: "Against nature, that is, against the order of nature, which created women's genitals for the use of men, and conversely, and not so women could cohabit with women." As Louis Compton points out, there are no early commentators that understood this passage "in other than a lesbian sense."[42] Bernadette Brooten has also shown how St. Paul not only located the source of what is unnatural in the women but identified the transgression itself as a gendered one.[43]

The writings of two of the most important and influential theologians of the thirteenth century confirm that the sin of sodomy is not simply a sin against reproduction, as is commonly claimed; it is also a crime against gender. Albert the Great (1206–80) broadly defines *luxuria* as "an experience of pleasure according to the reproductive power that does not comply with law," suggesting that the sins of lust are violations of the reproductive laws governing human genitals.[44] This would include all types of fornication, adultery, incest, masturbation (except female masturbation, which, because it does not involve generative matter, cannot be considered an abuse of reproduction), and sodomy. Albert's definition of sodomy, however, is not restricted to the usual reproductive prescription regarding the appropriate use of vessels and deposition of semen; instead, he carefully identifies it as "a sin against nature, man with man, or woman with woman."[45] His four reasons for condemning it are not confined to its violation of the laws of reproduction. Other natural laws are invoked, including that of desire: sodomy proceeds from a burning frenzy that subverts the natural order. It is especially disgusting and foul, and yet prevails among persons of high degree. It becomes an addiction for those who practice it, making them unable to free themselves of it, and it is contagious and spreads like a disease.[46] Clearly, there is more going on in Albert's condemnation than a crusade for reproduction and heteronormativity. The nature of the desire, which I have shown is often identified with the feminine in the first place, poses the greatest threat, and that threat is not confined to masculine same-sex acts.

Aquinas (1225–74) distinguishes four types of the vice against nature: 1) ejaculation without coitus (meaning pollution, which Aquinas equates with effeminacy); 2) bestiality; 3) copulation with an "undue sex" (*concubitus ad non debitum sexum*); and 4) deviation from the natural manner, as I have already discussed above in connection with William Peraldus.[47] On a scale of seriousness, Aquinas rates bestiality to be the worst, followed by sodomy (including the female variety), intercourse in an unnatural position, and pollution. In at least three of these, we can discern the gender irregularities that concern Aquinas as much as the reproductive dysfunctions because, as I have already pointed out, his entire rationale for gender difference depends on procreation. Without it, the threat of gender drifting is a very real one.

The early penitentials and summae for confessors also specified female same-sex acts in the category of sodomy. Theodore of Tarsus in the seventh century and Bede in the eighth century both prescribe a three-year penance "if a woman practices vice with a woman."[48] Theodore's penance for women's same-sex acts would be picked up by Ivo of Chartres (1091–1116) in his *Decretum* and in later summae based on Ivo's work, including the highly influential manual of penance, *Liber poenitentialis* by Robert of Flamborough. In his section on fornication, Robert assigns a seven-year penance for a "mulier, si cum muliere fornicate fuerit" (woman, if she commits fornication with a woman). Furthermore, although he cautions against speaking too specifically about sins against nature lest one suggest sins to one's penitents they would not otherwise have considered, he explicitly advocates interrogating women on sins of lust unsparingly, even as men are interrogated: "Just as I ask men whether they committed acts against nature, I likewise ask women about every type of fornication."[49]

Similarly in his *Decretum* (1140), a standard work of canon law that placed female sodomy on par with male sodomy, Gratian condemned "acts contrary to nature" as "more shameful and foul" in women and men than if they had sinned through "the natural use by adultery or fornication."[50] In his discussion of sins against nature, Thomas of Chobham also parallels the commission of "shameful acts," men with men and women with women.[51] In the fifteenth century, Jean Gerson includes sexual acts between women among the crimes against nature, along with the usual "semination in a vessel not ordained for it." In an echo of Gerson, St. Antonius (1381–1451) collapses the sins against nature with the sodomitic species, stating that "a man with a man, a woman with a woman, or a man with a woman outside of the fit vessel is called the sodomitic vice."[52] Another fifteenth-century confessional manual, the *Directoire des confesseurs*, which was attributed to Gerson but is probably not by him, singles out women who "have each other by detestable and horrible means which should not be named or written."[53]

The evidence of all of these works—canon literature, confessional manual, and theological treatise alike—is that sodomy was represented as a vice that afflicted women as well as men and in the same ways that it afflicted men. Some of the definitions also suggest that procreation was not the only moral principle at stake: another was gender difference and sexual hierarchy. St. Antonius lists women with women, men with men, *or* men with women outside the appropriate vessel; Aquinas writes of sex with an "undue sex," leaving aside the use or abuse of instruments and vessels. Preservation of gender roles is part of the overall strategy of the medieval indictments against crimes against nature, and it is a part that should not be subsumed into the procreative agenda. In medieval discourse about sodomy, procreation is only one aspect of a much larger concern with the natural, and it is crucially linked to that other major component of the natural, gender. Problematic as the category of the natural was for medieval medical and philosophical writers, it nevertheless structured the ways in which all sins of lust were conceived. Unlike the other six mortal sins— pride, envy, wrath, gluttony, sloth, and greed—the sin of lechery was a crime against the whole interrelated systems of gender and sexuality as they were divinely conceived and ordered in nature. Beyond the vessels and instruments involved, theologians were concerned about the maintenance of gender difference, and particularly of the hierarchy of man to woman as soul is to body. They sought in their baroque definitions of sins against nature to preserve that hierarchy, that difference between men and women used to explain procreation in the first place. There could be no sodomy without a gender ideology based on a presumed naturalness of the sexes, their purpose, and their natures. The women of Sodom, therefore, are as threatening to that natural order as the men of Sodom—even more so because of the medieval representation of femininity as already *un*natural.

From St. Paul to the Parson, the women of Sodom are never invisible or silent. Given the pervasive inclusion of women in medieval definitions of sodomy it is appropriate not to ask why the silence, because there wasn't exactly a silence on the subject, except for that of the Parson's, which was designed to contain its hazardous contaminating effects, but to ask how the comparatively extensive literature on male sodomy functions alongside a paucity of literature on female sodomy. The answer is not what Brundage claims or what most scholars seem to assume, that is, that female sodomy simply was less threatening to the social order. To make this evaluation is to ignore the complicated ways in which sodomy and gender vector each other.

Three scholars that I know of have suggested another reason for the medieval attention given to male sodomy over female sodomy. As I have already shown, Joan Cadden is one of the few scholars who have made legible the connection between sodomy and feminine desire in Alan of Lille's *Plaint of Nature*. She then wonders why Alan and others have little or nothing to say about female sodomy, and she finds an answer in the gender constraints of the period already operative in "the family in particular and society in general." She further speculates that the assigned passivity to women in sexual relations renders them both of lesser value and lesser concern.[54] The very passivity assigned to femininity — including sex and gender roles — renders it illegible in discussions of sodomy. This is another way in which cultural ideas about femininity and the silence that expresses those ideas reinforce and structure the discourse of sodomy.

The second scholar is Margaret Hunt, who in an "afterword" to the volume of essays *Queering the Renaissance* raises the question for the early modern period of why sodomy is "rarely applied to forbidden or 'antisocial' acts perpetrated by women." Her answer to this question leads her to chart a more subversive course for scholars of premodern sexuality than appears in current studies of sodomy:

Why is this [that sodomy rarely is applied to forbidden acts by women]? Plainly it is because there is an already well-established set of precepts, practices, and discursive conventions at both the elite and popular levels devoted to the supervision and confinement of women, and particularly to controlling their sexual and reproductive lives. If we really wish to understand sexuality and power in the Renaissance, it would be unwise either to proceed as if "sodomy" were a more gender-inclusive category than it actually is (or was), or to fall into the trap of idealizing a phenomenon like passionate male friendship, divorced from its gendered social context. Instead we should focus our attention precisely on the intersections between sodomy fears . . . and the domination of women, a more challenging and more deeply subversive course.[55]

Hunt proposes that the "relative silence" comes from a displacement rather than an absence. Women's sexuality and gender roles are already scripted, monitored, and supervised through an "already well-established set of precepts, practices, and discursive conventions at both the elite and popular levels," *in a way that men's sexuality and gender roles are not*, I would add.

Nevertheless, those same conventions that govern women's roles and sexual behavior elsewhere are deployed in the sodomitic discourse directed at men as well as the discourse about lechery in general aimed at men and women. Heterosex-acts are not exempt from it. In the first part of this chapter, I attempted to examine male sodomitic discourse within the larger analytic arena of medieval ideas about gender and sexuality, not just sexuality. I have also insisted on the inclusiveness of female sodomy in medieval thought, but I do not wish to imply that the category was more gender inclusive than it was. Hunt cautions against drawing such a conclusion. Medieval sodomy included female same-sex desire and sexual acts, but it would be a mistake to see that category as *equally* representative of male and female forms of sodomy. Female sodomy is neglected as a topic even if it is included in the medieval concept, and this fact forces us to return to those "intersections of sodomy fears . . . and the domination of women."

Finally, Thomas Laqueur offers a slightly different formulation of Hunt's analysis. After noting the disparity of literature on male and female sodomy, Laqueur argues that it is not heterosexuality but gender that is the issue and that male sodomy was perceived as more threatening because of the cultural power and prestige associated with masculinity. "Radical, culturally unacceptable reversals of power and prestige" were figured in terms of gender, rather than sexual, crime because the preservation of gender identity is what was most directly at stake in sodomy. Laqueur argues throughout his book that "*sex*, or the body, must be understood as the epiphenomenon, while *gender*, what we would take to be a cultural category, was primary or 'real.'" According to Laqueur, whether one is studying modernity or premodernity, "sex . . . is situational; it is explicable only within the context of battles over gender and thought."[56] While Laqueur bases most of his argument on evidence derived from the sixteenth century on, he parallels Hunt in his insistence on gender as crucial to the premodern and early modern understanding of sodomy. Whether gender is primary or not, it is inextricable from medieval discourse about sodomy—both the verbosity about male sodomy and the relative reserve on the subject of Sodom's women.

Having recognized the gendering of sodomy in its different forms—through pathologizing the feminine and excluding it—I wish to return to another aspect of sodomy's medieval construction: its complicity with heterosexuality. By focusing on gender as the primary category informing the medieval understanding of sodomy, my study of sodomy thus far already intimates that the lines between heterosexuality and sodomy — or between natural and unnatural sex — did not exist in any categorical sense. The gender pathologies that manifest themselves in sexual desires and behaviors seem to cross the modern binary divide between same-sex acts and heterosexuality. If what I have been arguing is correct, "heteronormativity" is not merely an unstable category; it is an illegible one for the Middle Ages.

Heterosexuality and Other Unnatural Acts

As we have seen, the category of sodomy is both set apart by its depravity and threat of contagion, requiring silence and caution on the part of priests in confessionals and fictional parsons in penitential treatises, and incorporated into the larger scheme of fornication. In its unnaturalness, however, it is not alone. Chaucer's Parson, following his sources, insists on the unnaturalness not only of sodomy but of all fornication, about which he has much more to say than he does about sodomy:

Of Leccherie, as I seyde, sourden diverse speces, as fornicacioun, that is bitwixe man and womman that been nat maried, and this is deedly synne and agayns nature. Al that is enemy and destruccioun to nature is agayns nature (X.864–65).

(Concerning Lechery, as I have said, diverse species arise, such as fornication, that is between a man and a woman who are not married, and this is a mortal sin and against nature. All that is an enemy and destructive to nature is against nature.)

This definition of what is "against nature" includes all forms of lust, not just the sodomitic variety. If fornication — as any kind of sex between unmarried men and women — is itself unnatural, so is what we would call heterosexuality, or heterosex-acts. As I have already shown, even sex between married people is, for the most part, unnatural, too. The band of "heterosexual" sex that is natural, and therefore normative, is so narrow as to be almost meaningless. Only sex in the proper vessels with the proper instruments in the proper positions with the appropriate procreative intentions in orderly ways and during times that are not otherwise excluded "counts" as natural and normative in medieval theology, canon law, and penitentials.[57] At the same time, most "heterosexual" sex occupies the same unnatural category as sodomy, the main difference being that same-sex acts were placed under the interdiction of secrecy, while other unnatural sex acts were not. Just as the

silence about female sodomy functioned alongside the verbosity about male
sodomy as part of what it means, so the secrecy governing sodomy "underlies and permeates" the whole discourse about *luxuria* in the Middle Ages,
making sodomy integral to, rather than opposed to or excluded from, that
discourse. At the same time, this "integrity" of natural and unnatural acts
renders "heteronormativity" as we know it illegible as a distinct category of
acts, desires, and behaviors.

Pierre Payer goes beyond arguing against a heterosexual category of
human action and behavior to assert:

In the strictest sense, there are no discussions of sex in the Middle Ages. . . . The
concept of sex or sexuality as an integral dimension of human persons, as an object
of concern, discourse, truth, and knowledge, did not emerge until well after the
Middle Ages.[58]

Instead of sex, the Middle Ages spoke of the vice of lechery (*luxuria*), the
unbridled lust, or desire (*libido*), and fleshly concupiscence (*concupiscen-
tia*). Pleasure (*ardor*) also played a role in the operations of lust in theological discussions, but it was the intentions, motivations, and manner of
seeking pleasure that were emphasized.[59] These are the same terms used
to classify and characterize the vices of lechery, both "heterosexual" and
"homosexual." There is no substantive difference between homosexual sex
and other acts against nature: both represent, in the Parson's language, "all
that is enemy and destructive to nature." This subversion of nature arises
not so much through specific acts entailed in the various categories of sins
but through the perversion of that desire that is the already corrupted
consequence of the Fall. The sodomite, like the "heterosexual" adulterer, is
guilty not only of seeking out non-procreative sexual acts, but of a re-
bellious libido that ignores reason and seeks unmeasured satisfaction of its
appetite and pleasure.

This is not to say that there are not degrees and hierarchies of lecherous
acts that often position acts against nature and sodomy in particular on the
most serious end of the continuum. The fact remains that the medieval
scheme of lechery is a continuum structured not according to the objects of
desire but according to the movements and permutations of that desire
itself. Some acts and desires may be more natural than others, but heterosexuality per se is not the determining factor in this taxonomy.

My argument about heterosexuality follows recent work on the topic
in studies of sexuality that claim that it, like homosexuality, is a nineteenth-

century invention.[60] Although medieval scholars have been busy applying Foucault's dismantling of homosexuality to medieval acts, there is little examination of heterosexuality as a construction and "invention" of the nineteenth century as well. In fact, in most discussions of sodomy, heterosexuality (under the name of heteronormativity) remains the assumed medieval norm against which all discussions of sodomy are measured and thought to be excluded. Yet my discussion of both sodomy and heterosexuality suggests something else, that perhaps there was no heteronormativity, much less heterosexuality, in medieval theological and penitential discourse. Instead, the operative categories of desire, lechery, concupiscence, and pleasure placed what we think of as heterosexual acts in the same general category as sodomy, with natural and unnatural being the crucial designators. Still, most sexual acts, heterosexual and sodomitic alike, fell into the category of unnatural, and what was often at stake besides procreation was the regulation of gender roles and all the social appurtenances those roles entailed.

I am not the first to insist that we need to think medieval sexual desire and activity differently than we do modern sexuality, but the structural relationship of heterosex-acts to other medieval categories of sex acts is often ignored in medieval scholarship. In the search for medieval histories and discourses about sexuality, heterosexuality should not be overlooked or assumed. The Middle Ages, after all, preceded the conception, invention, and normalization of heterosexuality as we know it and probably heteronomativity as well. As James A. Schultz reminds us, "In a world 'before heterosexuality' the hegemonic desire for the other sex does not exercise its tyranny in the same way it does today — perhaps because there is no competition in sight, perhaps because the identity of the individual is not at stake."[61] Thinking the Middle Ages *before heterosexuality* means also thinking sodomy before the binary polarization of homosexuality to heterosexuality in the modern period. There is ample cause, as this chapter has shown, for doing this.

If we begin to rethink sodomy as a discourse that deploys gender in a crucial way and rethink "natural" sex/desire as on a continuum with sodomy, intersecting and being intersected by it, we will be forced to rethink how we read sex and sexuality in medieval literary texts as well. The assumption of heteronormativity in medieval narratives already construes its own plot, which goes roughly like this: something queer escapes the otherwise vigilant heteronormative gaze of the text that the text finally realizes and resolves, usually through some heterosexual adjustment. If there are no such heteronorms or polarized sodomitic others in medieval literature, new possibilities for reading medieval sexuality emerge.

One such reading I have already implied in my argument about sodomy as a female perversion. Because the category of the feminine was both defined as perverse and allied with the natural, it already lodges a problem at the core of medieval gender and sexual ideologies. Jonathan Dollimore maintains in his book *Sexual Dissidence* that cultural ideas of perversion are based on "one of the most fundamental of all binaries, and one of the most violent of all hierarchies," natural vs. unnatural. Yet, as he also shows from the Renaissance to Freud and Foucault, the dominant term of this binary, nature, always contains the perverse within it.[62] In the Middle Ages this capacity of nature to exhibit perversions can be found in medical explanations of sodomy (particularly Peter of Abano's), the failure of Nature's argument against same-sex love in Alan of Lille because "the seeds of irregularity are planted in things," and in the theological categories of *luxuria* themselves, which segregate "acts against nature" from other "heterosexual" sins that are also inimical and hostile to nature, as the Parson insists.

An alternative to current studies of sodomy in the Middle Ages would be a tracking of the perverse as it slips and shifts from natural to unnatural, making not only sodomy but heterosexuality impossible to locate, even impossible. Medieval nature includes perversions in many forms, including Augustine's account of Original Sin and fleshly concupiscence and drives — a "perverse implantation" if there ever was one; the medieval notion of bestiality, which is both natural and unnatural; and the medieval construction of femininity, which was perverse from the very beginning and in need of rationalization by Albert, Aquinas, and other scholastic theologians.[63] This is where both heterosexuality and sodomy intersect, as I have shown, in the paradoxically perverse principle of nature, that is, femininity. The term *perversion* itself originally designated an erring, straying, or deviation from what is natural or right, and it was often associated with two groups, women and heretics. Those who erred, strayed or deviated from natural or divine law became both the examples and the parodies of nature — parodies because by deviating from nature's designs (and God's) they become monstrous, abominable versions these designs.[64]

If we take female perversions as one of our categories for understanding medieval sexuality, we are forced to revise our notions of a normative heterosexuality. Heterosexuality as we know it is finally unstable because it depends on the feminine, and the feminine is by nature perverse, straying, unbridled. Chaucer's Wife of Bath is an example of the way this perversity at the heart of the feminine comes to undo natural sexuality, including sex in appropriate vessels with appropriate instruments at appropriate times. The notoriously verbose and outspoken argument in her Prologue for frequent marriages, the role of genitals in paying the marriage debt, and her self-described love of things "venerian," all seem to identify her primarily and inescapably as a heterosexual woman, with emphasis on the sexual. Yet the Wife is the premier case study of medieval perversion if there ever was one, and this renders her classification as heterosexual problematic, if not irrelevant. For in her perverse pursuit of "her appetite," her generosity with her "chamber of Venus," her abuse of the sexual marriage debt, her fornication outside marriage, and her bragging celebration of her "likerousnesse" (lecherousness), she summons up all that strays from the natural in femininity — all that renders it perverse in the first place. She lurks like a memory trace in Streitfeld's film *Female Perversions*.

In fact, the Wife of Bath may be closer to the Pardoner than most scholars have realized so far. While the Wife's irrepressible spirit distinguishes her in character from the angry and self-destructive Pardoner, by the standards of medieval sexual ideology the two are companions in perversion. The unnatural sexualities so volubly defended and elaborated in the one case in the Wife's treatise of a Prologue and so venomously exposed in the Pardoner's self-disclosure are part of the same condition of gender pathology, the Wife's being expressed chiefly through a rampant and unchastened appetite and the Pardoner's through his feminized body, his spiritual depravity, and his invidious lust for money. Both characters would fit comfortably in the world of Streitfeld's film in which female perversions become one way of measuring society's own soul sickness and psychic pain.

Interrogating the supposed heteronormativity of the Middle Ages along with sodomy is just part of the project of defamiliarizing the past that I am suggesting in this chapter. A more radical approach to the study of medieval sexualities would require that we extricate ourselves from contemporary identity categories as well — from what we think we know about the present. The more valuable historicizing project for past sexualities would begin without the presumption that we know what sodomy is, much less what it meant for the Middle Ages. It would begin without the presumption of heteronormativity. And, finally, it would not restrict its study to the binary opposition of the sodomitic and the heteronormative.

When sodomy and heteronormativity "as we know them" disappear from the historicizing enterprise of queer medieval studies, a space is created for all sorts of interesting possibilities and problems, such as the question of what happens to gender categories as a result. If heteronormativity does not dictate gender categories, how did the Middle Ages conceive the relationship of gender to sexuality? I have already suggested some answers to this question in the medieval construction of sodomy.

A more important direction that sodomy studies could take has been sketched out by Janet Halley in her study of the *Bowers v. Hardwick* decision.[65] Instead of recuperating and celebrating premodern sodomitic discourse as an historical category that antecedes modern gay identities, we could explore how sodomy as a category in medieval and contemporary discourses remains resolutely and persistently a "definitionally unstable" one, to borrow Halley's words, and at the same time, how it has been deployed "as if" it had a stable, coherent, monolithic meaning and history. It was Foucault, after all, who called sodomy "that utterly confused category," though some recent studies of sodomy suggest otherwise.[66] Jonathan Goldberg reminds us that it is precisely because it was an utterly confused category that the term can be mobilized, but he adds, "this is also how the bankruptcy of the term, and what has been done in its name, can be uncovered."[67] By exposing the "referential complexity of sodomy" in the Middle Ages as well as the present, we can also begin to chart the exploitation of this complexity to target sinful or "criminal" persons or activities. And we begin to discern those perversions that are always seeming to be something or somewhere else.

Sodomy is also the effect of a medieval technology of secrecy that bears comparison with contemporary structures of the closet even though they also differ considerably. While covert operations marked sodomy as that abominable vice that threatened to contaminate all persons who spoke or heard its name, they did not designate a category of persons identified with the act. Nevertheless, traces of medieval coversion of sodomy survive in contemporary deployments of the closet and such policies as the military "Don't Ask, Don't Tell" policy — revealing "the distances they have traveled, the force of their passage, and the gashes they have left in the ongoing order of things."

A reframing of our study of medieval sexual categories and acts around medieval perversions affords us a larger arena in which to understand overlapping gender and sexual ideologies. It also renders visible some of the instabilities in these ideologies, perhaps even the impossibility of heteronormativity itself. The very incoherence of medieval ideas about love and lechery becomes visible in such texts as John Gower's *Confessio Amantis,* where perversions are everywhere and, as in Susan Streitfeld's film, they are never what they seem to be.

Confessio Amantis and the Limits of Heterosexuality

If perversions are never where or what they seem to be, perhaps we should not be surprised that they appear in a medieval text that is synonymous with morality. John Gower's *Confessio Amantis* displays "a taste for the lurid that might make Stephen King squeamish — not only incest, but adultery, rape, infanticide, parricide, beheadings, mutilations, and other manner of violence and brutality."[68] Yet few scholars seem to find perversion there. Instead, Chaucer and Gower scholars have an uncanny ability to ignore the perverse in the *Confessio Amantis*. It is Chaucer's characterization of John Gower as the "moral Gower" that has dominated Gower (and Chaucer) scholarship and caused Gower's marginalization by comparison with Chaucer. This insistence on Gower's comparative morality relative to Chaucer is puzzling because the *Confessio Amantis* is anything but moral. It is Chaucer, after all, who has his Man of Law condemn Gower's "unkynde abhomynacions," meaning his stories of incest, prompting Scanlon to remark that Chaucer seems to play the prude to Gower's willingness to broach taboo subjects.[69]

If medieval scholars fail to see Stephen King in John Gower's *Confessio Amantis*, it is in part because of its penitential structure and its confessional topos. The many stories that make up the *Confessio* function as exempla of the Seven Deadly Sins (except for the sin of Lechery) and as negative guidelines for Amans's pursuit of love. Taking the structure as the guide for reading Gower's text, some critics view the disjunction between the exempla and the sins they are designed to illustrate as evidence of Gower's critique of secular love and his goal of spiritual conversion not only of Amans but of the reader.[70]

But Gower's work has a habit of eluding its own penitential taxonomy and critical efforts to find a unified meaning in it. The exempla that Gower uses to illustrate the sins of Greed, Wrath, Gluttony, Sloth, and Pride, as well as their subcategories, often "do more, and sometimes do less, than elucidate the particular vice they are supposed to elucidate." This is an understatement because some of the exempla are rendered absurd by the application of the categorical sin. Aeneas's abandonment of Dido is explained as Sloth. The often cited story of brother-sister incest between

Canace and Machaire is not used as an exemplum of a subspecie of Lechery, as one might expect. Instead, the story excuses their love and reserves its condemnation for the pair's father, who responds to their love with rage. There are also many examples of rape that are excused in the name of the pressures of natures, as in the story of Mundus and Paulina. These are just a few examples of how "Gower's penitential taxonomy does violence to the tales he imposes it on."[71]

The many structural and thematic disjunctions in the poem draw attention to themselves, calling into question both the exemplary mode of narrative and the confessional taxonomy that gives the text its moral structure. Efforts to reconcile the two merely suppress the glaring misfittings of stories to *sentence*, or morals, and the misprision of Genius's treatise on love as a whole. Either critical move—to bring the Christian theology of the Seven Deadly Sins to bear on secular love or to take the moral naiveté of the stories as evidence of Gower's compassion for the sexual transgressions of his characters—attempts to do away with the problem.[72] I want to focus on the disjunction itself and to consider how Gower couches perversion in the kind of penitential treatises I have already examined here. My argument is that Gower's poem struggles with the very indistinguishability of types of love or "lust" that I have already shown in theological texts. In particular, it is the category of nature and the natural itself that proves unreliable in Gower's text, just as it does in theological arguments. Gower's text observes the breakdown in the crucial medieval binary of natural/unnatural, and it allows the perverse to erupt in its midst. In the process what we think of as heterosexuality or normativity disappears, becomes impossible. I am not so interested here in what Gower's intention was, whether moral or humane; instead, I want to explore how the *Confessio Amantis* lays bare the perverse in medieval love and religious ideologies, including the ways in which gender pathology and sexual perversion are embedded in the "natural" and hence "moral." Finally, I want to consider how medieval texts such as Gower's and modern movies such as Streitfeld's suggest that perversions are only as perverse as the cultural norms that produce them.

The "confession of Amans" alluded to in the title of Gower's poem is really a misnomer because the bulk of the work is devoted to Genius's exempla of the Six Deadly Sins: Pride, Envy, Wrath, Sloth, Greed, and Gluttony. The impetus for Genius's discourse is Amans's complaint to Venus in Book I, in which he pleads for her grace in his as yet unsuccessful love quest. Venus appears to Amans, inquires into his "sickness," and appoints Genius to perform the office of priest by shriving Amans. Genius's role as confessor requires him to inquire into each of the sins the way a priest would and to instruct Amans in the nature of each sin and its subspecies by means of moralizing stories derived mainly from classical tradition. Instead of illustrating the nature of each sin as it manifests itself in human behavior and affects the spiritual condition, Genius demonstrates how each sin betrays love or natural law as he interrogates Amans about his guilt on each score.

As other scholars have noted, one of the most blatant problems with Genius's taxonomy of sins against love is his contradictory account of the natural world that claims love as one of its operations. Nature, or *kinde*, seems to serve a Venus who drives all her servants mad, while at other times nature represents a love guided by reason. Gower's Latin epigram to Book I represents a natural love that is anything but regulated or normalized:

Created love subjects the world to the Laws of Nature, and incites all to be of one mind in being wild. Love seems to be the Prince of this world, and no matter what their estate, rich or poor, all are in need of him. Love and Fortune are equally matched: the one lures blind folk into snares, and both have their wheels. Love is health that is a sickness, a stillness without quiet, a truancy that is faithful, a peace that is all war, a refreshing wound, a sweet evil.[73]

A standard description of courtly love with its oxymoronic suffering, this epigram also assigns to natural love a lawlessness, wildness, and lack of regularity. The Latin phrase Gower uses here, *naturatus amor*, appears to be his own coinage, and it ambiguously points to some kind of relationship between love and nature.[74] Ironically, though, there is little to distinguish this type of love from unnatural love; or to put it another way, if this is natural love, then unnatural love must be orderly, reasoned, and consistent. Even though this reasoning would be wrong, it points to the problem with Genius's and the Parson's arguments from nature, that is, that nature is already disordered, and so is desire. The natural is, in a sense, already unnatural.

Genius reiterates this idea of the natural in a defense of the incestuous love of Canace and Machaire in his exposition on melancholy, the servant of Wrath. When nature, or *kinde*, assails the heart, not only is the lover bound to submit, but he does so against reason in order to "halt the lawes of nature" (hold the laws of nature).[75] Machaire and Canace first kiss,

And after sche which is Maistresse
In kinde and techeth every life
Withoute lawe positif,

Of which sche takth nomaner charge,
Bot kepth hire lawes al at large,
Nature, tok hem into lore
And tawht hem so, that overmore
Sche hath hem in such wise daunted
That thei were, as who seith, enchaunted (III.170–78).

(After which she who is mistress
In nature and teaches every life
Without positive law,
Of which she takes no heed,
But keeps her laws all at large,
Nature took them into her tutelage
And taught them so, that moreover
She had daunted them in such a way
That they were, as they say, enchanted.)

Nature, the mistress of *kinde*, is distinguished in her liberal keeping of laws "at large" from *law positif*, which referred in the Middle Ages to laws arbitrarily instituted by the Church, that is, laws that were culturally designed, in contrast to natural and divine law. Nature's largesse is set against the narrow morality of institutional laws established by the Church, which are explicitly associated in the poem's Prologue with the "war and strife" (Prol.247–49) that grips Gower's times. As in the opening epigram to Book I, Genius seems to triumph over a natural law, and by extension a natural love, that is not confined to the procreative parameters set by theologians or by Nature herself in other incarnations, such as Alan of Lille's *Plaint of Nature*.[76] Sexual perversion is "here" nowhere to be seen, in contrast to the summae and penitentials, where it is everywhere, even in so-called natural procreation. Instead, what is judged unnatural by Genius is the reaction of Eolus, the father, who drives Canace to suicide. His "horrible cruelty" is linked in the story to the fact that "he was to love strange" and therefore could not be merciful to the lovers. At the end of the tale, Amans is warned not to oppose "what nature hath set in hir lawe" (III.355). Canace as a figure of one in whom nature has set her law is ironic, too, because in Ovid's *Heroides* Canace represents "mad passion" rather than natural affection. Genius's revision of Canace surely would have been understood in the Ovidian context of Canace's "unkind abominations," as the Man of Law reads her.

Later Genius uses natural law precisely to condemn incest in Book VIII. In the account of creation that begins Book VIII, Genius explains that

incest was permissible until the time of Abraham, when the land was popu-
lated enough that it was no longer necessary. Genius invokes canon law that
expressly forbids incest and excoriates those who behave like a "cock among
the Hennes," taking "what thing comth next to honde" (VIII.159, 163).
Genius goes on to cite examples of this particular "loves lust," including
Caligula and Lot. The main tale, however, is the story of Apollonius, which
begins with the tale of Antiochus's incest with his daughter. That same
desire that Nature inspired in Canace and Machaire is here depicted as
transgressive of the same law. "How lust of love exceeds the law" becomes
the subject of the tale of Apollonius. Incest is no longer an obedience to
nature's law but "blind lust" inspired by "pleasure and concupiscence /
Without the insight of conscience" (VIII.293–94). Genius's whole argument about incest is thus incoherent because the category of the natural is
also incoherent.

This is the same problem that Alan of Lille's Nature has: namely, that
perversions are already part of the natural law she attempts to explain and
defend against perverse sexual practices.[77] As she recounts her betrayal by
Venus and Cupid, "it becomes clear that natural desire itself, and the language of myth in which she seeks to represent it, are pervaded by contradiction, their sacred purpose inseparable from a long history of intrigue, betrayal and violence," according to Winthrop Wetherbee.[78] Human desire,
far from being subsumed under Nature's plan and guidance, threatens
rather to betray that plan, to swerve from Genius's program of procreative sex, and to lodge a disruptive unnatural at the core of the human
condition.

Guided by this incoherent, contradictory, and discontinuous category
of the natural, Gower's Genius produces a narrative about love that admits
the medieval perverse in the forms of what are usually excluded categories
of sexual love. The model of this perversion is Venus herself. Alan's Nature
blames Venus for abandoning her instructions about the proper forms of
copulation and turning out of boredom and desire for difference to adultery
and fornication herself. Nature alleges that Venus thus corrupted all natural
sexuality through her own transgressions, forever contaminating natural
love with the disorder of desire. As Nature explains,

Trapped by the deadly suggestions arising from her own adultery, she barbarously
turned a noble work into a craft, a work governed by rule into something ruleless, a
work of refinement into something boorish, and studiously corrupting my precept,
she dispossessed the hammers of fellowship with their anvils and sentenced them to
counterfeit anvils.[79]

The metaphor of hammers and anvils, as I have already noted, refers to the appropriate masculine/active and feminine/passive roles in procreative sexuality. The barbarity of it all consists in the unnatural uses of desire that result from Venus's sport, yet what Nature also shows is that the unnatural seems to arise naturally out of desire itself, Venus's and humankind's alike.

Gower's take on this originary myth is quite different. Genius implicates Venus's femininity in the disordering of natural desires and the corruption of all women since. The story that he tells in Book 5 in response to Amans's request for information about the pagan gods assigns to the feminine the disordering of desire in a way that Alan's does not, at least not so explicitly. Prefacing his story with an admission of his own shame because he is, after all, her priest, Genius goes on to accuse Venus of "putting away Danger" and "find[ing] a way for lust." In addition to numerous affairs, Venus committed incest with her son, Cupid, and introduced diversity into the sexual practices of women in particular. Alan derives male same-sex love from Venus's straying, while Gower's Genius says nothing of same-sex desire, though the two are varieties of the same disorder, as I have already argued. Gower's variation on Alan of Lille is thus no coincidence. Instead of the conversion of hammers (males) into anvils (females), Gower's Genius derives from Venus the genealogy of disordered desire as it is manifested in the promiscuity of all women:

Sche made comun that desport,
And sette a lawe of such a port,
That every womman mihte take
What man hire liste, and noght forsake
To ben als comun as sche wolde.
Sche was the ferste also which tolde
That wommen scholde here bodi selle (V.1425–31).

(She made common that delight,
And set a law out of such behavior,
That every woman might take
Whatever man she pleased, and not give up
To be as common as she wished.
She was the first also who said
That women should sell their bodies.)

Ironically, Venus's pursuit of pleasure in defiance of Nature's law is itself a law — a law of unbridled desire that allows a woman to have any man she desires, to become as promiscuous as she pleases, and to sell her body. The unnatural, which Alan of Lille characterizes as the gender transgression of sodomy and Genius relates to the nature of desire itself, is not so easily excluded from Nature's domain. Errant feminine desire as it is hyperbolically represented in Venus's transgressions is a part of the natural order, following its own laws that Genius may condemn here, but that are triumphed elsewhere in his many exempla. This account of the unleashing of desire clearly contradicts the sympathetic treatment of such desire in the rest of Gower's work, including Genius's account of Venus's adulterous affair with Mars (V.635–75). All natural desire is thus perverse and, as the opening epigram insists, it subjects the world to the laws of nature at the same time that it incites "all to be of one mind in being wild."

The perverse is as much a part of "heterosexual" desire as it is of same-sex desire because desire itself is unstable, errant, and excessive, like Venus. Gower's Genius merely pursues a theological and philosophical contradiction to its logical conclusions in his exempla, resulting in the conscious collapsing of natural and unnatural types of love. The perverse itself becomes the norm, and the failure of Genius's moralizing either to comprehend the significance of his stories or to develop any consistent love ethos is the result of this basic incoherence of his subject, an incoherence that Alan of Lille also encountered in his treatise. Heterosexual love—or courtly love—is not so much critiqued through Genius's inept moralizing and narration as it is rendered incomprehensible by the collapse of natural/unnatural distinctions and placed in a league with incest, same-sex desire, rape, and adultery. The mark of Genius's instruction in the "nature" of love and sex is its persistent uncongeniality both to the love it models and to the morality it so superficially and ineptly illustrates.

The disjunction of morality and exemplum open up other problems in Genius's narrative of natural desire, including the threat of feminine desire and the instability of gender roles. I want to cluster a few of Genius's tales from the various books to examine the more troubling and interesting examples of how his insistence on models of natural desire ends up denaturalizing gender and sexuality at the same time. Far from being a radical agenda, however, this destabilizing of gender roles and sexual categories never mounts any kind of social critique of either, much less of courtly love. Instead, the narrative unwittingly exposes how necessary the sexual and gender displacements are to the patriarchal social order. In the final book of Gower's poem, Apollonius's ideal love triumphs over that of Antiochus, the incestuous father, but as Genius has already shown, the two loves are part of the same system of natural love. The one requires the other to exist.

One of the more curious collections of exempla is that found in Book IV, which is devoted to Sloth. Here are some of the stories that Chaucer tells in the *Legend of Good Women*, stories of Dido, Phyllis, Penelope, and Alcione, who represent the virtuous martyrs of love to unfaithful men.[80] Chaucer's women in the *Legend* offer medieval versions of Streitfeld's cinematic heroines of the female perverse. Their extreme submissiveness and self-sacrifice in the face of outright deception and rejection from their male lovers represents one extreme case of female perversion. Yet Gower's Genius uses the stories of Dido and Phyllis in particular as examples not of female virtue and masculine deception but of masculine passivity in the forms of sloth and forgetfulness. In contrast to Dido, who "loves Aeneas so hotly," desiring him more and more after he leaves her for Italy, Aeneas simply delays out of "thoghtes feinte" (sluggish thoughts, IV.88, 118). Similarly, a few stories later, Genius tells the story of Demephone and Phyllis as his example of the dangers of forgetfulness. As with Dido and Aeneas, separation between the two lovers causes Demephone to forget about Phyllis, while she pines, writes him a letter, and searches the sea for his ship. Finally, after cursing his sloth, she hangs herself; unlike Aeneas, Demephone lives to "curse his Sloth," but too late.

What is striking about these stories is their emphasis on masculine passivity. Sloth is the form that the abdication of masculinity takes in Aeneas and Demephone, and it renders the women of the tale the actors, the subjects of desire, not just martyrs of love. This curious reversal of roles, though, points to a larger problem in Genius's whole schema of natural desire: it is not so irrepressible as Genius has maintained. Desire is no longer desire if it becomes forgetful and listless; it no longer causes all to be of "one mind in being wild." It can simply evaporate in men's sloth, causing the heroic suicides of women. The absurdity of this idea is patent, and it does not, as some might claim, point to a critique of romantic love. Rather, it seems to allude to the impossibility of heterosexual romantic love altogether. Ulysses, however, is saved from Sloth by a letter from Penelope, reminding him that other men are "proving their hardiness" by wooing her. Somehow her letter so stimulates Ulysses out of his Sloth that "one day seems like a thousand years" until he sees her again whom "he desireth most of alle" (IV.222–23). Desire is undone in these stories because the men don't delay out of faithlessness but out of Sloth — laziness and procrastination — which is the absence of desire.

The impossibility of romantic male-female desire is further compli-
cated by Genius's later assertion in the same book that the lover's Sloth is
constituted by a failure to bear arms. He uses Ulysses again as an example,
describing the occasion when Ulysses tried to avoid joining the siege of
Troy so that he could remain with Penelope. Love itself is here a form of
Sloth, just as it might be said to be in the case of Aeneas. Had he stayed with
Dido, he would have been slothful, according to Virgil and Ovid. Later in
Book IV he too is praised for his military might when he fights Turnus to
get Lavinia (IV.2183–89).

Against the slothful infelicities of heterosexual romantic love, Genius
opposes the virtuous, active "business" of two lovers, Pygmalion and Iphis.
Pygmalion is a curious choice of the active, busy lover because he is usually a
figure of idolatry in late medieval literature, including the *Roman de la Rose*.
Genius describes all the symptoms of idolatry in Pygmalion's obsession
with his image. The "pure impression" made on his imagination is a sign
that his love has turned to idolatry. Yet in Genius's account, Pygmalion is a
model of perseverance and he is rewarded with the perfect woman, a "lusti
wif, / Which obeissant was at his wille" (IV.423–24). While some scholars
explain Genius's positive spin on Pygmalion by the fact that he produced
children through this wife, a more plausible explanation is that it represents
the correction of the gendering of desire.[81] Female desire of the type figured
in Dido and Phyllis is masculine and it renders men slothful, while the
persistent exertion of Pygmalion's desire on his statue literally creates the
perfect woman, both lusty and obedient. The active principles in the story
are Pygmalion's desire and his words in the form of a prayer to Venus. Even
the Middle Ages read the Pygmalion story as a particular kind of masculine
perversion fusing a desire for a specular reflection of himself with a fear of
femininity. Genius is not, of course, aware of this, but his reader should be,
and it alerts us to the incoherence of his entire discourse on sloth as well as
an increasingly disturbing emerging picture of idealized heterosexual love.

The other active, nonslothful lover is a woman passing as a man. In
one of the most curious tales of Gower's text—one that is rarely commented on—Genius revises the Ovidian tale of Iphis, who cross-dresses as
a man and is betrothed to a girl, Ianthe. In both Ovid's and Gower's
accounts, Iphis is disguised as a male from birth by her mother to save her
from her father's threat to kill the baby if it is not born a boy. In Ovid's
version of this story, however, once Iphis becomes betrothed to Ianthe, she
becomes keenly aware of the monstrosity of the situation. Comparing her
love for Ianthe to Pasiphaë's for a bull, she laments that "I have more

madness in my love than hers." She blames Nature for turning against her
and deceiving her, and she dreads the upcoming marriage night. Finally, Isis
comes to the rescue, transforming Iphis into a man. Gower changes the
story to make Iphis unaware of any problem with her love for Ianthe. In
fact, the sexual playfulness of the two girls (they are 10 years old) is viewed
as natural. As children, they lie "ofte abedde" together, "sche and sche,"
with no heterosexual imperative breathing down their necks or hindering
their pleasure. After a few years, the two girls suddenly feel the pricking of
Nature as they are lying together at night:

Nature, which doth every wiht
Upon hire lawe forto muse,
Constreigneth hem, so that thei use
Thing which to hem was al unknowe (IV.484–87).

(Nature, which causes every person
To reflect upon her law,
Compels them, so that they practice
That thing which was completely unknown to them.)

Interestingly enough, the little comment that there is on this passage is
widely divergent. Rosemary Woolf finds in this scene evidence of Gower's
"willingness to deal with or touch upon the subject of homosexuality . . .
and equally remarkably to do so with sympathy," while R. F. Yeager goes to
extreme lengths to rescue Gower from such a sympathy.[82] Clearly there is a
problem in the fact that Genius casts this love not only as natural but as
exemplary. Like the incest tales in the *Confessio*, this tale seems to normalize
medieval perversions in the name of that "naturatus amor" that renders all
"to be of one mind in being wild." Unlike the incest tales, however, this tale
of Iphis and Iante inverts the gender roles and renders the courtly love
model of most of the tales meaningless. More significantly, same-sex desire
occurs in all innocence, while the heterosexuality that saves the two lovers
requires drastic intervention.

It is at this crucial point in the tale that Cupid intervenes, taking pity on
their "grete love" and transforming Iphis into a man in mid-kiss so that
there was "to kinde non offence" (IV.505). The "problem" with their love is
not necessarily that nature takes offence, for as we have seen, she "constrains" them to commit what were otherwise considered to be unnatural
acts. Cupid's intervention should be unnecessary, but Genius explains in a
highly obfuscating passage:

Wherof Cupide thilke throwe
Toke pite for the grete love,
And let do sette kinde above,
So that hir lawe mai ben used,
And thei upon here lust excused.
For love hateth nothing more
Than thing which stant ayein the lore
Of that nature in kinde hath sett (IV.488–95).

(Cupid on this occasion
Took pity on their great love,
And caused "kinde" to be set above,
So that her law could be used,
And them excused with regard to their lust.
For love hates nothing more
Than a thing which stands against the teaching
Of what nature has classified [set in kind].)

The second part of this passage seems to suggest a moral condemnation of this love as one that opposes the teachings of nature, even though it was nature that was responsible for the love in the first place. The first part of the passage suggests something different guiding Cupid's intervention: the necessity of facilitating the *use* of nature's law, by which sexual intercourse is presumably meant. Cupid's intervention is simply a morphological adjustment to the lust that nature designed in the first place. Still, the air of "offense" to nature haunts the whole story before Genius inserts his misprized moral.

The moral of the story ignores its singularity and its challenge to Genius's moral structure: love is well disposed to those who pursue it with a "busy heart." Female busy-ness on behalf of a love for another woman violates all theological and courtly models of sexual love alike, not to mention the gender roles that make those models possible. The story of Iphis and Ianthe, like that of Pygmalion, shows neither a sympathy with homosexual love nor a critique of courtly love. Genius's moralizing here as elsewhere makes nonsense of both. Instead, what it points to is the instability of both, not only because of Nature's disregard for heterosexuality, but because gender itself proves to be merely a disguise in the story—it neither provokes the desire of the two girls for each other nor constrains them. Furthermore, the praise of Iphis's "business" or activity goes against all the moral and theological constraints applied to gender. Genius's praise for Iphis's activity is tantamount to Alan of Lille praising the conversion of hammers into anvils or the passivity of men who engage in sex with other men. The perverse is permitted not only to go unpunished in the narrative but to go unrecognized as well. In spite of Genius's unawareness, the story asserts the naturalness of what goes against nature and the unnaturalness of nature, requiring Cupid's intervention to enable this "great love" to make use of the laws of nature. What is also overlooked in the narrative throughout is the motivating factor behind this predicament of the two lovers: the decision of Iphis's mother to dress her as a boy to fool the father, who threatened to kill his child unless it were a boy. Iphis becomes a caricature not only of a "king's son," which she becomes by cross-dressing, but of the masculinity it implies.

Another cross-dresser who appears in the *Confessio* is Achilles in the tale of Achilles and Deidamia. In this case, Achilles is disguised as a girl by his mother, Thetis, in an effort to avoid the fulfillment of prophecy of his death in battle at Troy. "Clothed in the same fashion that belongs to womanhood," Achilles accepts his mother's disguise. Along with the clothing of a girl, Achilles also assumes all the feminine habits and behaviors that Thetis teaches him. Achilles not only learns how "with sober and goodly countenounce / He should his womanhood advance," but he delights in it:

Achilles, which that ilke while
Was yong, upon himself to smyle
Began, when he was so besein (V.3011–13).

(Achilles, who during that time
Was young, began to smile on himself
Whenever he was so equipped.)

The clothes make the man a woman, even to himself, and Achilles takes pleasure in his "womanhood." Not only was he "a woman to behold," but Genius suggests that Achilles effectively exchanges his manhood for womanhood (V.3050–55).

Nature, however, intervenes. When his mother sends Achilles to live with Deidamia, daughter of King Lichomede, Nature makes the two bedfellows "forto stere" until "al was don in dede" (V.3064, 3068). Once again, "kinde" directs the lovers toward natural (heterosexual) love under cover of unnatural (same-sex) love. It might seem as though the story is reinforcing the naturalness of heterosexual sex because the two lovers are drawn to each other in spite of their same-sex appearances. But Achilles is still identified with his cross-dressed womanliness. There is no suggestion by Genius that the sexual act changes Achilles's identity. In fact, the true test of his masculinity comes not here but later, when the Trojans try to flush him out from among the women at Lichomede's court so that they can enlist his help with the siege. Achilles is finally proven to be a man in spite of himself and his mother's outfitting him as a woman only when he is presented with a choice between beautiful women's clothing or armor and battle implements. Achilles, who is passing as a woman in Lichomede's court, reveals his true manhood when he steps forth to take the sword, hawberk, helmet, and shield sent by Agamemnon to expose his true masculinity. It is the battle that proves the man, while the clothing makes for the gender identity; nature seems to be less concerned with sexual object choices as proof of gender than with cultural codes of gender: armor vs. dresses.

The moral is again off the mark. Genius warns Amans of the treachery of "Falswitnesse" in Achilles's passing as a maid, and he blames Thetis (not Achilles) for the treachery. Such a moral does not begin to address the ease with which Achilles "becomes" a woman or the uncertain status of his masculinity, which cannot be discerned in him, so that Agamemnon and his privy council are forced to trick it out of him. The sexual encounter between Achilles and Deidamia, unlike that of Iphis and Iante, requires no adjustments from Cupid or Nature, even though Achilles maintains his feminine role even as he impregnates her. The prospect and accouterments of battle — not sexual acts — restore Achilles to his natural and proper masculinity. The perverse lingers, however, in the form of the nagging suggestion in this and the Iphis story that the natural is not what it seems. Nor are women or men, or sex for that matter. The fact that false witness in the form of gender-passing is so completely successful in the story of Achilles points to the instability of the cultural construction of gender, and Genius's moral against false witness does little to allay this problem.

If cross-dressing stories in the *Confessio Amantis* seem to undo its morality and courtly love ideals with a touch of the perverse, they can also function conservatively to reinforce those same ideals. Later in Book V, Genius discusses rape as a species of Avarice under three separate topics: ravine, or rape, robbery (of maidenhead), stealth, and thievery. The longest tale is of the rape of Philomela, in which Genius sacrifices Philomela's violation and tragedy to moralize that Amans should avoid "ravine" lest he end up like Tereus, eating his own children.[83] This story is followed by examples of robbery of virginity, which are described as the taking of "mennes good," his "chaffare" (V.6107, 6114, 6118), and the story includes high praise for virginity. Finally, Genius turns to the subject of stealth, which covers everything from the stealing of a kiss to rape. When Genius asks Amans if he is guilty of this sin, he responds that he is no thief, but not because he is morally opposed to it. As long as Daunger, or aloofness, guards his lady, no Stealth will prevail: "whil Daunger stant in his office, / Of Stelthe, which ye clepe a vice, / I schal be gultif neveremo" (while Daunger stands in his office, / Of Stealth, which you call a vice, / I shall never be guilty) (V.6643–45). The sinister suggestion here is that the lady's Daunger both necessitates a lover's stealth and disarms it. As in his handling of the story of Philomela, Genius in another story trivializes rape and the woman's suffering in particular. The tale is of Phoebus's rape of Leucothoe, which causes her father in outrage to have her buried alive in a pit "so that these maidens after this may take example of what it means to suffer her maidenhead to be stolen" (V.6767–69). Although Leucothoe is turned into a flower by Phoebus, there is no remorse for the rape or the father's revenge, much less pity for Leucothoe.

The story of Hercules and Faunus follows that of Leucothoe as a humorous example of failed rape through cross-dressing. Hercules and Iole are sporting in a cave together when she decides that they should exchange their clothes. She dons his tunic made from the skin of a lion and his mace until "sche was lich the man arraied," and he in turn wears her clothes. Later while they are asleep with their exchanged garments by their beds, Faunus enters the cave to rape Iole. Seeing the mace and tunic made of lion skin, Faunus assumes that Iole is Hercules and he steers clear of her bed. Turning to the other bed and finding a "bewimpled visage," Faunus undresses and jumps into the bed where Hercules is sleeping, "supposing well that it was she." When Hercules feels "a man above," he throws Faunus to the ground, and he becomes the joke of all the wood nymphs. Genius's moral continues the game of the tale, for he advises Amans to avoid theft unless he has better discernment than Faunus.

Cross-dressing in this story trivializes the subject of rape and Genius's supposed moral condemnation of it. Faunus is faulted not for attempting to rape Iole, but for mistaking Hercules for Iole and trying to rape him. Genius's suggestion that Amans should avoid stealthy acts such as Faunus's lest he make the same mistake and suffer the same ridicule is absurd. This absurdity is one in a series, including the juxtaposition of disturbing stories of rape with this one and the petty confessions they elicit from Amans, such as his fantasy about stealing into his lady's chambers. Cross-dressing in this tale serves to gloss over the violation of the women in the tales — or its threat — and to reinforce the conversion of rape throughout the *Confessio* into "desirable, idealized, elite love" or farce, in this case.[84] The complicity of rape with medieval love ideology is never recognized or acknowledged in the tale of Hercules's cross-dressing, nor is the threat of same-sex rape that it barely suggests.

One last example of Gower's perversions amidst the natural course of love's madness is his revision of the story of Narcissus. Narcissus is both the eponymous figure of self-love, and in Alan of Lille's version, the primary example of the perversion of masculinity into femininity and same-sex love. Genius's version of the Narcissus myth appears in Book I on Pride as an example of the species, "surquiderie," or presumption. Narcissus's pride is, of course, his refusal to love women because he sets his own beauty above all others. There is no mention of Echo's unrequited love for him, which in Ovid's version of the story determines his fate. In the key scene of the story, Gower's Narcissus comes upon a "lusty well" in the midst of a hunt. His fatal gaze into the well recapitulates Ovid but with a startling difference:

[A]nd as he caste his lok
Into the welle and hiede tok,
He sih the like of his visage,
And wende ther were an ymage
Of such a Nimphe as tho was faie,
Wherof that love his herte assaie
Began, as it was after sene,
Of his sotie and made him wene
It were a womman that he syh (I.2313–21)

(And as he cast his look
Into the well and took notice,
He saw the likeness of his face,
And supposed it was the image
Of such a nymph as then was endued with magic,
Causing that love to begin to assail his heart,
As it was afterwards seen,
And out of his folly made him think
It was a woman that he saw.)

Narcissus sees his own reflection as first a nymph and then a woman rather than a man. What does Gower mean by this significant alteration in what Narcissus sees? The Latin gloss of the *Confessio* identifies the female image with Echo, and this has led some scholars to credit Gower's Narcissus with undergoing "nothing more or less than the birth of love," like any courtly lover.[85] Whether Narcissus sees Echo or not in this scene, his folly lies in his taking his own image for that of a nymph. There are other possible interpretations than Gower's correction of Narcissus's self-love into love of a beauty other than himself. It is Narcissus's own folly, after all, that creates the illusion — a twist on his previous self-love. One might be tempted to see this as a heterosexual adjustment to the perversion of Alan's Narcissus, that is, that masculine self-love leads to same-sex love. Yet it is also possible that Gower renders concretely that very feminization of which Alan speaks. Narcissus sees himself as a woman in a sense because of his self-love, and this is the ultimate female perversion. Perhaps, too, there is a more potent suggestion in this version of the Narcissus story that the object of desire in all courtly love is the lover himself, who seeks and finds his reflection in the feminine object. Or perhaps the story points to the inevitable feminizing of the courtly lover whom the *Romance of the Rose* directs to "make his manners like hers," to imitate the habits and behaviors of the woman he loves.[86] All that Genius tells us is that like the flower that bears his name and blooms in the winter, Narcissus's folly was "contraire to kynde" (contrary to nature, I.2356–57). Narcissus's presumption is clearly the unnatural impulse of the story, but Narcissus's love for himself in the form of a woman is its result.

That Narcissus's love was a perverse madness Genius makes clear. He who held love most in disdain, Genius concludes, "he was least worthy in love's eye / And most mocked in his wit" (I.2362–63). The conversion of Narcissus's image to nymph and woman in his own eyes is the greatest of transgressions, representing even in the "wildness" that attends "naturatus amor" a truly errant desire that degrades him. Although the nymphs of the well take pity on Narcissus, Genius does not, and he further seals his tragedy by condemning him for his unworthiness and his self-deceived (*bejaped*) wit. The original Ovidian line that persists in most medieval redactions of the story of Narcissus — that he is guilty of self-love — is skewed in Gower so that Narcissus's pride is feminized and his wit degraded. Narcissus's madness is reflected back to him in the form of a nymph, and his story threatens to expose a link between desire and identity. What Narcissus desires is the figure of himself as a woman that is reflected to him in the well. What he grieves is both the "thing which he could never achieve" (I.2332) and the feminine that he dreaded in his disdain for love and has now "become." The tale exposes in a unique way how masculine identity in the form of Narcissus's disdain of love and preference for hunting actually masks this feminine longing and finally, his own melancholic estrangement from the feminine.

At the end of the *Confessio Amantis*, Gower himself will be forced, as

Narcissus was, to examine his own reflection, and like Narcissus, will see an alien being—not a nymph or a woman, but Age itself that has so disfigured his face that he is instantly cured of his love melancholy. Unlike Narcissus, he does not fall in love with his own image, but rather, he comes to the sudden realization that he is too old for love. While Narcissus's image is a fantasy produced by self-love, Gower's image releases him from his self-deception. Gower's sudden self-awareness also marks a clear shift in the tone of the whole work from serious moralizing to humorous self-depreca-tion. Venus laughs at Gower now that he has seen himself in his "heart's eye" and "asks as if it were a game what love was." Gower is silent and ashamed because he unable to answer. Gower subsequently abandons all "love's rage" after Venus advises that he should seek no more after love but instead should pursue peace and moral virtue because he is not up to the game of love (VIII.2908–31).

This solution to Amans's problem, as some critics have noted, is a rather sneaky and unsatisfactory one on Gower's part because the age of the poet, which is withheld through some 30,000 lines, renders the entire preceding poem irrelevant.[87] Although critics continue to accept Amans/Gower's rejection of love in view of his old age seriously, there is much to suggest that this, too, is a game. First, there is Venus's response to Gower's sudden change. There is also the complete abandonment of love altogether, which is humorous in view of the long discourse on love in the rest of the poem. But as I have been showing in some of the stories, there is a similar sort of game going on in the form of the radical disjunction of moralizing structure and stories and the riddling of natural love with the perverse. Although this sport is not without its purpose, the moralizing structure that critics continue to take seriously is as absurd as Amans's love and Genius's hermeneutics. Yet the very application of the penitential format to love renders the format itself absurd, even meaningless, as Genius warps it to fit everything from the petty infractions to the grand tragedies of love and in the process does violence to its stories. The sheer incongruity of story and penitential moral produces a range of effects from humorous to unsettling. There is hardly a clear moral trajectory to the entire work, much less a clear moral condemnation of courtly love.

What does this mean for the status of desire and sexuality in the work? As I suggested at the outset of this discussion, Gower's text fails to make clear distinctions between natural and unnatural forms of love, much less between heterosexuality and homosexuality. It also trivializes the violence, rape, and sacrifice of women to the cause of *fin amors*. In the course of making very detailed distinctions among the vices and virtues of love, it not only fails to produce any meaningful distinctions but actively renders its own distinctions nonsensical. In effect, Gower had no choice but to abandon love at the end because Genius had already so successfully riddled it with contradictions and incoherence. It is important to recognize, too, that the moral structure itself is rendered absurd by the exempla brought to bear on it. Even if Gower follows Venus's advice at the end and goes in search of moral virtue, the bulk of the poem has already obscured the moral route.

Furthermore, the much discussed Prologue to Gower's poem suggests the impossibility of the moral path designated at the poem's end. The condition of the world is one of diversity, division, fragmentation, and conflict. While Gower pointedly critiques the various institutions of society — the Church, State, and Commons, or people — he also insists upon the inevitability, even naturalness, of this state of divisiveness and change. Nature is, after all, the model of confusion and disorder in the changes of seasons, fluctuations of nature, the ocean's ebb and flow, and heavenly and meteorological anomalies (Prol.918–66). Division and diversity as they condition social upheavals are reflected in the physiological makeup of humans "for his complexioun / Is mad upon divisioun" (for their complexion is based upon division, Prol.975–76). The four humors that make up human beings — hot, cold, moist, and dry — are diverse elements, and man, therefore, exists in a state of "debate" and corruption. Likewise, Gower finds the same qualities of diversity and corruption in the spiritual condition of human beings because body and soul are in continual debate (995–1008). Original Sin, too, contributed to the internal division in people (996–1017). Finally, the fracturing of languages from a single tongue after the Tower of Babel estranged human beings from each other because "none knew what the other meant" (1024). In spite of his earlier critique of the lack of charity and the self-interested divisions in fourteenth-century society, Gower seems to acknowledge this chaotic fragmentation as part of the human condition.

Gower finds a unifying principle not in a clear moral direction, but in poetry itself. And not just any poetry, but the poetry of "lust and lore," which, like Chaucer's "ernest and game," promises instruction and pleasure in the same literary enterprise. He ends his Prologue with the story of Arion, whose song could tame beasts and make peace between warring species. Most importantly, his "lusti melodie" worked its wonders on human beings "when each man with ther other laughed" (1071). It is laughter that repairs what imperfect charity in a corrupt, divided, and restless human condition cannot, to "make peace where there now is hate" (1075). If Arion's song serves as Gower's exemplum for the poetic enterprise, it points to laughter as a means of repairing the estrangement of human beings from themselves and each other, even if it does not aspire to repair all the social ills that Gower chronicles in the Prologue.

Gower's humorous intention, though, does not mitigate the serious implications of the *Confessio* in the areas of gender and sexuality. The confusion of natural categories throughout the work and the misfitting of theological categories of sins to the subject of courtly love point to problems in both, regardless of Gower's intentions. The opening Latin epigram of Book I celebrating the power of love to subject all creatures to the laws of nature and render them wild of mind embraces a doubleness that is both problematic and instructive. It is problematic in that it fails to distinguish between moral and immoral or amoral types of love, leveling all under the rubric of natural law. It is instructive in that it exposes the intersection of the normative and the perverse, an intersection that we have already observed in penitential texts as well. Heterosexual love in its idealized form as courtly love both contains the perverse and is already perverted into those "unnatural" forms that nature seems to permit, including incest, same-sex love, rape, and self-love. The bland moralizing that glosses over these blatant perversions of medieval gender and sexual ideology only calls attention to the problem. At the end of the *Confessio*, Genius substitutes incest for the usual seventh sin of Lechery, and he attempts to assert the unnaturalness of Antiochus's incestuous rape of his daughter as against the "honest love" of Apollonius for his wife and child. While scholars would like to take this exemplum for the resolution of all the inconsistencies in the rest of the work and for a summation of its morality, the story simply cannot undo the contradictions demonstrated throughout the work. In fact, if anything, the story of Apollonius demonstrates how the incestuous anti-ideal of love *makes possible* the idealizing of Apollonius's "honest love," the final oxymoron in an acutely contradictory work. As in the story of the rape of Philomela, the violence done to the woman (Antiochus's daughter) is subsumed by the rivalry between Antiochus and Apollonius, and on a larger scale, between honest and "unkind" loves. Amans's dissatisfaction with Genius at this point, however, is understandable because the story is of no use to him or to the reader.

What is useful is the way in which Genius's instruction exposes the perverse within the normative and the very instability of the normative itself. The violence against women, the selfishness, the feminization of men,

the voraciousness of desire, the aberrant nature of sexuality, and the disor-
derliness of gender identity all speak through Genius's advocacy of an ordered, morally coherent guide for love. Idealized heterosexuality in the
form of courtly love is undone in the *Confessio* in the sense that its normativity is compromised, even rendered incoherent. At the end of the
poem, Gower dreams of a band of youthful lovers, including many of the
lovers who have appeared already as negative examples of desire. They
speak in unison "al of knyhthod and of Armes, / And what it is to ligge in
armes / With love, whanne it is achieved" (all of knighthood and of arms, /
And what it is to lie in arms / With love, when it is achieved, VIII.2498–
99). The perversion that is heterosexual, courtly love as it has been codified
in the *Confessio* clearly serves the narrative of masculine chivalric heroism
represented in the stories of these very exemplars of love. Because the perverse functions to authorize vital cultural myths and ideals, such as those of
love and masculine heroism, it is not only implicated in those ideals but it is
essential to them. Why else would the female group of four good wives be
singled out of this same group? Penelope, Lucrece, Alcestis, and Alcyone
are all praised along with the chivalric heroes of this visionary ensemble "by
example of all good / In Marriage" (VIII.2617–18). Lucrece's suicide "for
dread of shame" after her rape by Tarquin, Penelope's loyalty to Ulysses,
Alcestis's sacrifice of her own life for her husband's, and Alcyon's suicide in
response to her husband's death—these are the gender ideals that perversely underwrite courtly love in the Middle Ages and masculine chivalric
virtue. Alcestis and Lucrece are in fact used in Book VII to exemplify
chastity, with its concomitant qualities of submission and sacrifice, and to
rationalize masculine political authority. No appeal to a spiritual notion of
charity is capable of resolving this cultural perversion; after all, even Christian charity in the Middle Ages relied on the same cultural myths for its
figuration. The perverse is not bound by the secular when the language of
Christian love is borrowed from that of secular love.

　　For all its perversions, Gower's text is not finally subversive. The ideal-
ization of feminine chastity as a metaphor for political authority and integrity, the pairing of chivalric heroism with feminine sacrifice in the four good
wives, and the demonization of Venus and female desire all point to the
ways in which gender ideology secures a range of social, political, and
theological ideals. These ideals include the vision of a harmonized society
that Gower alludes to in his Prologue, the model of the self-restrained
monarchy in Book VII, and the turn away from secular love, "divisioun,"
and "lustes" to charity, "unite," "good governance," and masculine reason at

the end of the *Confessio*. For all his sympathy with the former, John Gower is on the side of order, unity, and social hierarchy.

What is interesting, though, is that heterosexuality itself is not at stake in Gower's vision. As I have tried to show, the categories of natural and un-natural sex become hopelessly confused in Genius's dialogue with Amans, as do the inviolability of gender roles. Yet this very incoherence is symptom-atic of a larger problem in medieval discourse about sexuality, an incoher-ence that can be seen in the failure to distinguish clearly the natural from the perverse, or in the Parson's words, the abominable, unmentionable sins from the merely unnatural, articulatable vices. Sodomy, same-sex desire, incest, rape, and "heterosexual" fornication are only partially explained and contained by medieval norms of what constitutes procreative sex. Gender norms function much more clearly than do sexual norms to define and regulate sexual behavior. Gower exploits this incoherence in his text. His only solution is no solution at all, though it is a mystification: to relegate sex and secular love to youth and charity to age.

The perverse remains with us in the Middle Ages and the present. The natural/unnatural conditions the medieval perverse, while heterosexuality vs. all others conditions the modern. There is a similarity, however, in the medieval and modern perverse in that gender ideology is crucial to both, perhaps more crucial to medieval ideas of sexuality than it is to modern ones. Louise Kaplan and Susan Streitfeld have taught us that "perversions are never what they seem to be"—that they are in fact sexual disguises for gender anxieties. Unlike modern psychology, the Middle Ages was not so confident about its distinctions between perversions and normal sexuality because its conception of sexuality itself was riddled with the perverse. Sodomy and heterosexuality were both symptomatic of concupiscence, a human condition that was both natural and already corrupted. Like Kaplan et al., the Middle Ages did render sexual pathologies in terms of gender pathologies, and it, too, attempted to define precisely the nature of perver-sions. Because of the implicit association of the feminine with desire and the pathologizing of all sexuality in medieval theology, though, the Middle Ages was in the peculiar position of vacuating the category of normal sex. Heterosexuality as a normative principle simply did not exist; fornication as a perversion that coexisted with sodomy and gender infractions did. In this area at least, nature seems to have created nothing but perversions.

That "abominable sin that no one ought to speak or write" proves to be only one of the secrets of medieval theology about sexuality. Normative heterosexuality's best kept secret is that it did not exist in the Middle Ages, or rather, that it existed as part of the same discourse that included sodomy. If sodomy was maintained as that secret about which no one should speak or write, this secrecy also disguised the fact that it was merely another form of the same discourse that produced "heterosexuality" in the Middle Ages.

The complicity of sodomy and "heterosexuality" in the Middle Ages is one of the conclusions to be drawn from this study. As I emphasized in the beginning of this chapter, my purpose has been to correct what I see as a dangerously narrow focus on sexuality in the Middle Ages that either excludes gender from its analysis or worse, posits gender as the conservative constraint that sexuality subverts. Not only do the operations of misogyny disappear from view in such a project, but the intersections between gender ideology and sexual oppression are rendered invisible. The questionable opposition of heterosexuality and sodomy also glosses over the way in which gender ideology sustains both discourses. Just as disturbing is the deeply conservative effect of such a framing of our discussion of medieval sexuality, for it preserves—rather than interrogates—medieval and contemporary structures of oppression, including the misogynistic rhetoric of sodomitic discourse in the Middle Ages and the heterosexual/homosexual framework of contemporary sexual identities. It is only by looking at the intersections of gender and sexuality in both medieval culture and contemporary queer theory that the lines of oppression, medieval and contemporary, can be made visible. The search for a queer Middle Ages, too, runs the risk that all queer theory runs of universalizing male sexuality and at the same time, of trivializing gender as either too obvious or too retrograde for comment.

If this book has shown anything about secrecy, it has demonstrated its pernicious ability to travel within medieval culture as well as across historical periods, the force of its passage, and the gashes it leaves on the past and the ongoing order of things. It is easy enough to become complicitous in the cultural secrets we study, particularly if our own categories contribute to the illegibility of those secrets. Our own desires as scholars of the past and of sexualities can restrict our optic even as they sometimes also powerfully transform restrictive histories and anthropologies. Eve Sedgwick suggests that secrecy is a crucial technology of contemporary culture that operates around and upon gay identity, in conjunction with other culturally significant formulations, such as the distinctions between public and private, disclosure and concealment, masculine and feminine, and knowledge and ignorance.[88] By examining the historical reach of this secrecy, including medieval covert operations that structured and gave meaning to confession, women's gossip, rhetorics of knowledge, legal terminology governing wives, and sodomitic discourse, we can, perhaps, begin to understand how secrecy functions in our culture, too. Discovering the secrets of history, or of our present, is not the goal of studying secrecy in the first place, for such a tactic only subjects one to the very operations that secrecy sets in motion. Beyond discovering the areas of historical periods that secrecy governs and how it works, we confront "what human beings care most to protect and to probe: the exalted, the dangerous, the shameful; the sources of power and creation; the fragile and the intimate." And in this recognition of secrecy's powerful reach, historically and ideologically, we can begin to imagine strategies of resistance.

Notes

Introduction

1. Oscar Wilde, *The Picture of Dorian Gray*, ed. Peter Ackroyd (New York: Penguin, 1949), p. 26.

2. Michel Foucault, *The History of Sexuality*, Vol. 1, *An Introduction*, trans. Robert Hurley (New York: Vintage, 1990), p. 27.

3. Sissela Bok, *Secrets: On the Ethics of Concealment and Revelation* (New York: Vintage Books, 1989), pp. xvii–xviii.

4. D. A. Miller, *The Novel and the Police* (Berkeley: University of California Press, 1988), p. 207. For his comments on studying the differing secrecies of cultures, see p. 206.

5. Eve Kosofsky Sedgwick, *Epistemology of the Closet* (Berkeley: University of California Press, 1990), pp. 70–71. For my discussion of this quote elsewhere, see my essay, "Don't Ask, Don't Tell: Murderous Plots and Medieval Secrets," in *Premodern Sexualities*, ed. Louise Fradenburg and Carla Freccero (New York: Routledge, 1996), pp. 138–40.

6. Kim Lane Scheppele, *Legal Secrets: Equality and Efficiency in Common Law* (Chicago: University of Chicago Press, 1988), p. 14.

7. Michel de Certeau, *The Mystic Fable*, Vol. 1, *The Sixteenth and Seventeenth Centuries*, trans. Michael B. Smith (Chicago: University of Chicago Press, 1992), p. 97. See Chapter 3 for a discussion of de Certeau's theory of secrecy.

8. Louise Fradenburg and Carla Freccero make a similar point about the need for reframing modernity as a "mutual construction" with premodernity in their "Introduction: Caxton, Foucault, and the Pleasures of History," in *Premodern Sexualities*, ed. Fradenburg and Freccero, p. xxi.

9. Carolyn Dinshaw also argues for the creative potential of the Middle Ages to reframe the present, but she emphasizes more its liberatory potential for forging "a new, post-identitarian and post-medieval ethos." In "Getting Medieval: *Pulp Fiction*, Gawain, and Foucault," in *The Book and the Body*, ed. Dolores Warwick Frese and Katherine O'Brien O'Keeffe (Notre Dame, Ind.: University of Notre Dame Press, 1997), pp. 137, 146, 155.

10. Scheppele, *Legal Secrets*, p. 5.

11. I am borrowing and combining the definitions of Bok, *Secrets*, pp. 5–9, and Scheppele, *Legal Secrets*, p. 5. See Bok for a more extensive distinction between secrecy and privacy, pp. 10–14.

12. Foucault, *History of Sexuality*, 1: 104; Lee Patterson, *Chaucer and the Subject of History* (Madison: University of Wisconsin Press, 1991), p. 386.

Chapter 1

1. Michel Foucault, *The History of Sexuality*, Vol. 1, *An Introduction*, trans. Robert Hurley (New York: Vintage, 1990), p. 59.

2. Celestine Bohlen, "The Good Word: Creature Comforts for Catholics," *New York Times*, 28 June 1996, natl. ed.: A4.

3. Ibid.

4. Foucault, *History of Sexuality*, 1: 59.

5. Foucault, *History of Sexuality*, 1: 19–20.

6. Foucault, *History of Sexuality*, 1: 20.

7. David M. Halperin, *Saint Foucault: Towards a Gay Hagiography* (New York: Oxford University Press, 1995), p. 6.

8. For this idea in Foucault, see the analysis of James Miller, *The Passion of Michel Foucault* (New York: Simon and Schuster, 1993), pp. 321–24, and Halperin, *Saint Foucault*, pp. 90–97. See also Foucault's ideal of the intellectual who is not bound by consistency and universalities, even as I have suggested that Foucault is not, "End of the Monarchy of Sex," in *Foucault Live (Interviews, 1961–1984)*, ed. Sylvère Lotringer, trans. Lysa Hochroth and John Johnston (New York: Semio-text[e], 1996), p. 225.

9. For a summary of these and other effects of Foucault's work, see Halperin, *Saint Foucault*, pp. 40–43, 56–62. Halperin finds one of the most important aspects of Foucault's work for gay and lesbian liberation to be his notion of *ascesis*; see pp. 76–79, 101–12, 115–19.

10. Foucault, *History of Sexuality*, 1: 35.

11. "On the Genealogy of Ethics: An Overview of Work in Progress," a 1983 interview with Michel Foucault in *Michel Foucault: Beyond Structuralism and Herme-neutics*, 2d ed., ed. Hubert L. Dreyfus and Paul Rabinow (Chicago: University of Chicago Press, 1983), p. 229.

12. Michel Foucault, "An Aesthetics of Existence," in *Foucault Live (Interviews, 1961–1984)*, p. 450. See also pp. 455, 461.

13. Foucault, *History of Sexuality*, 1: 33.

14. Both quotations come from Foucault's essay "A Preface to Transgression" in *Language, Counter-Memory, Practice: Selected Essays and Interviews*, ed. Donald Bouchard, trans. Bouchard and Sherry Simon (Ithaca, N.Y.: Cornell University Press, 1977), p. 29.

15. Foucault, "Preface to Transgression," pp. 29–30.

16. Ibid., pp. 30–33. It is important to note that Foucault looks toward a new discourse and not sexuality for this language of transgression (p. 33).

17. Carolyn Dinshaw also critiques Foucault's nostalgia as it reflects "a particu-lar desire for (as he sees it) a premodern realm of clearly apprehensible sexual acts as opposed to the hypocritical and surreptitious world of modern sexual identities," in "'Getting Medieval': *Pulp Fiction*, Gawain, Foucault," in *The Book and the Body*, ed. Dolores Warwick Frese and Katherine O'Brien O'Keefe (Notre Dame, Ind.: Uni-versity of Notre Dame Press, 1997), pp. 140–41. Such works as James Miller's biography of Foucault, *The Passion of Michel Foucault*, David Halperin's *Saint Fou-cault*, and queer theory that adopts Foucaultian principles of the historicity and

constructedness of sexuality nevertheless ignore the discourse that gives this sexuality speech in Foucault's analysis. This is, I think, a dangerous oversight that needs to be addressed in contemporary theory as well as in histories of sexuality. If there is no sex without confession, it is incumbent on those who use Foucault to acknowledge and further pursue his ideas about confessional discourse. Unfortunately, I suspect that scholars do not want to acknowledge this aspect of modern sexual discourse because it brings a negative framework to the liberatory scholarship some are trying to achieve.

18. Foucault, *History of Sexuality*, 1: 58.

19. Ibid., 59.

20. Foucault, "The Battle for Chastity," in *Western Sexuality: Practice and Precept in Past and Present Times*, ed. Philippe Ariès and André Bejin, trans. Anthony Forster (Oxford: Basil Blackwell, 1985), p. 25.

21. Foucault, "On the Genealogy of Ethics," p. 231.

22. Foucault's thinking on Cassian is developed primarily in his Howison lectures, which are not published; however, Mark Blasius has edited the lectures as they were given at Dartmouth on November 17 and 24, 1980, which he says are "more or less the same papers as the Howison Lectures at Berkeley on October 20–21" (p. 198), in "About the Beginning of the Hermeneutics of the Self: Two Lectures at Dartmouth," *Political Theory* 21, 2 (May 1993): 198–227. Also, James Miller summarizes these lectures in *The Passion of Michel Foucault*, pp. 322–23. Foucault discusses Cassian and the ascetic struggle with the flesh in "The Battle for Chastity," pp. 14–25; and in "Du gouvernement des vivants," in *Résumé des cours, 1970–1982* (Paris: Gallimard, 1989), pp. 123–28.

23. See "Power Affects the Body," in which Foucault claims that the "essential part" of the *History of Sexuality* is "a reworking of the theory of power," and "The Ethics of the Concern for Self as a Practice of Freedom," in which he proclaims his primary interest to be the "care of the self," in *Foucault Live*, ed. Lotringer, pp. 209, 432–49.

24. Foucault, "On the Genealogy of Ethics," p. 245. Foucault contrasts this Christian notion of the self with the classical "idea of a self which had to be created as a work of art" (p. 245). Foucault implies elsewhere, however, that the Christian self is just as much a "work of art," though in a different sense and with difference consequences.

25. Foucault, "The Subject and Power," in *Michel Foucault: Beyond Structuralism and Hermeneutics*, 2d ed., ed. Herbert L. Dreyfus and Paul Rabinow (Chicago: University of Chicago Press, 1983), p. 214.

26. Ibid., p. 248.

27. Foucault, "Battle for Chastity," p. 25.

28. I am borrowing Thomas Flynn's idea of the "Foucaultian triangle"—knowledge, power, and subjectivization—as a key formulation in his later works, "Foucault as Parrhesiast," in *The Final Foucault*, ed. James Bernauer and David Rasmussen (Cambridge, Mass.: MIT Press, 1988), p. 106.

29. Foucault, *History of Sexuality*, 1: 71. Foucault describes the modern phenomenon of *scientia sexualis*, but his analysis parallels his account of medieval confession as well. For the interaction of revealing and concealing, see 1: 61.

30. Foucault, "Du gouvernement des vivants," in *Résumé des cours*, p. 128. My translation.

31. James Bernauer, "Foucault's Ecstatic Thinking," in *The Final Foucault*, ed. James Bernauer and David Rasmussen (Cambridge, Mass.: MIT Press, 1988), p. 53. For this idea in Foucault, see also "Schizo-Culture: Infantile Sexuality," "Power Affects the Body," and "The Ethics of the Concern for Self as a Practice of Freedom," in *Foucault Live*, ed. Lotringer, pp. 155–67, 208–9, 432–35.

32. Foucault, "Sexuality and Solitude," in *Humanities in Review I*, ed. David Rieff (Cambridge: Cambridge University Press, 1982), p. 11.

33. Foucault, "Sexuality and Solitude," p. 16; Foucault, "Battle for Chastity," pp. 24–25; and Foucault, *History of Sexuality*, 1: 57–71.

34. Foucault, *History of Sexuality*, 1: 19–20.

35. Ibid., 1: 61–62.

36. Foucault, *History of Sexuality*, 1: 62. Basing her analysis on Foucault, Sissela Bok maps a similar dynamic in the power relationship of confession in *Secrets: On the Ethics of Concealment and Revelation* (New York: Vintage Books, 1989), pp. 73–88.

37. Pierre J. Payer critiques Foucault's reduction of the subject of confession to sex and maintains that the evidence for confession's influence on contemporary discourses of sex is "virtually nonexistent" in "Foucault on Penance and the Shaping of Sexuality," *Studies in Religion* 14 (1985): 313–20.

38. Michel Foucault, "About the Beginning of the Hermeneutics of the Self: Two Lectures at Dartmouth," ed. Mark Blasius, *Political Theory* 21, 2 (May 1993): 222. See also James Miller, *The Passion of Michel Foucault*, p. 324. See also Bernauer, "Foucault's Ecstatic Thinking," pp. 69–70. These are the only two Foucault scholars I know of who address this contradiction in Foucault's work.

39. Quoted in Miller, *Passion of Michel Foucault*, p. 324.

40. Michel Foucault, *The Archaeology of Knowledge and the Discourse on Language*, trans. A. M. Sheridan Smith (New York: Pantheon Books, 1972), p. 17. See Miller's discussion of this idea in Foucault's work, *Passion of Michel Foucault*, pp. 123–64, 324–25. Foucault plays on this idea in "The Masked Philosopher," where he discusses anonymity as a principle of truth, in *Foucault Live*, pp. 302–7.

41. This is a composite quotation from Foucault's lecture on "Christianity and Subjectivity," given first at Dartmouth and then as a Howison lecture at Berkeley, in which he expanded his idea, "Hermeneutics of the Self," pp. 222, 53n.

42. Foucault, "On the Genealogy of Ethics," p. 231. Elizabeth A. Clark also notes the shift in Foucault's later work toward the Christian hermeneutics of the self, and she critiques his argument for the discontinuity between pagan and Christian sexual ethics, "Foucault, the Fathers, and Sex," *Journal of the American Academy of Religion* 56 (1988): 619–41.

43. Bok, *Secrets*, pp. xvii–xviii.

44. Oscar D. Watkins, *A History of Penance* (New York: Burt Franklin, 1961), 2: 748–49.

45. See Jeremy Tambling, *Confession: Sexuality, Sin, the Subject* (Manchester: Manchester University Press, 1990), pp. 38–39; Thomas N. Tentler, *Sin and Confession on the Eve of the Reformation* (Princeton, N.J.: Princeton University Press, 1977), pp. 13–25, 61–62, 138–39; W. A. Pantin, *The English Church in the Fourteenth*

Century (Notre Dame, Ind.: University of Notre Dame Press, 1962), p. 192; and Henry Charles Lea, *A History of Auricular Confession and Indulgences in the Latin Church*, 3 vols. (Philadelphia: Lea Brothers, 1896), 1: 483–93; 2: 161, 414. For an argument against these effects, particularly that of the Church's consolidation of control over sinners through confession, see Lawrence Duggan, "Fear and Confession on the Eve of the Reformation," *Archiv für Reformationsgeschichte* 75 (1984): 153–75.

46. The "age of discretion" was variously interpreted and argued, ranging from 10 to 14. See Lea, *History of Auricular Confession*, 1: 400–402.

47. See Miri Rubin, *Corpus Christi: The Eucharist in Late Medieval Culture* (Cambridge: Cambridge University Press, 1991), pp. 64–66.

48. Quoted in Rubin, *Corpus Christi*, p. 66.

49. See my discussion of Foucault and confession in the first part of this chapter.

50. See, for example, Alan of Lille, *Liber poenitentialis*, PL 210: 285.

51. Lea, *History of Auricular Confession*, 1: 412. See 1: 12 for Lea's entire discussion of the seal of confession. See also Bertrand A. Kurtscheid, *A History of the Seal of Confession*, trans. F. A. Marks (London: B. Herder, 1927).

52. Tentler, *Sin and Confession*, pp. 16–27. For an overview of early Christian penance, see also Bernhard Poschmann, *Penance and the Anointing of the Sick* (London: Burns and Oates, 1964), pp. 5–121.

53. Lea, *History of Auricular Confession*, 1: 412. Duns Scotus and others also argue for this secrecy on the basis of natural and divine laws (pp. 412–14).

54. Watkins, *History of Penance*, 2: 736. For other examples of the priest's obligation to secrecy, see also Lea, *History of Auricular Confession*, 1: 417–20.

55. Lea, *History of Auricular Confession*, 1: 420.

56. Ibid., 1: 233.

57. See Poschmann, *Penance and the Anointing of the Sick*, p. 158; see pp. 157–93 for a full discussion of the problem.

58. This is obviously an oversimplified rendering of what was a complicated theological issue. For a more fully developed account of the declaratory vs. indicative roles of the priest in confession, see Tentler, *Sin and Confession*, pp. 22–27; and Lea, *History of Auricular Confession*, 1: 466–88.

59. *Speculum Sacerdotale*, ed. Edward H. Weatherly, EETS, o.s. 200 (London: Oxford University Press, 1936), p. 67. The text also warns that priests should not hear confessions of people from another parish without the parish priest's permission.

60. Lea, *History of Auricular Confession*, 1: 249–50. For discussions of this problem, see also Tentler, *Sin and Confession*, pp. 124–28; and Duggan, "Fear and Confession," pp. 165–69.

61. Robert Mannyng of Brunne, *Handlyng Synne*, ed. F. J. Furnivall, EETS 119 (London: Kegan Paul, Trench and Trübner, 1901), p. 126, and EETS 123 (London: Kegan Paul, Trench and Trübner, 1903), p. 35; and *The Book of Vices and Virtues*, ed. W. Nelson Francis, EETS, o.s. 217 (London: Oxford University Press, 1942), p. 180. For this idea in Aquinas, see Kurtscheid, *Seal of Confession*, p. 292.

62. Lea, *History of Auricular Confession*, 1: 432. See further examples of discussions of the situational ethics surrounding this problem of the violation of the seal of

confession on pp. 432–40. In his *Regulae Morales*, Jean Gerson states that "in no case, not even to save an entire nation, is it permitted to reveal the confession" (quoted in Kurtscheid, *Seal of Confession*, p.181).

63. "The Social History of Confession in the Age of the Reformation," *Transactions of the Royal Historical Society* 5th ser. 25 (1975): 24. Mary C. Mansfield also stresses that "Lenten confession was a surprisingly open affair," *The Humiliation of Sinners: Public Penance in Thirteenth-Century France* (Ithaca, N.Y.: Cornell University Press, 1995), p. 79.

64. *Speculum Sacerdotale*, ed. Weatherly, pp. 64–65.

65. Lea documents efforts from the twelfth century onwards to eliminate this old-fashioned formula, which accompanied an invocation to the Holy Ghost. Because the priest had the power of binding and loosing the soul through absolution, this was no longer necessary but apparently continued to be practiced, *History of Auricular Confession*, 1: 51–54. Tentler documents confusion about the practice, *Sin and Confession*, pp. 86–87.

66. The *OED* dates "shriving pew" in 1487, "shriving stool" in 1534, and "shriving cloth" in 1534. Mansfield finds other suggestions that this cloth might have been used in England to conceal men in confession, while women were still required to confess in the open for their own safety, *Humiliation of the Sinner*, pp. 79–80.

67. Lea, *History of Auricular Confession*, 1: 382–84, 394; Tentler, *Sin and Confession*, p. 82.

68. Lea, *History of Auricular Confession*, 1: 394–95; and Tambling, *Confession*, pp. 66–70, in which he applies Foucault's theory of the Panopticon to the confessional box.

69. "Fiat confessio coram oculis omnium, in patente loco, ne subintroeat lupus rapax in angulis suadens agere quae turpe est etiam cogitare." Quoted in Lea, *History of Auricular Confession*, 1: 394.

70. Foucault, *History of Sexuality*, 1: 27. Mary B. McKinley analyzes the "mastery of rhetoric" required by confession in Marguerite de Navarre's *Heptameron*, including the "shaping of their narratives, the way they told their *secrets*" in her chapter "Telling Secrets: Sacramental Confession and Narrative Authority in the *Heptameron*," in *Critical Tales: New Studies of the* Heptameron *and Early Modern Culture*, ed. John D. Lyons and Mary B. McKinley (Philadelphia: University of Pennsylvania Press, 1993), p. 156.

71. Foucault, *History of Sexuality*, 1: 61. This "what if" is more than a suggestion; it is a description of the discourse of confession.

72. Michel de Certeau, *The Mystic Fable*, Vol. 1, *The Sixteenth and Seventeenth Centuries*, trans. Michael B. Smith (Chicago: University of Chicago Press, 1992), p. 97. De Certeau is interested primarily in the ways that secrecy structures mysticism in the sixteenth and seventeenth centuries, but his theoretical insights about how secrecy works are useful for my discussion of confession.

73. De Certeau, *Mystic Fable*, 1: 98.

74. *John Mirk's Instruction for Parish Priests*, ed. Edward Peacock, EETS, o.s. 31 (London: K. Paul, Trench and Trübner, 1902), p. 24, ll. 777, 779.

75. At the heart of confession was "the interrogatory," according to Stephen

Haliczer, "which was designed to provide a highly structured way of examining the conscience of the penitent and eliciting appropriate replies," *Sexuality in the Confessional* (Oxford: Oxford University Press, 1996), p. 8.

76. See J. J. Francis Firth's introduction to *Robert of Flamborough: Liber Poenitentialis*, Studies and Texts 18 (Toronto: Pontifical Institute of Mediaeval Studies, 1971), p. 10; and Adrian Morey, *Bartholomew of Exeter, Bishop and Canonist* (Cambridge: Cambridge University Press, 1937), p. 170–71.

77. Thomas of Chobham, *Summa confessorum*, ed., F. Broomfield, Analecta mediaevalia Namurcensia 25 (Louvain: Editions Nauwelaerts, 1968), pp. xv and xvii.

78. Tentler, *Sin and Confession*, pp. 86, 116–20.

79. Lea, *History of Auricular Confession*, 1: 370.

80. Lea, *History of Auricular Confession*, 1: 371. For early efforts to classify the sins, see 2: pp. 235–48. Tentler discusses the massive detail of another summa for confessors, *Angelica*, "Interrogationes" (1486), which amasses an index of moral questions for some 20,000 words, *Sin and Confession*, p. 90.

81. "Non igitur in hac re perfectionem exspectetis; 'inscrutabile est' enim 'cor' hominis et 'quis cognoscet illud?'" *Robert of Flamborough: Liber Poenitentialis*, p. 54.

82. Lea, *History of Auricular Confession*, 2: 415.

83. Quoted and trans. by Tentler, *Sin and Confession*, pp. 91–92.

84. Quoted in Tentler, *Sin and Confession*, p. 88. See also James A. Brundage, *Law, Sex, and Christian Society in Medieval Europe* (Chicago: University of Chicago Press, 1980), p. 399. Nicholas of Lyra (d. 1349) is particularly concerned about confessors giving women "ideas for more adventurous sins" during confession, see Brundage, *Law, Sex*, p. 428.

85. *Robert of Flamborough*, ed. Firth, p. 196. See Brundage's discussion, *Law, Sex*, p. 399.

86. Lea, *History of Auricular Confession*, 1: 381.

87. Again, I am drawing from Michel de Certeau's discussion of the "problematics of secrecy," *Mystic Fable*, 1: 98.

88. Mirk, *Instruction for Parish Priests*, pp. 114, 147.

89. Quoted in Tentler, *Sin and Confession*, pp. 106–7. Tentler finds this same prescription in the works of St. Antoninus of Florence, Angelus de Clavasio, Sylvester Prierias, and Godescalc Rosemondt.

90. Quoted in Tentler, *Sin and Confession*, p. 109.

91. J.R.R. Tolkien, ed., *The Ancrene Wisse: The English Text of the Ancrene Riwle edited from MS. Corpus Christi College Cambridge 402*, EETS 249 (London: Oxford University Press, 1962), pp. 165–72.

92. See Tentler's discussion of this problem in *Sin and Confession*, p. 108.

93. *Mirk's Festial*, ed. Theodore Erbe, EETS, e.s. 96 (London: Kegan Paul, Trench, Trübner, 1905), p. 91. This story is followed by another like it of a man equally ashamed (pp. 92–93).

94. Robert Mannyng of Brunne, *Handlyng Synne*, pp. 351–86; *Book of Vices and Virtues*, pp. 173–81; Don Michel, *Ayenbit of Inwit or Remorse of Conscience*, ed. R. Morris, EETS o.s. 23 (London: Kegan Paul, Trench and Trübner, 1866), pp. 172–78; *Speculum Sacerdotale*, ed. Weatherly pp. 63–75.

95. *The Riverside Chaucer*, ed. Larry D. Benson, 3d ed (Boston: Houghton Mifflin, 1987).

96. *Speculum Sacerdotale*, ed. Weatherly, p. 66.

97. See Tentler, *Sin and Confession*, pp. 135–37. See also Lea, *History of Auricular Confession*, 1: 370–73.

98. See Tentler, *Sin and Confession*, p. 146. See also Lea's discussion of the problem of defining the two classes of sins, *History of Auricular Confession*, 2: 237–73.

99. Tentler, *Sin and Confession*, p. 154

100. Foucault, *History of Sexuality*, 1: 71.

101. This point is also made by Pierre Payer, "Foucault on Penance and the Shaping of Sexuality," pp. 313–20.

102. Thomas of Chobham, *Summa confessorum*, ed. Broomfield, pp. 330–404, as compared to the sins of Gluttony (pp. 405–13), Wrath (pp. 414–66), Avarice (pp. 487–534), Envy (pp. 535–36), Sloth (pp. 536–37), and Pride (pp. 537–58). For more on the subject of nocturnal emissions in Thomas and elsewhere, see Dyan Elliott, "Pollution, Illusion, and Masculine Disarray: Nocturnal Emissions and the Sexuality of the Clergy," in *Constructing Medieval Sexuality*, ed. Karma Lochrie, Peggy McCracken, and James A. Schultz (Minneapolis: University of Minnesota Press, 1997), pp.1–23.

103. Foucault, *History of Sexuality*, 1: 59.

104. Lee Patterson, *Chaucer and the Subject of History* (Madison: University of Wisconsin Press, 1991), p. 386. Patterson makes this remark in the course of his discussion of Chaucer's Pardoner's Prologue and Tale. See also his earlier essay, "Chaucerian Confession: Penitential Literature and the Pardoner," *Medievalia et Humanistica* 7 (1976): 153–73.

105. *Sir Gawain and the Green Knight*, in *The Complete Work of the Pearl Poet*, ed. Malcolm Andrew, Ronald Waldron, and Clifford Peterson, with facing translation by Casey Finch (Berkeley: University of California Press, 1993), ll. 2433–36. All quotations from this edition will appear in parentheses in the text hereafter; all translations are my own, unless otherwise noted.

106. Carolyn Dinshaw, "A Kiss Is Just a Kiss: Heterosexuality and Its Consolations in *Sir Gawain and the Green Knight*," *diacritics* 24, 2–3 (Summer–Fall 1994): 218.

107. See J. A. Burrow, *A Reading of Sir Gawain and the Green Knight* (New York: Barnes and Noble, 1966), pp. 122–63; Mary Flowers Braswell, *The Medieval Sinner: Characterization and Confession in the Literature of the English Middle Ages* (New York: Associated University Presses, 1982), pp. 95–100; A. C. Spearing, *The Gawain-Poet: A Critical Study* (Cambridge: Cambridge University Press, 1970), pp. 225–36.

108. I am borrowing a phrase from Geraldine Heng's incisive analysis of the poem, "A Woman Wants: The Lady, *Gawain*, and the Forms of Seduction," *Yale Journal of Criticism* 2/3 (1992): 104.

109. Burrow, *A Reading of Sir Gawain*, pp. 42, 104–6, 130–59. Spearing disputes Burrow's interpretation, citing the conflict between Gawain's dual commit-

ment to *clannesse* and *cortaysye* as the true dilemma of the poem, *Gawain-Poet*, pp. 205–9.

110. See Burrow, *Reading of Sir Gawain*, pp. 106–56, and Spearing, *Gawain-Poet*, pp. 225–30. Spearing argues against Burrows that Gawain fails to recognize his sin of covetousness as a sin and that is why he fails to confess it, not that he deliberately conceals it. For the idea of the incomplete confession, see also Braswell, *Medieval Sinner*, pp. 97–98.

111. See, for example, David Aers's critique of the "priestly caste" of scholars while at the same time recognizing a public/private split in consciousness that is key to the interpretations of those same scholars, " 'In Arthurus Day': Community, Virtue, and Individual Identity in *Sir Gawain and the Green Knight*," in *Community, Gender, and Individual Identity: English Writing, 1360–1430* (New York: Routledge, 1988), pp. 165–66, 169–77. Carolyn Dinshaw's analysis of the consolations of heterosexuality also depends upon Gawain's concealment of his winnings from Bertilak in "A Kiss Is Just a Kiss."

112. Dinshaw, "A Kiss Is Just a Kiss," p. 205.

113. Geraldine Heng provides an excellent analysis of the pleasures of speech about sex in this poem, particularly where it seems that Gawain is most resistant, "The Woman Wants," pp. 103–5. I am indebted to her examination of the seduction scenes — the "pull between pleasure and unpleasure" — and Gawain's identity crisis; she does not, however, consider the role that confession and the poetics of concealment play in this pleasurable discourse, as I do here.

114. For the connection between *ars erotica* and *scientia sexualis*, see Foucault, *History of Sexuality*, 1: 70. Heng also makes this distinction between discourse as the medium of desire and its object; see "A Woman Wants," p. 104. Foucault attributes this distinction to psychoanalysis, in which "speech is not merely the medium which manifests — or dissembles — desire; it is also the object of desire," *Archaeology of Knowledge and the Discourse on Language*, p. 216.

115. De Certeau, *Mystic Fable*, 1: 97–98.

116. Aers, " 'In Arthurus Day,' " pp. 162–65.

117. For an excellent analysis of Gawain's feminization, see especially Sheila Fisher, "Taken Men and Token Women in *Sir Gawain and the Green Knight*," in *Seeking the Woman in Late Medieval and Renaissance Writings: Essays in Feminist Contextual Criticism*, ed. Sheila Fisher and Janet E. Halley (Knoxville: University of Tennessee Press, 1989), pp. 71–105.

118. See, for example, the note on this passage in *Sir Gawain*, ed. Andrew, Waldron, and Peterson, 392n.

119. Heng describes the "flat narrative taciturnity" of the poem in "A Woman Wants," p. 107. I am indebted to her for this idea as well as for her description of narrative foreshortening in the poem.

120. Foucault, *History of Sexuality*, 1: 45.

121. For a discussion of the crisis in heterosexual identity produced by these exchanges, see Dinshaw, "A Kiss Is Just a Kiss," 215–19.

122. Burrow explains this passage, which seems to contradict his analysis of the penitential message of the poem, by distinguishing between the harm of the belt

itself and the hiding of it and between the sin and the memory of the sin. It is a strained and finally unconvincing argument, *Reading of Sir Gawain*, pp. 154–56.

123. Fisher and Dinshaw note this move in the poem towards the feminizing of the flesh. See Fisher, "Taken Men and Token Women," p. 94 and "A Kiss Is Just a Kiss," p. 219.

124. For these interpretations, see Burrow, *Reading of Sir Gawain*, p. 158; Johnson, *Voice of the Gawain-Poet*, p. 91; Aers, "'In Arthurus' Day,'" pp. 176–78.

125. Margo Jefferson, "Facing Incest, in Memoir and Novel," *New York Times*, 29 May 1997, natl. ed.: B7.

Chapter 2

1. Patricia Meyer Spacks, *Gossip* (New York: Knopf, 1985), p. 263. I have benefited greatly from Spacks's marvelously suggestive book on gossip, particularly her first two chapters elaborating its operations.

2. *The Riverside Chaucer*, 3d ed., ed. Larry D. Benson (Boston: Houghton Mifflin, 1987), p. 11.

3. Two important socio-linguistic studies of women's gossip are Deborah Jones, "Gossip: Notes on Women's Oral Culture," in *The Feminist Critique of Language: A Reader*, ed. Deborah Cameron (London: Routledge, 1990), pp. 193–98; and a critique and expansion of Jones by Jennifer Coates, "Gossip Revisited: Language in All-Female Groups," in *Women in Their Speech Communities: New Perspectives in Language and Sex*, ed. Jennifer Coates and Deborah Cameron (London: Longman, 1988), pp. 94–122.

4. Jan B. Gordon, *Gossip and Subversion in Nineteenth-Century British Fiction* (New York: St. Martin's Press, 1996), p. 71. My own analysis of gossip is indebted to Gordon's, although I am more interested in its significance for gender than Gordon is.

5. Recent studies include Deborah Jones, "Gossip"; Jennifer Coates, "Gossip Revisited"; and Jörg R. Bergmann, *Discreet Indiscretions: The Social Organization of Gossip*, trans. John Bednarz, Jr. (New York: Aldine de Gruyter, 1993). Bergmann summarizes the neglect of studies of gossip in anthropology, sociology, and linguistics, pp. 1–41.

6. Spacks makes this statement about gossip as a literary phenomenon with a view towards the "subversive implications" of gossip in *Gossip*, p.12. I am also interested in gossip's potential for subversion, but I think it is important first to consider how gossip often serves "our culture's dominant values" as well as posing a challenge to it.

7. I am borrowing the language of Teresa de Lauretis in *Technologies of Gender: Essays on Theory, Film, and Fiction* (Bloomington: Indiana University Press, 1987), to describe the possible positioning of feminist discourse in the "elsewhere" of the present: "the blind spots, or the space-off, of its representations. I think of it as spaces in the margins of hegemonic discourses, social spaces carved in the interstices of institutions and in the chinks and cracks of the power-knowledge apparati.

And it is there that the terms of a different construction of gender can be posed" (p. 25).

8. Spacks, *Gossip*, p. 22. The observations of this paragraph summarize some important ideas in Spacks's first chapter on the problematics of gossip. I only want to reserve from her analysis my own contentions about official uses of gossip apart from the subversive uses she implies throughout her analysis.

9. This is a term I have borrowed from Eve Kosofsky Sedgwick, who argues that it "can be harnessed, licensed, and regulated on a mass scale for striking enforcements," for example, in rape laws, where men and ignorance are privileged, *Epistemology of the Closet* (Berkeley: University of California Press, 1990), pp. 5–8. Privileged unknowing is especially visible in contemporary constructions of sexuality. See Sedgwick's discussion of this idea in "Privileges of Unknowing : Diderot's *The Nun*," in *Tendencies* (Durham, N.C.: Duke University Press, 1993), pp. 23–51. The idea that secrecy protects not knowledge but the knowledge of a knowledge is further discussed in D. A. Miller, *The Novel and the Police* (Berkeley: University of California Press, 1988), p. 206, and Sedgwick, "Privilege of Unknowing," p. 31. I have also discussed this policy in my essay "Don't Ask, Don't Tell: Murderous Plots and Medieval Secrets," in *Premodern Sexualities*, ed. Louise Fradenburg and Carla Freccero (New York: Routledge, 1996), pp. 137–40, 147–52. For a summary of the policy, see "Text of Pentagon's New Policy Guidelines on Homosexuals in the Military," *New York Times*, 20 July 1993, A12.

10. Spacks, *Gossip*, p. 5.

11. In her pioneering essay "Notes on Camp," Susan Sontag states that camp is a strategy for homosexual integration within the heterosexual community and that, as a "sensibility," it is "disengaged, depoliticized, or at least apolitical," *Against Interpretation and Other Essays* (New York: Dell, 1966), pp. 279, 289. For a more recent discussion of camp that disagrees with Sontag's view, see *Camp Grounds: Style and Homosexuality*, ed. David Bergman (Amherst: University of Massachusetts Press, 1993).

12. Miller, *The Novel and the Police*, p. 207.

13. The idea of epistemological transparency is developed in Rita Goldberg's study of the Suzanne in Diderot's *The Nun* appearing in *Sex and Enlightenment: Women in Richardson and Diderot* (Cambridge: Cambridge University Press, 1984), p. 194. She uses the term to describe Suzanne's desire to know the world's secrets, while I use it to describe the condition of gay subjectivity with respect to heterosexual privilege.

14. Spacks, *Gossip*, pp. 8, 6, 5–6.

15. Ibid., p. 3.

16. Martin Heidegger, *Being and Time*, trans. John Macquarrie and Edward Robinson (New York: Harper and Row, 1962), p. 212. For other discussions of Heidegger's view of "idle talk," see Gordon, *Gossip and Subversion*, p. 351. Spacks compares Heidegger's view with Kierkegaard's, which likewise indicts the triviality of gossip, see *Gossip*, pp. 17–18.

17. For a full study of the sociology of gossip, see Bergmann, *Discreet Indiscretions*. In fact, Bergmann disputes attempts such as Heidegger's to contrast norma-

tive conversation with gossip because they often fail to recognize the function, performance, and purpose of gossip as a mode of conversation; see pp. 1–41.

18. Heidegger, *Being and Time*, pp. 212–13. Spacks says that Heidegger "ignores a set of possibilities crucial to [a] full understanding of gossip," *Gossip*, p. 17.

19. Spacks argues that "surfaces are not superficial" and that Heidegger ignores the significant intimacies that gossip engenders, *Gossip*, p.17. In its aesthetics of the surface as against the depth model of identity and epistemology, gossip resembles camp; see Jonathan Dollimore, *Sexual Dissidence: Augustine to Wilde, Freud to Foucault* (Oxford: Clarendon Press, 1991), p. 311.

20. Spacks, *Gossip*, p. 6; the author also delineates a continuum of such functions, including malice (the least common), idle talk, and "serious" gossip that serves the purpose of creating intimacy between two people (pp. 4–6). She acknowledges the protean nature of gossip, that is, its ready modulation from one function to another (p. 6).

21. Chaucer draws upon Boethius's *Consolation of Philosophy*, trans. V. E. Watts (Baltimore: Penguin Books, 1969), III. 12, for the first idea quoted and attributed to Plato in the General Prologue (I.741–42); the second may be found expressed throughout the *Canterbury Tales*, particularly in the prologue to the Tale of Melibee and the Retraction. Of course, Chaucer is always challenging these ideas of the relationship of language to deeds, intentions, and meaning, as in the Pardoner's Tale.

22. Spacks, *Gossip*, p. 15.

23. See my discussion of the Miller's Tale in Chapter 4; Luce Irigaray, *This Sex Which Is Not One*, trans. Catherine Porter (Ithaca, N.Y.: Cornell University Press, 1985), pp. 170–97; and Clare A. Lees's analysis of Lady Meed in "Gender and Exchange in *Piers Plowman*," in *Class and Gender in Early English Literature: Intersections*, ed. Britton J. Harwood and Gillian R. Overing (Bloomington: Indiana University Press, 1994), pp.112–30.

24. Spacks writes that the fascination gossip elicits "bears some relation to that of pornography." She links gossip's effects to the erotic through its voyeurism, its titillation, and the "secret knowledge" it imparts, *Gossip*, p. 11.

25. Sigmund Freud, *Three Essays on the Theory of Sexuality*, vol. 7 of *The Standard Edition of the Complete Psychological Works of Sigmund Freud*, trans. James Strachey et al. (London: Hogarth Press, 1962), 7: 150.

26. For Freud's theory of the voyeur's scopophilia, see *Three Essays*, 7: 156–57.

27. Roland Barthes, *Roland Barthes*, trans. Richard Howard (New York: Hill and Wang, 1977), p. 169.

28. Quoted in J. R. Owst, *Literature and the Pulpit in Medieval England* (New York: Barnes and Noble, 1961), p. 456.

29. Foucault speaks of this proliferation of discourses "carefully tailored to the requirements of power" about sex in *History of Sexuality*, Vol. 1: *An Introduction*, trans. Robert Hurley (New York: Vintage, 1990), p. 72.

30. Spacks claims that the word does not become attached to women until the mid-eighteenth century, but she is wrong on this point. See her etymological discussion, *Gossip*, pp. 25–26.

31. *Middle English Dictionary*, ed. Hans Kurath and Sherman M. Kuhn (Ann Arbor: University of Michigan Press, 1968), J: 368–70.

32. Ibid., C: 294–95.

33. Ibid., B: 616.

34. *Piers Plowman: The B Version*, ed. George Kane and E. Talbot Donaldson (London: Athlone, 1975), passus 5: 87–88. All quotations are from this edition.

35. William Langland, *Will's Vision of Piers Plowman*, ed., Elizabeth D. Kirk and Judith H. Anderson, trans. E. Talbot Donaldson (New York: Norton, 1990), p. 44.

36. Langland, *Will's Vision of Piers Plowman*, p. 219.

37. John Mirk, *Mirk's Festial*, ed. Theodor Erbe, EETS 96 (London: Kegan Paul, Trench, Trübner, 1905), pp. 279–80.

38. For a discussion of Tutivillus in medieval drama, see G. R. Owst, *Literature and the Pulpit*, pp. 512–20.

39. For the exempla of Tutivillus as the accuser of negligent priests, see *The Exempla or Illustrative Stories from the "Sermones vulgares" of Jacques de Vitry*, ed. T. F. Crane, Folklore Society, vol. 26, no. 19 (London, 1890), pp. 6, 141.

40. Robert Mannyng of Brunne, *Handlyng synne*, ed. F.J. Furnivall, EETS 119, 123 (London: Kegan Paul, Trench, and Trübner, 1901–3), pp. 290–92; William Caxton, trans., *The Book of the Knight of the Tower*, ed. M. Y. Offord, EETS 217 (London: Oxford University Press, 1971), pp. 49–50. Yet another version in Caxton's text has the fiend attending to knights, squires, and ladies (pp. 48–49).

41. The Last Judgment (Wakefield) in *Medieval Drama*, ed. David Bevington (Boston: Houghton Mifflin, 1975), p. 643.

42. Woodburn O. Ross, ed., *Middle English Sermons*, EETS, o.s. 209 (London: Oxford University Press, 1960), p. 233.

43. Ross, ed., *Middle English Sermons*, pp. 24, 300. Another account of envious speech may be found in *Peter Idley's Instructions to His Son*, ed. Charlotte D'Evelyn (London: Oxford University Press, 1935), pp. 171–72.

44. Caxton, *Book of the Knight*, p. 106.

45. Ibid., p. 191.

46. *Peter Idley's Instructions*, p. 210, ll. 414–20.

47. Genius condemns the revealing of secrets to women in *The Roman de la Rose*, by Guillaume de Lorris and Jean de Meun, trans. Charles Dahlberg, 16322–16616. For the Wife of Bath's retelling of the Midas story, see *Riverside Chaucer*, ed. Benson, III.952–82.

48. I am quoting from "The Gossips," ed. James E. Masters (Shaftesbury, Dorset: High House Press, 1926). An earlier edition of the poem entitled "Good Gossipis Mine" appears in *Songs, Carols, and Other Miscellaneous Poems*, ed. Roman Dyboski, EETS 101 (London: Kegan Paul, Trench, Trübner, 1907), pp. 106–8. No specific date is given for this poem, but it exists in a manuscript that was compiled gradually ending in 1536. It is interesting that in the earlier version, the poem constructs a dialogue between two gossips, whereas in the Masters edition, this dialogue has been lost, and the result is that the substance of the gossips' conversation is overheard. Another key difference is that the earlier edition ends two stanzas before the Masters edition, and these two stanzas are crucial to the masculine perspective of the later version of the poem, as I will show.

49. "The Gossips," ed. Masters, p. 5. All further citations in the text are to this edition.

50. Jacques Derrida, "'To Do Justice to Freud': The History of Madness in the Age of Psychoanalysis," trans. Pascale-Anne Brault and Michael Naas, *Critical Inquiry* 20 (Winter 1994): 245. My quotation is a bit unfair to Derrida because it appears as his summary of Foucault's idea of the secret as it functions in psychoanalysis, and he is critical of Foucault's analysis. I only want, however, to use the ideas about secrecy that Derrida characterizes as Foucault's.

51. Spacks briefly discusses the speaker's placating tone at the end of the poem "lest women speak evil of men" and the "uneasy perception that something significant happens in gatherings of gossips," *Gossips*, pp. 35, 36.

52. The context for Foucault's discussion of this type of secrecy is the work of the writer Raymond Roussel in *Death and the Labyrinth: The World of Raymond Roussel*, trans. Charles Ruas (New York: Doubleday, 1986), p. 3. I am adapting Foucault's discussion to the gendered issue of women's gossip.

53. I am borrowing Eve Kosofsky Sedgwick's term "epistemological enforcement," although I am using it differently than she does in her analysis of sexual ignorance in Denis Diderot's novel *La Religieuse*, "Privilege of Unknowing," p. 48. She also discusses the cultural regime of the ignorance/knowledge binary logic in *Epistemology of the Closet*, pp. 1–12, 67–78. My analysis here as elsewhere in this book is indebted to her writing on the subjects of secrecy and the closet.

54. I am borrowing Domna C. Stanton's idea of recuperation in her analysis of sixteenth-century texts on women's gossip, "Recuperating Women and the Man Behind the Screen," in *Sexuality and Gender in Early Modern Europe: Institutions, Texts, Images*, ed. James Grantham Turner (Cambridge: Cambridge University Press, 1993), pp. 247–65.

55. Sedgwick, *Epistemology of the Closet*, p. 4; there is a mistake in the word order of this sentence that I have corrected. Part of the statement also appears at the beginning of her essay, "Privilege of Unknowing," p. 23.

56. See Foucault, *History of Sexuality*, 1: 27. For Sedgwick's analogy with secrecy, see *Epistemology of the Closet*, p. 3.

57. Sedgwick points out the "labor-intensive ignorance" of the main character Suzanne in Diderot's *The Nun* in "Privilege of Unknowing," p. 29.

58. Gesse M. Gellrich, *The Idea of the Book in the Middle Ages* (Ithaca, N.Y.: Cornell University Press, 1986), p. 169. This is also the view of Jacqueline T. Miller, *Poetic License: Authority and Authorship in Medieval and Renaissance Contexts* (New York: Oxford University Press, 1982), pp. 35–72. J. A. W. Bennett calls the poem "a vindication of poetry," *Chaucer's* Book of Fame (Oxford: Clarendon Press, 1968), p. xi; and Piero Boitani sees the poem as embodying Chaucer's idea of literature and literature's relationship to language and reality, *Chaucer and the Imaginary World of Fame* (Cambridge: D. S. Brewer, 1984), p.189. See also John M. Fyler's comments in the introduction to the poem in *Riverside Chaucer*, ed. Benson, p. 348.

59. Elaine Tuttle Hansen, *Chaucer and the Fictions of Gender* (Berkeley: University of California Press, 1992), p. 91. Hansen also asks what the narrator's "resemblance" to Dido means in the context of the poem, but this is a question I am less interested in because I do not see the narrator as in danger of being feminized, as Hansen does.

60. For example, see Sheila Delaney's argument for Chaucer's "skeptical fideism" that "grants the validity of conflicting truths and confronts the problem with no way of deciding between them" and that is exemplified in the narrator's doubt and confusion, *Chaucer's* House of Fame: *The Poetics of Skeptical Fideism* (Chicago: University of Chicago Press, 1972). See also John M. Fyler's argument that the poem poses the "limits of human understanding" in the narrator's unknowing, *Chaucer and Ovid* (New Haven, Conn.: Yale University Press, 1979), pp. 23, 27. Gellrich sees the conflicting views in the poems as part of Chaucer's effort to replace *auctores* and *auctoritas* with the voice of his text, *Idea of the Book*, pp. 170–200. Only Hansen suggests that the narrator's deferral of knowledge has links with the gender ideology of the poem, *Chaucer and the Fictions of Gender*, pp. 98–100, but again, she views this as part of the narrator's feminization.

61. In particular, see Jill Mann's argument for Chaucer's "acute sensitivity to his own responsibilities as a poet towards women," *Geoffrey Chaucer* (Atlantic Highlands, N.J.: Humanities Press, 1991), pp. 7–8. Hansen goes so far as to see a dangerous identification with Dido in the narrator's sympathy, *Chaucer and the Fictions of Gender*, pp. 100–101.

62. Spacks, *Gossip*, p. 233.

63. Hansen, *Chaucer and the Fictions of Gender*, p. 95. Hansen further argues that Geffrey identifies with Dido and is thus in danger of being feminized (pp. 98–101).

64. "Nec iam furtivum Dido meditatur amorem: / coniugium vocat; hoc praetexit nomine culpam" (IV.171–72). Quoted in Fyler, *Chaucer and Ovid*, p. 35. See also Bennett, *Chaucer's* Book of Fame, p. 34. Gellrich argues in *The Idea of the Book in the Middle Ages* that Aeneas's "heroism and duty are not forgotten or nullified; they exist in conflict with the portrait of him rendered by Ovid's Dido as callous betrayer" (p. 71).

65. For example, see Caxton, trans., *Book of the Knight of the Tower*, pp. 150–52, 165–68. Spacks also makes this connection between Dido's speech and the Knight's instruction on women's reputations, *Gossip*, p. 32.

66. Bennett shows how Virgil distinguishes the two types of fame in the *Aeneid*—*fama* (rumor) and *laus* (renown)—that Chaucer later develops in Book III; see *Chaucer's* Book of Fame, p. 39.

67. For example, see Gellrich's view that the art "is its own authority," *Idea of the Book*. pp. 198–99, and Miller's claim that it expresses "faith in self as artist," *Poetic License*, p. 64. Boitani notes that the passage both "limits the extent to which he knows his art" and expresses the "quiet self-assurance" of the poet, *Chaucer and the Imaginary World of Fame*, p. 207.

68. Britton J. Harwood, "Building Class and Gender into Chaucer's *Hous*" in *Class and Gender in Early English Literature*, ed. Britton J. Harwood and Gillian R. Overing (Bloomington: Indiana University Press, 1994), p. 98. Harwood's claim contrasts with the view of most scholars that the poem contests poetry against written authority. He is also the only critic I have read to link the portrait of Fame to that of Lady Meed (p.100), as I also hope to do.

69. See William Langland, *Piers Plowman: The B Version*, 3.122. 3.40–41. Harwood also notes the resemblance between Meed and Fame, "Building Class and

Gender into Chaucer's *Hous*," p.100. Hansen links Fame's femininity to "the paradoxical representation of women in Chaucer . . . and more generally in medieval culture," *Chaucer and the Fictions of Gender*, p.104n.

70. See Clare A. Lees, "Gender and Exchange," pp. 112–30.

71. Mann, *Geoffrey Chaucer*, p. 16. Mann goes on to say that Chaucer recuperates "the living individual" from this reduction, a reading I disagree with because Dido *is* her lament in Book I, and the narrator merely confirms her appropriation by gossip.

72. Bennett also notes the connection between these two allusions, *Chaucer's* Book of Fame, pp. 167–68.

73. Bennett, *Chaucer's* Book of Fame, p. 186.

74. Spacks describes the power of gossip to forge a "unity of talkers" and to create its own authority, *Gossip*, p. 212.

75. Spacks, *Gossip*, p. 233. Where I have inserted "poetry," Spacks uses "fiction."

76. I am paraphrasing Spacks: "The elevation of gossip to an expression of communal myth-making pays tribute to speech's unpredictability" (*Gossip*, p. 233).

77. William Eamon, *Science and the Secrets of Nature: Books of Secrets in Medieval and Early Modern Culture* (Princeton, N.J.: Princeton University Press, 1994), p. 44.

Chapter 3

1. Quoted from the catalogue for the Center for African Art's 1993 exhibit, "Secrecy: African Art That Conceals and Reveals," in Holland Cotter's review, "Discovering Secrets, Africa's Currency of Power," *New York Times*, 12 February 1976, Sec. B, p. 6, cols. 1–4. I should note that the quotation occurs in the context of the elder's statement to a tribal fraternity, not an audience of Western anthropologists, and the exhibit's focus on secrecy was designed to "consider the notion of secrecy itself, with its combination of discretion and self-aggrandizement and its tendency to set up social boundaries" (B6, col. 2). In addition, the review contrasts this exhibit's study of secrecy in African culture with Western imperializing habits of representing Africa as a secret.

2. Michel de Certeau, *The Mystic Fable*, Vol. 1, *The Sixteenth and Seventeenth Centuries*, trans. Michael B. Smith (Chicago: University of Chicago Press, 1992), p. 97. De Certeau's analysis of the "problematics of secrecy" is chiefly concerned with his description of the new meaning of mysticism in the sixteenth and seventeenth centuries. My own analysis of secrecy in this chapter is indebted to de Certeau's brilliant commentary on its operations in mystical discourse.

3. I am borrowing de Certeau's analysis of this "elementary structure" of secrecy, *Mystic Fable*, 1: 98. Michel Foucault describes a very different structure of power and dynamic in the act of confession, where the one who knows is obligated to speak to the one who does not. It is the latter, rather than the former, who holds the power in this case. See Michel Foucault, *The History of Sexuality*, Vol. 1, *An Introduction*, trans. Robert Hurley (New York: Vintage Books, 1990), pp. 61–65. See Chapter 1 for my discussion of Foucault's analysis of the use of secrecy in connection with confessional discourse.

4. Foucault, *History of Sexuality*, 1: 57–58.

5. De Certeau characterizes the secret as "a something which *is* without *appearing*." Thus, "it is dangerously close to the lie or fiction" (*Mystic Fable*, 1: 98). The hidden become "caught up in the labyrinthian relations of the fictions they produce with the realities they conceal." I have shortened his phrase to "labyrinthian fictions."

6. De Certeau, *Mystic Fable*, 1: 98.

7. De Certeau characterizes the force with which the assertion of a secret "imposes" itself on someone else: "It is an address: it repels, attracts, or binds the interlocutors; it is addressed to someone and acts upon him," *Mystic Fable*, 1: 98.

8. De Certeau, *Mystic Fable*, 1: 98.

9. De Certeau discusses the traps of language and recourse to authority in *Mystic Fable*, 1: 98–99.

10. The words of Georg Simmel, quoted in Sissela Bok, *Secrets: On the Ethics of Concealment and Revelation* (New York: Vintage Books, 1989), p. 36.

11. Foucault cautions us to think of silence as permeating discourses, rather than functioning as their limit, *History of Sexuality*, 1: 27. Eve Kosofsky Sedgwick also views silence as a kind of speech act in the case of closetedness, *Epistemology of the Closet* (Berkeley: University of California Press, 1990), p. 3.

12. Sedgwick describes the closet as "the defining structure for gay oppression in this century, *Epistemology of the Closet*, p. 71. I think that secrecy constitutes an analogous defining structure, as I have discussed in my Introduction.

13. *History of Sexuality*, 1: 72.

14. Roger Bacon, *Opus Majus*, 2 vols., trans. Robert Belle Burke (New York: Russell and Russell, 1962), 1: 11–12. For a discussion of this passage and Bacon's reading of the *Secret of Secrets*, see William Eamon, *Science and the Secrets of Nature: Books of Secrets in Medieval and Early Modern Culture* (Princeton, N.J.: Princeton University Press, 1994), pp. 45–53. Eamon's work is one of the first to undertake a serious study of the books of secrets, and I am indebted to it.

15. Eamon concludes that this is the agenda of the *Secret of Secrets*, and he speculates that this would have served the ideology of ruling classes and late-medieval intellectuals, *Science and the Secrets of Nature*, pp. 49–50.

16. Bacon, *Opus Majus*, 2: 621.

17. Steele dates Bacon's edition sometime before 1257, but recently Steven J. Williams has challenged Steele's dating and has argued instead for a later date of ca. 1270 to ca. 1292 in "Roger Bacon and His Edition of the Pseudo-Aristotelian *Secretum secretorum*," *Speculum* 69 (1994): 57–63. Speculation about why Bacon was so keen on the treatise varies. See Williams's summary of the views of Bacon's biographers (pp. 64–65). Eamon offers a new argument on the subject that Bacon valued the treatise for its reliance on experimentation, *Science and the Secrets of Nature*, pp. 45–53.

18. Eamon, *Science and the Secrets of Nature*, p. 45; and Eamon, "Books of Secrets in Medieval and Early Modern Science," *Sudhoffs Archiv* 69 (1985): 26. Lynn Thorndike calls it the "most widely influential upon the medieval mind of all the spurious works attributed to Aristotle," in *A History of Magic and Experimental Science* (New York: Macmillan, 1923), 2: 267.

19. See Eamon, *Science and the Secrets of Nature*, pp. 45–46; Lynn Thorndike,

History of Magic and Experimental Science, 2: 267; and W. F. Ryan and Charles B. Schmitt, eds., *Pseudo-Aristotle: The* Secret of Secrets: *Sources and Influences* (London: Warburg Institute, 1982), p. 2. The English versions have been edited by Robert Steele, *Three Prose Versions of the Secreta Secretorum*, EETS, e.s. 74 (London, 1898), and by M. A. Manzalaoui, *Secretum Secretorum: Nine English Versions*, vol. 1, EETS 276 (Oxford: Oxford University Press, 1977).

20. For example, see the fifteenth-century poem edited by Robert Steele, *Lydgate and Burgh's Secrees of Old Philosoffres*, EETS, e.s. 66 (London, 1884), and Piere d'Abernum's thirteenth-century poem, *Le Secre de Secrez*, in Steele, ed., *Opera hactenus inedita Rogeri Baconi* (Oxford: Oxford University Press, 1920), pp. 287–313.

21. Roger Bacon, *Secretum secretorum cum glossis et notulis*, vol. 5 of *Opera hactenus inedita Rogeri Baconi*, ed. Robert Steele (Oxford: Oxford University Press, 1920), p. 1. Stewart C. Easton claims in his biography of Bacon that the *Secret of Secrets* was "the most influential in his whole life, the book which perhaps more than anything else turned him from his life of philosophy to a study of natural science," *Roger Bacon and His Search for a Universal Science* (New York: Columbia University Press, 1952), pp. 24, 81.This was not Bacon's reason for promoting the work. According to Eamon, he saw in the treatise the foundation of experimental science, *Science and the Secrets of Nature*, pp. 47–48.

22. Eamon, *Science and the Secrets of Nature*, p. 44.

23. For an overview of this tradition first in Hellenistic culture and later in Arab culture, see Eamon, *Science and the Secrets of Nature*, pp. 16–45.

24. William Eamon, "From the Secrets of Nature to Public Knowledge," *Minerva* 23, 3 (Fall 1985): 323. Michael Scot, for example, draws upon the *Secret of Secrets* for his own treatise on *Physionomia*. See Danielle Jacquart and Claude Thomasset, *Sexuality and Medicine in the Middle Ages*, trans. Matthew Adamson (Princeton, N.J.: Princeton University Press, 1988), pp.143–44. For the tendency of medieval science to minimize its debt to Arab science, see Brian Stock, "Science, Technology, and Economic Progress in the Middle Ages," in *Science in the Middle Ages*, ed. David C. Lindberg (Chicago: University of Chicago Press, 1978), p. 12. For the roots of transmission of Arabic science to the West, see David C. Lindberg, "The Transmission of Greek and Arabic Learning to the West," in *Science in the Middle Ages*, pp. 52–90; and Charles H. Haskins, *Studies in the History of Mediaeval Science* (Cambridge, Mass: Harvard University Press, 1927).

25. Manzalaoui, ed., *Secretum Secretorum*, p. ix. Ryan and Schmitt consider the existence of a Greek original to be doubtful even though the Arabic texts contain "a good deal of Greek material," *Pseudo-Aristotle: The* Secret of Secrets: *Sources and Influences*, p.1. The Arabic text has been edited (see Manzalaoui, p. ix). Ismail Ali has produced a modern English translation of the Arabic in *Opera hactenus inedita Rogeri Baconi*, fasc. 5, pp. 176–283.

26. The short version survives in 150 manuscripts, while the long version exists in 350 manuscripts. See Manzalaoui's introduction to this English edition of the *Secretum Secretorum*, pp. xiv–xvi; Steele's introduction to Bacon's edition, *Secretum secretorum cum glossis et notulis*, pp. ix–xiv; and Eamon, *Science and the Secrets of Nature*, pp. 45–46. For a study of the evolution of the Arabic text, see M. Grignaschi, "L'Origine et les Métamorphoses du 'Sirr-Al-Asrâr,'" *Archives d'Histoire Doc-*

trinale et Littéraire du Moyen Age 43 (1976): 7–112, and "La Diffusion du 'Secretum Secretorum' (Sirr-Al-'Asrar) dans l'Europe occidentale," *Archives d'Histoire Doctrinale et Littéraire du Moyen Age* 47 (1980): 7–70.

27. The Latin version of the letter, *Epistola Alexandri ad Aristotelem*, was produced by Julius Valerius from the Greek Pseudo-Callisthenes. The popular medieval version of this letter that was translated into Old English was *Epistola Alexandri Macedonis ad Aristotelem magistrum suum de itinere suo et de situ Indiae*. For an overview of this tradition, see George Cary, *The Medieval Alexander* (Cambridge: Cambridge University Press, 1956), pp.14–16; and Dorothee Metlitzki, *The Matter of Araby in Medieval England* (New Haven, Conn.: Yale University Press, 1977), pp. 106–11. The Old English version is edited in Stanley Rypins, ed., *Three Old English Prose Texts*, EETS, e.s. 161 (London: Oxford University Press, 1924).

28. This is from the Arabic version, which differs from the Latin only its addition of the Persian ambition to rule, Bacon, *Secretum Secretorum*, ed. Steele, p. 177.

29. Bacon, *Secretum Secretorum*, ed. Steele, p. 40: "Preterea quod interrogasti et scire desideras est archanum tale quod humana pectora vix poterunt tollerare; quomodo ergo possunt in mortalibus pellibus depingi? Ad illud itaque quod te decet inquirere et mihi licitum est tractare, me oportet et teneor ex debito respondere, sicut tu teneris ex debito discreciones non exigere a me amplius ex hoc secreto quod tibi tradidi in hoc libro." All translations from the Latin are my own.

30. Bacon, *Secretum Secretorum*, ed. Steele, p. 41: "Causa quidem subest quare tibi figurative revelo secretum meum, loquens tecum exemplis enigmaticis atque signis, quia timeo nimium ne liber presencium ad manus deveniat infidelium et ad potestatem arrogancium, et sic perveniat ad illos ultimum bonum et archanum divinum, ad quod summus Deus illos judicavit immeritos et indignos."

31. The translation of the full title is given in Manzalaoui, ed., *Secretum Secretorum*, p. 1, and somewhat differently, in Metlitzki, *The Matter of Araby*, p.106.

32. See Chapter 1, where I discuss Foucault's theory about this interdependent obligation in connection with confession, Foucault, *History of Sexuality*, 1.

33. Sissela Bok discusses this intimacy and the dynamic of insider- and outsidership in *Secrets*, pp. 6–7.

34. Jacquart and Thomasset, *Sexuality and Medicine in the Middle Ages*, p.127. I should note, however, that Jacquart and Thomasset do not make the connections with Western scientific discourse that I am making here. Their description circumscribes the tradition of Arabic treatises on love and sexuality, pp. 87–138.

35. The Arabic version consists of ten discourses, which Bacon in his Latin edition grouped into parts. See Robert Steele, *Liber Secreti Secretorum Aristotilis ad regem Alexanderem*, vol. 5 of *Opera hactenus inedita Rogeri Baconi*, pp. 25–172. Not all versions contain these four sections. In addition, some contain an added section on alchemy (see Steele's edition).

36. Richard Kieckhefer places this text in the tradition of medieval magic, *Magic in the Middle Ages* (Cambridge: Cambridge University Press, 1990), pp. 140–44.

37. Or, as Judith Ferster puts it, "either the book is not really the secret of secrets, or it is unreadable," *Fictions of Advice: The Literature and Politics of Counsel in Late Medieval England* (Philadelphia: University of Pennsylvania Press, 1996), p. 49.

38. Evelyn Fox Keller, *Secrets of Life, Secrets of Death: Essays on Language, Gender and Science* (New York: Routledge, 1992), p. 40.

39. See Keller, *Secrets of Life, Secrets of Death*, pp. 15–72; and Evelyn Fox Keller, "Making Gender Visible," in *Feminist Studies/Critical Studies*, ed. Teresa de Lauretis (Bloomington: Indiana University Press, 1986), pp. 67–77.

40. Eamon, *Science and the Secrets of Nature*, p. 79.

41. The standard study of Natura's representation in the Middle Ages is that of George D. Economou, *The Goddess Natura in Medieval Literature* (Cambridge, Mass.: Harvard University Press, 1972); Carolyn Dinshaw shows how a similar feminine figure of the text is used to create a masculine poetics in *Chaucer's Sexual Poetics* (Madison: University of Wisconsin Press, 1989), pp. 3–27.

42. For secrecy in the medieval guilds, see Eamon, *Science and the Secrets of Nature*, pp. 81–82; George Unwin, *Gilds and Companies of London*, 4th ed. (New York: Barnes and Noble, 1964); and Pamela O. Long, "Invention, Authorship, 'Intellectual Property,' and the Origin of Patents: Notes Toward a Conceptual History," *Technology and Culture* 32 (1991): 846–84. I discuss guild secrecy more fully in Chapter 4.

43. See Foucault, *History of Sexuality*, 1: 61; for a discussion of this idea in medieval confession, see Chapter 1 of this book.

44. Bacon, *Secretum Secretorum*, ed. Steele, p. 60: "O Alexander recola factum regine Indorum, quando tibi mandavit causa amicicie multa xennia et dona venusta, inter que missa fuit illa venustissima puella que ab infancia imbuta et nutrita fuit veneno serpentum, ita quod de sua natura conversa fuit in naturam serpentum. Et nisi ego illa hora diligenter inspexissem in ipsam, et arte judicassem de puella, eo quod ita audacter et horribiliter et incessabiliter et inverecunde suum figebat visum in facie hominum, perpendi siquidem quod interfeceret homines solo morsu vel visu, quod tu experimento post probavisti."

45. Ibid., p. 192.

46. See Bacon, *Secretum Secretorum*, ed. Steele, pp. 60–62 and Manzalaoui, ed., *Secretum Secretorum*, pp. 46, 142, 330.

47. Cary claims that one of the chief purposes of the treatise is to teach kings to rely on their philosophers, *The Medieval Alexander*, pp.105–10.

48. Claude Thomasset summarizes the variations on the "la pucelle venimeuse" in the *Secret of Secrets* and a related text that I will discuss later in this chapter, *Placides et Timéo, une vision du monde à la fin du XIIIe siècle: Commentaire du Dialogue de Placides et Timéo* (Geneva: Droz, 1982), pp. 76–108. He points out that the Latin differs from the Arabic and Hebrew (and other versions) in this feature of the mortal female gaze (p. 81).

49. Bacon, *Secretum Secretorum*, ed. Steele, p.191; for the Hebrew account, see Thomasset, *Commentaire du Dialogue*, p. 76.

50. Thomasset, *Commentaire du Dialogue*, p. 81: "C'est précisément au XIIIe siècle que semble s'établir une tradition qui prête aux vieilles femmes un regard maléfique. La rétention du sang menstruel infecte le corps, se porte sur les yeux et leur communique un pouvoir mortel." My translation.

51. See Aristotle, *On Dreams*, in *On the Soul, Parva naturalia, On Breath*, ed. and trans. W. S. Hett (Cambridge, Mass.: Harvard University Press, 1957), II:

459b 28–31; and Pliny, *Natural History*, ed. and trans. H. Rackham, W. H. S. Jones, and D. E. Eicholz, Loeb Classical Library (Cambridge, Mass.: Harvard University Press, 1938–62), 7: vi–xiv. See also Janice Delaney, Mary Jane Lupton, and Emily Toth, *The Curse: A Cultural History of Menstruation*, rev. ed. (Urbana: University of Illinois Press, 1988), pp. 45–46.

52. Albert the Great, *Questiones super De Animalibus* in *Alberti Magni Opera Omnia* ed. E. Filthaut, vol. 9 (Münster: Aschendorff, 1955), 9: Q9. For further discussion of this idea, see Jacquart and Thomasset, *Sexuality and Medicine*, pp. 74–78.

53. For a few summaries of this idea in psychoanalytic theory, see Judith Butler, *Gender Trouble: Feminism and the Subversion of Identity* (New York: Routledge, 1990), pp. 43–57. Luce Irigaray draws on Freud's notion of the phallic gaze to show how masculinity depends on a specular structure and the feminine is placed outside representation, *This Sex Which Is Not One*, trans. Catherine Porter (Ithaca, N.Y.: Cornell University Press, 1985); and *Speculum of the Other Woman*, trans. Gillian C. Gill (Ithaca, N.Y.: Cornell University Press, 1985). For an analysis of the gaze in Lacan, see Judith Butler, *Bodies That Matter: On the Discursive Limits of Sex* (New York: Routledge, 1993), pp. 72–83.

54. The story does not appear in one of the two Arabic versions, see Bacon, *Secretum Secretorum*, ed. Steele, p. xv. For the Latin, see Bacon, *Secretum Secretorum*, ed. Steele, pp. 144–46; Middle English versions of the legend occur in Manzalaoui, *Secretum Secretorum*, pp. 81–82, 190–92. In the Hebrew version, the story is replaced by a warning against red-headed counsellors, Bacon, *Secretum Secretorum*, ed. Steele, p. xv.

55. Bacon, *Secretum Secretorum*, ed. Steele, p. 144: "et lege mea licitum est mihi tollere sanguinem suum, pecuniam suam et accidens suum, id est, uxorem, parentes et genitores. Insuper maledictum est mihi si . . . facio secum justiciam vel pareo ei." The Latin version identifies the one of Christian faith as *magus orientalis*; the Arabic version identifies him as a "fire worshipper" who nevertheless espouses Christian law, and later Middle English versions identify him as simply a Christian.

56. For the Latin version, see Bacon, *Secretum Secretorum*, ed. Steele, p. 165, and for the Arabic, see p. 219. In the Arabic version, Philemon is Aklaman. Steele explains in the introduction that the story was originally told of Socrates and Zopyrus (lxiii).

57. Bacon, *Secretum Secretorum*, ed. Steele, p. 165: "quia philosophia nichil aliud est quam abstinencia et victoria concupiscibilium."

58. R. I. Moore, *The Formation of a Persecuting Society: Power and Deviance in Western Europe, 950–1250* (Oxford: Basil Blackwell, 1987), p. 100; see also pp. 101–23. Moore draws upon the ideas of Mary Douglas, *Purity and Danger* (London: Ark Paperbacks, 1966), pp. 140–58, to show how these fears become projected on Jews, heretics, prostitutes, homosexuals, the poor, and other threatening groups. For the relationship of sexuality to race, see also Steven Kruger's essay "Conversion and Medieval Sexual, Religious, and Racial Categories" in *Constructing Medieval Sexuality*, ed. Karma Lochrie, Peggy McCracken, and James A. Schultz (Minneapolis: University of Minnesota Press, 1997), pp. 158–79.

59. For a discussion of the analogies between the feminine, language, and reading, see Dinshaw, *Chaucer's Sexual Poetics*, pp. 3–27.

60. See Bacon, *Secretum Secretorum*, ed. Steele, pp. 135–44. It is also significant that the Hebrew version substitutes a warning against red-headed counselors for this section (p. xv). Ferster notes the tenuousness of the moral of this story, *Fictions of Advice*, pp. 52–53.

61. Moore recounts the prejudice against Jews in the twelfth century that led to their persecution in the thirteenth century and later Middle Ages, *Formation of a Persecuting Society*, pp. 27–45.

62. *Þe Priuyté of Priuyteis* in *Secretum Secretorum*, ed. Manzalaoui, p. 121.

63. For the role of publishing in disclosing trade secrets as well as in transforming the field of science, see Elizabeth L. Eisenstein, *The Printing Press as an Agent of Change* (Cambridge: Cambridge University Press, 1979), 1: 270–80 and vol. 2.

64. Some of this alchemical information can be found in Bacon's edition of the *Secret of Secrets*; see *Secretum Secretorum*, ed. Steele, pp. 114–23. The 1500 Achillini edition of Bacon's text restores alchemical information previously omitted from the Latin text. Steele includes this in his edition of Bacon, pp. 73–75. For an overview of alchemy in the Middle Ages, see Kieckhefer, *Magic in the Middle Ages*, pp. 133–44.

65. *The Riverside Chaucer*, 3d ed., ed. Larry D. Benson (Boston: Houghton Mifflin, 1987), VIII.1442–47.

66. Quoted in Metlitzki, *Matter of Araby*, p. 91.

67. See Manzalaoui's discussion of the manuscript's affiliations, *Secretum Secretorum*, xix–xx.

68. J. Monfrin lists these different compilations in French translations of the treatise in "La place du *Secret des secrets* dans la littérature française mediévale," in *Pseudo-Aristotle, The Secret of Secrets: Sources and Influences*, ed. W. F. Ryan and Charles B. Schmitt (London: Warburg Institute, 1982), pp. 94–97.

69. This translation is the *Decretum Aristotelis* by John Shirley (with an interesting misreading of *decretum* for *secretum*) that is described in Manzalaoui, *Secretum Secretorum*, p. xxxiii.

70. *The English Works of John Gower*, ed. G. C. Macaulay, EETS, e.s. 82 (London: Oxford University Press, 1901), VII.233–85; *Lydgate and Burgh's Secrees of Old Philosoffres*, ed. Robert Steele, EETS, e.s. 66 (London, 1884). For an overview of the two works, see Charles F. Mullett, "John Lydgate: A Mirror of Medieval Medicine," *Bulletin of the History of Medicine* 22 (1948): 403–15.

71. Thomas Hoccleve, *Hoccleve's Works*, ed. F. J. Furnivall, EETS, e.s. 72 (London: Kegan Paul, Trench, and Trübner, 1897).

72. John Gower, *Confessio Amantis* in *English Works of John Gower*, ed. Macaulay, 2: VII.19–20. While Macaulay notes that Gower's source is not the *Secret of Secrets* but Brunetto Latini's *Livres dou tresor*, A. H. Gilbert argues that the former was more important than Macaulay thought, "Notes on the Influence of the *Secretum Secretorum*," *Speculum* 3 (1928): 84–98. More recently, M. A. Manzalaoui charts echoes of the Pseudo-Aristotelian text with Gower's *Confessio Amantis*, "'Noght in the Registre of Venus': Gower's English Mirror for Princes," in *Medieval Studies for J. A. W. Bennett*, ed. P. L. Heyworth (Oxford: Clarendon Press, 1981), pp. 159–83. John H. Fisher draws broad thematic connections between the erotic main

subject of the *Confessio* and those subjects of statecraft and learning in the *Secretum* in *John Gower: Moral Philosopher and Friend of Chaucer* (New York: New York University Press, 1964), p. 89.

73. John Gower, *Confessio Amantis* in *English Works*, 2: VII.5412–23.

74. Manzalaoui argues for the tranquilizing effect of Book VII, " 'Noght in the Registre of Venus,' " pp. 164–65.

75. See, for example, Larry Scanlon, *Narrative, Authority, and Power: The Medieval Exemplum and the Chaucerian Tradition* (Cambridge: Cambridge University Press, 1994), pp. 282–97.

76. D. A. Miller, *The Novel and the Police* (Berkeley: University of California Press, 1988), 207. Also quoted in Sedgwick, *Epistemology of the Closet*, p. 67. I am indebted to Sedgwick's analysis of Miller and the notion of the open secret as it relates to knowledge and ignorance (pp. 67–90).

77. See Monica Green, "Women's Medical Practice and Health Care in Medieval Europe," in *Sisters and Workers in the Middle Ages*, ed. Judith M. Bennett, Elizabeth A. Clark, Jean F. O'Barr, B. Anne Vilen, and Sarah Westphal-Wihl (Chicago: University of Chicago Press, 1989), p. 52.

78. See Green, "Women's Medical Practice," pp. 52–53, and Beryl Rowland, *Medieval Woman's Guide to Health: The First English Gynecological Handbook* (Kent, Ohio: Kent State University Press, 1981), p. 9. In fact, Félicie was correct, for the statute explicitly prohibits ignorant practitioners and Jews, but not women. See Lynn Thorndike's translation of the 1271 statute, *University Records and Life in the Middle Ages* (New York: Columbia University Press, 1944), pp. 83–85.

79. *Chartularium Universitatis Parisiensis*, ed. Henri Denifle (Paris, 1891), 2: 264: "Item melius est et honestius et par quod mulier sagax et experta in arte visitet mulierem infirmam, videatque et inquirat secreta nature et abscondita ejus, quam homo, cui non licet predicta videre, inquirere, nec palpare manus, mammas, ventrem et pedes, etc., mulierum; imo debet homo mulierum secreta et earum societates secretas evitare et fugere quantum potest. Et mulier antea permitteret se mori, quam secreta infirmitatis sue homini revelare propter honestatem sexus muliebris et propter verecundiam, quam revelando pateretur." My translation. Monica Green argues that Félicie employs the "rhetoric of [women's] modesty" in "a conscious attempt to actively turn the taboo [against women's revealing their 'secrets' to men] to their own advantage and thereby resist the increasing circumscription of women's sphere of medical practice." See "Women's Medical Practice," p. 74. She also critiques Beryl Rowland's position that "women's health was women's business" in the Middle Ages.

80. *History of Sexuality*, 1: 101.

81. Pseudo-Albert, *Women's Secrets: A Translation of Pseudo-Albertus Magnus's De Secretis Mulierum with Commentaries*, trans. Helen Rodnite Lemay (Albany: State University of New York Press, 1992), p. 1. Margaret Schleissner estimates the number of manuscripts at "nearly 100" and the number of Latin incunables at 55. See "A Fifteenth-Century Physician's Attitude Toward Sexuality: Dr. Johann Hartlieb's *Secreta mulierum* Translation," in *Sex in the Middle Ages: A Book of Essays*, ed. Joyce E. Salisbury (New York: Garland, 1991), p. 110.

82. Pseudo-Albert, *Women's Secrets*, trans. Lemay, p. vii.

83. Ibid., p. 59. All quotations are from Lemay's translation unless otherwise indicated.

84. Margaret Schleissner gives the example of Hartlieb's German translation of *De secretis mulierum*, in which the author claims to speak to married people but is in fact addressing an aristocratic bachelor named Siegmund, "A Fifteenth-Century Physician's Attitude Toward Sexuality," p. 114; for another German translation and its bourgeois audience, see Green, "Women's Medical Practice," p. 462n.

85. For example, some of the so-called Trotula texts were translated into the vernacular by women; the question still exists, however, whether women were the primary audience of these translations and what their status was with respect to "men's texts." See Green, "Women's Medical Practice," pp. 461–62. Margaret Schleissner characterizes the treatise as "a male-to-male discourse about women," and she describes the discourse's "atmosphere of intimacy," "A Fifteenth-Century Physician's Attitude," pp. 110, 113.

86. Quoted from Green's 1985 dissertation in Lemay's Introduction to *Women's Secrets*, p. 8.

87. Monica Green, "Female Sexuality in the Medieval West," *Trends in History* 4 (1990): 145.

88. Pseudo-Albert, *Women's Secrets*, trans. Lemay, p. 60. This commentary corresponds closely to the 1320 commentary of Utrecht 723, as it is summarized by Lynn Thorndike, "Further Consideration of the *Experimenta*, *Speculum astronomiae*, and *De secretis mulierum* ascribed to Albertus Magnus" *Speculum* 30 (1955): 430.

89. I am borrowing Eve Sedgwick's language in her analysis of Diderot's *The Nun*, in *Tendencies*, p. 48.

90. Pseudo-Albert, *Women's Secrets*, trans. Lemay, p. 60.

91. Ibid., p. 88.

92. Ibid., p. 88; see also pp. 102–3, 125, 128, 129–30.

93. Ibid., p. 107. Pseudo-Albert later claims to have "heard tell" about monstrous births based on sexual positions, again presumably from midwives or women patients (p. 114).

94. Thomasset, *Placides et Timéo*, pp. 290–97.

95. John Benton and Monica Green caution against assuming that Trotula's treatise, which was known under various titles, is the work of a "real woman." Benton argues that the treatise was written by a man under the figure of a woman; see Green, "Women's Medical Practice," pp. 62–74.

96. Thomasset, ed., *Placides et Timéo*, pp. 122–23: "Et quant plus en sent, plus en desire, de la quelle cose, quant vous arés este plus obeijssans anons et plus m'arés monstré samblant d'amours, je vous diray plus parfons secrés, qui ne sont mie a dire fors a son chier cuer et ami, les fleurs des secrés de nature qui ne font a escripre, ce dient les philosophes par leur judgement, fors de menue lettre, petite et soutiene et foible lettre et mal lisant, en parquemin foible et male appert et peu durant et en paroles couvertes, pour ce que cose abandonner est ville et cose a peines trouvee senee et chiere." My translation.

97. Jacquart and Thomasset comment on this same passage, noting the incongruity between Timéo's injunction to use poor quality manuscripts and the fine

quality of the manuscripts in which his injunction is preserved, *Sexuality and Medicine*, pp. 127–28.

98. See Joan Cadden, *Meanings of Sex Difference in the Middle Ages: Medicine, Science, and Culture* (Cambridge: Cambridge University Press, 1993), pp. 153, 150–62, and Thomas Laqueur, *Making Sex: Body and Gender from the Greeks to Freud* (Cambridge, Mass.: Harvard University Press, 1990), pp. 43–44, 46.

99. Pseudo-Albert, *Women's Secrets*, trans. Lemay, p. 68. Albertus Magnus's position is quoted in Cadden, *Meanings of Sex Difference*, p. 153.

100. Pseudo-Albert, *Women's Secrets*, trans. Lemay, p. 138.

101. For example, see Pseudo-Albert, *Women's Secrets*, trans. Lemay, pp. 102, 121; also, desire is connected with the retention of menses, p. 132.

102. Pseudo-Albert, *Women's Secrets*, trans. Lemay, p. 132.

103. *Galen On the Affected Parts*, trans. Rudolph E. Siegel (Basel: S. Karger, 1976), 6: V.185.

104. Helen Rodnite Lemay discusses the suppression of Galen's "cure" in the treatise of William of Saliceto, the thirteenth-century physician from Bologna, "William of Saliceto on Human Sexuality," *Viator* 12 (1981): 165–81.

105. Cadden, *Meanings of Sex Difference*, p. 116.

106. Cadden, *Meanings of Sex Difference*, p. 90. As Cadden points out, Salernitan questions often gave prominence to the subjects of sexuality and reproduction, pp. 90–91. For a study of this tradition, see Brian Lawn, *The Salernitan Questions: An Introduction to the History of Medieval and Renaissance Problem Literature* (Oxford: Clarendon Press, 1963).

107. For more on this practice, see Cadden, *Meanings of Sex Differences*, pp. 113–15.

108. Cadden notes that the "pedagogical practices and related literary forms had currency outside the university curriculum," citing as her main example, the *Secrets of Women*; see *Meanings of Sex Difference*, p. 115. Lemay also sketches the treatise's affinity with questions and problems literature, Pseudo-Albert, *Women's Secrets*, trans. Lemay, pp. 11–12. Claude Thomasset likewise links the French *Placides et Timéo* to the encyclopedias and the *quaestiones* format, *Placides et Timéo ou Li secrés as philosophes* (Geneva: Droz, 1980), p. xxviii.

109. Claude Thomasset makes this claim of the French *Placides et Timéo* in *Commentaire du Dialogue de Placides et Timéo*, p. 3. Lemay speculates that the *Secrets of Women* text might have been used as a basis for university lectures, *Women's Secrets*, p. 4.

110. For a summary of the work of Constantine the African and its contribution to the history of medicine, see Cadden, *Meanings of Sex Difference*, pp. 57–70.

111. See Cadden, *Meanings of Sex Difference*, pp. 88–93.

112. Pseudo-Albert, *Women's Secrets*, trans. Lemay, p. 13.

113. Pseudo-Albert, *Women's Secrets*, trans. Lemay, p. 12, and Cadden, *Meanings of Sex Difference*, pp. 175–76.

114. For a full survey of the literature of medicine and natural philosophy on women and reproduction, see Cadden, *Meanings of Sex Difference*.

115. Pseudo-Albert, *Women's Secrets*, trans. Lemay, p. 59.

116. Christine de Pizan, *The Book of the City of Ladies*, trans. Earl Jeffrey Rich-

ards (New York: Persea Books, 1982), pp. 22–23. Schleissner cites this very prohibition in a fifteenth-century Old French text, "A Fifteenth-Century Physician's Attitude," p. 113: "deffandus de reveler a fame par nostre sainct pere le pape sus paine descommuniement en la Decretal ad meam decretam."

117. Lemay writes, "For Pseudo-Albert, this term clearly refers to matters pertaining to sexual and reproductive life," Pseudo-Albert, *Women's Secrets*, trans. Lemay, p. 32, while Cadden views the title more generally to refer to "material relating to sexuality, reproduction, gynecology, and obstetrics," *Meanings of Sex Difference*, p. 115. Jacquart and Thomasset characterize the treatise as being about embryology with an air of "deceit about the character of the merchandise being purveyed," *Sexuality and Medicine*, p. 128. There is enough slippage in these three accounts to warrant suspicion, in my view, about the use of secrecy in the treatise and its mystification of the subject(s) treated.

118. Marie-Christine Pouchelle, *The Body and Surgery in the Middle Ages*, trans. Rosemary Morris (Cambridge: Polity Press, 1990), p. 191. Pouchelle's own analysis of the surgical treatise by Henri de Mondeville, *Chirurgie* (1306–1320), is a good example of the "profound equivocation" in medical views of the female body. Jacquart and Thomasset attribute this representation to masculine fear, *Sexuality and Medicine*, pp. 115, 129, 173–77, 188–93. Cadden is reluctant to draw a "grand synthetic scheme that captures the medieval concept of gender," but she does document what she calls a "cluster of gender-related notions," *Meanings of Sex Difference*, p. 9.

119. Translated in Beryl Rowland, *Medieval Woman's Guide to Health*, p. 59.

120. See Green, "Women's Medical Practices," pp. 52–56.

121. See Green, "Women's Medical Practices," p. 52; Vern L. Bullough, "The Medieval Medical University at Paris," *Bulletin of the History of Medicine* 31 (1957): 197–211, and "The Development of Medical Guilds at Paris," *Medievalia et Humanistica* 12 (1958): 33–40; and Robert S. Gottfried, *Doctors and Medicine in Medieval England, 1340–1530* (Princeton, N.J.: Princeton University Press, 1986). As Green points out, however, no study has been made of how this professionalization affected women in particular (p. 52n).

122. Denifle, ed., *Chartularium Universitatis Parisiensis*, 2: 266–67.

123. Jean Renart, *Galerent de Bretagne: roman du XIIIe siècle*, ed. Lucien Foulet (Paris: Champion, 1925), Classiques français du moyen âge, ll. 166–72: "Seigneurs, fait il, ma dame songe: / Ja vous diroit moult d'aventure, / S'elle congnoissoit la nature, / Des choses que clers ont aprises, / Qui a ce ont leurs estudies mises, / Qui sçavent les secrez des femmes / Mieulx qu'elles, ne n'est pas diffames." I am grateful to Peggy McCracken for bringing this story to my attention.

124. See Marie de France, *The Lais of Marie de France*, trans. Robert Hanning and Joan Ferrante (Durham, N.C.: Labyrinth Press, 1978), pp. 74–75.

125. Domna C. Stanton makes this argument for the masculine narrator's voyeuristic invasion of women gossips at the lying-in, "Recuperating Women and the Man Behind the Screen," in *Sexuality and Gender in Early Modern Europe: Institutions, Texts, Images*, ed. James Grantham Turner (Cambridge: Cambridge University Press, 1993), pp. 247–65, esp. p. 250.

126. Ross Chambers, "Histoire d'Oeuf: Secrets and Secrecy in a La Fontaine Fable," *Sub-stance* 32 (1981): 67.

127. Stanton, "Recuperating Women," p. 250.

128. For example, see R. Howard Block, "The Lay and the Law: Sexual/Textual Transgression in *La Chastelaine de Vergi*, the *Lai d'Ignaure*, and the *Lais* of Marie de France," *Stanford French Review* 14 (1990): 181–210.

129. Keller, *Secrets of Life*, p. 41.

130. Terri Kapsalis, *Public Privates: Performing Gynecology from Both Ends of the Speculum* (Durham, N.C.: Duke University Press, 1997).

Chapter 4

1. Catharine A. MacKinnon, "Feminism, Marxism, Method, and the State: Toward Feminist Jurisprudence," *Signs* 8.4 (Summer 1983): 656–57.

2. Georges Duby, "Private Power, Public Power," in *A History of Private Life*, Vol. 2, *Revelations of the Medieval World*, ed. Philippe Ariès and Georges Duby (Cambridge, Mass.: Belknap Press, 1988), p. 6.

3. Sissela Bok, *Secrets: On the Ethics of Concealment and Revelation* (New York: Vintage Books, 1989), pp. 10–11. Bok points out that although secrecy and privacy overlap, "secrecy hides far more than what is private" and "privacy need not hide" (p. 11).

4. Duby, "Private Power, Public Power," p. 4.

5. For a discussion of some examples of such secrecy, see R. Howard Bloch, "The Lay and the Law: Sexual/Textual Transgression in *La Chastelaine de Vergi*, the *Lai d'Ignaure*, and the *Lais* of Marie de France," *Stanford French Review* 14 (1990): 181–210.

6. Guillaume de Lorris and Jeun de Meun, *The Romance of the Rose*, trans. Charles Dahlberg (Princeton, N.J.: Princeton University Press, 1971), p. 276. Christine de Pizan counters this stereotype of women in her *Quarrel of the Rose*; see excerpt from her Letter to Jean de Montreuil (1401) in *Woman Defamed and Woman Defended: An Anthology of Medieval Texts*, ed. Alcuin Blamires (Oxford: Clarendon Press, 1992), pp. 286–87.

7. See Michel Foucault, *History of Sexuality*, Vol. 1, *An Introduction* (New York: Vintage, 1990), p. 27; and Eve Kosofsky Sedgwick, *Epistemology of the Closet* (Berkeley: University of California Press, 1990), pp. 3–4, and "Privilege of Unknowing: Diderot's *The Nun*" in *Tendencies* (Durham, N.C.: Duke University Press, 1993), pp. 23–25. I have already discussed this complicity of silence and verbalization in Chapter 2.

8. See J. H. Baker, *Manual of Law French*, 2d ed. (Hants: Scolar Press, 1992), p. 81. Also the *Anglo-Norman Dictionary*, Fascicle 1, ed. Louise W. Stone and William Rothwell (London: Modern Humanities Research Association, 1977), p. 120, which translates the phrase more literally: "covered by a husband."

9. Frederick Pollock and Frederic William Maitland, *The History of English Law Before the Time of Edward I* (Washington, D.C.: Lawyers' Literary Club, 1959), 2: 407.

10. Judith M. Bennett makes this case for wives in the Brigstock courts, who

as suitors, criminals, and litigants were "distinguished . . . from all other adults, regardless of age, sex, or marital status," *Women in the Medieval English Countryside: Brigstock Before the Plague* (London: Oxford University Press, 1987), p. 107.

11. Pollock and Maitland, *The History of English Law*, 2: 407n. I have been unable to verify this connotation of the term for Middle English.

12. For definitions of these words, see Baker, *Manual of Law French*, p. 81, and Stone and Rothwell, *Anglo-Norman Dictionary*, p. 120.

13. *Middle English Dictionary*, ed. Hans Kurath et al. (Ann Arbor: University of Michigan Press, 1959), C: 689.

14. Ibid., C: 694.

15. John Gower, *The English Works of John Gower*, ed. G. C. Macaulay, EETS, e.s., 82 (London: Oxford University Press, 1901), 1: 1.642–45.

16. Gower, *The English Works of John Gower*, ed. Macaulay, 1: 2.1879–1941.

17. John Lydgate, *The Pilgrimage of the Life of Man*, ed. F.J. Furnivall, EETS, e.s. 77 (London: Kegan Paul, Trench, and Trübner, 1899); 83 (London, 1901); 92 (London, 1904), l. 10627.

18. Geoffrey Chaucer, *Boece* in *The Riverside Chaucer*, 3d ed., ed. Larry D. Benson (Boston: Houghton Mifflin, 1987), bk. 5, meter 3, l. 24.

19. Pollock and Maitland, *History of English Law*, 2: 404. In northern France, by contrast, marital property was known as "acquest property," and spouses enjoyed joint tenancy of it. See James A. Brundage, *Law, Sex, and Christian Society in Medieval Europe* (Chicago: University of Chicago Press, 1987), p. 479.

20. Pollock and Maitland, *History of English Law*, 2: 404.

21. Glanvill, *The Treatise on the Laws and Customs of the Realm of England commonly called Glanvill*, ed. and trans. G. D. G. Hall (London: Nelson, 1965), bk. 11, par. 3. See also Kay E. Lacey, "Women and Work in Fourteenth and Fifteenth Century London," in *Women and Work in Pre-Industrial England*, ed. Lindsey Charles and Lorna Duffin (London: Croom Helm, 1985), p. 28.

22. Bennett makes this point in her analysis of the conjugal economy of Brigstock, *Women in the Medieval English Countryside*, p. 110. There was a provision for the widow to recover land of hers that her husband had alienated, but expedients were also developed to protect the husband's act against this challenge, such as stipulations of "urgent necessity" that could justify his alienating land against her will; see Pollock and Maitland, *History of English Law*, 2: 411–12.

23. Pollock and Maitland, *History of English Law*, 2: 404–5.

24. Lacey makes this point in "Women and Work in Fourteenth and Fifteenth Century London," p. 40.

25. Judith M. Bennett "Medieval Women, Modern Women: Across the Great Divide," in *Culture and History, 1350–1600: Essays on English Communities, Identities and Writing*, ed. David Aers (Detroit: Wayne State University Press, 1992), p. 153.

26. Glanvill, *The Treatise on the Laws and Customs*, bk. 6, par. 3.

27. Lee Holcombe argues that medieval common law originated out of this desire to create for husbands a "profitable guardianship of their wives' person and property," *Wives and Property: Reform of the Married Women's Property in Nineteenth Century England* (Toronto: University of Toronto Press, 1983), p. 19.

28. Glanvill, *The Treatise on the Laws and Customs*, bk. 7, par. 5. See also Pollock and Maitland, *History of English Law*, 2: 405, 428–29; Bennett, *Women in the Medieval English Countryside*, pp. 28–30, 110–14; and Lacey, "Women and Work in Fourteenth and Fifteenth Century London," pp. 26–29, 32–42.

29. Pollock and Maitland, *History of English Law*, 2: 405.

30. See Bennett's examples from Brigstock of the confusion of the wife's status as full litigant and as dependent in joint litigation cases, *Women in the Medieval English Countryside*, pp. 109–10.

31. Quoted in L. F. Salzman, *English Trade in the Middle Ages* (London: H. Pordes, 1964), p. 182.

32. Judith M. Bennett, "Medieval Women," p. 155. Bennett raises the possibility that instead of representing a liberation for women, as it might seem to us, the option of married woman as *femme sole* might have been "a means of freeing husbands from the debts and obligations of their wives; the custom, in other words, might have primarily benefited men" (p. 155). Diane Hutton gives one example where married women were treated under the law as *femme soles* even though they were not: butchers' wives in Shrewsbury were fined for leaving dung and entrails in the streets. In this case, wives were not protected by marriage, "Women in Fourteenth-Century Shrewsbury," in *Women and Work in Pre-Industrial England*, ed. Lindsay Charles and Lorna Duffin (London: Croom Helm, 1985), p. 95.

33. Quoted in Holcombe, *Wives and Property*, p. 25.

34. Holcombe, *Wives and Property*, p. 20.

35. Pollock and Maitland, *History of English Law*, 2: 436. I would like to thank Paul Strohm for bringing this to my attention, and I am indebted to his work on "Treason in the Household" for my own thinking on the petty treasons of wives, "Treason in the Household" in *Hochon's Arrow: The Social Imagination of Fourteenth-Century Texts* (Princeton, N.J.: Princeton University Press, 1992), pp. 121–44. Holcombe explains that only in the case of treason, felony, or adultery were widows compelled to forfeit their right to one-third of the real properties guaranteed to them in marriage, *Wives and Property*, p. 22.

36. Quoted in Paul Strohm, *Hochon's Arrow*, p. 124.

37. Strohm, *Hochon's Arrow*, pp. 126–27. Strohm cites two interesting cases where women who had murdered their husbands were tried for treason, and he extends his discussion to the literary example of the Wife of Bath.

38. Bennett, *Women in the Medieval English Countryside*, p. 188; she cautions elsewhere that even the private lives of medieval women were more public than we are used to (pp. 6–7). She refers to the "public disabilities" in this same work (p. 179). Bennett, too, speculates that her analysis of rural women might also apply to the lives of feudal and townswomen (p. 188).

39. *The Book of Margery Kempe*, ed. Sanford B. Meech and Hope Emily Allen, EETS, o.s. 214 (London: Oxford University Press, 1940), pp. 9–11.

40. For example, see the Parson's comments on women's pride of array in the Parson's Tale in *Riverside Chaucer*, ed. Benson, X.429–35. The Parson, however, also extends his discussion to men who are guilty of trying to enhance their sexual appeal in particular (X. 421–28).

41. Judith M. Bennett, *Ale, Beer, and Brewsters in England: Women's Work in a Changing World, 1300–1600* (New York: Oxford University Press, 1996), p. 128. See especially pp. 122–44.

42. Kempe, *The Book of Margery Kempe*, p. 129.

43. For discussions of the clothmaking trade and women's status in it, see Hutton, "Women in Fourteenth Century Shrewsbury," pp. 89–90; Maryanne Kowaleski, "Women's Work in a Market Town: Exeter in the Late Fourteenth Century," in *Women and Work in Preindustrial Europe*, ed. Barbara A. Hanawalt (Bloomington: Indiana University Press, 1986), p. 153; and Maryanne Kowaleski and Judith M. Bennett, "Crafts, Gilds, and Women in the Middle Ages: Fifty Years After Marian K. Dale," in *Sisters and Workers in the Middle Ages*, ed. Judith M. Bennett, Elizabeth A. Clark, Jean F. O'Barr, B. Anne Vilen, and Sarah Westphal-Wihl (Chicago: University of Chicago Press, 1989), p. 12.

44. "How the Good Wijf Tauȝte Hir Douȝtir," in *The Babees Book*, ed. F. J. Furnivall, EETS 32 (London: Kegan Paul, Trench, Trübner, 1868), p. 43, ll. 153–54.

45. Examples of both types of work may be found in Hutton, "Women in Fourteenth Century Shrewsbury," pp. 83–99; and Sue Wright, "'Churmaids, Huswyfes and Hucksters': The Employment of Women in Tudor and Stuart Salisbury," in *Women and Work in Pre-Industrial England*, ed. Charles and Duffin, pp. 100–21; Kowaleski, "Women's Work in a Market Town," pp. 145–66; and Bennett, "Medieval Women," pp. 152–53.

46. Kowaleski, "Women's Work in a Market Town," pp. 155–57. In addition to Kowaleski's study, my overview of women's work generalizes upon the two books of Judith Bennett, *Women in the Medieval English Countryside* and *Ale, Beer, and Brewsters in England*; P. J. P. Goldberg, *Women, Work, and Life Cycle in a Medieval Economy: Women in York and Yorkshire, c. 1300–1520* (Oxford: Clarendon Press, 1992); Hutton, "Women in Fourteenth-Century Shrewsbury"; Salzman, *English Trade in the Middle Ages*, Shulamith Shahar, *The Fourth Estate: A History of Women in the Middle Ages*, trans. Chaya Galai (London: Methuen, 1983); and other works.

47. Bennett compares fourteenth-century women with women of 1700 by using eight occupational categories, finding that there is little difference in the grouping of female trades, "Medieval Women," pp. 156–57. Other studies have also found women in the categories Bennett cites, including P. J. P. Goldberg, "Female Labour, Service and Marriage in the Late Medieval Urban North," *Northern History* 22 (1986): 28–29. Goldberg and Bennett disagree on their interpretations of the evidence, however. Goldberg finds evidence of a "full range of . . . occupations in which women can be found," while Bennett emphasizes the obstacles to such a range.

48. In fourteenth-century Shrewsbury, brewing was "virtually a female monopoly," according to Hutton, and those housewives who failed to pay the licensing fee also appear in court records, "Women in Fourteenth-Century Shrewsbury," p. 95. Bennett finds a similar monopoly among peasant women brewers in the town of Brigstock and generally in England, "The Village Ale-Wife: Women and Brewing in Fourteenth-Century England," in *Women and Work in Preindustrial Europe*, ed. Hanawalt, pp. 20–36. Bennett points out that wives only dominated brewing indus-

tries in rural economies when their husbands were engaged in other trades, p. 27. See also her book on female brewers, *Ale, Beer, and Brewsters in England*, pp. 14–36.

49. Bennett, "Medieval Women," p. 159. David Herlihy sums up his study of women and work in medieval Europe in this way: "Concentrated in household service, food sales, and petty retailing, they [women] tended to form the lowest, least trained, and least paid level of the urban work force," *Opera Muliebria: Women and Work in Medieval Europe* (New York: McGraw-Hill, 1990), pp. 178–79.

50. See Goldberg's argument, "Females in the Late Medieval Urban North," pp. 32–37. Goldberg lists other restrictions on women's labor in general, such as demand for labor, shifts in the economy, and marital status (p. 37). See also Goldberg, *Women, Work, and Life Cycle in a Medieval Economy*, pp. 82–157.

51. Women were forbidden in manorial courts from acting as personal pledges or tithing members, and thus, they were unable to form the community of economic support that men had. See Bennett, "Village Ale-Wife," p. 28; and Goldberg, "Females in the Late Medieval Urban North," p. 33.

52. This fact is noted by many, including Kowaleski, "Women's Work in a Market Town," pp. 155–58; Goldberg, *Women, Work, and Life Cycle*, pp. 101–18; and in the peasant economy of Brigstock, Bennett, *Women in the Medieval English Countryside*, pp. 177–98. This fact is not, however, noted in Hanawalt's argument for medieval marriage as a partnership, *The Ties That Bound: Peasant Families in Medieval England* (London: Oxford University Press, 1986).

53. Hutton, "Women in Fourteenth Century Shrewsbury," pp. 93, 96; Bennett, "Medieval Women," pp. 158–59. On the textile workshops of early medieval Europe, see Herlihy, *Opera Muliebria*, pp. 75–102.

54. See Shulamith Shahar's discussion of women and apprenticeship, *Fourth Estate*, pp. 198–200, 211. See also Bennett, "Medieval Women," p. 160. Goldberg writes in "Females in the Late Medieval Urban North" that "though there seems to have been no conscious policy to exclude women from the urban franchise with its associated right to retail trade, in effect access by apprenticeship and patrimony were closed" (p. 32). Barbara A. Hanawalt attributes the major differences between male and female apprenticeships to women's exclusion from guilds except through marriage and the unwillingness of families to spend much on the apprenticeship of daughters, *Growing Up in Medieval London: The Experience of Childhood in History* (New York: Oxford University Press, 1993), pp. 142–44. For sixteenth-century Lyon, see Natalie Zemon Davis, "Women in the Crafts in Sixteenth-Century Lyon," in *Women and Work in Preindustrial Europe*, ed. Hanawalt, pp. 169–72.

55. L. F. Salzman, *English Industries of the Middle Ages* (Oxford: Clarendon Press, 1923), pp. 328–29. Salzman notes that this statute relegates women to the level of "eternal amateurs," and Bennett concurs with this analysis, "Medieval Women," p. 153. Shahar sees the statute as allowing women to compensate for their exclusion from full membership in guilds and their society's refusal to recognize them as craftsmen, *Fourth Estate*, p. 197. Goldberg views "the full range" of women's occupations positively, even though he acknowledges the restrictions on their work, "Females in the Late Medieval Urban North," p. 30.

56. I am borrowing the characterization of the statute by Rodney Hilton,

"Women Traders in Medieval England," in *Class Conflict and the Crisis of Feudalism* (London: Hambledon Press, 1985), p. 135. See also Kowaleski's argument about the negative effect of women's multiple occupations, "Women's Work in a Market Town," p. 158.

57. "Ballad of a Tyrannical Husband," *Reliquiae Antiquae*, ed. Thomas Wright and James O. Halliwell (London, 1843), 2: 197.

58. Bennett, *Women in the Medieval English Countryside*, p. 116.

59. Unfortunately, the ballad fragment breaks off just as the wife and husband agree to exchange places for a day and the wife sets off to plow, so we do not know the outcome of this debate.

60. Hutton, "Fourteenth Century Shrewsbury," p. 97. Hilton also maintains that retail trade was essential to urban freedom, but retailers were regarded in the Middle Ages with suspicion, "Women Traders in Medieval England," p. 135.

61. Hilton includes another kind of retailer, forestallers, who would travel outside the market to buy raw materials and thereby avoid market tolls and restrictions. Then they would return to market to sell these materials — mostly grain, fish, and wool — "Women Traders in Medieval England," pp. 135–36.

62. For regulations aimed at brewsters, see Bennett, *Ale, Beer, and Brewsters in England*, pp. 98–121. For the general poor regard in which female hucksters were held, see Hilton, "Women Traders in Medieval England," pp. 144–45, and Kowaleski, "Women's Work in a Market Town," pp. 148–49.

63. John Gower, *The Complete Works of John Gower*, ed. G. C. Macaulay (Oxford: Clarendon Press, 1899), 2: 292: "Mais pour voirdire en cest endroit / As femmes plus partient du droit / Le mestier de Regraterie: / Mais si la femme au faire soit, / Molt plus engine et plus deçoit / Qe l'omme de sa chincherie" (ll. 26229–26334).

64. William Langland, *Piers Plowman: The C Text*, ed. Derek Pearsall (Berkeley: University of California Press, 1979), pp. 118–19. For the extremely negative images of brewsters in medieval literature, see Bennett, *Ale, Beer, and Brewsters in England*, pp. 122–44.

65. Antony Black, *Guilds and Civil Society in European Political Thought from the Twelfth Century to the Present* (Ithaca, N.Y.: Cornell University Press, 1984), p. 14. Richard Mackenney also emphasizes the importance of guilds in medieval cities, *Tradesmen and Traders: The World of the Guilds in Venice and Europe, c. 1250–1650* (Totowa, N.J.: Barnes & Noble, 1987), p. 1.

66. Herlihy, *Opera Muliebria*, p. 162.

67. In Paris, female guilds existed for such female work as spinning silk, making purses, producing head coverings, and washing, dyeing, and weaving wool and flax; see Shahar, *Fourth Estate*, p. 191. Cologne had four exclusively female guilds for yarnmakers, gold spinners, silk spinners, and silk weavers; see Martha C. Howell, *Women, Production, and Patriarchy in Late Medieval Cities* (Chicago: University of Chicago Press, 1986), pp. 124–58. See also Kowaleski and Bennett, "Crafts and Gilds," pp. 18–21.

68. See Bennett's summary of this view, "Medieval Women," p. 151. Goldberg says that "there is no evidence that women were generally excluded from any of the welfare benefits or social activities of these associations [guilds]," in *Women, Work,*

and Life Cycle, p. 322. Richard Mackenney argues from the evidence of women in guilds that "status groups within a guild were by no means rigidly defined," but he has very little to say specifically about the membership of women in guilds in his book as a whole, *Tradesmen and Traders*, p. 23. Bennett recounts how the status of women in medieval guilds has been inflated by its comparison with the apparent decline in female participation in guilds after the sixteenth century, "Medieval Women," pp. 159–60.

69. Bennett, "Medieval Women," p. 160; Lacey, "Women and Work in Fourteenth and Fifteenth Century London," p. 45; see also Kowaleski and Bennett, "Crafts, Gilds," pp. 11–13.

70. Goldberg, "Females in the Late Medieval Urban North," p. 32. Other accounts of the restrictions on women in guilds include Bennett, "Medieval Women, Modern Women," pp. 159–60; Herlihy, *Opera Muliebria*, pp. 161–62; Lacey, "Women and Work in Fourteenth and Fifteenth Century London," pp. 45–46; Shahar, *Fourth Estate*, pp. 190–200; and Martha C. Howell, "Women, the Family Economy, and the Structures of Market Production in Cities of Northern Europe During the Late Middle Ages," in *Women and Work in Preindustrial Europe*, ed. Hanawalt, pp. 208–14.

71. Shahar, *Fourth Estate*, p. 196. Goldberg finds this to be true of northern England, too, "Females in the Late Medieval Urban North," p. 32.

72. Norwich, for example, banned women weavers from teaching apprentices, Shahar, *Fourth Estate*, p. 197; Herlihy finds restrictions on women in Flanders in 1374, *Opera Muliebria*, p. 178; for other examples, see Howell, "Women, the Family Economy," p. 213.

73. It is true that the social bonds of religious guilds also depended on secrecy, with rules against revealing the counsels of the guild; however, this use of secrecy is, I would argue, less tied to the group identity than is the secrecy of craft guilds.

74. Toulmin Smith, ed., *English Gilds*, EETS, o.s. 40 (London: N. Trübner, 1870), p. 317. I have expanded the abbreviations.

75. Pamela O. Long, "Invention, Authorship, 'Intellectual Property,' and the Origin of Patents: Notes Toward a Conceptual History," *Technology and Culture* 32 (1991): 870. William Eamon likewise argues for the developing notion of intellectual property in the guild trade secrets, *Science and the Secrets of Nature: Books of Secrets in Medieval and Early Modern Culture* (Princeton, N.J.: Princeton University Press, 1994), pp. 81–82.

76. Merry E. Wiesner argues that German guilds began in the fifteenth century to systematically exclude women in the interest of "male bonding" in "Guilds, Male Bonding and Women's Work in Early Modern Germany," *Gender and History* 1 (Summer 1989): 125–37. I think this kind of exclusion is already in place in medieval guilds even if it is not so explicit as it is in later guild documents. Feminist historians have argued that women posed a threat to masculine authority in guilds and that guilds sought to discourage their participation as a result or to limit it to a secondary role as "sisters" of husbands in guilds; see Kowaleski and Bennett, "Crafts and Gilds," pp. 21–22; Howell, *Women, Production, and Patriarchy in Late Medieval Cities*, pp. 124–37, 152–58, 168–73; Davis, "Women in the Crafts," pp. 167–97; Judith C. Brown, "A Woman's Place Was in the Home: Women's Work in Renais-

sance Tuscany," in *Rewriting the Renaissance: The Discourses of Sexual Difference in Early Modern Europe*, ed. Margaret W. Ferguson, Maureen Quilligan, and Nancy J. Vickers (Chicago: University of Chicago Press, 1986), pp. 206–24.

77. Kowaleski and Bennett, "Crafts, Gilds," p. 13.

78. Marian K. Dale, "The London Silkwomen of the Fifteenth Century," in *Sisters and Workers in the Middle Ages*, ed. Bennett et al. (Chicago: University of Chicago Press, 1989) pp. 26–38.

79. Dale makes this point, "London Silkwomen," pp. 37–38, and Kowaleski and Bennett concur, "Crafts, Gilds," pp. 17–18.

80. Dale, "London Silkwomen," pp. 37–38.

81. Kowaleski and Bennett, "Crafts, Gilds," p. 23n. The complaint of the Yeoman Weavers of 1595 arose, according to Kowaleski and Bennett, from the competition that resulted from women's access to craft secrets.

82. Kowaleski and Bennett see it as "a somber reminder of how some medieval notions of 'community' worked to the disadvantage of women" in "Crafts, Gilds," p. 24.

83. On the indispensability of female retailers, see Hilton, "Women Traders," pp. 144–45; and Hutton, "Women in Fourteenth-Century Shrewsbury," p. 97.

84. See Black, *Guilds and Civil Society*, p. 14.

85. This is Wiesner's argument, "Guilds, Male Bonding," p. 131.

86. See Kowaleski and Bennett, "Crafts, Gilds," p. 20.

87. See Margaret Wood, *The English Medieval House* (London: Ferndale Editions, 1981); Georges Duby, "The Aristocratic Households of Feudal France: Communal Living," in *A History of the Private Life*, Part 2, ed. Philippe Ariès and Georges Duby, pp. 56–63, 77–85; and Charles de La Roncière, "Tuscan Notables on the Eve of the Renaissance," in *A History of the Private Life*, Part 2, ed. Philippe Ariès and Georges Duby, pp. 216–20.

88. Peter Brooks, *Body Work: Objects of Desire in Modern Narrative* (Cambridge, Mass: Harvard University Press, 1993), p. 37. For this idea as it applies to secrecy, see R. Howard Bloch, "The Lay and the Law: Sexual/Textual Transgression in *La Chastelaine de Vergi*, the *Lai d'Ignaure*, and the *Lais* of Marie de France," *Stanford French Review* 14 (1990): 191–96. Bloch's version is "The secret endures only to be revealed" (p. 196).

89. Other scholars have discussed privacy as a key issue in the poem, including William F. Woods, "Private and Public Space in the *Miller's Tale*," *ChauRev* 29 (1994): 166–78; Peter Goodall, "'Allone, withouten any Compaignye': Privacy in the First Fragment of the *Canterbury Tales*," *ELN* 29 (1991): 5–15; and R. W. Hanning, "Telling the Private Parts," in *The Idea of Medieval Literature: New Essays on Chaucer and Medieval Culture in Honor of Donald R. Howard*, ed. James M. Dean and Christian K. Zacher (Newark: University of Delaware Press, 1992), pp. 108–25 ; and Thomas J. Farrell, "Privacy and the Boundaries of Fabliau in the *Miller's Tale*," *ELH* 56 (1989): 773–95.

90. See Farrell's discussion of the Middle English word, "Privacy and the Boundaries of Fabliau," p. 775.

91. For some discussions on this issue, see Farrell, "Privacy and the Boundaries of the Fabliau," p. 735; Hanning, "Telling the Private Parts," pp. 108–25; Goodall,

"Allone, withouten any Compaignye," pp. 12–13. Laura Kendrick makes an unconvincing argument for the "pryvetees" of the passage working in the other direction, from wife's private parts to the divine, using Leo Steinberg's arguable thesis about the sexualizing of Christ, in *Chaucerian Play: Comedy and Control in the Canterbury Tales* (Berkeley: University of California Press, 1988), pp. 5–19. Sarah Stanbury offers a different kind of argument, that Chaucer "marks a wife's 'pryvetee' as sacred ground," suggesting that "women in Chaucer's fictions could indeed claim privacy as a territory of the person, "Women's Letters and Private Space in Chaucer," *Exemplaria* 6 (1994): 279.

92. For a theory of the feminizing of the text in medieval ideas of reading and authoring, see Carolyn Dinshaw, *Chaucer's Sexual Poetics* (Madison: University of Wisconsin Press, 1989), pp. 3–27.

93. Goodall also makes this argument more fully in terms of late medieval architecture and living conditions of university students, "'Allone, withouten any Compaignye,'" pp. 5–8.

94. Woods and Stanbury also argue that Alisoun represents privacy, including the anxiety that it generated. Woods fails, however, to consider how gender ideology is involved, "Private and Public Space," pp. 166–78; Stanbury thinks that "women's privacy takes on a life of its own as a territory of the self, however subject to invasion that space may be" in "Women's Letters," p. 285. Since female privacy implies its own invasion, I do not see how it can be construed as evidence of female subjectivity in this tale at least.

95. For a critique of this view of the tale's innocence and the reading of Alisoun's sensuality, see Elaine Tuttle Hansen, *Chaucer and the Fictions of Gender* (Berkeley: University of California Press, 1992), pp. 224–25. The readings of Alisoun range from D. W. Robertson's portrait of her as an "object of lust," *Preface to Chaucer* (Princeton, N.J.: Princeton University Press, 1962), p. 249, to E. T. Donaldson's "complacent target of a lewd whistle," *Speaking of Chaucer* (New York: Norton, 1970), p. 25, to V. A. Kolve's "free, instinctive, sensual, untamed" animal nature, *Chaucer and the Imagery of Narrative: The First Five Canterbury Tales* (Stanford, Calif.: Stanford University Press, 1984), p. 163, to Lee Patterson's embodiment of "the vitality and resourcefulness of the natural world," *Chaucer and the Subject of History* (Madison: University of Wisconsin Press, 1991), p. 258.

96. I am borrowing the unironic language of Woods, "Private and Public Space," p. 177n. Patrick J. Gallacher shows how, in the comparison of Alisoun's mouth to a hoard of apples "the rotund depth of the store of apples intimates the unseen, unfelt, secret life of what is perceived. What is inviting to taste and sight here is potential, not actually tactile or visible and hence part of the perceptually transcendent." In "Perception and Reality in the *Miller's Tale*," *ChauR* 18 (1983): 40. And so the Miller's conversion of Alisoun for masculine use is extended and perpetuated in modern scholarship.

97. Luce Irigaray, *The Sex Which Is Not One*, trans. Catherine Porter (Ithaca, N.Y.: Cornell University Press, 1985), p. 175, her emphasis.

98. For another argument about masculine madness at the end of the tale as representative of the punishment of each man's ego, see Woods, "Private and Public Space," pp. 172–73.

99. I am indebted here to Hansen's summary and critique of the critical commentary, *Chaucer and the Fictions of Gender*, pp. 227–28. While my analysis of this passage is similar to Hansen's, including a consideration of the heterosexual panic it produces, it differs from hers in its broader analysis of secrecy in relation to the tale's gender ideology.

100. Kim Lane Scheppele, *Legal Secrets: Equality and Efficiency in Common Law* (Chicago: University of Chicago Press, 1988), p. 5.

Chapter 5

1. Louise J. Kaplan, *Female Perversions: The Temptations of Emma Bovary* (New York: Doubleday, 1991), p. 9.

2. Kaplan, *Female Perversions*, p. 14.

3. See my discussion of this at the end of Chapter 4. Kim Lane Scheppele, *Legal Secrets: Equality and Efficiency in Common Law* (Chicago: University of Chicago Press, 1988), p. 5.

4. *The Riverside Chaucer*, 3d ed., ed. Larry D. Benson (Boston: Houghton Mifflin, 1987), X.909. All citations will be to this edition, and translations are my own.

5. For early modern discusssions of sodomy, see Jonathan Goldberg, *Sodometries: Renaissance Texts, Modern Sexualities* (Stanford, Calif.: Stanford University Press, 1992); and Judith C. Brown, *Immodest Acts: The Life of a Lesbian Nun in Renaissance Italy* (Oxford: Oxford University Press, 1986). Valerie Traub considers the problem of the absence of Englishwomen from the category, "The (In)Significance of 'Lesbian' Desire in Early Modern England," in *Queering the Renaissance*, ed. Jonathan Goldberg (Durham, N.C.: Duke University Press, 1994), pp. 62–83. For studies of sodomy in the Middle Ages, see Mark D. Jordan's excellent study, *The Invention of Sodomy in Christian Theology* (Chicago: University of Chicago Press, 1997). Jordan notes in his "Postlude" that misogyny is key to the medieval theology of sodomy, but he does not explore it anywhere in his book (p. 169). See also Allen J. Frantzen's essay, "The Disclosure of Sodomy in *Cleanness*," *PMLA* 3 (May 1996): 451–64. There are no studies of female sodomy in the Middle Ages, nor are there any studies such as Traub's or Brown's for the Renaissance.

6. As other scholars have noted, Old Testament references to Sodom associate it variously with divine judgment and the sin of self-indulgence. See Derrick Sherwin Bailey, *Homosexuality and the Western Christian Tradition* (London: Longman, Green, 1955; rpt. Hamden Conn: Archon Books, 1975), pp. 9–10; and Jordan, *Invention of Sodomy*, pp. 30–31. The two other New Testament references to the sin of Sodom in connection with sexual sin are 2 Peter 2: 9–10 and Jude 7–8.

7. Lorraine Daston and Katharine Park make this argument in their study of early modern models of hermaphroditism, "The Hermaphrodite and the Orders of Nature: Sexual Ambiguity in Early Modern France," in *Premodern Sexualities*, ed. Louise Fradenburg and Carla Freccero (New York: Routledge, 1996), pp. 117–36. See also Pierre J. Payer, *The Bridling of Desire: Views of Sex in the Later Middle Ages* (Toronto: University of Toronto Press, 1993), pp. 76–83; James A. Brundage, *Law,*

Sex, and Christian Society in Medieval Europe (Chicago: University of Chicago Press, 1987), pp. 7, 212–14, 286–87, 398–401.

8. For a summary of the different definitions of the term unnatural, see John T. Noonan, *Contraception: A History of Its Treatment by the Catholic Theologians and Canonists* (Cambridge, Mass.: Harvard University Press, 1965), pp. 187–88, 224–39.

9. Payer, *Bridling of Desire*, p. 77.

10. See Jordan's discussion of each writer, *Invention of Sodomy*, pp. 125–30, 146–47.

11. Payer, *Bridling of Desire*, pp. 76–77.

12. I am summarizing a range of scholarship too vast to cite fully here. For a sample of the arguments on the medical evidence, see Joan Cadden, *Meanings of Sex Difference in the Middle Ages: Medicine, Science, and Culture* (Cambridge: Cambridge University Press, 1993), and Thomas Laqueur, *Making Sex: Body and Gender from the Greeks to Freud* (Cambridge, Mass.: Harvard University Press, 1990), pp. 1–62; and on the theology, see Caroline Walker Bynum, *Holy Feast and Holy Fast: The Religious Significance of Food to Medieval Women* (Berkeley: University of California Press, 1987), and "The Female Body in Religious Practice," in *Fragmentation and Redemption: Essays on Gender and the Human Body in Medieval Religion* (New York: Zone Books, 1991), pp. 181–238.

13. Raymond of Peñafort, *Summa de poenitentia et matrimonio* (Rome, 1603; rpt. Farnborough: Gregg Press, 1967), 3.5.42, pp. 474–75. For parallels between the Parson's treatise and Raymond's *Summa*, see W. F. Bryan and Germaine Dempster, *Sources and Analogues of Chaucer's Canterbury Tales* (Chicago: University of Chicago Press, 1941), pp. 729–41.

14. For parallels between the Parson's Tale and Peraldus's *Summa*, see Kate O. Petersen, *The Sources of the Parson's Tale* (Boston: Ginn, 1901); and Bryan and Dempster, *Sources and Analogues*, pp. 741–45. For a discussion of two sources produced in England based on William Peraldus, see Siegfried Wenzel, "The Source of Chaucer's Seven Deadly Sins" *Traditio* 30 (1974): 351–78.

15. See Jordan's discussion of Peraldus, *Invention of Sodomy*, p. 110, and of the associations of lechery and sodomy with luxury in general, pp. 33–34.

16. Quoted in Jordan, *Invention of Sodomy*, p. 39. Jordan shows how Ambrose, too, locates the sin of Sodom in a fleshly indulgence (p. 34).

17. Quoted in Payer, *Bridling of Desire*, p. 77. Jordan also discusses this passage but dismisses as "bland" Peraldus's reference to women on top, *Invention of Sodomy*, pp. 110–11. For other condemnations of unnatural positions, see Thomas N. Tentler, *Sin and Confession on the Eve of the Reformation* (Princeton, N.J.: Princeton University Press, 1977), p. 204n. See also Noonan, *Contraception*, pp. 223–26.

18. Payer, *Bridling of Desire*, p. 79. I am indebted to Payer's entire discussion for this part of my argument. Noonan points out that the argument about position in heterosexual sex seemed to contradict the scholastic definition of natural because "insemination does not seem at issue," though writers like Peraldus tried to make it the issue, *Contraception*, pp. 238–39.

19. Quoted from Sylvester's sixteenth-century work, the *Sylvestrina* in Tentler, *Sin and Confession*, p. 201.

20. Peter Comestor, "Sexcentesimo vero anno mulieres in vesania versae super-

gressae viris abutebantur," *Historia scholastica, PL* 198, col.1081. For other examples of this moral condemnation using Peter Comestor, see Tentler, *Sin and Confession*, p. 192.

21. Payer, *Bridling of Desire*, p. 79. Jordan translates this same passage, *Invention of Sodomy*, p. 111.

22. Natalie Zemon Davis has made this same argument for early modern women, claiming that the popular fear of gender inversion could even serve women as a means of resistance, "Women on Top," in *Society and Culture in Early Modern France* (Stanford: Stanford University Press, 1975), pp. 124–51.

23. See Payer's discussion of the question of why women were created in the Garden of Eden and the answers of Albert and Aquinas, namely, that "the whole reason for gender differences is to provide an active principle (male) and a passive principle (female) without which there could not be any reproduction among the higher animals," *Bridling of Desire*, pp. 27–28.

24. See my analysis of the medieval link between the flesh and the feminine, *Margery Kempe and Translations of the Flesh* (Philadelphia: University of Pennsylvania Press, 1991), pp. 13–55; and also an earlier version of this chapter, "The Language of Transgression: Body, Flesh, and Word in Mystical Discourse," in *Speaking Two Languages: Traditional Disciplines and Contemporary Theory in Medieval Studies*, ed. Allen J. Frantzen (Albany: State University of New York Press, 1991), pp. 115–40.

25. Both definitions appear in Payer, *Bridling of Desire*, pp. 47, 55.

26. See Cadden's discussion in *Meanings of Sex Difference in the Middle Ages*, pp. 214–15, and especially her "Sciences/Silences: The Natures and Languages of 'Sodomy' in Peter of Abano's *Problemata* Commentary," in *Constructing Medieval Sexuality*, ed. Karma Lochrie, Peggy McCracken, and James A. Schultz (Minneapolis: University of Minnesota Press, 1997), pp. 40–57.

27. Translation is from Peter Damian, *Book of Gomorrah: An Eleventh-Century Treatise Against Clerical Homosexual Practices*, trans. Pierre J. Payer (Waterloo, Ont: Wilfrid Laurier University Press, 1982), p. 64; Peter Damian, *Liber Gomorrhianus — Epistola 31*. In *Die Brief des Petrus Damiani*, vol. 1, ed. Curt Reindel, MGH vol. 4 (Munich: Monumenta Germaniae Historica, 1983), 310.9–17. For a fine discussion of Damian's representation of sodomy, see Jordan, *Invention of Sodomy*, pp. 45–66.

28. Damian, *Book of Gomorrah*, pp. 68, 70, 79, 82, and *Liber Gomorrhianus*, vol.1: "vir evirage," "homo effeminate," 313.13–15; "virilis vite fortia facta relinquere et feminee conversationis illecebrosam mollitiem exhibere," 315.3–4; "lenocinantem libidinis lasciviam viriliter edomare, petulantia carnis incentiva reprimere," 320.8–9; "te in vires collige, viriliter excute, fortia temptare praesume," 322.24–25. For another discussion of how Damian views sodomy in terms of gender transgression and conflation, see David Lorenzo Boyd, "Disrupting the Norm: Sodomy, Culture and the Male Body in Peter Damian's *Liber Gomorrhianus*," in *Essays in Medieval Studies*, vol. 11, ed. Allen J. Frantzen and David J. Robertson (Chicago: Illinois Medieval Association, 1994), pp. 63–74.

29. Damian, *Book of Gomorrah*, p. 29; *Liber Gomorrhianus*, 1: 287.19–21.

30. Damian, *Book of Gomorrah*, p. 78; *Liber Gomorrhianus*, vol. 1: "Neque enim legitur, quod illi Sodomorum incole solummodo in aliena posteriora sint lapsi, sed

potius credenden est, quod iuxta effrenatae libidinis impetum diversis modis tur-
pitudinem sunt in se vel in alios operati," 320.1–4.

31. Alan of Lille, *The Plaint of Nature*, trans. James J. Sheridan (Toronto:
Pontifical Institute of Mediaeval Studies, 1980), meter 1, p. 69. Alan of Lille, "De
planctu naturae," ed. Nicholas Häring, *Studi Medievali* ser. 3, 19/2 (1978): 807.25–
30: "Hic nimis est logicus per quem conuersio simplex / Artis nature iura perire
facit. / Cudit in incude que semina nulla monetat. / Horret et incudem malleus ipse
suam. / Nullam materiem matricis signat idea / Sed magis in sterili litore uomer
arat." For some of the many other hammer/anvil references, see prose 4, pp. 136,
140, and prose 5, pp. 155–56, in Payer's translation of Damian's *Book of Gomorrah*.

32. Alan of Lille, *Plaint of Nature*, trans. Sheridan, prose 4, pp. 135–36, and
"De planctu naturae," ed. Häring, 835.68–80.

33. Alan of Lille, *The Plaint of Nature*, meter 5, p. 152. Häring, "De planctu
naturae," 843.37–844.44: "Quodlibet in facinus mulier discurrit et ultra, / Eius si
mentem morbidet iste furor. / Nata patrem fratremque soror uel sponsa maritum /
Fraude necat, fati preueniendo manum. /. . . Cogitur ipsa parens nomen nescire
parentis / In partuque dolos dum parit ipsa parat."

34. Cadden, *Meanings of Sex Difference*, p. 223.

35. See Cadden, *Meanings of Sex Difference*, pp. 21–26, 30–37; Laqueur, *Making Sex*, pp. 25–32; and Brundage, *Law, Sex, and Christian Society*, pp. 64–65, 350–
51, 425–28.

36. For a summary of Bossi's and Gerson's ideas about sodomy in *De stupro
detestabili in masculos 1*, see Brundage, *Law, Sex, and Christian Society*, pp. 533–34. See
Gerson, *De confessione mollitiei*, in *Oeuvres complètes*, ed. Palémon Glorieux, (Paris:
Desclée, 1960), 8: 72.

37. Ruth Mazo Karras and David Lorenzo Boyd, "'Ut cum muliere': A Male
Transvestite Prostitute in Fourteenth-Century London," in *Premodern Sexualities*, ed.
Louise Fradenburg and Carla Freccero (New York: Routledge, 1996), pp. 101–16.

38. Karras and Boyd, "'Ut cum muliere,'" pp. 109, 111–12.

39. Brundage, *Law, Sex, and Christian Society*, p. 400. Brundage is actually less
guilty than others of ignoring what he calls "lesbian" sex in his discussion of sins
against nature. In fact, his notes and discussions of female sexuality elsewhere in this
book have been invaluable to my own study.

40. Michel Foucault, *History of Sexuality*, Vol. 1, *An Introduction*, trans. Robert
Hurley (New York: Vintage, 1990), p. 27.

41. John Chrysostom, *Chrysostom: Homilies on the Acts of the Apostles and the
Epistle to the Romans*, ed. Philip Schaff, Nicene and Post-Nicene Fathers 11 (Christian Literature Publishing Co., 1889), p. 356.

42. Ambrose, *Commentaria in Epistolas B. Pauli*, PL 17: col. 60: "Haec irato
Deo propter idololatriam humano generi provenisse testatur, ut mulier mulierem
turpi desiderio ad usum appeteret"; Peter Abelard, *Expositio in epistolam Pauli ad
Romanos*, PL 178: col. 806: "Contra naturam, hoc est contra naturae institutionem,
quae genitalia feminarum usui virorum praeparavit, et e converso, non ut feminae
feminis cohabitarent." Translations are from Louis Compton, "The Myth of Lesbian
Impunity: Capital Laws from 1270 to 1791," in *Historical Perspectives on Homo-*

sexuality, ed. Salvatore J. Licata and Robert P. Petersen (New York: Haworth Press, 1981), p. 14.

43. Bernadette J. Brooten, *Love Between Women: Early Christian Responses to Female Homoeroticism* (Chicago: University of Chicago Press, 1996), p. 213.

44. Albert the Great, *Quaestio de luxuria* 1 vol., quoted in Jordan, *Invention of Sodomy*, p. 126. Jordan's main argument is that Albert defines sins against nature as sins against the reproductive faculty and teleology, that is, procreation, pp. 114–35.

45. "Sodomia est peccatum contra naturam, masculi cum masculo, vel foeminae cum foemina," in Albert the Great, *Opera Omnia*, vol. 33, ed. Auguste Borgnet (Paris: Vivès, 1895), p. 400. See also his *In evangelium Lucae, 17.29* in *Opera Omnia*, ed. Bognet, vol. 23 (Paris: Vives, 1895), p. 488.

46. Albert the Great, *In Evangelium Lucae*, 17.29, p. 488. For discussions of this passage in Albert, see Vern L. Bullough, "The Sin Against Nature and Homosexuality," in *Sexual Practices in the Medieval Church*, ed. Vern L. Bullough and James Brundage (Buffalo, N.Y.: Prometheus Books, 1982), p. 64; and Jordan, *Invention of Sodomy*, pp. 133–34.

47. For a summary of Aquinas's ideas on unnatural sin, see Bullough, "The Sin Against Nature and Homosexuality," in *Sexual Practices in the Medieval Church*, ed. Bullough and Brundage, p. 65; and Jordan, *Invention of Sodomy*, pp. 136–58.

48. *The Penitential of Theodore*, in *Medieval Handbooks of Penance: A Translation of the Principal Libri Poenitentiales*, trans. John T. McNeill and Helena M. Gamer (New York: Columbia University Press, 1990), p. 185; Bede, *De remediis Peccatorum*, *PL* 94: 570B.

49. *Robert of Flamborough: Liber Poenitentialis*, ed. J. J. Francis Firth, Studies and Texts, vol. 18 (Toronto: University of Toronto Press, 1971), pp. 229, 197: "Sicuti etiam quaesivi de masculo si contra naturam aliquid egerit, ita quaero de muliere, immo de omni genere fornicandi." See Michael Goodich's discussion, *The Unmentionable Vice: Homosexuality in the Later Medieval Period* (Santa Barbara, Calif.: ABC-Clio, 1979), pp. 56–57.

50. Quoted in Compton, "The Myth of Lesbian Impunity," p. 14.

51. Thomas of Chobham, *Summa confessorum*, ed. F. Broomfield. Analecta Mediaevalia Namurcensia 25 (Louvain: Editions Nauwelaerts, 1968), pp. 398–99.

52. Jean Gerson, *Regulae Morales*, XCIX, "De Luxuria," in *Opera Omnia*, ed. Ellies Du Pin (Antwerp, 1706), III, col. 95. St. Antonio is quoted in Bullough, "Sin against Nature," p. 66.

53. Quoted in Brown, *Immodest Acts*, p. 19.

54. Joan Cadden, *Meanings of Sex Difference*, pp. 223–24.

55. Margaret Hunt, "Afterword" in *Queering the Renaissance*, ed. Jonathan Goldberg (Durham, N.C.: Duke University Press, 1994), p. 373.

56. Laqueur, *Making Sex*, pp. 8, 11. For Laqueur's argument see, Chapter 2, especially pp. 50–53.

57. For a humorous illustration of the impossibility of natural heterosexual sex, see Brundage, *Law, Sex, and Christian Society*, p. 162.

58. Payer, *Bridling of Desire*, p. 14. Payer agrees with Foucault's thesis in the *History of Sexuality*, 1, that sex and sexuality are a relatively recent invention. In this respect, Payer follows a Foucaultian analysis of sexuality, such as those by David

Halperin and others, in insisting that sexuality was not an ontological category before the nineteenth century. He does not, however, adhere to the Foucaultian emphasis on acts either; rather, he claims for the Middle Ages that such concepts as lust, concupiscence, and desire are the categories of understanding.

59. For the terminology, see Payer, *Bridling of Desire*, pp. 19, 47–50; for the problematic nature of pleasure, see pp. 18–19, 30–34, 82–83.

60. The classic statement of Foucault about the invention of homosexuality in the nineteenth century appears in *History of Sexuality*, 1: 43; for a recent argument about the constructedness of heterosexuality as well, see Jonathan Ned Katz, *The Invention of Heterosexuality* (New York: Dutton, 1995). The word did not come into English until eight years after the term homosexuality was first used in 1892. See David M. Halperin, *One Hundred Years of Homosexuality and Other Essays on Greek Love* (New York: Routledge, 1990), pp. 15–18.

61. James A. Schultz, "Bodies That Don't Matter: Heterosexuality Before Heterosexuality in Gottfried's *Tristan*," in *Constructing Medieval Sexuality*, ed. Lochrie, McCracken, and Schultz (Minneapolis: University of Minnesota Press, 1997), p. 105.

62. Jonathan Dollimore, *Sexual Dissidence: Augustine to Wilde, Freud to Foucault* (Oxford: Clarendon Press, 1991), p. 109; for his discussion of the contradictions in nature, see pp. 108–30; for the perverse in Augustine's theology, pp. 131–47; for his analysis of Freud's "paradoxical perverse" and Foucault's "perverse dynamic," see pp. 103–6.

63. I am playing on Foucault's notion of "perverse implantation" as a product and instrument of power, *History of Sexuality*, 1: 36–49.

64. See Dollimore's discussion of the term, *Sexual Dissidence*, p. 120. He points out that many of the *OED* citations for perversion and its cognates associate this straying with women and religious heretics. Most of the citations date from 1500 onwards, but a few from the fifteenth century provide only suggestive evidence for the Middle Ages.

65. Janet E. Halley, "Bowers v. Hardwick in the Renaissance," in *Queering the Renaissance*, ed. Goldberg, pp. 15–39.

66. Foucault, *History of Sexuality*, 1: 101.

67. Jonathan Goldberg, "Sodomy in the New World: Anthropologies Old and New," *Social Text* 46 (1991): 29.

68. Larry Scanlon, *Narrative, Authority, and Power: The Medieval Exemplum and the Chaucerian Tradition* (Cambridge: Cambridge University Press, 1994), p. 247.

69. Scanlon, *Narrative, Authority, and Power*, pp. 246–47. For critics who argue for Gower's consistently moral and philosophical perspective, see John H. Fisher, *John Gower: Moral Philosopher and Friend of Chaucer* (New York: New York University Press, 1964); Patrick Gallacher, *Love, the Word, and Mercury: A Reading of John Gower's "Confessio Amantis"* (Albuquerque: University of New Mexico Press, 1975); Kurt Olsson, *John Gower and the Structures of Conversion: A Reading of the "Confessio Amantis"* (Cambridge: D. S. Brewer, 1992); and Russell A. Peck, *Kingship and the Common Profit in Gower's "Confessio Amantis"* (Carbondale: Southern Illinois Press, 1978). For an analysis of how this scholarly tradition of comparing the two writers attempted to establish Chaucer's masculine authority, see Carolyn Dinshaw, "Ri-

valry, Rape, and Manhood: Gower and Chaucer," in *Chaucer and Gower: Difference, Mutuality, Exchange*, ed. R. F. Yeager (Victoria, B.C.: English Literary Studies, 1991), pp. 130–52.

70. See Kurt Olsson, *John Gower*; for another version of this argument, see R. F. Yeager, *John Gower's Poetic: The Search for a New Arion* (Cambridge: D. S. Brewer, 1990), pp. 230–79. Scanlon offers a different analysis of Gower's critique of secular love in terms of the contingency of romance; see *Narrative, Authority, and Power*, pp. 267–82. See also Winthrop Wetherbee's discussion of how the tales "resist their overt moral purpose," in "Genius and Interpretation in the 'Confessio Amantis,'" in *Magister Regis: Studies in Honor of Robert Earl Kaske*, ed. Arthur Groos (New York: Fordham University Press, 1986), pp. 243–45.

71. Olsson, *Gower and the Structures of Conversion*, p. 11, and Scanlon, *Narrative, Authority, and Power*, p. 272.

72. I have already cited the theological strain of critical scholarship on the *Confessio Amantis*. Rosemary Woolf was the first to try to rewrite Gower's epithet from "moral" to "kindly" based on her reading of his sympathy for the sexual sins depicted in his work, "Moral Chaucer and Kindly Gower," in *J.R.R. Tolkien, Scholar and Storyteller: Essays in Memoriam*, ed. Mary Salu and Robert T. Farrell (Ithaca, N.Y.: Cornell University Press, 1979), pp. 221–45. For another assessment of Gower's compassion (as opposed to morality) in the incest story, see Derek Pearsall, "Gower's Narrative Art," *PMLA* 81 (1966): 481.

73. Translation from John Gower, *Confessio Amantis*, ed. Russell A. Peck (Toronto: University of Toronto Press, 1980), I.1–8. "Naturatus amor nature legibus orbem / Subdit, et vnanimes concitat esse feras: / Huius enim mundi Princeps amor esse videtur, / Cuius eget diues, pauper et omnis ope. / Sunt in agone pares amor et fortuna, que cecas / Plebis ad insidias vertit vterque rotas. / Est amor egra salus, vexata quies, pius error, / Bellica pax, vulnus dulce, suaue malum," John Gower, *The English Writings of John Gower*, ed. G. C. Macaulay, EETS 81 (London: Oxford University Press, 1900), I.i–viii.

74. For a discussion of the various possible meanings of the term *naturatus amor*, see Winthrop Wetherbee, "Latin Structure and Vernacular Space: Gower, Chaucer and the Boethian Tradition," in *Chaucer and Gower: Difference, Mutuality, Exchange* (Victoria, B.C.: English Literary Studies, 1991), p. 7.

75. John Gower, *The English Works*, III.157. Hereafter all references cited in the text will be to this edition.

76. In Alan's *Plaint*, Nature blames Venus for introducing disorder into natural procreation through lust and other corruptions. See Alan of Lille, *Plaint of Nature*, prose 5.

77. See Jordan's excellent discussion of this incoherence, particularly on the subject of sodomy, *Invention of Sodomy*, pp. 80–91.

78. Wetherbee, "Latin Structure and Vernacular Space," p. 14.

79. Alan of Lille, *Plaint of Nature*, trans. Sheridan, prose 5, pp. 163–64.

80. For an analysis of the appropriation of the feminine through its caricature, see Carolyn Dinshaw, *Chaucer's Sexual Poetics* (Madison: University of Wisconsin Press, 1989), pp. 65–87.

81. For example, see Olsson, *John Gower and the Structures of Confession*, p. 136.

My reading of the story is closer to Scanlon's, though I don't agree that this is an example of Gower's critique of courtly love; see Scanlon, *Narrative, Authority, and Power*, p. 273.

82. Woolf, "Moral Chaucer and Kindly Gower," p. 224; Yeager makes a labored distinction between Nature and *kinde* in this tale, "Learning to Speak in Tongues: Writing Poetry for a Trilingual Culture," in *Chaucer and Gower: Difference, Mutuality, Exchange*, ed. R. F. Yeager (Victoria, B.C.: English Literary Studies, 1991), pp. 120–26.

83. See Dinshaw's analysis of the way in which rape in this story reinforces patriarchal notions of the exchange of women and obscures the consequences for the women themselves, "Rivalry, Rape and Manhood: Gower and Chaucer," in *Chaucer and Gower*, ed. Yeager, pp. 130–52.

84. Dinshaw, "Rivalry, Rape, and Manhood," p. 140.

85. See Wetherbee, "Genius and Interpretation," p. 247, 248. Olsson agrees with Wetherbee; Olsson, *John Gower*, p. 84. .

86. Guillaume de Lorris and Jean de Meun, *The Romance of the Rose*, trans. Charles Dahlberg (Princeton, N.J.: Princeton University Press, 1971), p. 145.

87. For examples of this discomfort with Gower's ending, see Olsson, *John Gower*, p. 230, and J. A. Burrow, "The Portrayal of Amans in 'Confessio Amantis,'" in *Gower's Confessio: Responses and Reassessments*, ed. A. J. Minnis (Cambridge: Cambridge University Press, 1983), pp. 14–15.

88. Eve Kosofsky Sedgwick, *Epistemology of the Closet* (Durham, N.C.: Duke University Press, 1990), pp. 71–72. See my discussion of this idea in the Introduction.

Bibliography

PRIMARY SOURCES

Abelard, Peter. *Expositio in epistolam Pauli ad Romanos. PL* 178: cols. 735–923.
Alan of Lille. *De planctu naturae*, ed. Nicholas Häring. "Alan of Lille, 'De Planctu naturae.'" *Studi Medievali*, ser. 3. 19/2 (1978): 797–879.
———. *Liber poenitentialis. PL* 210: cols. 279–304.
———. *The Plaint of Nature*, trans. James J. Sheridan. Toronto: Pontifical Institute of Mediaeval Studies, 1980.
Albert the Great. *In evangelium Lucae*. In *Opera omnia*, ed. Auguste Borgnet. Vol. 23. Paris: Vivès, 1895.
———. *Opera Omnia*, ed. Auguste Borgnet. Paris: Vivès, 1890–99.
———. *Questiones super De Animalibus*. In *Alberti Magni Opera Omnia*, ed. E. Filthaut. Vol. 9. Münster: Aschendorff, 1955.
———. *Summa theologiae*. In *Opera omnia*, ed. Auguste Borgnet. Vol. 33. Paris: Vivès, 1895.
Pseudo-Albert. *Women's Secrets: A Translation of Pseudo-Albertus Magnus's* De Secretis Mulierum *with Commentaries*, trans. Helen Rodnite Lemay. Albany: State University of New York Press, 1992.
Ambrose. *Commentaria in Epistolas B. Pauli. PL* 17: cols. 45–504.
The Ancrene Wisse: The English Text of the Ancrene Riwle edited from MS. Corpus Christi College Cambridge 402, ed. J. R. R. Tolkien. EETS 249. London: Oxford University Press, 1962.
Aristotle. *On Dreams*. In *On the Soul, Parva naturalia, On Breath*, rev. ed., ed. and trans. W. S. Hett. Cambridge, Mass.: Harvard University Press, 1957.
Pseudo-Aristotle. *Secretum Secretorum: Nine English Versions*, ed. M. A. Manzalaoui. Vol. 1. EETS 276. Oxford: Oxford University Press. 1977.
Bacon, Roger. *Opus Majus*, trans. Robert Belle Burke. 2 vols. New York: Russell and Russell, 1962.
———. *Secretum secretorum cum glossis et notulis*, ed. Robert Steele. In *Opera hactenus inedita Rogeri Baconi*. Vol. 5. Oxford: Oxford University Press, 1920.
Bede. *De remediis Peccatorum. PL* 94: cols. 567–76.
Bevington, David, ed. *Medieval Drama*. Boston: Houghton Mifflin, 1975.
Blamires, Alcuin, ed. *Woman Defamed and Woman Defended: An Anthology of Medieval Texts*. Oxford: Clarendon Press, 1992.
Boethius. *The Consolation of Philosophy*, trans. V. E. Watts. New York: Penguin Books, 1969.

The Book of Vices and Virtues, ed. W. Nelson Francis. EETS o.s. 217. London: Oxford University Press, 1942.

Bryan, W. F. and Germaine Dempster. *Sources and Analogues of Chaucer's Canterbury Tales*. Chicago: University of Chicago Press, 1941.

Caxton, William, trans. *The Book of the Knight of the Tower*, ed. M. Y. Offord. EETS 217. London: Oxford University Press, 1971.

Chaucer, Geoffrey. *The Riverside Chaucer*. 3d ed., ed. Larry D. Benson. Boston: Houghton Mifflin, 1987.

Christine de Pizan. *The Book of the City of Ladies*, trans. Earl Jeffrey Richards. New York: Persea Books, 1982.

Chrysostom, John. *Chrysostom: Homilies on the Acts of the Apostles and the Epistle to the Romans*, ed. Philip Schaff. Nicene and Post-Nicene Fathers 11. New York: Christian Literature Publishing Co., 1889.

Comestor, Peter. *Historia scholastica*. PL 198: cols. 1045–1721.

Damian, Peter. *Book of Gomorrah: An Eleventh-Century Treatise Against Clerical Homosexual Practices*, trans. Pierre J. Payer. Waterloo, Ont.: Wilfrid Laurier University Press, 1982.

——. *Liber Gomorrhianus = Epistola 31*. In *Die Briefe des Petrus Damiani*, vol. 1, ed. Kurt Reindel. Monumenta Germaniae Historica: Die Briefe der deutschen Kaiserzeit, vol. 4. Munich: Monumenta Germaniae Historica, 1983.

Denifle, Henri, ed. *Chartularium Universitatis Parisiensis*. Vol. 2. Paris, 1891.

Furnivall, F. J., ed. *The Babees Book*. EETS 32. London: Kegan Paul, Trench, Trübner, 1868.

Galen. *Galen On the Affected Parts*, trans. Rudolph E. Siegel. Basel: S. Karger, 1976.

Gerson, Jean. *De confessione mollitiei*. In *Oeuvres complètes*, ed. Palémon Glorieux. Vol. 8. Paris: Desclée, 1960.

——. *Regulae Morales*. In *Opera Omnia*, ed. Ellies Du Pin. Vol. 3. Antwerp, 1706.

Glanvill. *The Treatise on the Laws and Customs of the Realm of England commonly called Glanvill*, ed. and trans. G. D. G. Hall. London: Nelson, 1965.

"The Gossips," ed. James E. Masters. Shaftesbury, Dorset: High House Press, 1926.

Gower, John. *The Complete Works of John Gower*, ed. G. C. Macaulay. Vol. 2. Oxford: Clarendon Press, 1899.

——. *Confessio Amantis*, ed. Russell A. Peck. Toronto: University of Toronto Press, 1980.

——. *The English Works of John Gower*, ed. G. C. Macaulay. EETS e.s. 81 and 82. London: Oxford University Press, 1901.

Guillaume de Lorris and Jean de Meun. *The Romance of the Rose*, trans. Charles Dahlberg. Princeton, N.J.: Princeton University Press, 1971.

Hoccleve, Thomas. *Hoccleve's Works*, ed. F. J. Furnivall. EETS e.s. 72. London: Kegan Paul, Trench, Trübner, 1897.

Jacques de Vitry. *The Exempla or Illustrative Stories from the "Sermones vulgares" of Jacques de Vitry*, ed. T. F. Crane. Folklore Society, vol. 26, no. 19. London, 1890.

Kempe, Margery. *The Book of Margery Kempe*, ed. Sanford B. Meech and Hope Emily Allen. EETS o.s. 214. London: Oxford University Press, 1940.

Langland, William. *Piers Plowman: The B Version*, ed. George Kane and E. Talbot Donaldson. London: Athlone, 1975.

——. *Piers Plowman. The C Text*, ed. Derek Pearsall. Berkeley: University of California Press, 1979.

——. *Will's Vision of Piers Plowman*, ed. Elizabeth D. Kirk and Judith H. Anderson. Trans. E. Talbot Donaldson. New York: Norton, 1990.

Lydgate, John. *The Pilgrimage of the Life of Man*, ed. F. J. Furnivall. EETS, e.s. 77 (London: Kegan Paul, Trench, Trübner, 1899), 83 (1901), and 92 (1904).

McNeill, John T. and Helena M. Gamer, trans. *Medieval Handbooks of Penance: A Translation of Principal Libri Poenitentiales*. New York: Columbia University Press, 1990.

Mannyng, Robert, of Brunne. *Handlyng Synne*, ed. F. J. Furnivalle. EETS 119, 123. London: Kegan Paul, Trench, Trübner, 1901–1903.

Marie de France. *The Lais of Marie de France*, trans. Robert Hanning and Joan Ferrante. Durham, N.C.: Labyrinth Press, 1978.

Michel, Don. *Ayenbit of Inwit or Remorse of Conscience*, ed. R. Morris. EETS o.s. 23. London: Kegan Paul, Trench, Trübner, 1866.

Middle English Sermons, ed. Woodburn O. Ross. EETS o.s. 209. London: Oxford University Press, 1940.

Mirk, John. *John Mirk's Instructions for Parish Priests*, ed. Edward Peacock. EETS 31. London: Kegan Paul, Trench, Trübner, 1902.

——. *Mirk's Festial*, ed. Theodore Erbe. EETS, e.s. 96. London: Kegan Paul, Trench, Trübner, 1905.

Peter Idley's Instructions to His Son, ed. Charlotte D'Evelyn. London: Oxford University Press, 1935.

Petersen, Kate O. *The Sources of the Parson's Tale*. Boston: Ginn, 1901.

Pliny. *Natural History*, ed. and trans. H. Rackham, W. H. S. Jones, and D. E. Eicholz. Vol. 7. Loeb Classical Library. Cambridge, Mass.: Harvard University Press, 1938–62.

Raymond of Peñafort. *Summa de poenitentia et matrimonio*. Rome, 1603; rpt. Farborough: Gregg Press, 1967.

Renart, John. *Galerent de Bretagne: roman du XIIIe siècle*, ed. Lucien Foulet. Paris: Champion, 1925.

Rypins, Stanley, ed. *Three Old English Prose Texts*. EETS e.s. 161. London: Oxford University Press, 1924.

Robert of Flamborough. *Robert of Flamborough:* Liber Poenitentialis, ed. J. J. Francis Firth. Studies and Texts 18. Toronto: Pontifical Institute of Mediaeval Studies, 1971.

Rowland, Beryl, ed. *Medieval Woman's Guide to Health: The First English Gynecological Handbook*. Kent, Oh.: Kent State University Press, 1981.

Sir Gawain and the Green Knight. In *The Complete Works of the Pearl Poet*, ed. Malcolm Andrew and Ronald Waldron, Clifford Peterson, trans. Casey Finch. Berkeley: University of California Press, 1993.

Smith, Toulmin, ed. *English Gilds*. EETS o.s. 40. London: N. Trübner, 1870.

Songs, Carols, and other Miscellaneous Poems, ed. Roman Dyboski. EETS 101. London: Kegan Paul, Trench, Trübner, 1907.

Speculum Sacerdotale, ed. Edward H. Weatherly. EETS o.s. 200. London: Oxford University Press, 1936.

Steele, Robert, ed. *Lydgate and Burgh's Secrees of Old Philosoffres*. EETS e.s. 66. London, 1884.

——. *Three Prose Versions of the Secreta Secretorum*. EETS e.s. 74. London, 1898.

Thomas of Chobham. *Summa confessorum*, ed. F. Broomfield. Analecta mediaevalia Namurcensia 25. Louvain: Editions Nauwelaerts, 1968.

Thomasset, Claude Alexandre, ed. *Placides et Timéo ou Li secrés as philosophes*. Geneva: Droz, 1980.

Thorndike, Lynn. *University Records and Life in the Middle Ages*. New York: Columbia University Press, 1944.

Wilde, Oscar. *The Picture of Dorian Gray*, ed. Peter Ackroyd. New York: Penguin, 1949.

Wright, Thomas and James O Halliwell, eds. *Reliquiae Antiquae*. Vol. 2. London, 1843.

SECONDARY SOURCES

Aers, David. *Community, Gender, and Individual Identity: English Writing, 1360–1430*. New York: Routledge, 1988.

Ariès, Philippe and Georges Duby, eds. *A History of Private Life*. Part 2, *Revelations of the Medieval World*. Trans. Arthur Goldhammer. Cambridge, Mass.: Belknap Press, 1988.

Bailey, Derrick Sherwin. *Homosexuality and the Western Christian Tradition*. London: Longman, Green, 1955; rpt. Hamden, Conn.: Archon Books, 1975.

Baker, John Hamilton. *Manual of French Law*. 2d ed. Hants: Scolar Press, 1992.

Barthes, Roland. *Roland Barthes*. Trans. Richard Howard. New York: Hill and Wang, 1977.

Bennett, J.A.W. *Chaucer's* Book of Fame. Oxford: Clarendon Press, 1968.

Bennett, Judith M. *Ale, Beer, and Brewsters in England: Women's Work in a Changing World, 1200–1600*. New York: Oxford University Press, 1996.

——. "Medieval Women, Modern Women: Across the Great Divide." In *Culture and History, 1350–1600: Essays on English Communities, Identities and Writing*, ed. David Aers, pp. 147–75. Detroit: Wayne State University Press, 1992.

——. *Women in the Medieval English Countryside: Brigstock Before the Plague*. London: Oxford University Press, 1987.

Bennett, Judith M., Elizabeth A. Clark, Jean F. O'Barr, B. Anne Vilen, and Sarah Westphal-Wihl, eds. *Sisters and Workers in the Middle Ages*. Chicago: University of Chicago Press, 1989.

Bergman, David, ed. *Camp Grounds: Style and Homosexuality*. Amherst: University of Massachusetts Press, 1993.

Bergmann, Jörg R. *Discreet Indiscretions: The Social Organization of Gossip*, trans. John Bednarz, Jr. New York: Aldine de Gruyter, 1993.

Bernauer, James and David Rasmussen, eds. *The Final Foucault*. Cambridge, Mass.: MIT Press, 1988.

Black, Antony. *Guilds and Civil Society in European Political Thought from the Twelfth Century to the Present*. Ithaca, N.Y.: Cornell University Press, 1984.

Bloch, R. Howard. "The Lay and the Law: Sexual/Textual Transgression in *La Chastelaine de Vergi*, the *Lai D'Ignaure*, and the *Lais* of Marie de France." *Stanford French Review* 14 (1990): 181–210.

Bohlen, Celestine. "The Good Word: Creature Comforts for Catholics." *New York Times*, 28 June 1996, natl. ed: A4.

Boitani, Piero. *Chaucer and the Imaginary World of Fame*. Cambridge: D. S. Brewer, 1984.

Bok, Sissela. *Secrets: On the Ethics of Concealment and Revelation*. New York: Vintage Books, 1989.

Bossy, John. "The Social History of Confession in the Age of the Reformation." *Transactions of the Royal Historical Society* 5th ser. 25 (1975): 21–38.

Boyd, David Lorenzo. "Disrupting the Norm: Sodomy, Culture and the Male Body in Peter Damian's *Liber Gomorrhianus*." In *Essays in Medieval Studies*, Vol. 11, ed. Allen J. Frantzen and David J. Robertson, pp. 63–74. Chicago: Illinois Medieval Association, 1994.

Braswell, Mary Flowers. *The Medieval Sinner: Characterization and Confession in the Literature of the English Middle Ages*. New York: Associated University Presses, 1982.

Brooks, Peter. *Body Work: Objects of Desire in Modern Narrative*. Cambridge, Mass.: Harvard University Press, 1993.

Brooten, Bernadette J. *Love Between Women: Early Christian Responses to Female Homoeroticism*. Chicago: University of Chicago Press, 1996.

Brown, Judith C. *Immodest Acts: The Life of a Lesbian Nun in Renaissance Italy*. New York: Oxford University Press, 1986.

——. "A Woman's Place Was in the Home: Women's Work in Renaissance Tuscany." In *Rewriting the Renaissance: The Discourses of Sexual Difference in Early Modern Europe*, ed. Margaret W. Ferguson, Maureen Quilligan, and Nancy J. Vickers, pp. 206–24. Chicago: University of Chicago Press, 1986.

Brundage, James A. *Law, Sex, and Christian Society in Medieval Europe*. Chicago: University of Chicago Press, 1987.

Bullough, Vern L. "The Development of Medical Guilds at Paris." *Medievalia et Humanistica* 12 (1958): 33–40.

——. "The Medieval Medical University at Paris." *Bulletin of the History of Medicine* 31 (1957): 197–211.

——. "The Sin Against Nature and Homosexuality." In *Sexual Practices in the Medieval Church*, ed. Vern L. Bullough and James Brundage, pp. 55–71. Buffalo, N.Y.: Prometheus Books, 1982.

Burrow, J. A. "The Portrayal of Amans in 'Confessio Amantis.'" In *Gower's Confessio: Responses and Reassessments*, ed. A. J. Minnis, pp. 5–24. Cambridge: Cambridge University Press, 1983.

——. *A Reading of Sir Gawain and the Green Knight*. New York: Barnes and Noble, 1966.

Butler, Judith. *Bodies That Matter: On the Discursive Limits of Sex*. New York: Routledge, 1993.

——. *Gender Trouble: Feminism and the Subversion of Identity*. New York: Routledge, 1990.

Bynum, Caroline Walker. "The Female Body in Religious Practice." In *Fragmentation and Redemption: Essays on Gender and the Human Body in Medieval Religion*, pp. 181–238. New York: Zone Books, 1991.

———. *Holy Feast and Holy Fast: The Religious Significance of Food to Medieval Women*. Berkeley: University of California Press, 1987.

Cadden, Joan. *Meanings of Sex Difference in the Middle Ages: Medicine, Science, and Culture*. Cambridge: Cambridge University Press, 1993.

———. "Sciences/Silences: The Natures and Languages of 'Sodomy' in Peter of Abano's *Problemata* Commentary." In *Constructing Medieval Sexuality*, ed. Lochrie et al., pp. 40–57.

Cary, George. *The Medieval Alexander*. Cambridge: Cambridge University Press, 1956.

de Certeau, Michel. *The Mystic Fable*, Vol. 1, *The Sixteenth and Seventeenth Centuries*. Trans. Michael B. Smith. Chicago: University of Chicago Press, 1992.

Chambers, Ross. "Histoire d'Oeuf: Secrets and Secrecy in a La Fontaine Fable." *Sub-stance* 32 (1981): 58–75.

Charles, Lindsey and Lorna Duffin, eds. *Women and Work in Pre-Industrial England*. London: Croom Helm, 1985.

Clark, Elizabeth A. "Foucault, the Fathers, and Sex." *Journal of the American Academy of Religion* 56 (1988): 619–41.

Coates, Jennifer. "Gossip Revisited: Language in All-Female Groups." In *Women in Their Speech Communities: New Perspectives in Language and Sex*, ed. Jennifer Coates and Deborah Cameron, pp. 94–122. London: Longman, 1988.

Compton, Louis. "The Myth of Lesbian Impunity: Capital Laws from 1270–1791." In *Historical Perspectives on Homosexuality*, ed. Salvatore J. Licata and Robert P. Petersen. New York: Haworth Press, 1981.

Cotter, Holland. "Discovering Secrets, Africa's Currency of Power." *New York Times* 12 February 1976: B6.

Dale, Marion K. "The London Silkwomen of the Fifteenth Century." In *Sisters and Workers*, ed. Bennett et al., pp. 26–38.

Daston, Lorraine and Katharine Park. "The Hermaphrodite and the Orders of Nature: Sexual Ambiguity in Early Modern France." In *Premodern Sexualities*, ed. Fradenburg and Freccero, pp. 117–36.

Davis, Natalie Zemon. "Women in the Crafts in Sixteenth-Century Lyon." In *Women and Work in Preindustrial Europe*, ed. Hanawalt, pp. 167–97.

———. "Women on Top." In *Society and Culture in Early Modern France*, pp. 124–51. Stanford, Calif.: Stanford University Press, 1975.

Delaney, Janice, Mary Jane Lupton, and Emily Toth. *The Curse: A Cultural History of Menstruation*. Rev. ed. Urbana: University of Illinois Press, 1988.

Delaney, Sheila. *Chaucer's House of Fame: The Poetics of Skeptical Fideism*. Chicago: University of Chicago Press, 1972.

Derrida, Jacques. "'To Do Justice to Freud': The History of Madness in the Age of Psychoanalysis," trans. Pascale-Anne Brault and Michael Naas. *Critical Inquiry* 20 (Winter 1994): 227–66.

Dinshaw, Carolyn. *Chaucer's Sexual Poetics*. Madison: University of Wisconsin Press, 1989.

———."Getting Medieval: *Pulp Fiction*, Gawain, and Foucault." In *The Book and the Body*, ed. Dolores Warwick Frese and Katherine O'Brien O'Keeffe. Notre Dame, Ind.: University of Notre Dame Press, 1997.

———. "A Kiss Is Just a Kiss: Heterosexuality and Its Consolations in *Sir Gawain and the Green Knight*." *diacritics* 24, 2–3 (Summer–Fall 1994): 205–24.

———. "Rivalry, Rape, and Manhood: Gower and Chaucer." In *Chaucer and Gower: Difference, Mutuality, Exchange*, ed. Yeager, pp. 130–52.

Dollimore, Jonathan. *Sexual Dissidence: Augustine to Wilde, Freud to Foucault*. Oxford: Clarendon Press, 1991.

Donaldson, E. Talbot. *Speaking of Chaucer*. New York: Norton, 1970.

Douglas, Mary. *Purity and Danger*. London: Ark Paperbacks, 1966.

Duby, Georges. "The Aristocratic Households of Feudal France: Communal Living," pp. 35–85. In *A History of Private Life*, Vol. 2, ed. Ariès and Duby.

———. "Private Power, Public Power." In *A History of Private Life*, Vol. 2, pp. 3–31.

Duggan, Lawrence. "Fear and Confession on the Eve of the Reformation." *Archiv für Reformationsgeschichte* 75 (1984): 153–75.

Eamon, William. "Books of Secrets in Medieval and Early Modern Science." *Sudhoffs Archiv* 69 (1985): 26–49.

———. "From the Secrets of Nature to Public Knowledge." *Minerva* 23, 3 (Fall 1985): 321–46.

———. *Science and the Secrets of Nature: Books of Secrets in Medieval and Early Modern Culture*. Princeton, N.J.: Princeton University Press, 1994.

Easton, Stewart C. *Roger Bacon and His Search for a Universal Science*. New York: Columbia University Press, 1952.

Economou, George D. *The Goddess Natura in Medieval Literature* Cambridge, Mass.: Harvard University Press, 1972.

Eisenstein, Elizabeth L. *The Printing Press as an Agent of Change*. 2 vols. Cambridge: Cambridge University Press, 1979.

Elliott, Dyan. "Pollution, Illusion, and Masculine Disarray: Nocturnal Emissions and the Sexuality of the Clergy." In *Constructing Medieval Sexuality*, ed. Lochrie, McCracken, and Schultz, pp. 1–23.

Farrell, Thomas J. "Privacy and the Boundaries of Fabliau in the *Miller's Tale*." *ELH* 56 (1989): 773–95.

Ferster, Judith. *Fictions of Advice: The Literature and Politics of Counsel in Late Medieval England*. Philadelphia: University of Pennsylvania Press, 1996.

Fisher, John H. *John Gower: Moral Philosopher and Friend of Chaucer*. New York: New York University Press, 1964.

Fisher, Sheila. "Taken Men and Token Women in *Sir Gawain and the Green Knight*." In *Seeking the Woman in Late Medieval and Renaissance Writings: Essays in Feminist Contextual Criticism*, ed. Sheila Fisher and Janet E. Halley. Knoxville: University of Tennessee Press, 1989.

Flynn, Thomas. "Foucault as Parrhesiast." In *The Final Foucault*, ed. James Bernauer and David Rasmussen, pp. 102–18. Cambridge, Mass.: MIT Press, 1988.

Foucault, Michel. "About the Beginning of the Hermeneutics of the Self: Two Lectures at Dartmouth." Ed. Mark Blasius. *Political Theory* 21, 2 (May 1993): 198–227.

——. *The Archaeology of Knowledge and the Discourse on Language*, trans. A.M. Sheridan Smith. New York: Pantheon Books, 1972.

——. The Battle for Chastity." In *Western Sexuality: Practice and Precept in Past and Present Times*, ed. Philippe Ariès and André Bejin, trans. Anthony Forster, pp. 14–25. Oxford: Basil Blackwell, 1985.

——. *Death and the Labyrinth: The World of Raymond Roussel*, trans. Charles Ruas. New York: Doubleday, 1986.

——. *Foucault Live: Collected Interviews, 1961–1984*, ed. Sylvère Lotringer, trans. Lysa Hochroth and John Johnston. New York: Semiotext(e), 1996.

——. *The History of Sexuality*, Vol. 1, *An Introduction*, trans. Robert Hurley. New York: Vintage, 1990.

——. *Language, Counter-Memory, Practice: Selected Essays and Interviews*, ed. Donald Bouchard, trans. Donald Bouchard and Sherry Simon. Ithaca, N.Y.: Cornell University Press, 1977.

——. *Michel Foucault: Beyond Structuralism and Hermeneutics*. 2d ed., ed. Hubert L. Dreyfus and Paul Rabinow. Chicago: University of Chicago Press, 1983.

——. *Résumé des cours, 1970–1982*. Paris: Gallimard, 1989.

——. "Sexuality and Solitude." In *Humanities in Review I*, ed. David Rieff, pp. 3–21. Cambridge: Cambridge University Press, 1982.

Fradenburg, Louise and Carla Freccero, eds. *Premodern Sexualities*. New York: Routledge, 1996.

Frantzen, Allen J. "The Disclosure of Sodomy in *Cleanness.*" *PMLA* 3 (May 1996): 451–64.

Freud, Sigmund. *Three Essays on the Theory of Sexuality*. Vol. 7 in *The Standard Edition of the Complete Psychological Works of Sigmund Freud*, trans. James Strachey et al. London: Hogarth Press, 1962.

Fyler, John M. *Chaucer and Ovid*. New Haven, Conn.: Yale University Press, 1979.

Gallacher, Patrick J. *Love, the Word, and Mercury: A Reading of John Gower's "Confessio Amantis.*" Albuquerque: University of New Mexico Press, 1975.

——. "Perception and Reality in the *Miller's Tale.*" *ChauRev* 18 (1983): 38–48.

Gellrich, Jesse. *The Idea of the Book in the Middle Ages*. Ithaca, N.Y.: Cornell University Press, 1986.

Gilbert. H. H. "Notes on the Influence of the *Secretum Secretorum.*" *Speculum* 3 (1928): 84–98.

Goldberg, Jonathan, ed. *Queering the Renaissance*. Durham, N.C.: Duke University Press, 1994.

——. *Sodometries: Renaissance Texts, Modern Sexualities*. Stanford, Calif.: Stanford University Press, 1992.

——. "Sodomy in the New World: Anthropologies Old and New." *Social Text* 46 (1991): 46–56.

Goldberg, P J.P. "Female Labour, Service and Marriage in the Late Medieval Urban North." *Northern History* 22 (1986): 18–38.

——. *Women, Work, and Life Cycle in a Medieval Economy: Women in York and Yorkshire, c. 1300–1520*. Oxford: Clarendon Press, 1992.

Goldberg, Rita. *Sex and Enlightenment: Women in Richardson and Diderot*. Cambridge: Cambridge University Press, 1984.

Goodall, Peter. "'Allone, withouten any Compaignye': Privacy in the First Fragment of the *Canterbury Tales*." *ELN* 29 (1991): 5–15.

Goodich, Michael. *The Unmentionable Vice: Homosexuality in the Later Medieval Period*. Santa Barbara, Calif.: ABC-Clio, 1979.

Gordon, Jan B. *Gossip and Subversion in Nineteenth-Century British Fiction*. New York: St. Martin's Press, 1996.

Gottfried, Robert S. *Doctors and Medicine in Medieval England, 1340–1530*. Princeton, N.J.: Princeton University Press, 1986.

Green, Monica. "Female Sexuality in the Medieval West." *Trends in History* 4 (1990): 127–58.

———. "Women's Medical Practice and Health Care in Medieval Europe." In *Sisters and Workers*, ed. Bennett et al., pp. 39–78.

Grignaschi, M. "La diffusion du 'Secretum secretorum' (Sirr-Al-'Asrar) dans l'Europe occidentale." *Archives d'Histoire Doctrinale et Littéraire du Moyen Age* 47 (1980): 7–70.

———. "L'origine et les métamorphoses du 'Sirr-al-asrâr.'" *Archives d'Histoire Doctrinale et Littéraire du Moyen Age* 43 (1976): 7–112.

Haliczer, Stephen. *Sexuality in the Confessional*. Oxford: Oxford University Press, 1996.

Halley, Janet E. "Bowers v. Hardwick in the Renaissance." In *Queering the Renaissance*, ed. Goldberg, pp. 15–39.

Halperin, David M. *One Hundred Years of Homosexuality and Other Essays on Greek Love*. New York: Routledge, 1990.

———. *Saint Foucault: Towards a Gay Hagiography*. New York: Oxford University Press, 1995.

Hanawalt, Barbara A. *Growing Up in Medieval London: The Experience of Childhood in History*. New York: Oxford University Press, 1993.

———. *The Ties That Bound: Peasant Families in Medieval England*. London: Oxford University Press, 1986.

———, ed. *Women and Work in Preindustrial Europe*. Bloomington: Indiana University Press, 1986.

Hanning, R. W. "Telling the Private Parts." In *The Idea of Medieval Literature: New Essays on Chaucer and Medieval Culture in Honor of Donald R. Howard*, ed. James M. Dean and Christian K. Zacher, pp. 108–25. Newark: University of Delaware Press, 1992.

Hansen, Elaine Tuttle. *Chaucer and the Fictions of Gender*. Berkeley: University of California Press, 1992.

Harwood, Britton J. "Building Class and Gender into Chaucer's *Hous*." In *Class and Gender in Early English Literature: Intersections*, ed. Britton J. Harwood and Gillian R. Overing. Bloomington: Indiana University Press, 1994.

Haskins, Charles H. *Studies in the History of Mediaeval Science*. Cambridge, Mass.: Harvard University Press, 1927.

Heidegger, Martin. *Being and Time*, trans. John Macquarrie and Edward Robinson. New York: Harper and Row, 1962.

Heng, Geraldine. "A Woman Wants: The Lady, *Gawain*, and the Forms of Seduction." *Yale Journal of Criticism* 2, 3 (1992): 101–33.

Herlihy, David. *Opera Muliebria: Women and Work in Medieval Europe*. New York: McGraw-Hill, 1990.

Hilton, Rodney. *Class Conflict and the Crisis of Feudalism*. London: Hambledon Press, 1985.

Holcombe, Lee. *Wives and Property: Reform of the Married Women's Property in Nineteenth Century England*. Toronto: University of Toronto Press, 1983.

Howell, Martha C. "Women, the Family Economy, and the Structures of Market Production in Cities of Northern Europe During the Late Middle Ages." In *Women and Work in Preindustrial Europe*, ed. Hanawalt, pp. 198–222.

———. *Women, Production, and Patriarchy in Late Medieval Cities*. Chicago: University of Chicago Press, 1986.

Hunt, Margaret. "Afterword." In *Queering the Renaissance*, ed. Goldberg, pp. 359–77.

Hutton, Diane. "Women in Fourteenth-Century Shrewsbury." In *Women and Work in Pre-industrial England*, ed. Charles and Duffin, pp. 83–99.

Irigaray, Luce. *Speculum of the Other Woman*, trans. Gillian C. Gill. Ithaca, N.Y.: Cornell University Press, 1985.

———. *This Sex Which Is Not One*, trans. Catherine Porter. Ithaca, N.Y.: Cornell University Press, 1985.

Jacquart, Danielle and Claude Thomasset. *Sexuality and Medicine in the Middle Ages*, trans. Matthew Adamson. Princeton, N.J.: Princeton University Press. 1988.

Jefferson, Margo. "Facing Incest, in Memoir and Novel." *New York Times*, 29 May 1997, natl. ed.: B7.

Johnson, Lynn Staley. *The Voice of the Gawain-Poet*. Madison: University of Wisconsin Press, 1984.

Jordan, Mark D. *The Invention of Sodomy in Christian Theology*. Chicago: University of Chicago Press, 1997.

Jones, Deborah. "Gossip: Notes on Women's Oral Culture." In *The Feminist Critique of Language: A Reader*, ed. Deborah Cameron, pp. 242–58. London: Routledge, 1990.

Kaplan, Louise J. *Female Perversions: The Temptations of Emma Bovary*. New York: Doubleday, 1991.

Kapsalis, Terri. *Public Privates: Performing Gynecology from Both Ends of the Speculum*. Durham, N.C.: Duke University Press, 1997.

Karras, Ruth Mazo and David Lorenzo Boyd. "'Ut cum muliere': A Male Transvestite Prostitute in Fourteenth-Century London." In *Premodern Sexualities*, ed. Fradenburg and Freccero, pp. 99–116.

Katz, Jonathan Ned. *The Invention of Heterosexuality*. New York: Dutton, 1995.

Keller, Evelyn Fox. "Making Gender Visible." In *Feminist Studies/Critical Studies*, ed. Theresa de Lauretis, pp. 67–77. Bloomington: Indiana University Press, 1986.

———. *Secrets of Life, Secrets of Death: Essays on Language, Gender and Science*. New York: Routledge, 1992.

Kendrick, Laura. *Chaucerian Play: Comedy and Control in the Canterbury Tales*. Berkeley: University of California Press, 1988.

Kieckhefer, Richard. *Magic in the Middle Ages*. Cambridge: Cambridge University Press, 1990.

Kolve, V. A. *Chaucer and the Imagery of Narrative: The First Five Canterbury Tales.* Stanford, Calif.: Stanford University Press, 1984.

Kowaleski, Maryanne. "Women's Work in a Market Town: Exeter in the Late Fourteenth Century." In *Women and Work in Preindustrial Europe*, ed. Hanawalt, pp. 145–66.

Kowaleski, Maryanne and Judith M. Bennett. "Crafts, Gilds, and Women in the Middle Ages: Fifty Years After Marian K. Dale." In *Sisters and Workers in the Middle Ages*, ed. Bennett et al., pp. 11–18.

Kruger, Stephen F. "Conversion and Medieval Sexual, Religious, and Racial Categories." In *Constructing Medieval Sexuality*, ed. Lochrie, McCracken, and Schultz, pp. 158–179.

Kurtscheid, Bertrand A. *A History of the Seal of Confession*, trans F. A. Marks. London, 1927.

Lacey, Kay E. "Women and Work in Fourteenth and Fifteenth Century London." In *Women and Work in Pre-Industrial England*, ed. Charles and Duffin, pp. 24–82.

Laqueur, Thomas. *Making Sex: Body and Gender from the Greeks to Freud.* Cambridge, Mass.: Harvard University Press, 1990.

de Lauretis, Teresa. *Technologies of Gender: Essays on Theory, Film, and Fiction.* Bloomington: Indiana University Press, 1987.

Lawn, Brian. *The Salernitan Questions: An Introduction to the History of Medieval and Renaissance Problem Literature.* Oxford: Clarendon Press, 1963.

Lea, Henry Charles. *A History of Auricular Confession and Indulgences in the Latin Church.* 3 vols. Philadelphia: Lea Brothers, 1896.

Lees, Clare A. "Gender and Exchange in *Piers Plowman*." In *Class and Gender in Early English Literature: Intersections*, ed. Britton J. Harwood and Gillian R. Overing, pp. 112–30. Bloomington: Indiana University Press, 1994.

Lemay, Helen Rodnite. "William of Saliceto on Human Sexuality." *Viator* 12 (1981): 165–81.

Lindberg, David C., ed. *Science in the Middle Ages.* Chicago: University of Chicago Press, 1978.

——. "The Transmission of Greek and Arabic Learning to the West." In *Science in the Middle Ages*, ed. Lindberg, pp. 52–90.

Lochrie, Karma. "Don't Ask, Don't Tell: Murderous Plots and Medieval Secrets." In *Premodern Sexualities*, ed. Fradenburg and Freccero, pp. 137–52.

——. "The Language of Transgression: Body, Flesh, and Word in Mystical Discourse." In *Speaking Two Languages: Traditional Disciplines and Contemporary Theory in Medieval Studies*, ed. Allen J. Frantzen, pp. 115–40. Albany: State University of New York Press, 1991.

——. *Margery Kempe and Translations of the Flesh.* Philadelphia: University of Pennsylvania Press, 1991.

Lochrie, Karma, Peggy McCracken, and James A. Schultz, eds. *Constructing Medieval Sexuality.* Minneapolis: University of Minnesota Press, 1997.

Long, Pamela O. "Invention, Authorship, 'Intellectual Property,' and the Origin of Patents: Notes Toward a Conceptual History." *Technology and Culture* 32 (1991): 846–84.

Mackenney, Richard. *Tradesmen and Traders: The World of the Guilds in Venice and Europe, c. 1250–1650*. Totowa, N.J.: Barnes and Noble, 1987.

MacKinnon, Catharine A. "Feminism, Marxism, Method, and the State: Toward Feminist Jurisprudence." *Signs* 8, 4 (Summer 1983): 635–58.

McKinley, Mary B. "Telling Secrets: Sacramental Confession and Narrative Authority in the *Heptameron*." In *Critical Tales: New Studies of the* Heptameron *and Early Modern Culture*, ed. John D. Lyons and Mary B. McKinley, pp. 146–71. Philadelphia: University of Pennsylvania Press, 1993.

Mann, Jill. *Geoffrey Chaucer*. Atlantic Highlands, N.J.: Humanities Press, 1991.

Mansfield, Mary C. *The Humiliation of Sinners: Public Penance in Thirteenth-Century France*. Ithaca, N.Y.: Cornell University Press, 1995.

Manzalaoui, M. A. "'Noght in the Registre of Venus': Gower's English Mirror for Princes." In *Medieval Studies for J.A.W. Bennett*, ed. P. L. Heyworth, pp. 159–83. Oxford: Clarendon Press,1981.

Metlitzki, Dorothee. *The Matter of Araby in Medieval England*. New Haven, Conn.: Yale University Press, 1977.

Miller, D. A. *The Novel and the Police*. Berkeley: University of California Press, 1988.

Miller, Jacqueline T. *Poetic License: Authority and Authorship in Medieval and Renaissance Contexts*. New York: Oxford University Press, 1982.

Miller, James. *The Passion of Michel Foucault*. New York: Simon and Schuster, 1993.

Monfrin, J. "La place du *Secret des secrets* dan la littérature française mediévale." In *Pseudo-Aristotle, The* Secret of Secrets: *Sources and Influences*, ed. W. F. Ryan and Charles B. Schmitt, pp. 73–115. London: Warburg Institute, 1982.

Moore, R. I. *The Formation of a Persecuting Society: Power and Deviance in Western Europe, 950–1250*. Oxford: Basil Blackwell, 1987.

Morey, Adrian. *Bartholomew of Exeter, Bishop and Canonist*. Cambridge: Cambridge University Press, 1937.

Mullett, Charles F. "John Lydgate: A Mirror of Medieval Medicine." *Bulletin of the History of Medicine* 22 (1948): 403–15.

Noonan, John T. *Contraception: A History of Its Treatment by the Catholic Theologians and Canonists*. Cambridge, Mass.: Harvard University Press, 1965.

Olsson, Kurt. *John Gower and the Structures of Conversion: A Reading of the "Confessio Amantis."* Cambridge: D. S. Brewer, 1992.

Owst, J. R. *Literature and the Pulpit in Medieval England*. New York: Barnes and Noble, 1961.

Pantin, W. A. *The English Church in the Fourteenth Century*. Notre Dame, Ind.: University of Notre Dame Press, 1962.

Patterson, Lee. *Chaucer and the Subject of History*. Madison: University of Wisconsin Press, 1991.

——. "Chaucerian Confession: Penitential Literature and the Pardoner." *Medievalia et Humanistica* 7 (1976): 153–73.

Payer, Pierre J. *The Bridling of Desire: Views of Sex in the Later Middle Ages*. Toronto: University of Toronto Press, 1993.

——. "Foucault on Penance and the Shaping of Sexuality." *Studies in Religion* 14 (1985): 313–20.

Pearsall, Derek. "Gower's Narrative Art." *PMLA* 81 (1966): 475–84.

Peck, Russell A. *Kingship and the Common Profit in Gower's "Confessio Amantis."* Carbondale: Southern Illinois University Press, 1978.

Pollock, Frederick and Frederic William Maitland. *The History of English Law Before the Time of Edward I.* 2 vols. Washington, D.C.: Lawyers' Literary Club, 1959.

Poschmann, Bernhard. *Penance and the Anointing of the Sick.* London: Burns and Oates, 1964.

Pouchelle, Marie-Christine. *The Body and Surgery in the Middle Ages*, trans. Rosemary Morris. Cambridge: Polity Press, 1990.

Robertson, D. W. *Preface to Chaucer.* Princeton, N.J.: Princeton University Press, 1962.

Roncière, Charles de La. "Tuscan Notables on the Eve of the Renaissance." In *A History of Private Life*, Vol. 2, ed. Philippe Ariès and Georges Duby, pp. 157–309.

Rubin, Miri. *Corpus Christi: The Eucharist in Late Medieval Culture.* Cambridge: Cambridge University Press, 1991.

Ryan, W. F. and Charles B. Schmitt, eds. *Pseudo-Aristotle: The Secret of Secrets: Sources and Influences.* London: Warburg Institute, 1982.

Salzman, L. F. *English Industries of the Middle Ages.* Oxford: Clarendon Press, 1923.

———. *English Trade in the Middle Ages.* London: H. Pordes, 1964.

Scanlon, Larry. *Narrative, Authority, and Power: The Medieval Exemplum and the Chaucerian Tradition.* Cambridge: Cambridge University Press, 1994.

Scheppele, Kim Lane. *Legal Secrets: Equality and Efficiency in Common Law.* Chicago: University of Chicago Press, 1988.

Schleissner, Margaret. "A Fifteenth-Century Physician's Attitude Toward Sexuality: Dr. Johann Hartlieb's *Secreta mulierum* Translation." In *Sex in the Middle Ages: A Book of Essays*, ed. Joyce E. Salisbury, pp. 110–25. New York: Garland, 1991.

Schultz, James A. "Bodies That Don't Matter: Heterosexuality before Heterosexuality in Gottfried's *Tristan*. In *Constructing Medieval Sexuality*, ed. Lochrie, McCracken, and Schultz, pp. 91–110.

Sedgwick, Eve Kosofsky. *Epistemology of the Closet.* Berkeley: University of California Press, 1990.

———. *Tendencies.* Durham, N.C.: Duke University Press, 1993.

Shahar, Shulamith. *The Fourth Estate: A History of Women in the Middle Ages*, trans. Chaya Galai. London: Methuen, 1983.

Sontag, Susan. *Against Interpretation and Other Essays.* New York: Dell, 1966.

Spacks, Patricia Meyer. *Gossip.* New York: Knopf, 1985.

Spearing, A. C. *The Gawain-Poet: A Critical Study.* Cambridge: Cambridge University Press, 1970.

Stanbury, Sarah. "Women's Letters and Private Space in Chaucer." *Exemplaria* 6 (1994): 271–85.

Stanton, Domna. "Recuperating Women and the Man Behind the Screen." In *Sexuality and Gender in Early Modern Europe: Institutions, Texts, Images*, ed. James Grantham Turner, pp. 247–65. Cambridge: Cambridge University Press, 1993.

Stock, Brian. "Science, Technology, and Economic Progress in the Middle Ages." In *Science in the Middle Ages*, ed. Lindberg, pp. 1–51.

Strohm, Paul. *Hochon's Arrow: The Social Imagination of Fourteenth-Century Texts.* Princeton, N.J.: Princeton University Press, 1992.

Tambling, Jeremy. *Confession: Sexuality, Sin, the Subject*. Manchester: Manchester University Press, 1990.

Tentler, Thomas N. *Sin and Confession on the Eve of the Reformation*. Princeton, N.J.: Princeton University Press, 1977.

"Text of Pentagon's New Policy Guidelines on Homosexuals in the Military." *New York Times*, 20 July 1993: A12.

Thomasset, Claude. *Placides et Timéo: une vision du monde à la fin du XIIIe siècle: Commentaire du Dialogue de Placides et Timéo*. Geneva: Droz, 1982.

Thorndike, Lynn. "Further Consideration of the *Experimenta, Speculum astronomiae*, and *De secretis mulierum* ascribed to Albertus Magnus." *Speculum* 30 (1955): 413–33.

———. *A History of Magic and Experimental Science*, Vol. 2. New York: Macmillan, 1923.

Traub, Valerie. "The (In)Significance of 'Lesbian' Desire in Early Modern England." In *Queering the Renaissance*, ed. Goldberg, pp. 62–83.

Unwin, George. *Gilds and Companies of London*. 4th ed. New York: Barnes and Noble, 1964.

Watkins, Oscar D. *A History of Penance*. 2 vols. New York: Burt Franklin, 1961.

Wenzel, Siegfried. "The Source of Chaucer's Seven Deadly Sins." *Traditio* 30 (1974): 351–78.

Wetherbee, Winthrop. "Genius and Interpretation in the 'Confessio Amantis.'" In *Magister Regis: Studies in Honor of Robert Earl Kaske*, ed. Arthur Groos, pp. 243–52. New York: Fordham University Press, 1986.

———. "Latin Structure and Vernacular Space: Gower, Chaucer and the Boethian Tradition." In *Chaucer and Gower: Difference, Mutuality, Exchange*, ed. Yeager, pp. 7–35.

Wiesner, Merry E. "Guilds, Male Bonding and Women's Work in Early Modern Germany. *Gender and History* 1 (Summer 1989): 125–37.

Williams, Steven J. "Roger Bacon and His Edition of the Pseudo-Aristotelian *Secretum secretorum*." *Speculum* 69 (1994): 57–73.

Wood, Margaret. *The English Medieval House*. London: Ferndale Editions, 1981.

Woods, William F. "Private and Public Space in the *Miller's Tale*." *ChauRev* 29 (1994): 166–78.

Woolf, Rosemary. "Moral Chaucer and Kindly Gower." In *J. R. R. Tolkien, Scholar and Storyteller: Essays in Memoriam*, ed. Mary Salu and Robert T. Farrell, pp. 221–45. Ithaca, N.Y.: Cornell University Press, 1979.

Wright, Sue. "'Churmaids, Huswyfes and Hucksters': The Employment of Women in Tudor and Stuart Salisbury." In *Women and Work in Pre-industrial England*, ed. Charles and Duffin, pp. 100–21.

Yeager, R. F. *John Gower's Poetic: The Search for a New Arion*. Cambridge: D. S. Brewer, 1990.

———. "Learning to Speak in Tongues: Writing Poetry for a Trilingual Culture." In *Chaucer and Gower: Difference, Mutuality, and Exchange*, ed. Yeager, pp. 115–29.

———, ed. *Chaucer and Gower: Difference, Mutuality, Exchange*. Victoria, B.C.: English Literary Studies, 1991.

Index

Acknowledgments

A book about secrets is under immense pressure to keep none, including those who have made important contributions to it. The thing about secrets is that they flourish only in community among their keepers, and the same is true of this book. This project would have been impossible without the conversations and discussions of others who kept it from becoming my own well-kept secret. I am indebted not so much to keepers of my secrets but to those friends and colleagues who have pushed my thinking on the subject of secrecy or otherwise encouraged me to finish a project that sometimes daunted me, including Sarah Beckwith, Judith M. Bennett, Carolyn Dinshaw, Louise Fradenburg, Carla Freccero, Gail Gibson, Ruth Mazo Karras, Clare Lees, E. Ann Matter, Peggy McCracken, Gillian Overing, and James A. Schultz. I am particularly grateful to Mechthild Hart for her support, encouragement, and intellectual integrity, which kept me from veering away from the driving passions of this book. To Mary Dye I owe special thanks for her intellectual enthusiasm, which was invaluable to the writing of my first book, and her knowledge of dark matter and quantum weirdness, which has expanded my thinking about secrecy even beyond the scope of this book. I am also grateful to Jerome E. Singerman and Alison A. Anderson at the University of Pennsylvania Press for their many helpful suggestions.

In the Fall of 1997, I was fortunate to receive a paid leave of absence from Loyola University Chicago in order to complete this book. During that time, I also benefited enormously from my tenure as a Resident Scholar at the Center for Cultural Studies, University of California, Santa Cruz. The Center, my fellow scholars, my hosts, Patti and Richard Fitchen, as well as the amazing California environs gave me just the hospitality and inspiration I needed to complete this project.

Portions of Chapters 1, 3, and 4 appeared elsewhere, though in very different forms. An earlier version of my discussion of Foucault in Chapter 1 appeared in "Desiring Foucault," *Journal of Medieval and Early Modern Studies* 27, 1 (Winter 1997): 3–16. Some of my ideas about the Secrets of Women first appeared in my article, "Don't Ask, Don't Tell: Murderous

Plots and Medieval Secrets," which was published in a special volume of *GLQ: Journal of Lesbian and Gay Studies* 1 (1995): 405–17, edited by Louise Fradenburg and Carla Freccero. This essay was reprinted in *Premodern Sexualities*, ed. Fradenburg and Freccero (New York: Routledge, 1996). *Exemplaria* published a much earlier version of my analysis of the Miller's Tale in Chapter 4, "Women's 'Pryvetees' and Fabliau Politics in the Miller's Tale," 6, 2 (Fall 1994): 287–304. I am grateful to these publications for the opportunity to develop my ideas about secrecy and permission to republish these essays here.

Finally, to Lia Gaty, Pat Zak, and others, I owe an enormous personal debt for their role in teaching me my secrets, without which I could never have gone searching for medieval ones.